Game Changers

The Rousing Legacy of Louisiana Sports

Marty Mulé

Game Changers

The Rousing Legacy of Louisiana Sports

Marty Mulé

2013
University of Louisiana at Lafayette Press

FRONT COVER

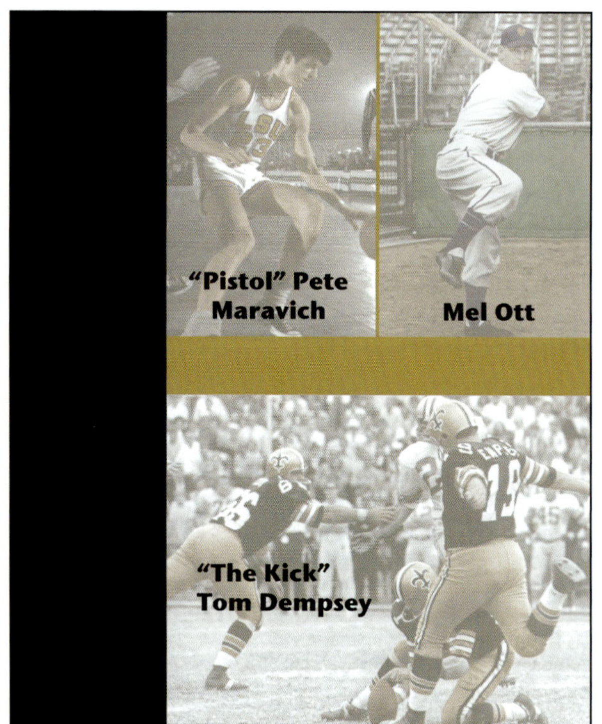

REAR COVER

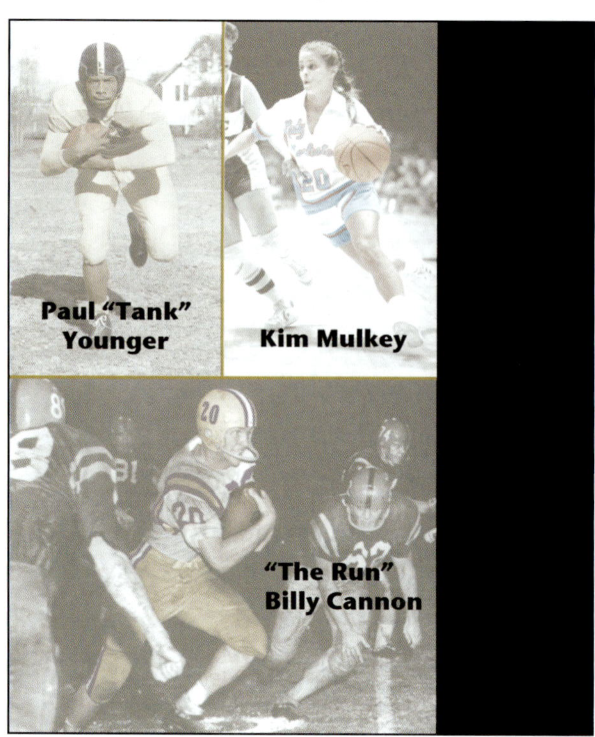

University of Louisiana at Lafayette Press
P.O. Box 40831
Lafayette, LA 70504-0831
http://ulpress.org

ISBN 13 (hardcover): 978-1-935754-25-1

Library of Congress Cataloging-in-Publication Data:

Mulé, Marty.
Game changers : the rousing legacy of Louisiana sports / by Marty Mule.
pages cm
ISBN 978-1-935754-25-1 (alk. paper)
1. Sports--Louisiana--History. 2. Athletes--Louisiana. I. Title.
GV584.L8M85 2013
796.09763--dc23
2013023851

Printed in Canada.

Contents

Foreword by Tim Brando . . . vii
Preface by Marty Mulé . . . ix

Acknowledgments . . . x

FOOTBALL . . . 1
- New Orleans Saints (2009) . . . 7
- Eddie Robinson . . . 11
- Terry Bradshaw . . . 16
- Ace Mumford . . . 19
- Chris Cagle . . . 22
- Marshall Faulk . . . 24
- LSU (1958) . . . 26
- LSU (2003) . . . 28
- LSU (2007) . . . 30
- Northeast Louisiana University (1987) . . . 32
- National Champions by Louisiana Schools . . . 34
- Billy Cannon . . . 36
- Eddie Price . . . 39
- Doug Williams . . . 42
- Louisiana Super Bowl Quarterbacks . . . 44
- Tom Dempsey . . . 46
- LSU (1908) . . . 48
- Collie Nicholson . . . 50
- Buddy Davis and R. L. Stockard . . . 52
- Paul "Tank" Younger . . . 54
- New Orleans Saints (2006) . . . 56
- Jim Taylor . . . 58
- Centenary College (1932) . . . 60
- Heisman Trophy Candidates from Louisiana . . . 62
- Tulane University (1931) . . . 63
- Super Bowls in New Orleans . . . 66
- Tulane Beats LSU (1973) . . . 69
- Southeastern Louisiana University (1954) . . . 71
- LSU (1965) . . . 73
- Sugar Bowl . . . 75
- Tulane University (1934) . . . 77
- Paul "Bear" Bryant . . . 79
- McNeese State University (1976) . . . 82
- Steve Van Buren . . . 84
- Shaun King . . . 86
- Louisiana High School Football . . . 88
- J. T. Curtis . . . 91
- LSU Night Football . . . 94
- New Orleans Saints . . . 96
- Dave Dixon and the Superdome . . . 99
- Bayou Classic . . . 101

BASEBALL . . . 103
- Lou Brock . . . 110
- Ron Guidry . . . 112
- Joe Adcock . . . 115
- Ted Lyons . . . 117
- Mel Ott . . . 119
- Ron Maestri and UNO (1984) . . . 122
- Warren Morris and LSU (1996) . . . 124
- Nicholls State University (1970) . . . 126

MEN'S BASKETBALL . . . 128
- NCAA Final Four in New Orleans . . . 132
- LSU (1935) . . . 134
- Loyola University (1945) . . . 137
- LSU (2006) . . . 138
- Karl Malone . . . 140
- Bill Reigel and McNeese State University (1956) . . . 142
- Bob Pettit . . . 144
- Pete Maravich and LSU . . . 147
- Pete Maravich and the New Orleans Jazz . . . 149
- Willis Reed . . . 150
- Xavier University (1973) . . . 152
- UNO and the Shot-Clock . . . 154
- Jesuit and St. Augustine (1965) . . . 155

WOMEN'S BASKETBALL . . . 157
- Baskin High School . . . 160
- Louisiana Tech University . . . 162

BOXING . . . 164
- John Sullivan vs. Jim Corbett (1892) . . . 167

HORSE RACING . . . 170
- Lexington and Lecomte . . . 174
- Black Gold . . . 176

GOLF . . . 179
- Tommy Bolt . . . 181
- Freddie Haas . . . 182
- Dick Mayer and the Greater New Orleans Open . . . 184

TRACK AND FIELD . . . 186
- LSU (1933) . . . 189
- Audrey "Mickey" Patterson . . . 191

LAGNIAPPE . . . 193
- Hamilton "Ham" Richardson . . . 194
- Claude Hamilton "Grits" Gresham Jr. . . . 196
- Southern Yacht Club . . . 198
- Billy Allgood and Louisiana College . . . 200
- Jesuit High School (1946) . . . 202
- University Nicknames . . . 205

POSTSCRIPT
- Louisiana Sports Hall of Fame Museum by Doug Ireland . . . 209

To Hap Glaudi, Bob Roesler, Buddy Diliberto, and Pete Finney, who all opened holes for me to run through.
And to the athletes and sports figures they covered with such keen insights.

Marty Mulé

McDonogh #14 track team, winners of the 1910 *Daily Picayune* Trophy, which represented the New Orleans City Championship.

FOREWORD
BY TIM BRANDO

Through the years the question most asked of me has been, "How did you get where you are in sportscasting as a native of Shreveport, Louisiana?"

My inner reaction always is, "While it's nice that you asked, what kind of a backhanded compliment is that?" The truth is I've been blessed throughout my career, and first and foremost, being a native of Louisiana probably helped as much as anything.

Going to school in Monroe and working in my twenties in both Baton Rouge and New Orleans, covering sports "all over the boot," contributed greatly in the pursuit of my career goals.

I grew up in west Shreveport right across the street from an All-State combo guard named Jimmy Pruett. He was a great player on a fantastic Fair Park High School basketball team that won the state Class 3A championship in 1963. At the age of seven, I knew not just Charles Beasley, David Worthington, Andy Fullerton, and Roger Hicks who started along with my hero Jimmy at Fair Park, but the first fives for just about every team in their district. In my early days the Top 20 State High School Basketball Tournament was played in Shreveport's Hirsch Coliseum, and thanks to my uncle and dad's help, I never missed a play in the Classes C, B, A, AA, and AAA state semifinals and title games. I was there to witness whether the iron was kind or unkind!

The names still resonate. The stories I heard about those I did not have the good fortune to see, like Hall of Famer Jackie Moreland, still dance in my head. There was Fabian Mang of traditional power Jesuit-New Orleans, then a few years later and a couple hours down the road in Alexandria at Rapides Parish Coliseum, we watched the incomparable combination of Hall of Famer Greg Procell, who set national prep scoring records, and his wingman, Walter "Tootsie Roll" Meshell, sparkle for tiny Ebarb High. Hall of Famer Scotty Robertson, later the head coach of three NBA teams AND a big league baseball scout, coached in Shreveport at Byrd High School. Robert Parish, who played more NBA games than anybody, got his start in Shreveport at Woodlawn High and Centenary College. This all fueled my life-long passion for basketball.

During football season, I watched prep phenoms Terry Bradshaw and Joe Ferguson throw the football for Shreveport's Woodlawn High. A few miles to the east, the Ruston Rifle, Bert Jones, was making his own name as the son of Hall of Famer Dub Jones. The legendary Eddie Robinson was stacking up wins for the Grambling College Tigers, shaping a national legacy and producing Hall of Famers like Buck Buchanan, Ernie Ladd, Willie Davis, Willie Brown, and Sammy White, with trailblazing quarterbacks James "Shack" Harris and ultimately Doug Williams at the forefront.

Tim Brando with Warwick Dunn.

It was my incredible good fortune as a ninth grader at Lakeshore Jr. High and tenth grader at Fair Park to have the chance to be part of a father/son broadcast team in 1971 and '72 for the Neville High Tigers over in Monroe. I was fourteen years old and it was amazing working with my dad, Hub, and watching legends in the making. Neville's head coach was Charlie Brown, and his defensive coordinator was "Chick" Childress, both future Louisiana Sports Hall of Fame inductees.

The first high school football game I broadcast on radio was between Neville and a new Shreveport school, Captain Shreve, that had opened four years earlier. Lee Hedges, the man for whom the Gators' stadium is now named, was on the opposite sideline from Coach Brown that evening. He was Bradshaw's high school coach. Great coaches, and some future college stars and NFL players like the Bengals' linebacker Bo Harris, were on the field while I was right where I wanted to be, in the booth.

Fast forward a dozen years to the first statewide telecast of the high school state championship games, a new concept called The Superdome Classic, created by state prep sports commissioner Tommy Henry, yet another former high school coach in my neighborhood and a future Hall of Fame inductee. There was Coach Brown leading yet another Tiger team to a title against South Terrebonne from down along the bayous in Houma. I was working in local TV in Baton Rouge at the time and the opportunity came my way to call the game on television. What a thrill that was for me!

A year later, Neville was back in the Superdome, taking on Ruston in the 4A state final—with the Bearcats led by Childress, their hometown hero, who was raised in an orphanage and played at RHS for another Hall of Fame coach, "Hoss" Garrett, who also produced the aforementioned Bert Jones.

As a young reporter in Baton Rouge I cut my teeth on Hall of Fame coach Dale Brown, his first Southeastern Conference title team, and later his first Final Four team in 1981. I stayed in the state's capital city through 1986 when his Tigers made a miracle run as an eleven-seed on the road to Dallas for the Final Four. It was during that time that I gained attention from the folks at ESPN and got my first big break onto the national stage. "Daddy Dale" made people around the country sit up and notice LSU basketball, due to his colorful style and recruiting success. He remains one of my heroes, for his values and principles and impact on people even more so than for his great coaching accomplishments. I was proud to make the presentation speech for his Hall of Fame induction in 1999.

During my time in Baton Rouge, I also covered the New Orleans Saints, as unbeknownst to us, they neared the end of their lean years. I got to know and became close friends with the legendary Archie Manning, a consummate Hall of Famer in the game of life and now a colleague of mine at CBS Sports.

That's only a snapshot of my good fortune. Safe to say, without Louisiana's sports legends I would not be where I am today! I still pinch myself at times. I proudly wear on my sleeve my pride in my home state, and particularly our incredible sports legacy that just keeps rollin' along like the mighty Mississippi River. You survey the national sports scene week after week, year after year, and Louisiana supplies a disproportionate number of great stars, exciting teams, and passionate fans who may not have invented tailgating, but have perfected it!

When I moved to Baton Rouge, I covered sports alongside another Hall of Famer, whose work you're about to savor like a great gumbo. My friend Marty Mulé has detailed much of Louisiana's sports greatness in this magnificent book. As you turn these pages, you'll be amazed by the fascinating stories, mesmerized by the fabulous feats, and inspired by the unforgettable nature of our state's finest sports figures, teams, and events.

Congratulations and thanks go to Marty, who poured himself and his life's library of Bayou State sports knowledge into this remarkable book. I thought I knew many of the names and the events, but chapter after chapter, he's unveiled tales that have deepened my appreciation for the astounding power-packed punch that Louisiana delivers daily to sports fans everywhere.

As the sparkling Louisiana Sports Hall of Fame Museum opens in beautiful, appropriately historic Natchitoches (hometown of Joe Dumars and the college town of football greats such as Bobby Hebert, Joe Delaney, Mark Duper, Jackie Smith, Charlie Tolar, and Charlie Hennigan), I'm looking forward to cruising an hour down Interstate 49 from Chateau Brando to visit. When you make the pilgrimage, many of the stories in *Game Changers* will be yours to witness.

Wherever you are, you can feel the electricity of Saturday night in Tiger Stadium, hear the squeak of Pistol Pete's Chuck Taylor's in the old Cow Barn, marvel at the audacity of the Saints' onside kick to trigger their win in Super Bowl XLIV, read how the fabled Sullivan vs. Corbett world heavyweight fight of 1892 captivated the world, imagine the pop of the catcher's mitt receiving a fastball from Louisiana Lightning, Ron Guidry . . . those adventures and many more are yours in these pages.

Tim Brando
CBS Sports, Shreveport, La.

Preface
by Marty Mulé

A Little Bit of Sports Heaven

A television ad used to run in New Orleans in which, with a backdrop of a church steeple, a deep voice reminded us that someday we'll meet again in the only place better than Louisiana.

There's a kernel of truth in that embellishment. The Pelican State really is a little bit of heaven—sports heaven.

And sports always has been something of a sideline religion in Louisiana, with outcomes that sometimes elicit choruses of "Hallelujah," "Hosanna," and "Glory Be!" from a segment of the followers.

Believe me, it's not that rare an occurrence, which is the purpose of this chronicle.

For a medium-sized state most renowned for its cuisine, culture, charm, and, above all, colorful history, the sports legacy of Louisiana is astounding.

Think about this: In a state dwarfed by some of the population giants of the country, Louisiana was home to the first college coach to exceed four hundred football victories, Eddie Robinson of Grambling, and to one of the only two men to coach more than five hundred football victories on any level (prep, college, or pro), J. T. Curtis of Curtis Christian School. Another illustration are two specks on the map of the state. In the northeast corner of Louisiana two towns—villages really—Bernice and Summerfield, stand about thirteen miles apart with a combined population of fewer than four thousand. And each has a native son in the Basketball Hall of Fame, Willis Reed and Karl Malone.

It really is kind of amazing, isn't it?

Not only does Louisiana produce more than its share of professional football athletes—and a disproportionate share of Super Bowl quarterbacks—but it's notable that the first touchdown scored in the Super Bowl was by a player with Pelican State ties, Max McGee of Tulane. And the second touchdown, and the first rushing, came from another, Jim Taylor of LSU.

Pete Maravich, a touchstone of the modern basketball player, scored 3,667 points in his three years at LSU, the *major*-college record, but only second in Louisiana. Bob Hopkins scored 3,759 points, ninety-two more than the Pistol, in his four-year career at Grambling.

The first father-son combination to be entered into the NFL record book came from a north Louisiana family. On November 25, 1951, William "Dub" Jones, a Cleveland Browns flanker, scored a record-tying six touchdowns against the Chicago Bears. On December 15, 1974, Dub's son Bert, the quarterback of the Baltimore Colts, completed a then-record seventeen consecutive passes against the New York Jets.

Louisiana Tech's Terry Bradshaw set the gold standard for Super Bowl quarterbacks, steering the Pittsburgh Steelers to four victories in four appearances, but the Manning boys of New Orleans left an imprint almost inconceivable of ever being duplicated: back-to-back MVP performances by brothers in the Super Bowl.

In the days when the pros played only twelve games, the Philadelphia Eagles' Steve Van Buren, out of LSU, was the first player to rush for a thousand yards twice, in 1947 and '49; the latter being the same season another alum of Van Buren's prep alma mater, New Orleans's Warren Easton High, Eddie Price of Tulane (1946-49), also ran for one thousand yards on the college level (1,137)—at a nation-leading, and stupefying, 6.6 yards per carry.

The first NFL player from a predominantly African American school was Tank Younger of Grambling, who more than justified the confidence of his college coach, Robinson.

Louisiana is also where John L. Sullivan and Gentleman Jim Corbett changed the rules of boxing and where Muhammad Ali won his last championship; where North Carolina coach Dean Smith clinched his first national basketball championship and where Indiana's Bobby Knight coached his last; where one of the most significant football games ever played, Super Bowl IV, was held and where an exorbitant number of pro football teams afterward won their crowns.

In track there is, of course, LSU's famed five-man team, Olympics hurdler Rod Milburn, and sprinter Mickey Patterson-Tyler, the first African American woman to medal in the Olympics. A core of superb multi-sport athletes (Joe Delaney, Mark Duper, Victor Oatis, along with runner Mario Johnson) provided Louisiana with one of its greatest track thrills in 1981 when Northwestern State's football-playing sprinters outran a relay unit of world-class runners.

Mel Ott grew up in Gretna, across the Mississippi River from the Big Easy, then went on to play as a teen near the Hudson River in the Big Apple—and became one of the greatest hitters in the history of the National League. Other baseball greats include fellow Hall of Famer Ted Lyons of Lake Charles, who led the American League with a 2.10 ERA—at the age of forty-one—and Ron Guidry of Southwestern Louisiana, who retired with a career record approximating that of Sandy Koufax's.

In golf, when Byron Nelson was winning everything there was to win, it was New Orleanian Freddie Haas who put a stop to it. A decade later Shreveport's Tommy Bolt led the game's most prestigious tournament, the U.S. Open, from practically the opening tee to his closing putt.

The longest victory streak in any sport or team—outside of the Harlem Globetrotters—was set in Louisiana, 218 by the Baskin High School girls basketball team. The girls don't get all the glory, though. Karl Malone of Summerfield and Louisiana Tech, Joe Dumars of Natchitoches and McNeese State, Willis Reed of Bernice and Grambling, and Bob Pettit of Baton Rouge and LSU head an impressive group of state-raised athletes to leave deep dents in the NBA.

Among influences of the sport, there is also Clara Gregory Baer of Newcomb College, who wrote the original rules of girls' "basquette ball"; the University of New Orleans, which played a role in implementing the shot clock in men's college basketball; and Dave Dixon, who changed Louisiana's sportscape with his twin quests of securing an NFL franchise and taking a vision out of his brain and anchoring it on New Orleans's Poydras Street, meaning, of course, the Superdome.

These are feats, folks, and facts worth remembering. From the Lexington-Lecompe match races of 1854—covered like the World Series is today—to the Saints' scintillating return to the Superdome after Hurricane Katrina, the first step in New Orleans's ultimate triumph in Super Bowl XLIV, Louisiana has a compelling story to tell in sports.

These accounts are revived through variations of stories I wrote during my time at the *Times-Picayune* and other outlets; they are also compilations of eye-witnesses, other reportage, and observers of other places and times—and through some miracle of circumstance—the honor of their recounting fell to me.

Glory Be.

MAJOR ASSISTS
(Acknowledgments)

No one person could possibly have been the repository of all the athletes, coaches, or major figures and their feats in the rich sports history of Louisiana—or put those achievements in clear focus.

Those with firsthand knowledge, and a willingness to share their facts, insights, and asides of the subject, not only have my thanks, but also should have the gratitude of the generations of sports fans who follow this one.

Ted Lewis of the *Baton Rouge Advocate* provided an outline and in many ways was the guiding spirit of the project. A battery of others pointed the way to sources of information and background. That group included: the *Ruston Daily Leader*'s Buddy Davis, whose own compelling story is included, and deserved, in this text, and who saw and shared some of the biggest sports moments—and some of the biggest names—of north Louisiana up close and personal; Bobby Dower of the *Lake Charles American-Press* was on the scene with the intriguing story of Coach Jack Doland and McNeese State football in the first Independence Bowl and provided material to put the Cowboys' national championship basketball team of the mid-1950s in context, as did the *Shreveport Times*' Scott Ferrell who filled in the amazing story of Centenary football in the 1920s and '30s.

Some stories would have been incomplete—or remained untold—without the added insights and suggestions of Louisiana's patron saint of sportswriters, Peter Finney of the *Times-Picayune*, who spent a distinguished career covering more than half the current 120-year history of the LSU Tigers and covered the New Orleans Saints from their birth, through their long "Ain'ts" era and on to their Super Bowl championship.

Major assists for their suggestions and editing notations are credited to the *Times-Picayune*'s Bill Bumgarner, Robert Steckel, and Darrell Williams. Ro Brown and Ronnie Virgets of various media outlets each contributed their expertise, as well as Bob Tompkins of the *Alexandria Town Talk*, Brent St. Germain of the *Houma Courier*, Butch Muir of the *Baton Rouge Advocate*, Ron Brocato of the *Clarion-Herald*, John Ventola, Mike Detillier, and the Louisiana Sports Hall of Fame's Doug Ireland.

There were also the long ago writings and observations of Bob Roesler and George Sweeney of the *Times-Picayune*, Dan Hardesty of the *Baton Rouge State-Times*, Jerry Byrd of the *Shreveport Journal* and Truman Stacy of the *Lake Charles American-Press*, whose works are intertwined with my own reportage over the course of three decades along with updated interviews for this project. James Wilson and the staff of ULL Press did a masterful job catching glitches, making useful suggestions, and generally improving the project.

Finally, there was the figure, whose involvement came about purely by happenstance but whose commitment was total, and who in some ways became the most indispensable of all: Nico Van Thyn, a proud Dutchman who grew up in Shreveport, then wrote and edited sports there. He now toils in the foreign land of Fort Worth, Texas, but his heart remains in the Sports Fan's Paradise of Louisiana.

Marty Mulé
Mandeville, La.

Now a free-lance writer, Marty Mulé spent more than thirty years on the sports staff of the *New Orleans Times-Picayune*, often writing in-depth feature stories. Mulé has been the recipient of first-place national writing awards from the Associated Press Sports Editors, Football Writers of America, and the National Sportscasters and Sportswriters Association. He has also been voted Louisiana Sportswriter of the Year eleven times by his peers. A graduate of Louisiana State University, this is Mulé's eighth book.

The Kickoff

January 1, 1890
Sportsman's Park, New Orleans, La.

Tom Bayne.

Plop.

Tom Bayne made quite a splash on the Louisiana sporting scene.

In a town where such diverse pastimes as fencing, bicycling, boxing, chess, card games, and horse racing were the leisure preoccupations of the citizenry, he brought a new sport to their attention.

The first toddling steps of football in New Orleans—indeed, in Louisiana—were the direct result of the fascination, labor, and sportsmanship of Bayne, a young lawyer who had been a noted quarterback under Walter Camp at Yale and whose passion for the game had never subsided—though nowhere in the South did it arouse much interest.

Football interest was growing elsewhere, especially in the East where many colleges would challenge each other to this odd game, more of a scrum than finesse. But it brought little more than indifference in New Orleans, where very few even had a rudimentary knowledge of football.

The Flying Wedge and Double V were the formations then in vogue, the field was 110 yards long, and offenses had three downs to gain five yards. Touchdowns counted for four points, and points after for two.

It was a different game in the 1880s than it is today.

But it was Bayne who started Louisiana towards the passionate fixation the state now has on the sport.

After several years of starts and stops at New Orleans's Southern Athletic Club, in which he devised games between two five-man teams (because there weren't enough athletes familiar enough with football for full complements), Bayne came up with the idea (interestingly enough, since this was a dozen years before the first Rose Bowl) of a New Year's Day game in New Orleans "with the object of having young athletes of our city take hold of it, and attain the same perfection, and have the game as popular as it is in the North."

Two teams, one called "Yale," the other "Princeton," were manned by Louisiana students home for the holidays from eastern schools. They played on January 1, 1890, in what the New Orleans *Daily Picayune* billed as the city's "first intercollegiate football game."

With the grandstand of Sportsman's Park reportedly "filled with the choicest flowers of New Orleans society," the first game with a semblance of organization in the way football was being played elsewhere was held in Louisiana. It was even played with a ball described as "oval-shaped and cased in leather."

The *Picayune's* coverage breathlessly said, "The collisions between the teams were true tests of strength, skill and endurance."

After a scoreless half, Yale scored a touchdown and a goal-after touchdown to win 6-0. The game was cut short because in making the PAT (point after touchdown) the kicker—a Half Back identified as "Mr. Le Sassier"—booted the only ball into the waters of the canal that bordered the park.

Thus, the first Big Game ever played in Louisiana ended not with a bang but a ripple.

☆ ☆ ☆

Three years later, Bayne was not only still playing for Southern Athletic Club but also coaching Tulane's first football team—each against the other.

The players, from today's perspective, are striking. Only two weighed as much as two hundred pounds. Both teams wore nondescript outfits with mismatched jerseys and stockings of various colors and stripes. The athletes wore bushy pompadours, which the men in the rush-line delighted in poking into the eyes of the opposition.

1899 LSU squad.

It was a perplexing dual assignment for Bayne because he played against his pupils and helped beat them, despite the fact that between plays he would coach them.

With SAC camped at the Tulane 5, Bayne tried to skirt left end but was hit by Walter Castenado. But before Bayne hit the ground, he tossed the ball to a player named Schwartz, who took it in for the touchdown.

Tulane lost its first game 12-0 in part because of its own coach's prowess on the field.

A game seven days later would be far more important and completely demonstrate Bayne's sportsmanship.

Bayne had scheduled what actually would be the first college game played in the Pelican State with Louisiana State University, where a team was being formed by Dr. Charles Coates, a young chemistry professor from Baltimore who had played the sport at Johns Hopkins and who, as a child, had been in attendance at the Rutgers-Princeton game in New Brunswick, New Jersey, in 1869, regarded as the first game of American football ever played.

Bayne must have been pretty confident that his team was ready to play LSU. He laid out the playing field at Sportsman's Park, helped plant the goalposts, helped sell tickets (fifty cents) and, incredibly, helped Coates prepare the fledgling LSU squad, which had never played before, making the long, arduous trip to Baton Rouge several times.

"The LSU boys knew little or nothing about it," Bayne said later, "and Dr. Coates and I had to practice them plenty to get them started."

Because there was only one football available, it was kept in Baton Rouge half the week and in New Orleans the other half.

There were extraordinarily fine relations between the schools when they first met on the field, on November 25, 1893. LSU gave Tulane the honor of choosing the umpire, and it picked Tom Bayne, while LSU was accorded the right to select the referee—Coates.

Both used some "ringers," players with no actual ties to the universities. Tom's younger brother Hugh had graduated from Yale, and members of the Southern Athletic Club also played for Tulane.

The *Daily Picayune* described the proceedings thusly: "Tulane . . . began the game with a formation of the flying wedge. It was prettily done. The ball was passed to Lombard and as the wedge was blocked, he started around right end. The next play was equally as good. (Hugh) Bayne went through the line, the Baton Rouge (line) melting away before the onset of Castenado and Foster. Through their aid, Bayne made a clean run to the goal and accomplished the first touchdown of the match in something under two minutes."

Despite lime, with which the field was marked, getting into Hugh's eyes, in short order he also scored a second touchdown, the first two in

Charles "Peggy" Flournoy.

Hank Lauricella.

Tulane history, en route to a 34-0 victory.

Tom Bayne's Tulanians lost their debut season finale to Ole Miss 12-4 to finish with a 1-2 record.

For getting the school started in football, Tulane showed its appreciation to Bayne, who coached without remuneration, by presenting him with an umbrella.

☆ ☆ ☆

The New Orleans Saints, of course, would become Louisiana's pro team of choice. But neither they nor the parade of professional teams to play exhibition football in the 1950s and '60s while Dave Dixon chased a franchise were the first pros ever to put a cleat in Louisiana turf. That was none other than the Chicago Bears and their just signed gate attraction, the Galloping Ghost, Harold "Red" Grange.

Promoter C. C. ("Cash 'n Carry") Pyle included New Orleans on a barnstorming tour of the country, and on January 10, 1926, at the Heinemann Park baseball stadium, the Bears played a hastily assembled team called the New Orleans All-Stars, beating the locals 14-0 before a crowd of ten thousand.

Pyle was the embodiment of the shady image pro football had at the time, as described by Lester Lautenschlaeger, a former Tulane quarterback then practicing law but assisting Coach Clark Shaughnessy on the side.

"He asked me to get a team together to play the Bears," Lautenschlaeger said of Pyle in George Sweeney's book, *The Green Wave*. "He promised to pay me $6,000 (to be split among the players, recruited from across the South)."

Pro football was frowned upon at Tulane, and administrators let it be known that anyone associated with the game had no place at their school. "Brother" Brown, also a former stellar athlete and at that time a Green Wave assistant coach, was upset with Tulane's attitude and quit to join the All-Stars. Lautenschlaeger said he didn't have a chance to quit. Tulane summarily fired him.

"Pyle had this horrible reputation about fulfilling his financial obligations, so I demanded $3,000 a day before the game," Lautenschlaeger said. "He wouldn't budge. I told him we wouldn't play . . . I told him no money, no game. He got me the $3,000 and I demanded the rest between halves. My dad, who was an attorney, told me I better watch Pyle. I couldn't find C. C after the second quarter so I went and sat in the press box. The writers asked what I was doing up there and I told them if I didn't get the $3,000 Pyle owed me, there would be no second half. Pyle rushed up from the stands when he found what was going on.

"He demanded we play. I told him to give me the money he owed and we would. My dad had a black bag with him and Pyle put the $3,000 in cash in the bag (to be dispersed to the players) and we finished the game."

Tulane, however, was firm. The school would not take the tainted Lautenschlaeger back into its employ.

☆ ☆ ☆

Of course, the reputation of pro football greatly improved over the decades, and the sport grew into a multi-billion dollar business—and Louisiana's passion for Anything Football also seemed boundless with practically every gridiron venture finding an audience in the state.

The Shreveport Steamer of the World Football League lasted two seasons (1974-75). The New Orleans Night (1991-92) and the New Orleans Voodoo (2004 to the present) operate in the spring to give Louisiana its fix of the sport when the colleges and NFL are out of action.

Dave Dixon was as instrumental in another interesting concept as he was in bringing the Saints and the Superdome to fruition. Dixon envisioned a spring/summer league (not in competition with the NFL) that would be both entertaining and a seasoning experience for players with NFL potential. In 1983 that became the United States Football League.

When the Boston Breakers, a charter member, couldn't make

Y. A. Tittle.

Bert Jones.

Mel Blount (left) and Charlie Joiner (right).

Danny Abramowicz.

a go of the venture in New England, Joe Canizaro, a New Orleans real estate mogul, bought the club and moved it to the Crescent City.

It was in most ways a success. Canizaro brought in Marcus Dupree, a budding superstar back who had left the University of Oklahoma early, and home state hero Buford Jordan of McNeese State, who was the leading rusher with 1,276 yards. The team finished the 1984 season with an 8-10 record, and drew an average 30,557 fans, seventh in the eighteen-team league.

But, in a move foreshadowing the collapse of the USFL, New Jersey Generals owner Donald Trump started pushing a move to fall football in competition with the NFL—the precise opposite of why the USFL was conceived and founded in the first place.

Knowing there was no way he could compete head-to-head with the New Orleans Saints, Canizaro sold the Breakers to interests in Portland.

After three years of its owners following Trump and swerving away from Dixon's precept of not bucking the NFL, the USFL was pronounced dead.

* * *

The imprint of the Pelican State on football would be incalculable, not even taking into account its producing Hall of Fame players such as Steve Van Buren, Jim Taylor, and Y. A. Tittle, all of whom played at LSU; or Willie Davis, Buck Buchanan, Charlie Joiner, and Willie Brown, who all played at Grambling; Louisiana Tech's Terry Bradshaw and Fred Dean, New Orleans's Marshall Faulk, Mel Blount of Southern, Jackie Smith of Northwestern State, Willie Roaf of Louisiana Tech and the Saints, or Canton-worthy athletes such as Aeneas Williams (Southern), Johnny Robinson (LSU), the Manning boys, Peyton and Eli, and Reggie Wayne of New Orleans, Brian Mitchell (UL Lafayette), or Destrehan's Ed Reed, Kevin Mawae (LSU), Alan Faneca (LSU), and Baton Rouge's Warrick Dunn. There's even Cal Hubbard, not from Louisiana but who played in the glory days at Centenary, then went on to become "the most feared lineman in the NFL" in the 1920s and '30s. Hubbard, named to the NFL's all-time team in 1969, is enshrined in both the College Football Hall of Fame and the Pro Football Hall of Fame.

Not even Heisman Trophy recipients such as Springhill's John David Crow or LSU's Billy Cannon or other No. 1 professional draft picks such as Tommy Mason (Tulane), Buchanan, Bradshaw, and the Manning boys, not even JaMarcus Russell who had a tremendous college career at quarterback at LSU but fizzled as a pro.

And not to be overlooked are stalwarts such as perennial All-Pro linebacker Isiah Robertson out of Southern; Heisman Trophy runners-up Jerry Stovall of LSU and New Orleanian Hank Lauricella; or Ernie Ladd (Grambling), a defensive stonewall in the early days of the AFL; Mark Duper (Northwestern State) of the famed Miami Dolphins' Marks Brothers; LSU's Kevin Faulk, described as "Mr. Reliable" by Coach Bill Belichick on multiple Super Bowl-winning New England squads; Roy Winston (LSU), who started at linebacker in four Super Bowls; noted quarterback Joe Ferguson of Shreveport; Gary Reasons (Northwestern State), an integral part of two Super Bowl-winning clubs; Pro Bowl defensive back Charles Tillman (UL Lafayette); or defensive end Rich "Tombstone" Jackson from Southern, and an original inductee in the Denver Broncos' Ring of Fame; Tulane's Matt Forté; New Orleans's Mike Wallace; Lardarius Webb of Nicholls State, who became the only player in NCAA Division I history to receive awards of Player of the Week on offense, defense, and special teams in the Southland Conference in the same season, 2007.

There are also major contributors such as Jake Delhomme of UL Lafayette who quarterbacked the Carolina Panthers to the Su-

per Bowl, and his college teammate Brandon Stokley, a receiver who played on two Super Bowl teams; Gary Barbaro, who went from Nicholls State to a Pro Bowl career as a safety with the Kansas City Chiefs, and who, despite playing just one season in the fledgling league, was named to the all-time USFL team.

Northwestern State left a big impression in the early days of the AFL through the exploits of receiver Charlie Hennigan, who quit teaching high school biology to become one of the league's brightest stars. Hennigan scored the first touchdown in Houston Oilers history and in 1961 accumulated 1,746 yards receiving—a pro record that stood for thirty-four years. His pro and college teammate Charlie Tolar was known as the "human bowling ball" for his five-foot-six, 210 pound physique. A perennial AFL All-Star running back, Tolar was named to the Oilers' 30th anniversary team.

Northwestern State's Joe Delaney played just two years with the Kansas City Chiefs before an untimely death, but set four franchise records. Southeastern's Billy Andrews, who played eleven seasons at linebacker in the NFL, left his mark on the very first Monday Night Football game, on September 21, 1970, when he intercepted Joe Namath and returned it for a touchdown, a key play in a 31-21 Cleveland Browns victory over the New York Jets.

Charles "Peggy" Flournoy, Tulane's first All-American, led the nation in scoring with 129 points in 1925, the year the undefeated Green Wave turned down the Rose Bowl, opening the way for Alabama's first appearance in Pasadena.

The next season another player at a Louisiana college, Elton "Bucky" Moore, known as the "Dixie Flyer," not only spearheaded a 10-0-0 record at Loyola of New Orleans in 1926, but also helped the Wolfpack ring up 335 points—an astounding figure for the time. Moore not only scored fourteen touchdowns and twenty-one PATs, a total of 105 points, but he also ran for 1,304 yards, almost twice as many as Red Grange (743) did in his best season of 1924.

The list might not be boundless . . . but it sure seems like it.

Kevin Mawae.

Matt Forté.

Brian Mitchell.

WHO DAT!

February 7, 2010
Sun Life Stadium, Miami, Florida

This couldn't have been scripted any better. Three native sons converged to seal what arguably could be considered the No. 1 moment in the three centuries-long sports history of Louisiana.

The favored Indianapolis Colts were driving for a tying touchdown late in the fourth quarter of Super Bowl XLIV against the New Orleans Saints. Quarterback Peyton Manning, raised in the Crescent City and the scion of an old Saints hero, threw to teammate Reggie Wayne of Marrero.

The Saints' Tracy Porter, of Port Allen, "jumped" the pass, intercepted and returned it seventy-four yards for a touchdown to seal the 31-17 New Orleans victory.

In a game replete with memorable plays—including a gutsy onside kick to open the second half—Porter's was the one that meant the Saints had really gone marching in.

It meant they actually had won a Super Bowl.

This was the crowning touch in the more than four decades long odyssey of a star-crossed team based in a city that four years earlier was ground zero for the most calamitous natural disaster to strike the North American continent.

This was a team that was supported and loved unconditionally through the worst days of the franchise, but also a team that looked ready to abandon the city in the devastating aftermath of Hurricane Katrina.

The high point of the Saints came in the wake of New Orleans's lowest point.

Defensive tackle Charles Grant, asked why that victory in Miami's Sun Life Stadium seemed to mean so much to the Saints, responded: "You have to look at how far we've come."

* * *

The Road to Super Bowl XLIV was a breathtaking four-month ride through the fall of 2009, jockeyed by Saints' coach Sean Payton and his quarterback Drew Brees. Together they would keep opposing defenses on their heels, and the Saints would go from 2008's 8-8 and last place in the NFC South to thirteen consecutive victories—the longest season-opening run for an NFC team since the merger with the American Football League in 1970—to begin the 2009 season before going into cruise control into the playoffs.

Brees was the fuse for everything that happened in their air-oriented offense, steering the Saints to 510 points, most in the NFL, completing 363 of his 514 passes, a then-NFL record 70.6 percentage, for 4,620 yards and 34 touchdowns.

But offense wasn't the whole story.

Payton brought in new defensive coordinator Gregg Williams—a man he so wanted on his staff he was willing to forgo $250,000 of his own money to facilitate the difference in the necessary compensation to lure Williams—who was obsessed with the art of taking the ball away.

Overall, the Saints' new 4-3 attacking defense was just as mediocre as it ever had been, ranking 20th of the thirty-two NFL teams, but Williams brought in a major weapon: turnovers. He preached it, practiced it, *willed* it. Suddenly, almost as if stardust was cast on Williams's unit, the Saints were swooping in for interceptions and scooping up fumbles. Their total of thirty-nine was seventeen more than they had in 2008, one behind league-leading Green Bay, and New Orleans's eight touchdown returns of turnovers were highest in the NFL. Safety Darren Sharper tied for the lead with nine interceptions for a record 376 yards and three touchdowns.

Now, of course, we know Williams's hiring was a huge miscalculation. He added little to the team and brought much to question. After his consistently average-at-best defenses hastened his departure from New Orleans, Williams would be implicated in an arrangement whereby he and players kicked in money for bonuses for big defensive plays, a pay-for-pain compact not unusual in the NFL but forbidden for coaches.

Commissioner Roger Goodell would make an example of the Saints, suspending both Williams and Payton for "bounties" on opposing players, even though it was part of the culture of NFL football. He wanted to make an example of a high-profile team—the Saints.

Williams changed the Saints from one of the most popular champions ever to one perceived as tainted. But it should be noted that physicality played a minimal role in the march to the Super Bowl title. The aggressiveness Williams wanted never truly translated into a major weapon for the Saints, and the stat sheet indicated that defense was never a "dirty" unit. In the three 2009 playoff games against the Arizona Cardinals, Minnesota Vikings, and Indianapolis Colts, the Saints were flagged a total of two times for personal fouls. And over the course of Williams's three years with the Saints, New Orleans ranked as the eighth-most penalized team in the NFL—meaning seven other teams were guilty of more transgressions.

In 2009, though, the story was turnovers, and in the postseason the Saints added eight more, and another touchdown.

Things were going so unbelievably well, Saints opponents didn't come within two touchdowns of them for the season's first six weeks. The Miami Dolphins were their first speed bump, going ahead 24-3 in the second quarter before Brees brought the Saints back to a 46-34 victory. Against the Washington Redskins seven weeks after that, Brees threw an interception, and in trying to bring the defender down, receiver Robert Meachem stripped the ball out for another turnover—and returned the fumble forty-four yards for a touchdown in another improbable 33-30 Saints victory, this one in overtime.

Only in the last three games, when Payton took his foot off the pedal with the playoffs assured, did the Saints come up short on the scoreboard.

The danger, as many in the national press harped on constantly, was no team had ever lost its last three regular season games and then won a Super Bowl.

With their unbeaten bubble burst, the Saints couldn't make history . . . could they?

Despite putting a touchdown on the scoreboard in the first fifteen seconds of its history—thanks to John Gilliam's ninety-four-yard opening kickoff in 1967—this was one woe-begotten pro football franchise, mismanaged in the front office and misplayed on the field for decades.

Consider this. The Saints:

- didn't have their first winning season for twenty-one years;
- didn't make the playoffs for twenty-one years;
- didn't win their first divisional title for twenty-five years;
- didn't win their first playoff game for thirty-three years;
- were the first team to lose to the expansion team Tampa Bay Buccaneers; and
- were the first team to lose to the expansion team Cleveland Browns.

It's the kind of thing that, in hindsight, could be expected from a franchise that once traded its entire draft to get one player, in part so the coach could hit the golf course; once hired an astronaut as general manager; passed on thirty-three future Hall of Fame players in its first fifteen drafts; and had thirteen head coaches in its first thirty-nine years of existence, an average tenure of three seasons, with only one leaving with a winning record.

Whew. These weren't so much "Saints" as they were martyrs.

This is how bad things could go for the Saints. On December 3, 1979, what was then perceived as the biggest game in franchise history was scheduled at the Superdome. It was the first Monday Night Football game in New Orleans in five years. In compiling their previous 0-3 Monday Night Football record, the team had been outscored 88-27.

The Saints, at 7-7 and in first place in the NFC West, lined up against the Oakland Raiders. New Orleans was: (1) eying the club's first winning season and (2) expecting to make the playoffs for the first time. In fact, the NFL had informed the Saints that with a victory that night they could start printing playoff tickets.

The fired-up Saints came out and truly impressed the national audience, waylaying the Raiders 35-14—in the first half. With that twenty-one-point Saints lead, the click of televisions being turned off echoed across America.

But when those viewers woke up the next day, the news on the morning shows reported a stunning 42-35 Raiders comeback.

Yeah, these were the same old Saints. They finished 1979 without their first winning season, going 8-8, and again sitting at home to watch the playoffs. A year later they went 1-15, finally winning in the fifteenth week of the season.

It's no wonder their fans, taking the lead of sportscaster Buddy Diliberto, soon took to wearing grocery bags over their heads at games and re-christened their team the "Ain'ts."

The mission of general manager Mickey Loomis was to transform the team. First, he had to hire a new coach after Jim Haslett was fired (though no one could realistically hold the 3-13 record in 2005 against him), get the facility up and running, and rebuild his football team in a rebuilding city.

One candidate piqued Loomis's interest. A boyish-looking forty-two-year-old assistant who turned down his first shot as a head coach when offered the job at Oakland and then missed out at Green Bay.

That, of course, was Sean Payton. And Loomis would later say the key to all that happened was that hire.

"If we don't sign Sean," Loomis said, "then we probably don't get Drew to come. In hiring Sean, we got the best offensive mind in the NFL, and we got one of the best quarterbacks. He's made all of this work."

Taking a circuitous route, the dominoes were falling into place. In the last game of the 2005 season, Brees, then the San Diego Chargers' quarterback, was hit in the end zone trying to recover a fumble and tore the labrum in his throwing shoulder.

Chargers coach Marty Schottenheimer, smitten with young backup Philip Rivers, didn't want the damaged Brees anymore, and the only two teams showing any interest after his surgery were the Miami Dolphins and storm-dilapidated New Orleans.

Dolphins doctors told Coach Nick Saban that a full recovery was iffy, and he passed on Brees to go with Daunte Culpepper.

Payton had no such qualms. He wanted Brees, and told him so.

So the Saints fell into a quarterback who would throw for a league-leading 18,238 yards and 122 touchdowns over the next four years, complete an NFL-record percentage of his passes, and ignite a once disparaged team to two NFC Championship Games—and the Super Bowl title.

After hiring Payton and signing Brees, Loomis drafted running back Reggie Bush, guard Jahri Evans, and receiver Marques Colston, all contributors from the start to the considerable progress the Saints made.

In 2006, Payton's first season, the team went 10-6 in the regular season, and made the NFC Championship Game, losing 39-14 to the Chicago Bears and coming up one step short of a Super Bowl appearance.

From there Payton began a concerted effort of collecting all the essential pieces he needed for a complete team. Accumulating castoffs such as former All-Pro safety Darren Sharper and linebacker Jonathan Vilma, viewed as damaged goods by the New York Jets, doing whatever and getting whoever it took, Payton filled in the holes.

And with a team with seventeen players that went undrafted coming out of college, the Saints, the unlikeliest franchise, began their ascent to the throne of professional football.

Nobody promised any rose gardens. In order to become the first club to lose its last three regular season games then win the Super Bowl, the Saints had to overcome three future Hall of Fame quarterbacks. It started with the Arizona Cardinals and Kurt Warner. New Orleans won 45-14.

Then came the NFC Championship Game with the Minnesota Vikings and Brett Favre, the quarterback from just over the state line in Kiln, Mississippi.

The Vikings were the real stumbling block. For most of the night, Minnesota was the better team, out-numbering the Saints in first downs (31-15), plays (82-55), and yards (475-257), and generally just outplaying the home team.

But five turnovers, including two in the fourth quarter, doomed the Vikings' mission.

With nineteen seconds to play, the score tied at 28, on 3rd and 10 at the Saints' 33, and the din in the Dome reaching crescendo proportions, the Vikings were simply trying to get better field goal range position. But with all the noise in the Superdome, they had a communication mix up. A twelfth man was in the huddle, which Saints tackle Remi Ayodele quickly brought to the attention of the officials.

Five yards farther back after the penalty, and with the Saints ignoring the run and hanging back, Favre, who could have dashed for five to seven yards—enough for a long-range kick attempt—rolled right, then threw across his body toward receiver Sidney Rice in the middle of the field.

Porter read the play, stepped in front, and picked off the pass at the Saints' 22.

Four minutes and forty-five seconds into overtime, rookie Garrett Hartley kicked a forty-yard field goal for the Saints' 31-28 victory

As the ball sailed through the crossbars, Saints longtime radio voice Jim Henderson shouted dramatically into his mike, "Pigs have flown; hell has frozen over!"

It was his way of overstating the fact that the Saints were in the Super Bowl.

"I think Jim has been practicing that line for about ten years," said Henderson's friend, longtime on-the-air partner and former Saints quarterback Archie Manning laconically. "He was just starting to wonder if he'd ever be able to use it."

Two Hall of Fame QBs down and one to go: that season's MVP, Archie's son, Peyton Manning of the Indianapolis Colts.

Super Bowl XLIV was a memorable game, with derring-do feats and drama enough to hold the record-television audience in their seats to the end—or, at least, until close to the finish.

But no play was talked about more across the country the

Garrett Hartley kicks one of his three 40-plus yard field goals. Although Hartley's kicking performance set a Super Bowl record, it was overshadowed by Thomas Morstead's onside kickoff at the start of the second-half.

next day than the opening of the second half. Payton gave his twenty-three-year-old rookie kicker Thomas Morstead a one-word play: "Ambush," their code word for an onside kick.

With the Saints down 10-6 on the biggest stage in sports, Morstead toe-tapped the ball toward Colts' up-man Hank Baskett. It took a bounce, then ricocheted off his chest, setting off a scrum that literally lasted minutes. Saints safety Chris Reis came out of it with raw, burning forearms—and with the ball.

Saints coaches had noticed in film studies some of the Colts' kickoff team "bailing before the kick," leaving the front line to set up their return blocks.

"I thought it was 60 to 70 percent that we'd recover," said Payton, "and keeping the ball away from Peyton Manning one more time is huge in a game like this. Once I decided we'd do it, it was just a matter of time."

From there the Saints went to their first lead of the night, 13-10.

Keeping the ball from Manning was good thinking. The first two times the Colts had the ball that night Manning staked them to a 10-0 lead, including a 96-yard drive that ended with a touchdown pass to Pierre Garçon.

Meanwhile, Brees started off with a *clink*. In the first quarter he was a miserly 3-of-7 for 27 yards. Then he roared into form, completing 29-of-32 for 261 yards and two touchdowns the rest of the way. And two of the three incompletions were spikes to stop the clock.

The man was on fire.

In the fourth quarter, with the Colts again ahead 17-16, Brees went on a memorable fifty-nine-yard drive, completing seven straight passes—to seven different receivers—to inch ahead. A two-point conversion pass to Lance Moore made the sequence eight passes to eight different receivers. And that last one—which had to be reviewed—was very important because with 5:42 to play, the Colts were driving for a tying touchdown, not the winning points.

That's where we were two minutes and eighteen seconds later, with Manning lined up in the shotgun on 3rd and 5 at the Saints' 31, and Porter positioned across from Wayne.

The instant Porter saw a man go in motion, he sensed what was coming. Hurried by Williams's all-out blitz, Manning fired a pass to the slanting Wayne, and Porter stepped right in front.

"Everything slowed down," the cornerback said. "The spiral on the ball slowed down. The guys around me slowed down. The crowd noise stopped. It was just me and the football."

Seventy-four yards later Porter was in the end zone, and the Saints' miracle run was secured.

Hell had frozen over again.

The New Orleans Saints were Super Bowl champions.

Tracy Porter's fourth-quarter interception secured the Saints' Super Bowl victory.

COACH ROB

October 7, 1995
Robinson Stadium, Grambling, La.

Coach Eddie Robinson on the Grambling sideline.

Who could have ever imagined it at the beginning?: Eddie Robinson atop the Mount Olympus of college football coaching.

In the midst of the Great Depression, before the bombs fell on Pearl Harbor, the newly married Robinson left a job at a Baton Rouge feed mill making twenty-five cents an hour to begin toiling at a small African American institution that was little more than a vo-tech school in the segregated South. Barely older than the players he inherited, Robinson became head football coach, trainer, grounds keeper, basketball coach, and instructor of an etiquette class he instituted for the poor, rural black kids that attended Louisiana Negro Normal and Industrial Institute.

This was a one-man operation. No assistants, and not much assistance. Rob, as he was known, even had to mark off the yard lines himself.

Almost six decades later, he retired from the sidelines having transformed Louisiana's smallest football-playing school into one of the state's biggest names and having gone where no football coach had gone before, further even than his friends and role models Paul "Bear" Bryant of Alabama and Woody Hayes of Ohio State. With 408 victories, nine black national championships, and seventeen Southwestern Athletic Conference titles, "Coach Rob" left gigantic footprints on the game as the builder of a football arsenal that became a conduit to the pros and a household name across the sporting world.

Robinson was an unabashed flag-waver who trekked through his life's journey with wife Doris and their kids at their side, and with a legion of young men who were not only better football players but better men because they played under him.

As much as anything, Eddie Robinson was a man of unyielding values—but he was a heck of a football coach, too, one of the best who ever diagrammed a play.

★ ★ ★

The secret to such extraordinary success, Robinson would say, was being prepared. On the sidelines, he always carried a briefcase rather than a sheaf of papers on a clipboard with tendencies of opposing coaches and teams.

He picked up that career-long practice from the most influential person in his life.

It's said we all stand on the shoulders of those who came before us. The shoulders of Reuben S. Turner held the weight not only of Robinson but the modern history of college football.

★ ★ ★

Robinson, always infatuated with the strategies of the sport, learned the game from Coach Julius Kraft at Baton Rouge's McKinley High.

Afterward, he got the chance to play quarterback for the renowned Ace Mumford at Southern University. But his career as a Jaguar didn't last long. He wasn't given a room on campus, and although he felt that he was holding his own, the only praise he said he heard went to "the great guys from Texas." He added, "Heck, I didn't have a car and it got kind of old having to thumb rides back and forth, especially after practice."

A close friend enrolled at Leland College, a small denominational school in Baker, a few miles from Baton Rouge, and Eddie, feeling unwanted, was talked into transferring. Leland football was a disaster, and before Robinson's junior year a coaching change was made.

"I remember coming home from my summer job and my mama telling me the new coach was waiting to see me. Mama said he was a 'preacher, too, but the way he taps his feet to music, he can't be much of one.'"

Reuben Turner was a football-playing Virginia Methodist preacher when, in 1939, he was asked to assume the coaching duties at Leland. "I felt I could do more preaching and more good to young men on the field than in a pulpit," Turner said in a 1985 interview.

The first day on the job, Turner, barely in his thirties, visited the home of Leland's junior quarterback, who had decided not to

Preparation—Coach Robinson's key to success on the football field and in life.

return to his woeful football team, or even to school.

"Eddie wasn't home," said Turner. "He had a job on an ice wagon making $3.50 a week. He thought he was rolling in the money and wanted to quit school. But I talked to his mother and we prayed on it."

Perhaps the decision came at the end of their orison. Turner recalled, "His mother told me, 'Reverend, you be sure that boy goes to church.'" Turner chuckled at the memory and said, "'Course, I was going to see to that in any case.'"

Eddie didn't take his mother's decision easily. He wanted his job and was peeved. Mrs. Robinson made Eddie accompany Turner on a recruiting trip around the state. "I think mama was hypnotized," Eddie said.

Turner said the petulant youngster wouldn't speak to him for days. "He was sullen," Turner said.

☆ ☆ ☆

Turner would preach at night in order to make a few dollars to finance the trip, and one evening in Jennings, in Louisiana's rice belt, he impulsively introduced his silent quarterback—who the sports world eventually would come to know as a near-nonstop speaker—to the congregation "as an example of the fine young people we have at Leland," Turner said. "Brother Eddie Robinson is now going to give you some of his thoughts."

"I don't know what possessed me to do it," Turner said, "and Eddie got up very hesitantly. He started to speak slowly and very softly, but he started gathering momentum and, once he got started, I thought he would never stop."

For several weeks the two meandered throughout Louisiana, living on what Robinson termed "the good will of the Lord," and finding a carload of prospects. When drills opened in the fall, Turner made the players buy composition books and copy plays that he drew on the blackboard, producing the first playbook Eddie had ever seen.

"Before this, all we ever called was 'Notre Dame left' or 'Notre Dame right,' but Turner installed several formations and various plays from each. I didn't know there was that much football in the world!" Robinson said with a laugh.

Turner's debut was spoiled on the game's final play. Bishop College pulled out a 12-7 win and Eddie swore his coach cried all the way back from Marshall, Texas, to Baker.

"I wondered why a grown man would act like this," Robinson recalled, "but he told me later he felt he made the proper preparations for the game and didn't believe we should have lost. Turner felt very strongly about football."

Next up was Alcorn, considered the strongest opponent on the schedule. This time Turner's preparations paid off. He scouted his opponent, rare for the time, and charted tendencies in every situation.

"We ran Alcorn right off the field and I knew right there [there] was something to this preparation business," Robinson remembered with a wink. Leland was to lose only once more in two years, both championship seasons.

☆ ☆ ☆

Turner used Eddie as an assistant as well as a quarterback. At the Turner home, all phases and situations of the sport were discussed. The two studied technique books from beginning to end, then over again. Whenever Turner had business elsewhere, he'd turn the practices over to his quarterback, who accepted the task zealously.

"I felt a responsibility to [do] more than when Coach was present," Eddie said solemnly. "If he wanted us to do twenty-five laps, I'd order thirty-five. If I saw a guy throw a block wrong, I'd make him do it over and over. I felt we should do more simply because Coach wasn't there.

"Later I found out that the first few times he left the team to me, he'd hide and observe the practice. He said he didn't blame the team for resenting me because I tried to kill them—and me, too. Still, he didn't come out to help them."

Nobody knew it at the time, of course, but Turner was preparing Rob for his life's work.

Jobs weren't plentiful in the summer of 1941, and Robinson, newly graduated and newly married, couldn't be choosy about work. He accepted employment unloading trucks at a Baton Rouge feed mill. Then an aunt learned about a coaching position opening up in north Louisiana.

This wasn't at Howard or Morehouse, or even Southern, historically black schools with a pedigree and a standing among African Americans. This wasn't even yet Grambling College. It was Louisiana Negro Normal and Industrial Institute, more of a trade school than an academic citadel.

Ralph Waldo Emerson Jones, the baseball-coaching president of the school whose sister was close friends with Rob's aunt, granted Eddie an interview. "Those two women worried the president so much," Robinson exclaimed, "I believe he hired me to save his sanity."

"But talk about a happy man. I was on top the world with my bride and a coaching job."

The older players Robinson inherited had competed on the field against their new coach just the year before and apparently resented his appointment. Winless through eight games, Robinson decided to drop the seniors from his squad. A tie and Robinson's first victory closed the season.

"It was tough for a while," he said. "Fans were openly saying I didn't know what I was doing, and to tell the truth, I wondered a little myself. But President Jones, although he was not aware of it, gave me the confidence to stick to my plans."

Eating in a side room of the cafeteria, Eddie overheard two faculty members criticizing his strategy. Jones joined the men for lunch and immediately was asked about firing the coach. Eddie froze. "I couldn't move," he recounted. "It seemed like an eternity before the president answered, but to this day I remember his reply word for word: 'Well, I'm going to have to give Coach Robinson a chance, the same way I gave you a chance. Even though I can't measure it, you probably didn't do a great job in the classroom your first year. I expect you're doing better now. Eddie Robinson will win next year.'"

The Tigers went unbeaten, untied, and unscored upon in 1942.

Paul "Tank" Younger was the first of Robinson's players to reach the NFL, and the first prospect from a predominately black college to be given the opportunity. Once he made it, the pros began taking further notice of Grambling players, especially as they began excelling at football's highest level.

Four members of Robinson's unbeaten 1955 club eventually went on to All-Pro fame, and thirteen Tigers made pro rosters in 1963. Four of Robinson's players (Willie Brown, Junious "Buck" Buchanan, Charlie Joiner, and Willie Davis) have been inducted into the Pro Football Hall of Fame.

The wire services, networks, national magazines, and newspapers were suddenly in daily contact with Grambling. The Tigers became a big name in the world of sports.

Robinson not only taught football, he taught life, too. He'd hit the dormitory hall at 6:00 a.m. every morning clanging a bell in order to get the players up for breakfast, on the theory that if they were up and about for their morning meal they'd also find their way to class.

"You know people always ask us how many boys we have in pro ball," Rob once noted. "But seldom are we asked how many of our players graduate. Not all Grambling men play professional football, and we have a responsibility to prepare them for other careers."

That wasn't all. Robinson's teams were required to wear coats and ties on trips, taught to respect the flag, required to keep their rooms clean, and forced to take his etiquette class for proper table manners and the correct way in which to shake hands and leave a room.

"He teaches values," the late defensive tackle Buck Buchanan said. "More than anything he passed on [to] me, Rob taught me respect."

Spotting the Grambling president strolling to the practice area one hot August afternoon, Buchanan cursed under his breath. The president's presence meant extra plays. Buchanan remembered the otherwise inconsequential session, held more than two decades beforehand, vividly. "After the president spoke to the squad," he said, "Rob told me to take off my blue jersey, meaning I was no longer on first team, and made me stand on the sidelines." The humiliation lasted three days, and Buck was too

embarrassed to tell his teammates why.

When Robinson finally told Buchanan he could put his blue jersey back on, the defender had come to the startling realization he wasn't the only big man on campus.

They all learned.

Quarterback Doug Williams recalled four years of listening to Robinson lecture on the American Dream and work ethic, saying, "I felt like I'd received a degree in philosophy."

Turner had Robinson pegged from the start. Not only did every Grambling player attend Sunday morning church services, they attended vespers every Sunday evening. That was when they used to receive their scholarship money, before the NCAA disallowed the stipend. Now the first football meeting of the week followed the service.

"The longer I live, I swear the more I appreciate what Rob has given to us," Williams said. "More than football, he's given us direction in life."

With much stacked against him, Robinson rolled up a 408-165-15 record in fifty-seven years of coaching, at the time the most wins in college football history and still all-time at his beloved Grambling. He reached a milestone no one thought any football coach could, his 400th victory, with a 42-6 win over Mississippi Valley State at age seventy-six.

How good of a coach was Eddie Robinson? Lost in the aura of what became his legend is the fact that in fifteen years of coaching football and basketball simultaneously, he had a 89-37-7 record on the field and a 288-120 record on the court, approximately a 70 percent winning percentage in both sports.

Even more meaningful to Robinson was that the man who spawned the finished coach and man almost a half-century after the fateful prayer session with Eddie's mother was pleased with the result. Reuben S. Turner's most treasured possession in his final years was a handwritten letter from his protégé.

"Coach," wrote Rob to Turner, "it never would have happened without you. I tremble to think of what my life would have been without you."

Coach Robinson before his final home game, November 15, 1997. Robinson led the Tigers to 408 victories during his fifty-seven year tenure.

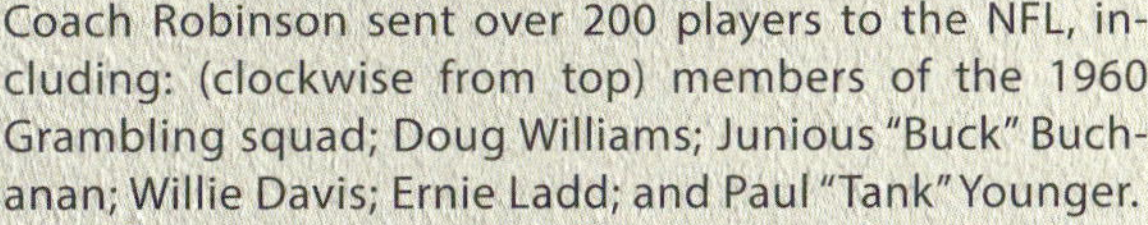

Coach Robinson sent over 200 players to the NFL, including: (clockwise from top) members of the 1960 Grambling squad; Doug Williams; Junious "Buck" Buchanan; Willie Davis; Ernie Ladd; and Paul "Tank" Younger.

THE LAST WORD

January 21, 1979
Orange Bowl, Miami, Florida

Terry Bradshaw led the Pittsburgh Steelers to four Super Bowl victories between 1975 and 1980.

This was nothing short of an amazing moment. Terry Bradshaw was setting Super Bowl records—and the halftime show had yet to begin.

Bradshaw simply was unstoppable in Super Bowl XIII, causing the Dallas Cowboys to stumble all over the field and his critics to stutter incoherently across America.

After thirty minutes of football, Bradshaw had passed for 253 yards and three touchdowns as the Pittsburgh Steelers led Dallas 21-14 in the Big Game of 1978. It was the Pittsburgh defense, not the Pittsburgh quarterback, who was having problems, much to the surprise of most of the sporting press.

It's kind of easy now to see what a great quarterback Bradshaw was, lifting a woe-begotten franchise to a championship level. But at the time Bradshaw was a whipping boy for Easterners who clung to the stereotype that anyone who spoke with a Southern drawl must be dim-witted. It should be noted, though, that Bradshaw played along, trying too hard to fit in and saying things meant to be cute but falling flat. Though he always called his own plays, Terry was maybe never able to shake a Li'l Abner image until he became a first-ballot Hall of Famer.

But Terry Bradshaw stands tall in the pantheon of pro quarterbacks, setting an almost impossible standard: four Super Bowl appearances and four Super Bowl championships. Nobody has ever done better.

★ ★ ★

The Blonde Bomber defused Tom Landry's football machinemind for the second time in four years.

Pittsburgh won the American Conference championship with a 14-2 record as Bradshaw turned in a brilliant season, completing 53 percent of his passes for 2,995 yards and 28 touchdowns. After two victories in the playoffs, the Steelers were on the brink of their third Super Bowl title in three appearances, including one in Super X when Pittsburgh also defeated Dallas. Everything in Bradshaw's career was falling into place after a rocky beginning. "It all comes down to this," he said after the game, "God gave me some ability, and He gave me some faith. I've been trying to put them both to work."

After throwing two touchdowns of twenty-eight and seventy-five yards to John Stallworth, Bradshaw was able to somehow zip another scoring pass to secondary receiver Rocky Bleier, who made the catch barely in bounds just before the half to give the Steelers a touchdown lead.

After Franco Harris went in on a twenty-two-yard run to make the score 28-17, the Cowboys fumbled the kickoff. Smelling blood, Bradshaw hit Lynn Swann for an eighteen-yard touchdown that jacked the margin to 35-17 with less than seven minutes to play. The Cowboys, fighting to the end, scored two touchdowns in the remaining time, but it was Terry Bradshaw's day, the kind that generally silences the critics, if only for a while. "Maybe it's because of my personality, but I don't think I'll ever get the recognition from the media," he reflected. "They make excuses for the other guys; they don't for me. I lose, I go back to being a dummy."

Though he didn't have a perfect game, with an interception and two fumbles, Bradshaw finished with 17 completions in 30 attempts for 318 yards and 4 touchdowns. He was named MVP for the first of two times.

★ ★ ★

Terry was always a hard-working kid growing up in Shreveport, spending hours throwing footballs (in football season) and baseballs (in baseball season) through a swing and into a bucket and rubber tire in his backyard. Despite being a year ahead of his age in school, making him a bit gawky compared to his classmates, Bradshaw built himself into a promising athlete, setting a

Bradshaw's #12 is retired after his senior year at Louisiana Tech.

national high school javelin record with a toss of 244 feet and 11 inches.

But he wasn't a quarterback yet at Woodlawn High, which from the late 1950s to late 1960s was a gold mine for passers under Coach Lee Hedges. Billy Laird, who played briefly with the Boston Patriots, was the first, followed by Trey Prather (whose promise was snuffed out in Vietnam), Bradshaw, then long-time pro Joe Ferguson.

"(Terry) wasn't a scarecrow," Hedges said in the 1970s, "but he didn't have near the muscle definition he has today. He didn't turn seventeen until midway through his senior year. But that arm of his was already of age." Bradshaw offered his own secret of success. "I was the kind of kid that worked every day, every day. No one had to tell me I was clumsy and needed to run the hurdles. I did it on my own. I wanted to excel, and I realized my abilities were limited because I was awkward. So the Good Lord gave me the capacity to work, work, work."

When he finally got his chance to quarterback Woodlawn he threw twenty-one touchdown passes and his team reached the state finals.

Then he made a big mistake.

Because of growing pressure to go to LSU, which he did not wish to attend because Trey Prather was there and Terry did not want to sit on the bench for another three years, he just went through the motions of taking his entrance exam.

Though he graduated in the top third of his class with a B-minus average, that was the start of Terry's slow-witted reputation.

After some disillusionment with Baylor, his first choice, Terry went to nearby Louisiana Tech where he led the NCAA in passing yardage (2,890) in 1969.

"I just came into my own about then," Terry said of the months just before his junior year. "I had grown to six-foot-three, 215-pounds, and my motor skills had come together. I could run now; I had speed and quickness, and the strength to shake off tacklers. I could run and throw."

None other than Steelers' owner Art Rooney took a personal trip to Ruston to see for himself what sort of athlete could throw for 6,586 career yards and set twenty team and conference records for a Division II school.

With the first pick of the 1970 draft, Rooney selected Bradshaw.

You'd think Terry didn't know what he was getting into. The woeful Steelers had only one win in its last twenty-eight games, and their quarterback history was harrowing. Such eventual luminaries as Johnny Unitas, Earl Morral, Jackie Kemp, Bill Nelson, and Lenny Dawson all paid their dues in Pittsburgh on their way to success elsewhere. But, with the exuberance of the young, Bradshaw was undeterred—even elated. He viewed the Steelers as a team he had a chance to grow with and told reporters he wanted to play even if his team was ahead—or behind—70-0. Starting with a loser, he said, was a blessing, because that was the kind of team he wanted to lead to a championship.

The Eastern press tried to hide smirks and grins at this open country kid who didn't realize he wasn't supposed to be this honest. They began to mock him in print, and because things didn't work out on that dreadful team from the start, Terry started getting all the blame. Culture shock must have set in as the drawling youngster incurred the wrath of blue collar Pittsburgh. A construction worker actually booed the rookie as he signed his first contract at midfield in unfinished Three Rivers Stadium—the start of what Terry came to believe was a chorus.

Every miscue by the rookie was accompanied by disapproving roars, almost as if the crowd wanted a chance to vent. Stories circulated of Terry forgetting snap counts and of teammates occasionally having to make the calls in the huddle. Terry had to be helped from the field once because of an injury and a mighty cheer went up from the fans.

"That first year was horrible," he recalled. "I was embarrassed and ashamed. But we won five games, and I got some understanding of what was going on, the hardships, the cold truth, the bitterness about this game. I learned it wasn't rah-rah college anymore. 'If you lose, doggone tough. We'll win next week.' Now it was, 'Hey, you SOB, I lost two bucks on you!'"

Things got worse before they got better. There was a time when the Steelers alternated quarterbacks. Then he lost his job to Joe Gilliam. "He put on the pressure and kept it on, and I was shut out," Bradshaw said. "I was benched, not playing, and I could

Bradshaw on the Louisiana Tech sideline with his brother Gary.

never even imagine that. I always thought I was a good quarterback, and that someday I could be a real good quarterback. But it seemed I was the only one felt that way."

Matters came to a head one night in Terry's apartment. He sat alone, absorbed in self-pity, trying to sort things out. In the long, gloomy night, he began reading his Bible, and something changed. In him, and in his game. Terry didn't just suddenly play well, but Coach Chuck Noll decided to stick with Bradshaw and things started clicking in a game against New England. "Terry really came of age in that game," said teammate Ray Mansfield, "just the things he said and did. He had complete control, and he knew it, and we knew it." Of the second series against the Patriots, Mansfield continued, "he came into that huddle and he was in complete charge. He's been that way ever since."

Indeed. Pittsburgh surged from that point to a pulverizing defeat of Minnesota in Super Bowl X, and followed that up by the thumping of Dallas a year later

By the time of Super Bowl XIII, the third of the Bradshaw's four championships, he was finally getting his due. "We knew Bradshaw was the key," said Cowboys safety Cliff Harris. "They are really a good team, but Bradshaw made them great today."

What happened that long night in his apartment to cause that dramatic turnaround? "It was what we as Christians call re-dedication, where I re-dedicate my life to the Lord and He forgives me of my sins. That's what I did that night," Bradshaw explained. "What it did was give me peace of mind, the reassurance that I wasn't getting from anyone else. It allowed me to readjust, to cope with the problem. If I played, fine. If I didn't, well, the Lord would take care of me. The main thing was just to stop worrying. I realized this wasn't the greatest thing in the world. It's football, just a game."

DRAWING AN ACE

December 5, 1948
Kezar Stadium, San Francisco, California

Today, the game would engender screaming headlines from coast to coast. In those days of the late 1940s, the first pairing of a predominantly white school and a predominantly black school, San Francisco State and Southern University, didn't raise an eyebrow.

Either we've come a long way or maybe we've regressed.

The Fruit Bowl was played in the City by the Bay in Kezar Stadium, and put an exclamation point on the Jaguars' 1948 12-0-0 season, the fourth of Coach Arnett W. Mumford's six black national championship teams.

"We had a great trip going out there," quarterback Warren "Jug" Braden recalled. "We all gained ten or fifteen pounds because we had a big dining car all to ourselves on the train. It was just another ballgame to us, and we were treated fine the whole time. They even had a dance for us after the game. Nobody ever played against a white team before, but it was just another game against a well-seasoned team. Race was never brought up. We had played the best teams in our league and we were glad to get the competition."

The Fruit Bowl was played in a quagmire, and Southern won 30-0 with Braden being named MVP.

It's a long since forgotten football game, but it really was history in the making. Fittingly, "Ace" Mumford, a black football pioneer, showed the way—just as he did throughout his career.

★ ★ ★

As one who saw them come and go over the course of decades, former Southern University assistant football coach and longtime Jaguars observer John Brown made a flat evaluation almost forty years after his old boss died in 1962: "Mumford was the best coach they've had there."

Maybe one of the best anybody ever had anywhere.

Mumford coached four schools to an overall 235-82-25 record and the half-dozen black national championships. His Southern teams were 169-57-14—with five of those championships and eleven Southwestern Athletic Conference titles in his twenty-five-year tenure on the bluff. There was one eleven-year stretch under Mumford when the Jaguars didn't lose more than one conference game a season.

Clearly, Mumford was a Coaches' Coach.

The most used word for describing the driven Mumford by those who knew him best was a variation of "perfect." Eddie Robinson, the iconic coach at Grambling, said of his one-time mentor, "he worked for perfection." Emory Hines, a lineman for Mumford at Texas College and later an assistant for him at Southern, said, "he was a perfectionist."

At the core of Mumford's uncommon success was an obsession for flawless execution. He was never satisfied until he got it. "We didn't have lights on the practice field," Hines continued, "but Coach Mumford would get the players down by the end of the field near the street lights and work until he got what he wanted."

Braden, one of thirty-five All-Americans Mumford developed in his thirty-six-year career, said, "I can still see him standing behind the offense, puffing on a cigarette, making us run the same play over and over until we could practically run it with our eyes closed."

R. L. Stockard, who was the sports information director at Southern during Mumford's tenure, revealed that at practice the coach would tip off the defense on what plays the offense was going to run, then make the offense repeat the play time after

Coach Mumford on the Southern sideline.

time until it finally gained ten yards. "So just what would this accomplish?" Stockard asked. "Well, there is only one thing that can make an offense successful while running against a defense that knows what's coming: blocking. Mumford, who preferred smaller but quicker athletes, always had teams with superior blocking. That overcomes a lot of obstacles."

And he was a strategist, employing the man-in-motion, flankers and wideouts, and variations of the T-formation, including the wing-T, long before they were widely popular.

Mumford wanted to know all there was about football. In the Jim Crow world of the first two-thirds of the twentieth century, when blacks weren't allowed to sit in on some coaching clinics, Mumford would visit the hotels where the major coaches were staying to pick some of the game's most advanced minds. Glenn "Pop" Warner spent much time going over his tactics and philosophies with Mumford.

"I'm telling you all this," Warner is said to have admitted, "because I know I'll never be playing you."

Hines remembered Alabama's Paul "Bear" Bryant and Arkansas's Frank Broyles trading ideas with Mumford. "I can recall Coach Mumford sitting down with them here at Southern, moving soda tops in offensive and defensive patterns until the wee hours of the morning," Hines said.

A model of coaching consistency, Mumford, a gruff man and incessant smoker, took a circuitous route to Baton Rouge. He was born in Buckhannon, West Virginia, and went to Wilberforce University in Xenia, Ohio. During his succession of head coaching jobs—starting at Jarvis Christian when he was twenty-six, then at Bishop and Texas College and Southern—he did it all.

When he came to Southern—after coaching Texas College to the 1935 black national championship season, in which Southern was counted among his victims—Mumford took over several positions in the financially strapped athletic department. He was not only head football coach, but also basketball (coaching the 1941 black national championship team), baseball, and track coach, athletics director, and chairman of the physical education department, where he also taught.

The late Dean Jones, who played center and linebacker under Mumford in 1937-41 and who later became the Jaguars' athletic director, said the latter assignments should not be downplayed.

"He taught so many folks so many things about football," Jones said. "He learned from others, but he also did his share of teaching. He was also an academician. He was one of the few football coaches who taught kinesiology. And it was from him I learned about logarithms in a course called 'Tests and Measurement.'"

In those tough economic times of the Great Depression, Southern had to improvise to make ends meet. Once when the Jaguars' basketball team was stuck without a team bus, he got a chauffeur for the players—his wife.

Still, more than anything, Mumford was a football coach.

"It's all he thought about," Stockard said. "Next to his family, football was the big love of his life."

His earliest teams at Southern were not memorable. The Jaguars were 2-5-2 in 1936, and 4-4-1 in 1937. Then the Mumford touch began kicking in. Southern was 7-0-1 in 1938. From then on, Southern was a force to be reckoned with in black football circles—and beyond.

★ ★ ★

Perhaps by chance, perhaps by a confluence of just the right blend of talent and coaching acumen, the program truly flowered in the late 1940s when a smallish ballhandler from New Orleans first put on a blue Jaguar jersey.

Braden, five-foot-eight, 140 pounds, helped Xavier Prep win two state championships before matriculating to Southern in 1945.

Mumford had spent part of his summer traveling to coaching clinics and had a surprise for his team when he returned. He was junking his old single wing for the T-formation, which would prove ideal with Braden at quarterback. With Mumford constantly tinkering with his new offense and Braden's execution, the Jaguars uncoiled records of 9-2-1, 10-2-0, 12-0-0, and 10-0-1 over the next four seasons and won black national championships in 1948 and '49.

It was a glorious time for Southern University football.

★ ★ ★

Eddie Robinson, who would become the face of black college football, briefly was a part of Mumford's program before transferring to a nearby denominational school, Leland College.

"Southern had about thirteen quarterbacks," Robinson said, "and I was on the bottom of the list. Mumford did try to talk me into staying, but at the time I felt I had to make my own way."Robinson's admiration for Mumford never left, however. Six times over the years Robinson's Grambling teams played Mumfor's Jaguars, and Southern won five times. "He put a few knots on my head," Robinson would say later.

Thinking back on the trailblazing coach at Southern, Coach Rob once reflected, "I truly believe Mumford taught life as much as he coached football."

Lesson learned.

ONWARD, CHRISTIAN

November 27, 1926
Soldier Field, Chicago, Illinois

"How could a halfback be a breath of fire and streak of flame," Dan Jenkins asked in the September 15, 1969, issue of *Sports Illustrated* commemorating the one-hundredth season of college football, "playing, for, say, Southwestern Louisiana for example?"

And yet Chris Cagle became something akin to that when he went on to Army for four more years of college ball in the 1920s when you could do that sort of thing.

Christian Keener Cagle of Merryville in Beauregard Parish was all that and more.

A 1929 issue of *Time* magazine featured Cagle on the cover and reported in fevered prose that he was "As elusive as a god." In the national press, Cagle, for his sandy-colored hair, was the "Red Thunderbolt of West Point" (shortened to "Red" by his teammates), the "Louisiana Jackrabbit," and other monikers trying to capture his spectacular play.

But mostly he was just "Onward Christian," for an almost unfailing ability to advance the ball.

A triple-threat at both Southwestern Louisiana Institute and then, after he graduated, at Army, Cagle was the first football player selected on Grantland Rice's All-American team three straight years. He was college football's 1929 Player of the Year, which a few years later would equate to the Heisman Trophy. In Jenkins's essay, in which the evolution of the game was divided by decades, Cagle was shoulder pad-to-shoulder pad with some giants of the era—George Gipp of Notre Dame, Red Grange of Illinois, and Ernie Nevers of Stanford—in the mythological backfield of the '20s.

His credentials to be included in that select company? In four years at SLI (where he returned ten kickoffs for touchdowns), through a combination of TDs, PATs, and field goal kicking, Cagle scored 235 points—a school record that was not broken until 1989, sixty-four years later. At West Point, where he averaged 6.4 yards a carry and 26.4 yards a kickoff return, Cagle scored 169 points, giving him a total of 404 in his eight years of varsity football. He ran for 2,664 yards from scrimmage at Army and passed for 1,432—pretty heady stats for the time.

This says as much about Cagle as anything: He was captain of both schools where he played. And he made an impression at both as reflected in the won-loss columns. Over his two careers, Cagle's teams went 53-19-7 (23-11-2 at SLI, 30-8-5 at West Point).

It's fair to say that not until the fabled touchdown twins of Doc Blanchard and Glenn Davis in the mid-1940s did West Point have anyone to compare with Chris Cagle.

SLI teammate Bernard Lange would assess decades later of what he saw close up: "He was the greatest player ever. When Chris would run, you were never sure where his next step would land. He had thighs as big as watermelons, and they allowed him to change directions in mid-air."

★ ★ ★

One of eight children, Cagle got his name from an uncle who had been named for Christian Keener, a Methodist bishop.

At five-foot-ten, 175 pounds in his prime, on the surface there was nothing to indicate there was anything particularly special about Cagle. But he was a natural athlete who developed his extraordinary hand-eye coordination roping calves and colts while growing up in Southwest Louisiana, and he developed amazing speed and endurance after being caught in a boyhood prank at school.

Or at least that's how the story goes.

Instead of being suspended from classes, Cagle was kicked off the school bus. He turned his punishment into a conditioning drill by racing the bus the four-mile distance between his house and school, and back again after practice. He'd catch up each time the vehicle stopped to pick up other students. The speed, power, and endurance Chris developed on those daily jaunts are said to have been the secret to his immense athletic prowess.

Cagle would develop into a formidable football player, shot-put champion, and baseball hitter at Southwestern, in 1922 the closest college to Merryville.

★ ★ ★

At SLI he began gaining notoriety with surprising performances given the limitations of the time. In 1923, when the ball was shaped more like a pumpkin than the missile we play with today, he kicked a field goal against LSU that staked Southwestern to a 3-0 lead that held to late in the fourth quarter. That afternoon the eighteen-year-old tailback kept the ball away from the Tigers by completing 22 of 33 passes for 233 yards. LSU avoided the upset 7-3, though SLI out-gained the Tigers 278-198.

The following year, Cagle, who almost always played with his chin strap either dangling from his helmet or snapped around the back, had a mind-bending rushing average of 12.3 yards (752 yards in 61 attempts), and completed 53.9 percent of his passes for 859 yards. He also made 20 of 25 dropkick field goals.

He led SLI to a 7-2 record and the Louisiana Intercollegiate Athletic Association championship in 1925, scoring 93 points, rushing for 1,048 yards, and passing for 904 yards.

How do you put those feats in words? New Orleans sportswriter Charles "Pie" Dufour tried after covering a Tulane team that would finish 8-1-0 being hard-pressed to beat "small-time" SLI 14-0 in 1924. "When a player is captain, quarterback, No. 1 runner, No. 1 passer, No. 1 punter and No. 1 field- goal kicker," wrote Dufour, "he has to be pretty good in whatever league he plays in."

After he graduated, SLI officials, including the school president, used their influence to get Cagle an appointment to West Point to continue his career. In those days Army often would extend the playing careers of athletes from other schools. It was sort of like being drafted. West Point coach Lawrence "Biff" Jones—later to coach at LSU and have a memorable, unpleasant relationship with Louisiana governor Huey Long—was most happy to obtain Cagle's services.

Cagle almost changed history in one of college football's most famed moments—Notre Dame's "Win One for the Gipper" game at Yankee Stadium on November 10, 1928. Army was a heavy favorite, but Coach Knute Rockne pulled a psychological ploy by telling his team of the final request of George Gipp, the first Irish All-American who died of pneumonia shortly after his last game in 1920.

"The day before he died," Rockne said, "George asked me to wait until the situation seemed hopeless—then for a Notre Dame team to go out and beat Army for him. This is the day, and you're the team."

After a scoreless first half, Cagle seemingly took control, fueling an Army drive with runs of eight and ten yards, then throwing a perfect forty-yard pass that set up a Cadet touchdown. But inspired Notre Dame came back with two scores to take a 12-6 lead.

Army wasn't finished. Cagle gave the Cadets a shot to pull it out with a fifty-five-yard kickoff return in the final minutes. But the exhausted Cagle, who had played the entire game, collapsed at the 10-yard line and had to be carried from the field. The game ended two plays later—with Army one yard away from the tying touchdown and winning PAT.

Just a little more energy and one of the most intriguing stories in college football lore could have had a different outcome.

There was another game, the 1926 Army-Navy game in Chicago in which Soldier Field was dedicated. Cagle played a pivotal role before what was then the biggest crowd ever to see a college football game, 110,000. That meeting, a 21-21 tie, is still considered the greatest in the series. Down 14-0, Cagle broke off a key twenty-one-yard run that ultimately led to an Army touchdown. Later, a long kick return by Cagle put the ball at the Navy 44 from where he would shortly burst through the line for a touchdown that made the score 21-14, Army.

Navy came back for the tying touchdown, but Cagle and Army played the national champion Middies off their cleats.

★ ★ ★

Chris Cagle was a glittering figure in the Golden Age of Sport, but there would be no happy ending to his story.

Playing at Army extended his playing days, but he couldn't stand being away from Louisiana, where a certain Miss Marian Mumford Haile awaited. They were secretly married, violating the academy's honor code that specified no cadet could possess "a horse, mustache or wife."

Found out, Cagle was dismissed from West Point a month before he was to graduate.

Life went on with Chris playing pro ball for six seasons, then coaching for a season at Mississippi State, before partnering with John "Shipwreck" Kelly as owners of pro football's Brooklyn Dodgers.

In a few years, though, Cagle was a department manager of a New York insurance company. In December of 1942, on his way home to his wife and kids from work, he slipped on the steps of a subway and fractured his head. Cagle died of complications and pneumonia three days later. He was only thirty-seven.

In 1954, Louisiana's "Streak of Flame" became part of the second class to be inducted into the College Football Hall of Fame.

ONE CAME RUNNING

January 30, 2000
Georgia Dome, Atlanta, Georgia

What were they thinking? All those hot-shot coaches at Miami, Nebraska, and LSU knew of Marshall Faulk and wanted him with their respective programs.

They just didn't want him in their backfields.

We're talking about a player who in time would be considered the greatest all-purpose back in NFL history; the first man to run for twelve thousand yards and catch passes totaling more than six thousand yards; the only player to run for more than seventy touchdowns and catch passes for thirty more.

So exactly what did all those college talent evaluators miss?

Not much, really.

No matter what position Faulk lined up in, he was going to be exceptional. He did it all for Coach Wayne Reese's Carver High Rams, at various times playing quarterback, cornerback, tight end, flanker, split end, and kicker. That versatility was his strength—and weakness as far as the recruiters were concerned. Carver stats were murky, and on offense he was plugged in at every skill position, meaning he did not compile eye-raising numbers at any single one. Limited play at any of them was not enough to say definitively "that's where he belongs," even though he clearly could run, catch, and block.

On defense, though, he played one position, and did so exceedingly well. On the perimeter, he literally controlled the flow of a game, basically sealing off as much as half the secondary from opponents. Even Reese would later crack that his protégé could have been the No. 1 overall draft choice as a cornerback. "He really was better there," Reese said, "hard as that is to believe."

Of course, he was the No. 2 overall pick as a running back, and that's where he wanted to play.

Colleges were drooling at the thought of Faulk in their secondaries, and that's where they all lost him. "I knew I wanted to run the ball," he said later. "I knew I could run the ball."

★ ★ ★

Only by happenstance did Marshall get some encouragement about his ball-carrying aspirations. Curtis Johnson, a New Orleans-area native then an assistant on the staff at San Diego State (and later head coach at Tulane), was on a recruiting mission to check out another prospect and by sheer chance saw Carver's team—and Faulk.

Salivating, Johnson brought film back to Aztecs coach Al Luginbill, who said without hesitation, "We need this kid."

Johnson made an offer young Marshall couldn't refuse: A chance to run to daylight—right out of the squalor, crime, and hopelessness of the Desire Street housing project in New Orleans's notorious Ninth Ward.

Marshall was the fifth and last son of Roosevelt and Cecile Faulk, who after a divorce was singlehandedly trying to keep her baby on the straight and narrow. Not easy in an area where drug dealers were omnipresent and shootings and stabbings almost daily occurrences. She already had lost one son to the penitentiary, and she worked almost around the clock to provide material and moral support for her youngest.

Not always a model kid, especially in the classroom, Marshall nevertheless was able to sidestep the serious pitfalls of his environment, thanks to the influences of a sixth-grade teacher named Mrs. Porter and, later, Reese. Mrs. Porter started sending reports of Marshall's classroom behavior home to Cecile, with the danger of too many demerits costing him the opportunity to suit up for his playground team. That very real possibility got Marshall's attention.

The relationship of Faulk and Reese seems almost like fate in retrospect. Almost certainly Marshall's life would have been different without the longtime public school coach, who became a surrogate father—and role model—to the youngster, who would even become a regular at dinner at the Reese household.

Reese could see that Marshall had great potential, as an athlete and as a person. It was Reese walking the halls of Carver one day who spotted a stocky freshman finding his way around. Always looking for a potential prospect, Reese said "I went up to him and asked why he was not playing football." Next day he reported to practice.

When Faulk, an all-around athlete who excelled at basketball, baseball, and track, as well as football, told his coach he hoped to develop into a pro point guard, Reese stopped him cold with

a question: "How many five-foot-nine point guards are there in the NBA?" From then on, Marshall played basketball for the fun of the game.

When Faulk came to him as a fifteen-year-old and told the coach he had to quit the team because his mom was ill and he needed to make money at his brother's barbeque stand, Reese arranged a job for him—as a part time janitor at Carver that required him to report to work at 6:00 a.m., hours before classes began. He was mopping floors, cleaning sinks, scrubbing commodes, all before school and football practice.

That turned into one of life's lessons.

"I made a little money," Marshall reflected later, "and I learned something, too. I learned that when I grew up I didn't want to work a normal job."

By the time he left Carver, Reese suspected he wouldn't have to.

"He had a 49-inch vertical jump, he was drafted as an outfielder in baseball, he ran a 20.9 for 220 meters in track," Reese recalled. "When he first came out, he did not look like the typical football player with a great big neck and bulging muscles. The kids teased him about his (lack of) strength."

So Reese gave the motivated Marshall keys to the weight room.

"When he left Carver he could squat five hundred pounds," Reese said, and the increased muscle and speed showed up on the football field, one opposing coach saying that trying to tackle Faulk was like trying "to catch a bullet in the dark," another calling him "Superman."

☆ ☆ ☆

It didn't take long at San Diego State for Faulk to make headlines. Filling in for an injured starter in the second game of his college career against Pacific, Faulk broke loose for an NCAA-record 386 yards and seven touchdowns.

In three years as an Aztec (1991-93), Faulk amassed 4,589 yards rushing and scored sixty-two touchdowns, second all-time in NCAA history. An All-American all three seasons, he was also twice a Heisman Trophy finalist, finishing second in 1992.

Still, Marshall had to prove himself to some NFL observers who believed either he wasn't big enough at five-foot-ten, 207 pounds, or that perhaps his college success was as much a product of second-tier Western Athletic Conference opposition as of his own skills.

But Indianapolis Colts' general manager Bill Tobin—who almost two decades before made the call to pick Walter Payton from Jackson State—saw Marshall as the total package and selected him second in the 1993 draft.

The best was yet to come.

In twelve professional seasons with the Colts (1994-98) and the Rams (1999-2005), Faulk earned pro football's biggest honors: the NFL Most Valuable Player in 2000 and the Offensive Player of the Year from 1999 to 2001. In those first three seasons with "The Greatest Show on Turf," as the Rams' offense was dubbed for its pinball-like quality, Faulk was a key contributor to two Super Bowl appearances. In that period he rushed for 4,122 yards, averaging 5.4 yards a carry, while scoring 59 touchdowns.

Statistics don't always tell the full story. In Super Bowl XXXIV, Tennessee Titans coach Jeff Fisher geared his defense to stopping the Rams' running game—meaning Faulk. In ten carries Marshall could only gain seventeen yards, which still made him his team's leading rusher. But he caught five passes for ninety yards, loosening the Tennessee defense. Three of his receptions came on drives that led to two field goals and a touchdown in the Rams' 23-16 victory.

Defensive tackle D'Marco Farr, who saw Faulk as both a teammate and an opponent, put Marshall's talents in focus.

Farr said, "For a while he was the best weapon in the NFL. He could catch, run for power, run for speed. He was smart like a head coach. He was absolutely indefensible for a period of time."

"WE'RE NO. 1"

Fall 1958
Southland, U.S.A.

You'd think, considering this was as perfect a blueprint as any coach ever masterminded for his football team, that it came like a thunderbolt out of the blue.

Not so. "It was more like getting whacked with a 4x4 over the head," cracked Paul Dietzel, then the coach of the LSU Tigers.

What he was referring to—the genesis of what would transform a so-so ball club in 1957 to national championship status in 1958—was a drubbing the Tigers took at Ole Miss two years before. In that game, LSU led the powerful Rebels 17-14 at the half. "We played as well as we could play," Dietzel recalled, "but by the time we got to the dressing room we were worn out."

The Rebels routed LSU in the second half, running away with a 46-17 victory.

If necessity is the mother of invention, this was it for LSU football, which had a core of superior athletes, such as superstar halfback Billy Cannon, but lacked depth—especially crucial in those days of archaic substitution rules, exacerbated by a new precept put in before the '58 season that stipulated if a player was in a game at the start of a quarter, he could be replaced and then return, but no more than twice during that period.

After that runaway defeat at Ole Miss, Dietzel started tinkering with ways to overcome his team's greatest deficiency.

Two years later he was able to put in his acclaimed three-unit system that became the cornerstone of a national championship. Seldom if ever has a game plan been so flawlessly executed, and over a four-month span. The result was the first truly great team of modern SEC football.

In those days when players would play on both offense and defense, the LSU team was divided into three units: The White Team, comprised of the Tigers' best athletes and who played both ways; The Go Team, offensive specialists; and the Chinese Bandits, defensive specialists.

In a nutshell, Dietzel felt his starters (named for the color of their practice jerseys) could play with anybody in the country. He also knew that few, if any, of the specialists on the Go Team (originally the Gold Team, but misinterpreted by a sportswriter) or Bandits could. But if he could get ten good minutes out of each specialty unit in each game, then the rested White team theoretically would be in position to win games in the fourth quarter.

Against a schedule pocked with Hall of Fame coaches, here's how it worked out:

- LSU opened on the road against defending Southwest Conference champion Rice under Jess Neely. LSU won 26-6.
- Alabama, playing its first game under Bear Bryant, already respected for preeminent coaching jobs at Kentucky and Texas A&M, was next at Mobile. LSU won 13-3.
- Hardin-Simmons, a pass-happy threat which would go on to win the Border Conference under fabled TCU and Redskins quarterback Sammy Baugh, was the Tigers' first home opponent. LSU won 20-6.
- Miami, coached by the respected Andy Gustafson. LSU won 41-0.
- Kentucky, coached by Blanton Collier, one of the finest tacticians in football history. LSU won 32-7.
- Florida, under Bob Woodruff, was LSU's homecoming opponent. LSU won a nail-biter 10-7.
- Ole Miss, under legendary coach Johnny Vaught and ranked sixth in the nation, came in for the first hard sellout since Tiger Stadium was expanded to 67,510 four years before. LSU won 14-0.
- Duke, under Bill Murray, fell to the Tigers 50-18.
- Mississippi State provided the Tigers' closest call. On a rain-soaked and muddy field, LSU squeaked by 7-6.
- Tulane fell under a fourth-quarter onslaught of four

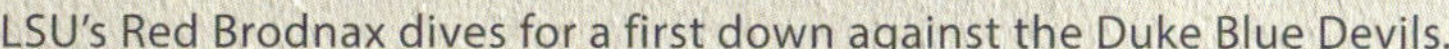
LSU's Red Brodnax dives for a first down against the Duke Blue Devils.

LSU's Johnny Robinson scores one of his four touchdowns against Tulane.

touchdowns. The ultimate outcome was LSU 62, Tulane 0.

- Clemson, under Frank Howard, in a Sugar Bowl that became a football slug-fest, fell to LSU 7-0.

It's impossible to compare the conditions of different eras, though anyone would have to conclude the '58 Tigers were as efficient as any team ever to wear the purple and gold.

Aside from those three relatively close games, as a general rule the Tigers performed as the proverbial well-oiled football machine.

Their efficiency is illustrated in the SEC's final statistics: Auburn led the league in total offense in 1958, averaging 319.4 yards a game. LSU was fourth at 278.0 yards. Yet LSU out-scored Auburn by more than a hundred points (275-173).

Auburn led the nation in total defense, giving up 157.5 yards a game. LSU was second in the SEC, yielding 191.4. But LSU led the SEC in scoring defense (53 points to 62).

Dietzel's theoretical three-team concept worked out perfectly. Over the course of the season, the White Team averaged thirty-five minutes a game. The Go Team and Chinese Bandits divided the remaining twenty-five minutes of game time almost evenly. The back-up troops kept the front line fresh enough to overrun all eleven opponents.

And the Chinese Bandits, throughout that magical season, more than held up their end. In perhaps the most stunning statistic in sports that year, every time an opponent ran a play against them, less than a yard (0.9) was gained.

Unlike the 2003 and 2007 LSU national champions, the '58 Tigers left no argument about who was No. 1. In fact, they were voted the Associated Press' Team of the Year over such professional championship teams as baseball's New York Yankees, the NFL's Baltimore Colts, and the NBA's St. Louis Hawks.

It may be unfair to compare eras, but taking everything into account, could a strong case be made that the 1958 Tigers were LSU's all-time team? Don Purvis, a Go team halfback that year and later an assistant coach for many years under Charlie McClendon, said yes.

"There have been a lot of teams at LSU with more talent, some with a lot more talent," Purvis said. "But as far as utilization of personnel, and the execution by that personnel, I believe the 1958 Tigers are the No. 1 team in the history of LSU."

TIGERS TO THE TOP - AGAIN

January 4, 2004
Louisiana Superdome, New Orleans, La.

What brought on the advent of the Bowl Championship Series, with its series of factors—knowledgeable observations and the data from various polls fed into computers—was an effort to have as close to a true No. 1 game as possible, while preserving the bowl system, and not, as was the case for most of the twentieth century, a championship based on opinion. Educated opinions for the most part, but opinions nevertheless.

Yet that's exactly what was at the heart of the great college football debate of 2003.

Here's the crux of the matter: Oklahoma spent the entire regular season at the top of the two polls, then when it was released in October, the BCS standings. OU obliterated the other contenders, and was talked about and written about as perhaps the greatest team of all time—until the Sooners stunningly lost 35-7 to Kansas State in the Big Twelve Championship Game. Southern Cal had a remarkably fine season, losing once to a so-so California squad, but finishing atop the sportswriters' and coaches' polls. Not flashy but efficient LSU came out of nowhere after losing to Florida at midseason and then stampeding the rest of its way to the SEC Championship Game.

The trio were obviously the nation's best college football teams, all with one defeat.

The BCS formula was a combination of computer rankings, schedule comparisons, quality-win bonuses, and a composite of the AP writers and *USA Today*/ESPN coaches polls.

The human opinion polls had USC ranked No. 1 at the end of the regular season, but the cold, calculating, dispassionate seven computers that figured the BCS standings had Oklahoma and LSU ranked 1 and 2, based largely on strength of schedule, a factor that was not determined until the last weekend of the season with Syracuse defeating Notre Dame and Boise State beating Hawaii. Both of the losing teams had been USC opponents and deflated the Trojans' accomplishments.

Those games turned out to mean everything because, coupled with LSU beating Georgia in the SEC title match, the Trojans suddenly trailed both OU and LSU in six of the seven computer rankings and in overall schedule strength. In the final BCS rankings, Oklahoma, 12-1, was first with 5.11 points based on its No. 1 position in five of the seven computers. LSU, 12-1, was second at 5.99, edging USC (11-1) by 0.16 in the second-closest finish in the BCS's six-year history. (Nebraska nipped Colorado by 0.05 in 2001.)

The howl that went up in Los Angeles (home base of the Trojans) and by voting sportswriters made the weeks leading up to the bowls a media spitting match. Southern Cal, No. 1 in the AP poll, was set to play fourth-ranked Michigan in the Rose Bowl. A victory would give the Trojans first place in at least one poll.

But Oklahoma and LSU were ticketed to play for the BCS national championship in the Sugar Bowl, a title, site, and formula designated years before and agreed to by every school in the NCAA's Division 1-A, including Southern California.

An irony is that the system was tweaked the previous year to take margins of victory out of the computers' computations because of thinking that the equation shouldn't be a factor, that a victory was just a victory and a defeat was just a defeat. So Oklahoma's lopsided loss to Kansas State had no more weight than USC's or LSU's. Also, as opposed to years gone by, a late-season defeat was no worse than an early setback. USC lost in September, LSU in October, and Oklahoma in December.

Had those computations remained in the equation (and apparently they did in the minds of the sportswriters), it's very likely LSU would have been playing Southern Cal in the Sugar Bowl.

But all the computers could factor was one defeat for each of the contenders, and one fewer victory for USC than Oklahoma or LSU. If the argument was difficulty of schedule, the Trojans came up short there, too. USC and LSU had two common opponents, Auburn and Arizona. The Trojans beat Auburn 23-0 in the opening game of the season; LSU defeated Auburn 31-7 eight weeks later. LSU beat Arizona 59-13 in its second game. USC whipped Arizona 45-0. Diplomatic Auburn coach Tommy Tuberville said he wouldn't want to be playing LSU right now (at the end of the regular season when the LSU defense was performing with the cold precision of an execution squad). Arizona senior Clay Hart was asked to make a comparison and said, "I thought they were really good," of the Trojans, "but I personally think LSU was the best team we've faced since I've been a Wildcat."

"Everybody wants to sit here and say they got screwed," Oklahoma defensive tackle Dusty Dvoracek said of Southern Cal, "but they actually got the easier row to hoe. They got to stay at home (in the Rose Bowl), play the lesser team (Michigan)."

So here was Tigers' coach Nick Saban's task: find a way to contain the highest-scoring team in college football, averaging an eye-popping 45.2 points. And the Sooners were also the nation's third-best overall defensive team, giving up an average of 255.7 yards a game.

Consider this heady statistic: In its first twelve games, Oklahoma was behind for fewer than six of the 720 minutes played.

Not only did the Sooners have seven first-team All-Americans, but they practically swept the major individual awards that go to the sport's crème de la crème, including the Heisman Trophy to quarterback Jason White.

Next to the Sooners, the Tigers just had two All-Americans,

defensive tackle Chad Lavalais and cornerback Corey Webster.

Conversely, despite its relative anonymity, LSU was a complete team, scoring an average of thirty-five points behind Matt Mauck, a twenty-four-year-old former minor-league catcher who had the SEC's highest passer rating, along with a dangerous combination of running backs and receivers and a big, fast offensive line that combined for 156 starts.

It was on defense, though, where LSU separated itself from the rest of college football. The Tigers led the nation in rushing defense, yielding a miniscule 68.2 yards, and were atop the statistical list in scoring defense, allowing a paltry 10.5 points a game.

And that's really where LSU won its first football national championship in forty-five years, on defense.

LSU got its winning points fifty-six seconds into the third quarter when defensive player Marcus Spears tipped a pass thrown by OU's White, brought it into his body, and ambled twenty yards to the end zone to give the Tigers an ultimate 21-14 advantage.

On the last meaningful play, with White searching for someone—anyone—open enough to get fingers on the ball and tie things up, Tigers' linebacker Lionel Turner fired through the middle on a delayed blitz and flattened the quarterback and any OU hopes.

In retrospect, this might have been the biggest seven-point rout in football history. Put this in focus: LSU held Oklahoma, which averaged 461 offensive yards coming into the Sugar Bowl, to 154 total yards—52 of that rushing, with only an average of 1.8 yards a try; LSU held OU, which averaged those forty-five points coming into the Sugar Bowl, to a couple of touchdowns, arrived at on a combined thirty-three yards (courtesy of a blocked punt and an interception).

The AP kept USC atop its poll, though the Tigers collected the BCS's crystal trophy.

But there was something else that should convince any disbelievers who made preseason bets on the eventual No. 1 team: Las Vegas paid off on Sugar Bowl champion LSU.

That was as official as any poll.

LIVING RIGHT

January 7, 2008
Louisiana Superdome, New Orleans, La.

How does it happen?

Not since 1965, when the Alabama Crimson Tide (with a 9-1-1 record) surpassed three teams with better credentials, had a more than one-loss team finished a college football season ranked No. 1.

Yet here was a two-loss LSU squad squeezed into position to win the national championship.

The problem was not LSU. It was the rest of college football, where all serious contenders except one, Ohio State, had two defeats, too.

The title gates were flung open for the Bayou Bengals when second-ranked West Virginia lost to four-touchdown underdog Pittsburgh. The Tigers were ranked No. 7 at the time but with a body of work that dwarfed the other contenders. LSU was a national-best 6-1 against ranked opponents, a résumé that rightfully put the Tigers in the title game in New Orleans.

In the craziest season in the almost 140-year history of college football—which opened with an upset of No. 5-ranked Michigan by lower-division opponent Appalachian State, and featured the biggest upset of all time with 41-point underdog Stanford beating Southern California, ranked No. 1 in the ESPN and Harris polls, used to determine Bowl Championship Series standings.

It was a season in which:

- Top-10 teams lost to unranked teams a staggering twenty times;
- Top-5 teams lost to unranked opponents an unprecedented thirteen times;
- The No. 1- and No. 2-ranked teams both lost on the final day of the regular season, each a step short of a chance to hoist the Waterford crystal ball, emblematic of the BCS title.

And, in the end, after the stunning developments on the last weekend of the Season of the Upset, the last teams standing were Ohio State and LSU—both of which had been previously ranked No. 1 and lost; the Tigers twice.

Just as incongruous, both also lost at home in November, until this zany season a certain killer of high aspirations for elite standing. But when Missouri and West Virginia lost, the Big Ten champion Buckeyes (11-1), then in third place in the BCS rankings, were lifted to the top spot. LSU (11-2), which had dropped to seventh, rose to second, passing five other contenders.

LSU coach Les Miles thoughtfully offered, "It's as if the Lord wanted these two teams to play."

The apparent reason for LSU's ascension: Missouri (10-2), Kansas (11-1), and Georgia (10-2) failed to win their league championships; the defeat of West Virginia (10-2) at the hands of a pronounced underdog; and the little matter of the 48-7 trouncing of Virginia Tech (11-2) by LSU.

Oklahoma (11-2) and Southern Cal (10-2) could, and would, make arguments that they were as worthy, but LSU's résumé (not only playing [seven]—and beating [six]—more ranked opponents than anyone in the country, but having beaten five teams in the Top 15 while the Trojans defeated none) appeared to be the deciding factor.

Still, the Bayou Bengals kept winning with a hell-bent-for-leather style, overcoming a plethora of obstacles. During the season they went for it on fourth down fifteen times, and made the necessary yardage an astounding twelve times (80 percent)—including a memorable five-for-five night in a win against Florida. Opponents were successful on only four-of-eighteen (22 percent) fourth downs. The Tigers also scored a touchdown in the waning seconds of a 30-24 victory over Auburn.

The morning of the SEC Championship Game, two hours before kickoff, Miles had to publicly refute an erroneous ESPN report by Kirk Herbstreit that he was leaving for the coaching job at Michigan, his alma mater. In addition, LSU had to not only win the league title game with its backup quarterback, but one who was also injured when Ryan Perrilloux deeply cut his index finger.

Plus, Miles not only coached the Tigers to victories against a backbreaking schedule, but in the process of fighting severe injuries and outside distractions, he also defeated five coaches with national championship credentials: South Carolina's Steve Spurrier, Florida's Urban Meyer, Alabama's Nick Saban, Tennessee's Phil Fulmer, and, now, Ohio State's Jim Tressel.

Ohio State jumped to a 10-0 lead, momentarily silencing the Superdome crowd, but from that point, at 9:12 to go in the first quarter to the half, LSU:

- had fifteen of the next nineteen first downs;
- ran thirty-six of the next fifty-five plays;
- converted eight of its next nine third downs and stopped Ohio State on four of its next five;
- outgained the Buckeyes 212-101 in taking a 24-10 halftime lead.

The outcome was never seriously in doubt after that.

The Bayou Bengals' not-as-close-as-the-final-score 38-24 victory over Ohio State made LSU the first two-game losing champion since Minnesota in 1960. Thinking back on it from his spot on the postgame podium, Miles mused of his team of domination, drama, and second chances, "It was like divine intervention."

A TEAM OF DESTINY

December 19, 1987
The Minidome, Pocatello, Idaho

"I think, when I look back on it," Stan Humphries reflected, "that maybe that (college) championship game was the high point of my athletic career."

That was truly a mouthful because Humphries, who quarter-backed Northeast Louisiana to the 1987 NCAA Division I-AA title, also quarterbacked the San Diego Chargers to Super Bowl XXIX, where they lost to the San Francisco 49ers.

"You know, it's hard getting to the Super Bowl," Humphries said, thinking back on all the blood, sweat, and tears it takes to get that close to football's ultimate crown, "and I wouldn't trade the experience for anything. But the fact is, we didn't win the Super Bowl. We did win the national championship. That's what separates the two in my mind."

There was nothing to separate for those who were at the title game in Idaho. Humphries and Marshall University's Tony Petersen put on dazzling performances in a shootout won by the Northeast Indians (now the ULM Warhawks) 43-42. The I-AA passing record was 419 yards set by Georgia Southern's Tracy Ham in 1985, and Humphries (436) and Petersen (474) each broke it that afternoon. The announcement was made that Humphries had eclipsed the record while he was on the field. Later, standing on the sideline, he heard that Petersen had broken his minutes-old record.

Still, Humphries had the bigger prize, the championship, though even that would not be assured until the last tick of the clock.

☆ ☆ ☆

Fans should have been warned to strap themselves in for the 1987 season. It was a bumpy ride. Northeast played a series of down-to-the-wire games, including three one-point victories and a three-point margin as the Indians went 13-2, a record that didn't show the travails the team endured all the way through.

"That championship game was really kind of a reflection of our season as a whole," Humphries said. "There was never a dull moment."

Using their new one-back, pro-style offense, the Indians cruised through their first three games.

Then things started getting tough. Northeast needed what seemed to be divine intervention to beat Northwestern State with a forty-eight-yard Humphries pass to Jackie Harris that was tipped twice on the last play to pull out a 33-32 victory.

The next week NLU was crushed 48-28 by Lamar. With the two shaky performances, Coach Pat Collins yanked Humphries and inserted backup Walter Phythian at QB to face defending national champion Georgia Southern, a 26-17 win.

That was followed by another loss, 17-7 to Southwestern Louisiana. Phythian and Humphries each played, but the Indians gained just 226 yards.

"Sloppy wasn't the word for it," Collins assessed. "I don't know if there is a word for it."

Finally Humphries got his job back, "and was able finish it off," he said.

The tipping point came the next week against Southern Mississippi and its budding superstar quarterback Brett Favre. The Indians won 34-24.

"Going over there, to a Division I-A school, and winning gave us a big shot of confidence," Humphries said. "That carried us a long way."

Against North Texas, Humphries threw for 310 yards and NLU built a 21-0 lead. But the Mean Green came storming back and a touchdown with 1:23 remaining cut the Indians' lead to 24-23. UNT coach Corky Nelson decided to play it straight with kicker Keith Chapman, who had not missed a PAT all season. But Chapman's kick hit the right upright and bounced back on the field.

"God was with us tonight," Collins recounted later. "That was one we don't practice every Thursday."

After beating Arkansas State, it was off to the playoffs, where more of the same awaited. In a rematch, NLU again beat North Texas, this time convincingly, 30-9. Then kicker Teddy Garcia, who had missed twice earlier, hit a forty-eight-yard field goal with fourteen seconds remaining to beat Eastern Kentucky 33-32. That heartstopper was followed by a double-overtime—after NLU squandered a 35-14 halftime lead—44-41 semifinal win over

Northern Iowa, relegated to Division I-AA also-ran status despite gaining 547 yards against the Indians.

All that was left was the championship game against Marshall on the campus of Idaho State University.

Perhaps if nudged in a slightly different direction, Humphries's moment in the sun might have come on the hardwood instead of the gridiron. He had the genes to excel in both. "My mom was a really, really good basketball player," he said. "My dad played football at (Louisiana) Tech for a while. The only thing they pushed me in was to be the best I could be."

He succeeded there on all levels. Stan was a prep All-American quarterback at Shreveport's Southwood High School, but he was also outstanding at his favorite sport.

"I loved basketball more than I ever loved football," he said. "I grew up loving and playing the game. But around my junior year in high school, I realized that I could probably go a little further in football."

Humphries signed with LSU, but after a couple of years transferred to Northeast, where in two seasons he passed for 4,395 yards and 29 touchdowns. In that span he also had eight games in which he passed for 300-plus yards—including the one for the national championship.

Taken in the sixth round of the NFL draft by Washington, Humphries was on the 1991 Redskins team that won the Super Bowl, though he was still on the sidelines learning the pro game. He got his big break when the 'Skins traded him to the Chargers a year later.

Almost immediately he became the starter, where he remained for six years, completing 1,431 of 2,516 passes for 17,191 yards and 89 touchdowns—and guiding San Diego to the Super Bowl.

Leaving an indelible impression wherever he's been, Humphries was inducted into both the ULM and Chargers halls of fame.

"It is nice to be remembered," he said.

The crowd of 11,513 got their money's worth that afternoon. The Indians and the Thundering Herd, fueled by Humphries and Petersen, produced more than a thousand yards of offense in a nationally televised game that featured thrilling plays and—befitting NLU's season—comebacks galore.

Humphries staked the Indians to a 21-13 halftime lead, then watched as Petersen rallied his troops with three touchdown passes. The Thundering Herd got another rushing TD to take what seemed to be safe 42-28 lead after three quarters.

It was time for Humphries to go to work. He took the Indians on an eight-play, seventy-four-yard drive to begin the fourth quarter, capped by a ten-yard TD pass to Kenneth Johnson on a screen pass. That cut the deficit to 42-34. NLU then went for two points, scoring when Humphries passed to Harris to make the score 42-36 with 13:34 left.

Before quarterbacking the San Diego Chargers in Super Bowl XXIX, Stan Humphries led the NLU Indians to a Division I-AA championship in 1987.

Next time NLU had the ball, Humphries completed five passes on an eleven-play, eighty-yard drive that resulted in a two-yard touchdown on a rollout. Garcia's PAT put the Indians back ahead 43-42.

Tighten those seat belts. Petersen still had three minutes to work with. And he used the remaining time well. He got the Thundering Herd to the Indians' 7—where they lost a fumble with two and a half minutes to play. Marshall did get the ball back, but an interception by Perry Harper with a minute to go preserved NLU's national championship.

Asked if he had a sense of déjà vu when Marshall came charging back, Collins said the thought hadn't crossed his mind, adding, "We've been in that situation so many times. I knew our players wouldn't panic."

Humphries put it all in clear context. "Look back at that game, at our whole season," he said, "and I think I'm right when I say we were like a Team of Destiny."

1987 NLU results

44	Louisiana Tech	7
44	Texas State	7
26	Nicholls State	14
33	Northwestern State	31
28	Lamar	48
26	Georgia Southern	17
7	Southwestern Louisiana	17
37	McNeese State	10
34	Southern Mississippi	24
24	North Texas	23
31	Arkansas State	21
30	North Texas	9
33	Eastern Kentucky	32
44	Northern Iowa	41
43	Marshall	42

ATOP THE COLLEGE FOOTBALL WORLD

National football championships might be rare elsewhere, but they're nothing out of the ordinary for Louisiana schools.

LSU has won several major college football titles. Louisiana Tech also has reigned over college football in what was then called the small college division, and ULM (then Northeast Louisiana) won the 1987 Division 1-AA playoffs. Grambling and Southern University have combined for double-digit black national champion titles.

Note: This speaks to the overall quality of the football played in Louisiana: In 1973, the dawn of integrated schools in the South, predominantly white and black schools did not play each other, and that was the first season NCAA Division II schools went to a playoff system to determine the national champion. Louisiana Tech, with a 12-1-0 record, swept past Western Illinois, Boise State, and then Western Kentucky to win the title in the Camellia Bowl in Sacramento, Calfornia.

But in one of those "what if" scenarios, Tech could have played Grambling for the championship. Eddie Robinson's Tigers lost 28-20 to Western Kentucky in the semifinals. Had things gone slightly different, both north Louisiana teams would have traveled 2,000 miles to play for the No. 1 pennant. And it would have been the first game between the two schools located five miles apart.

McNeese State deserves an honorable mention when it comes to titles. Twenty-three points in the right spots and the Cowboys would be included on this list. Coach Bobby Keasler's 'Pokes lost 10-9 in the 1997 NCAA Division I-AA championship game to Youngstown State. Five years later, in 2002, Coach Tommy Tate's McNeese team lost in the national championship 34-14 to Western Kentucky.

LSU also had a chance to add to its collection when the undefeated Tigers went to the 2012 BCS National Championship Game in New Orleans. But they lost 21-0 to Alabama, a team LSU beat 9-6 in overtime on the road during the regular season.

Coach Paul Dietzel (top row, right) and his LSU coaching staff.

Coach Eddie Robinson won nine black college national championships.

Coach Maxie Lambright (top row, center) and his La. Tech coaching staff, which included future NLU head coach Pat Collins (bottom row, right).

National Football Championships by Louisiana Schools

Major College or BCS National Championships:

Season	School	Record	Coach
1958	LSU	11-0-0	Paul Dietzel
2003	LSU	12-1-0	Nick Saban
2007	LSU	12-2-0	Les Miles

Small College National Championships:

Season	School	Record	Coach
1972	Louisiana Tech	12-0-0	Maxie Lambright
1973	Louisiana Tech	12-1-0	Maxie Lambright
1974	Louisiana Tech	11-1-0	Maxie Lambright

Division 1-AA National Championships:

Season	School	Record	Coach
1987	Northeast Louisiana (now ULM)	14-1-0	Pat Collins

National Black Championships:

Season	School	Record	Coach
1948	Southern University	12-0-0	Arnett Mumford
1949	Southern University	10-0-1	Arnett Mumford
1950	Southern University	10-0-1	Arnett Mumford
1954	Southern University	10-1-0	Arnett Mumford
1955	Grambling State University	10-0-0	Eddie Robinson
1960	Southern University	9-1-0	Arnett Mumford
1967	Grambling State University	9-1-0	Eddie Robinson
1972	Grambling State University	11-2-0	Eddie Robinson
1974	Grambling State University	10-2-0	Eddie Robinson
1975	Grambling State University	10-2-0	Eddie Robinson
1977	Grambling State University	10-1-0	Eddie Robinson
1980	Grambling State University	10-2-0	Eddie Robinson
1983	Grambling State University	9-1-0	Eddie Robinson
1992	Grambling State University	10-2-0	Eddie Robinson
1993	Southern University	11-1-0	Pete Richardson
1995	Southern University	11-1-0	Pete Richardson
1997	Southern University	11-1-0	Pete Richardson
2000	Grambling State University	10-1-0	Doug Williams
2001	Grambling State University	10-1-0	Doug Williams
2002	Grambling State University	11-2-0	Doug Williams
2003	Southern University	12-1-0	Pete Richardson
2005	Grambling State University	11-1-0	Melvin Spears
2008	Grambling State University	11-2-0	Rod Broadway

A CANNON BLAST

October 31, 1959
Tiger Stadium, Baton Rouge, La.

It's become a part of us, part of Louisiana's cultural DNA.

Always accompanied with J. C. Politz's staccato delivery, "Billy Cannon watches it bounce . . . He takes it at his own 11 . . ." each Halloween Cannon makes that same eerie and bewitching run in grainy black-and-white film, across Death Valley, beating Ole Miss every time in the most classic football game ever staged in Tiger Stadium.

Those seventeen seconds are the highpoint of LSU football, the signature play of a storied program, the orgasmic height of a golden two-year run in which the Tigers reached the pinnacle of college football with a national championship in 1958 and a string of nineteen consecutive victories.

No higher ranked teams—LSU No. 1, Ole Miss No. 3—ever squared off in Tiger Stadium before or after that night, and Cannon's epic eighty-nine-yard punt return through and around a horde of diving Rebels for an ultimate 7-3 Tigers victory was as much the difference as one man can be in a football game.

"I still get goose bumps watching it," said Lynn LeBlanc, who then was an All-SEC tackle for LSU and the team captain, "and I *played* in the doggone game."

Every single Tiger alive at the time, or born since October 31, 1959, seems to have been imbued with a genetic code that conveys the sheer drama and near-theatrical backdrop of that memorable game against a formidable opponent in 1959's Game of the Century, a game that all this time later not only still has that kind of sheen but legitimately could be considered as truly the Game of the Twentieth Century.

"It had what all great games have," Cannon reflected, "every man on both teams giving his best on every play, knowing they had to because any one play could decide the outcome."

The credentials of both teams were impeccable. Both teams were undefeated with 6-0 records, built largely on near-impregnable defenses. A combined total of thirteen points had been scored on them—two field goals against the Tigers, one touchdown against the Rebels.

"Ole Miss," Cannon stated, "was as good of a football team that could have been fielded in those days." LSU, too. No opponent had crossed the Tiger goal for thirty-eight consecutive quarters, going back to the previous season.

★ ★ ★

The backdrop was almost surreal. The brightness of the Tiger Stadium floodlights had increased since the year before. With a seventy-three-degree temperature and one hundred percent humidity for the 8:00 p.m. kickoff, the foggy field took on an unearthly quality under the lights—a perfect setting for Halloween night.

Early on it looked as if Ole Miss was playing trick-or-treat. Starting on the game's fifth play, LSU lost the first of its four first-half fumbles—one a Cannon bobble on the LSU 21 that led to the Rebels' field goal—and Ole Miss took advantage of the bottled-up Tigers to inch to the LSU 20, 20, 3, 5, and 7. After all that, all LSU gave up was the lone field goal by Robert Khayat, who would later serve as chancellor of Ole Miss.

Every game of this magnitude has heroes and near-heroes. In an era when players played both offense and defense, one of Ole Miss's was quarterback/defensive back Billy Brewer (later the head coach of the Rebels). He recovered each of LSU's lost fumbles. But he missed on one turnover that could have sealed the outcome, a third-quarter interception in the open field.

On the other side, as the half was winding down, with the Rebels on the Tiger 7, Chinese Bandit end Andy Bourgeois threw quarterback Bobby Franklin for a four-yard loss, causing the Rebels to screw up a snap in an effort to stop the clock, and failing to get off a field-goal attempt.

"That was crucial," LeBlanc said in discussing several critical plays obscured by time that could have altered everything that occurred later. "If they had gotten that field goal just before the half, then at the end of the game they could have beaten us with just another field goal. That's how close everything was that night."

With LSU showing a propensity for dropping the ball, and with the field slick and damp from the high humidity, once his team took the lead Rebels coach Johnny Vaught opened himself up to a perpetual second-guess by switching strategies. He called for punts early, frequently on third down, but even, maddening to Ole Miss fans, on first down.

Vaught's reasoning seems to have been two-fold: The Rebels were ahead and he was confident in his defense. Vaught's angle was to just let the Tigers try to handle the slippery ball. And wait.

Another strong consideration was that Vaught thought he could foil LSU with its own innovative three-platoon system. In order to circumvent the restrictive substitution rules of the day, in which a player could only enter a game twice in a quarter, Tigers coach Paul Dietzel used one unit to play both offense and defense (the White Team), another for defense (the Chinese Bandits), and a third (the Go Team) strictly for offense. Ole Miss's chances would be enhanced if Vaught could trap the Tigers with a specialist unit forced to play against its strengths, the Chinese Bandits on offense or, much worse, the Go Team on defense. At the very least, Vaught might force the White Team to play too much and tire it out.

From the LSU 20, Cannon punted on third down to the Rebel 39, and Jake Gibbs returned it to the 49.

That was the prelude to the most remembered play in LSU history. What isn't remembered is what directly led to it.

Ole Miss gained three yards to the LSU 48, making it second and seven. On that down, LeBlanc made the play that made Cannon's return possible. Gibbs took the snap and rolled out—all of a sudden there was LeBlanc running him down and dropping him for a 10-yard loss.

"I remember it vividly," said LeBlanc, later an LSU assistant for eleven years under Charlie McClendon. "I thought they were going to pass, I came free and shot straight to Gibbs."

That made it 3rd and 17 from the Ole Miss 42. Clearly without that sack the Rebels probably wouldn't have been kicking on the next play from midfield, or, if they did, the ball would have been spiraling into the end zone. Even though he had tried a return earlier from the 8, surely with time running out, in a game where every possession was precious, Cannon wouldn't try to return another within spitting distance of his own goalposts . . . would he?

Gibbs's punting was a potent Ole Miss weapon, averaging forty-eight yards that night, a major factor in keeping the Tigers hemmed in, and he got a good one off here, too—forty-seven yards.

"I was trying to kick out of bounds," Gibbs said, "expecting the ball to come down and roll out." Gibbs did exactly that earlier. "Instead," he recalled, "it took a high bounce—right to Billy."

All Gibbs could see through the fog was a jumble of blue-and-red and purple-and-gold colors, then a lone figure busting out of the cluster and streaming right toward him.

Cannon was hit at the 15, almost losing his balance, but shook off the tackle and maintained his footing. LeBlanc threw the first block, giving Cannon some room. Two Rebels made futile attempts to bring him down by the time he reached the 19. At the 25 a mob briefly encased Cannon, but in a millisecond he again came flying out. One Rebel slipped from Cannon's shoulders to his ankles in a five-yard ride before dropping off at the 30.

Seeing him run straight through the Ole Miss defenders, with the Rebels seemingly grasping at thin air, Dan Hardesty of the *Baton Rouge State-Times* wrote that Cannon resembled "a white-shirted ghost wearing jersey No. 20."

By the time he passed Vaught at midfield at least eight Rebels had gotten a hand on Cannon. Gibbs was the last man in the way. "I figured Jake was waiting for me to cut back on him," Cannon said, "so I gave him a little juke and went inside. . . . I know people say you can't think like that during the heat of a game, but that's how I got past Gibbs."

"I tried to hit him in his upper body," Gibbs said. ". . . Not a good thing to do with someone as strong and powerful as Billy Cannon."

Billy Cannon with LSU Coach Paul Dietzel.

Brewer added, "Only Billy Cannon could run and break tackles as he did. The man was a physical freak."

Hall of Fame sportswriter Fred Russell of *The Nashville Banner* summed up the sentiments of almost all who witnessed the play when he described it as a "superhuman feat."

☆ ☆ ☆

There were exactly ten minutes to play when Cannon crossed the goal line. Ole Miss would retain possession of the ball for an excruciating nine minutes and forty-two seconds of that time. Vaught again changed tactics. He inserted sophomore Doug Elmore, and his fresh pair of legs, at quarterback.

Starting at the Rebel 32, Elmore ignited a long, arduous march, flinging his backs against the Chinese Bandits, passing only once, and slowly worming his team into position to snatch away the victory.

"I was getting oxygen on the sidelines," Cannon said, "watching Doug pick up first down after first down. I thought to myself, 'Here's the best run I ever made in my life and we're going to lose!'"

LeBlanc admits he was thinking along the same lines. "The thought (of losing) started creeping into our minds," he said.

When Ole Miss penetrated the LSU 23, Dietzel sent the White Team back in. But the advance continued. The Rebels picked up their fifth first down of the drive at the 7 with ninety seconds remaining. In the three ensuing plays, Ole Miss worked its way to the LSU 2, forcing a win-or-lose, fourth-and-goal situation.

Ole Miss, of course, had been well-scouted, and the Tigers knew that at pivotal times the Rebels almost always relied on their quarterback. Elmore slammed off-tackle, where guard John Langan slowed him, Warren Rabb stopped his forward progress, and Cannon finished the job one yard short of the goal. Ironically, on a defensive play Cannon himself helped preserve what would become the enduring legend of Billy Cannon's Run—and LSU's most famed victory.

Cannon and Warren Rabb stop Ole Miss quarterback Doug Elmore one yard short of the goal line to preserve one of LSU's most famed victories.

The most electrifying play in Louisiana sports history, Billy Cannon's 1959 punt return against Ole Miss.

PRICE WAS RIGHT

November 5, 1949
Tulane Stadium, New Orleans, La.

Sometimes things happen despite logic. In this case, Tulane fullback Eddie Price was sick as the proverbial dog most of the week with the flu. He couldn't even practice until two days before a game with Navy.

Then he went out on Saturday and, in a 21-21 tie, put on a dazzling one-man show, scoring three touchdowns on runs of sixty-eight, twenty-five, and one yard. On that afternoon, Price averaged 10.8 yards rushing, 238 yards on 22 carries. He also had 3 yards receiving and 48 yards in kick returns for a total of 289 yards—Tulane's all-purpose record.

What, it makes one wonder, might have happened had Price been healthy in preparing for the Middies?

Decades after his last game as a collegian, it's not a stretch to put Price near the top of any list of Louisiana's all-time football players, rushing for more than 1,000 yards twice during a time when that achievement was a rarity, scoring 31 career touchdowns, and averaging an astonishing and still-school record 6.0 yards per carry for his four seasons with the Green Wave.

To put Price in context, consider that his peer, Doak Walker of Southern Methodist University, was the recipient of the Heisman Trophy in 1948 and ran for 532 yards that season. Price ran for 1,178 yards. Walker, a three-time All-American, had 1,954 career yards; Price had 3,095.

★ ★ ★

Early on, Price said later, nobody could have believed he would develop into an extraordinary athlete. Certainly not Johnny Brechtel, coach of New Orleans's Warren Easton High School Eagles, who first saw Eddie as a 145-pound sixteen-year-old in 1941. Brechtel put the prospect in the secondary for the first practice of the season.

"He sent the varsity backfield over me on an off-tackle play," Price said with a laugh years later. "I made the tackle, but that's all I remember. The next thing I knew, Coach was standing over me with smelling salts. 'You'll never make a football player,' he was yelling and laughing. I stayed on the B team that year. I got knocked silly a couple of times that year, and Coach would laugh and tell me I'd never make it.

"Now don't get me wrong, he wasn't sadistic. It was just his way of separating the men from the boys. Nobody else could have developed whatever football talent I had in those days."

After intense work on a weight program, Price reported for his junior season at a muscled 180 pounds. He scored three touchdowns in the Golden Eagles' first game, and he finished as the city's leading scorer with fifty-four points, as Easton won the Louisiana state championship in a 6-0 victory over Jennings—the difference being a Price halfback pass to Freddie Brechtel.

The Eagles didn't win state in 1943, but at the end of that season there wasn't a college coach in the country that wasn't trying to lure Eddie Price to his campus. Coach Brechtel had done

his job well, for he had brought out abilities in Eddie no one, not even the boy himself, realized existed.

The piston-like drive in his now heavily muscled legs and an inordinate smell for the goal line forced Notre Dame coach Frank Leahy to gush that he was the finest prep prospect he'd ever seen. Had it not been for the little matter of World War II, Price might have followed in the long and proud tradition of the Fightin' Irish.

Leahy, on a Sugar Bowl visit to New Orleans, corralled Eddie, Brechtel, and Holy Cross's Ray Espenan on the Holy Cross school grounds to make a pitch.

"Coach Leahy asked us to take a walk with him," Price recalled. "He said he always wanted to get a good view of the Mississippi River, so we went for a stroll on the levee back of Holy Cross. It was really funny. He spoke about the river, and then about Notre Dame. He talked about the protection levee and the first thing you know, he's telling us about Knute Rockne. He was selling us Notre Dame. But he didn't have to. We were sold already."

Price and Brechtel accepted a trip to South Bend and while they were there, the crafty Leahy had Price take his military tests in Chicago. He was accepted in the Navy's V-5 program, to be assigned to the Notre Dame unit. The service program allowed a recruit to attend—and play football for—the college where his unit was based. But not in this case; shortly afterward Price received a telegram from his mother telling him he'd been drafted.

Eddie hurried home, and straight to the induction board.

"I explained I had passed entrance requirements for the Navy V-12 training program," Price said, "and that I was only awaiting orders. Notre Dame assured me everything was all right, that the papers had been forwarded to New Orleans."

"That's fine," came the reply. "We'll just go ahead and swear you into the Navy, and you can report when your papers arrive from Notre Dame."

Two days later, Price was on his way to San Diego, and five months after that he was in the South Pacific. After taking part in the landings at Saipan, Leyte, Luzon, and Guam over the course of two years, Price returned home and found New Orleans and—a certain Miss Joyce Prats—far more enticing than South Bend or Frank Leahy.

"My whole perspective had changed in those two years," Eddie reflected. "Sure, Coach Leahy wanted me at Notre Dame, but I had been away from New Orleans, and I didn't want to leave again."

Tommy O'Boyle, a Tulane assistant coach, offered Eddie a grant-in-aid in the summer of 1946, and it was quickly accepted.

★ ★ ★

The twenty-one-year-old freshman was Coach Henry Frnka's third-string running back in the 1946 Tulane single wing, but moved up when Johnny Sims was injured against Florida in the second game of the season. Price scored two touchdowns playing behind Hoyt Moncrief.

A week later Price rushed for 80 yards, 70 coming on a touchdown run, as the Greenies fell to Rice 25-6, and held Tulane to 132 yards rushing. Tulane finished 3-7, but Price, still a sub, averaged 5.8 yards a carry, 335 yards on 57 carries.

The most important date of 1946 to Price, though, was the Christmas-break day he married Joyce Prats, sister of his high school and college teammate Ray Prats.

Joyce hugged her new husband the morning of the 1947 season opener against Alabama and requested softly, "Run one back all the way for a touchdown today for me, honey." Price didn't get into the game until just after a Crimson Tide touchdown in the final minute of the half when Frnka yanked Eddie from the bench and ordered, "Get in there and run that kickoff back for me, son."

The ball rolled through his legs and into the end zone.

"I was going to let it roll," Price recalled three decades later. "I hadn't realized I had touched it. But Don Fortier yelled to me to get the ball. I was three yards into our end zone when I picked it up. The delay caused the Alabama end to overshoot me, so I got by him. When I hit the 30-yard line there was a hole a block wide. Only (Tide quarterback) Harry Gilmer stood between me and the goal line. I faked him off balance and went all the way."

Bama fumbled the following kickoff, and Tulane gained possession with time for one play. Bennie Ellender completed a fifty-four-yard pass to Eddie's brother-in-law, Ray Prats, and the Greenies went on to a 21-20 victory.

It was one of two 1947 wins for Tulane, which had switched to the T-formation. Price averaged 4.4 yards a carry, 471 yards on 106 attempts. But Frnka soon came to the conclusion that Eddie was playing out of position.

★ ★ ★

Frnka moved Price from halfback to fullback for 1948, the season the Green Wave truly began blossoming. In preseason polls, the highest national ranking accorded Tulane was 49th, and the Greenies were generally fixed for a 10th-place finish in the twelve-team Southeastern Conference.

By the end of the season Tulane was ranked among the nation's best, 13th, its highest standing since 1939, and was a legitimate major bowl contender with a 9-1-0 record.

Among the Wave's victims was LSU, buried under an orgy of touchdowns in a 46-0 victory. Though Price surpassed his 116 yards and two touchdowns many times, the hard-driving fullback always said, this was his most memorable game.

"I had some better afternoons than that," he said with satisfaction, "but that's the one I like to remember best."

The Orange Bowl was plenty interested in Tulane, but SEC champion Georgia was its most coveted entrant, and Bulldogs' coach Wally Butts was adamant he would not take a chance on sullying his team's own 9-1 record against another SEC team.

By the time Tulane realized what was happening in those days of only a handful of postseason games, the Orange Bowl was filled with Georgia and Texas, the hometown Sugar Bowl was also filled, and the Green Wave was shut out.

In 1949, Tulane, with a 7-2-1 record, was able to accomplish one thing it failed to do in '48—win the SEC, the last title the Greenies would ever claim in the league.

After gaining 151 yards in a 28-14 victory against Alabama in the opener, Price tore a ligament in his foot during an 18-0 win over Georgia Tech. Despite missing two games, including a 40-0 romp in a "breather" against Southeastern Louisiana College, Eddie enjoyed his second 1,000-yard season (1,137), and led the nation in yards per average, an incredible 6.6.

Drafted by the New York Giants, Price went on to an All-Pro career in Gotham, where he also rewrote the Giants' record book.

Tulane football has produced highly-gifted ball-carriers in the decades since he hung up his cleats—Tommy Mason, Mewelbe Moore, Matt Forté—but Eddie price is still the measuring stick of Green Wave runners.

GROOMED FOR THE MOMENT

January 31, 1988
Jack Murphy Stadium, San Diego, California

Doug Williams led the Washington Redskins to victory in Super Bowl XXII.

The President of the United States gave a verbal salute: "Way to go, Doug."

The greeting came after a parade in Washington, D.C., a celebration of a Super Bowl victory by the team representing the nation's capital.

But Ronald Reagan's singling out of Doug Williams was recognition not only of his being the linchpin in Washington's smashing 42-10 upset of the Denver Broncos—overcoming a smarting injury to fire the Redskins to five touchdowns in one quarter—but also of his sudden status as a social pioneer.

Williams, playing on a hyperextended knee, was the first African American to quarterback a team in the Super Bowl.

Reagan said Williams' exploits against the Broncos were "one of the most inspiring performances displayed by any quarterback in football history."

It's almost as if Doug Williams had been groomed to be on this stage. He was a protégé of Coach Eddie Robinson at Grambling, the small black college where social impact was made through football. Robinson coached Tank Younger, the first player from a traditionally black school to play in the NFL, and Robinson coached James "Shack" Harris, the first black to open an NFL season as a starting quarterback.

Williams, who grew up in Zachary as the sixth of the eight children of Laura and Robert Williams, a veteran wounded at Pearl Harbor, played for Robinson from 1974-77. Doug left Grambling after accounting for 8,411 yards and 93 touchdowns, and became a first-team All-American selection by the Associated Press—the first time an African American was named to such an honor. He also finished fourth in the Heisman Trophy balloting, the highest anyone from a predominantly black program ever had.

Grambling was in Tokyo after a game with Temple when the results were announced. "Our team gathered in the locker room and Coach Robinson got up and told the entire team about how the Heisman balloting had come out," Williams recalled. "He said I finished fourth. But he added that as far as he was concerned, Grambling State had the Heisman Trophy winner.

"That's something I'll never forget. Coach Robinson saying that meant as much to me as winning that Heisman."

☆ ☆ ☆

And now here was Williams, Robinson's coaching pride and joy, thrust into the limelight of NFL history with the start in Super Bowl XXII. The game itself almost became a sidebar.

Williams's race became a major pregame focal point.

Out of the media contingent surrounding Doug one day before the 1988 game came a stunning inquiry: "How long have you been a black quarterback?" a reporter asked Williams, then thirty-two.

Williams answered patiently that he recognized his complexion as a child, and he played quarterback for years before reaching the Super Bowl. Yet, amid the guffaws and perplexed looks of the nation's sports media, Williams said he sort of understood the question.

"I think I understood where he was coming from, it just came out wrong," Williams explained. "I think he was trying to ask me how long people had been referring to me as 'a black quarterback.'"

It was the first time, but certainly not the last, the subject was broached. It became an ever-present Super Bowl topic. At the interview session it wasn't even posed as a question. One reporter merely said, "Black, Doug," and Williams responded with his usual answer: "(Coach) Joe Gibbs and (general manager) Bobby Beathard didn't bring me in to be the first black quarterback in the Super Bowl. They brought me in to be the quarterback of the Washington Redskins"

★ ★ ★

Williams took a roundabout route to Super Bowl history. He led the Tampa Bay Buccaneers to the playoffs three times in his first five seasons in the NFL before leaving in a contract dispute. Then he played in the United State Football League before Gibbs called to see if Williams was interested in a job as a backup to Jay Schroeder in 1986.

When Schroeder got hurt late in the '87 season, Williams got his chance, guiding the Redskins to victories against the Chicago Bears and Minnesota Vikings—and into the Super Bowl.

With the famed "Hogs," Washington's offensive line, in front of him and "the Posse," the Redskins' receiving corps, spread across the field, Williams was confident. Gibbs didn't even add any wrinkles to the offense for the game against the Broncos.

"Coach Gibbs wanted me to run his offense," Williams said. "He wanted to do certain things we did well, and didn't want to get away from those things."

The only thing to fear was the unexpected.

It came when Williams had to have an emergency root canal on Saturday, the day before the Super Bowl. "That evening I had trouble talking, but I went back to the hotel and watched TV while the painkillers worked," he said. "After that I didn't have a problem."

Indeed not. On Super Bowl Sunday, the Broncos took a 10-0 lead after the first quarter. Then Williams fired the Redskins to their shining second period.

In their five possessions of the quarter, Williams gunned the 'Skins to thirty-five points. He completed 9 of 11 passes for 228 yards and 4 touchdowns. His scoring passes covered 80, 27, 50, and 8 yards. Total time of possession: 5:54.

It was an amazing performance, especially since Doug had to leave the game in the first quarter with the hyperextended left knee. But Williams shortly returned to steer Washington to a then-record 356 yards of offense.

Williams now says that while he is proud it fell to him to be the first African American quarterback to start a Super Bowl, he is just as proud to be part of another exclusive group—a winning Super Bowl quarterback.

A SUPER LEGACY

Terry Bradshaw set the standard. The Blonde Bomber not only quarterbacked the Pittsburgh Steelers to the ultimate football game four times, he quarterbacked them to four Super Bowl championships.

Nearly a half-century later, nobody has surpassed that accomplishment.

But then, he had the background. He grew up in Louisiana, and that gave Bradshaw an edge.

Here's a thought worth pondering: In the first forty-six years of the game, seven different Louisiana athletes have quarterbacked their teams into Super Bowl berths (and an astonishing six times that quarterback was the game's MVP, Bradshaw and Eli Manning each receiving the honor twice).

Only California, with a population of more than 38 million, and Pennsylvania, with a population of 12.6 million have had more Super Bowl quarterbacks than Louisiana, with a pool of 4.5 million people. A scan of much more populous states shows Texas with one and Florida with none.

Put it this way, in that time span, those Louisiana quarterbacks started a total of twelve title games, meaning 26 percent of all Super Bowls opened with a Louisianan under center.

Bradshaw started four, followed by Peyton Manning (2), Eli Manning (2), David Woodley (1), Stan Humphries (1), Doug Williams (1), and Jake Delhomme (1).

Clearly, Louisiana packs a punch far more powerful than its weight class would indicate. But what accounts for Louisiana quarterbacks' success?

Must be something in the boudin.

Archie Manning, the former New Orleans Saints hero who runs an annual passing academy for players from across the country and who is the father of two Super Bowl-winning MVPs, said it's an unanswerable question.

"Louisiana has always produced good quarterbacks," Manning said. "A lot of very good quarterbacks have come from here who never even got to the Super Bowl. For some reason Louisiana has been a good place for growing quarterbacks."

He should know.

An intriguing part of the equation is that each one of the Louisiana QBs in the Super Bowls attended different colleges. Bradshaw was a product of Louisiana Tech, Woodley of LSU, Humphries of Northeast Louisiana, Williams of Grambling, Peyton Manning of Tennessee, Eli Manning of Ole Miss, and Delhomme of Southwestern Louisiana.

They had left legacies already at their respective college programs. Bradshaw was the NCAA's leading passer in 1968, and Williams was part of three black national championship teams at

Dave Woodley of LSU, who later led the Miami Dolphins in Super Bowl VII.

Grambling. Woodley was at the helm of Coach Charlie McClendon's last LSU teams and was MVP of the Tangerine Bowl in Mac's final game. Humphries quarterbacked Northeast Louisiana (today's ULM) to the 1987 Division II national title. Peyton Manning steered the Tennessee Vols to the 1997 SEC championship, and his brother Eli made Ole Miss an extremely dangerous opponent in the early years of the twenty-first century. Delhomme left USL (now UL Lafayette) as the school's all-time leader in passing yards and touchdown passes.

As a collective group in the NFL title game they also left deep impressions:

- In Super Bowls XIII and XIV, Bradshaw became the first player to be voted MVP in back-to-back title games since Bart Starr in the first two.
- In 1982, when Woodley was at the helm of the Miami Dolphins in a 27-17 losing effort against the Washington Redskins, he was, at age twenty-four, the youngest quarterback ever to start a Super Bowl.
- Williams, of course, was the first African American to start at quarterback when he was the MVP in the Redskins' 42-10 beat-down of the Denver Broncos.
- Humphries guided the San Diego Chargers to their only Super Bowl (XXIX), although his team lost 49-26.

- Despite throwing for three touchdowns and no interceptions (achieving a QB rating of 113.6), Delhomme—an undrafted free agent and former New Orleans Saint—and his Carolina Panthers were beaten 32-29 in Super Bowl XXXVIII by the New England Patriots.

- Perhaps the Super Bowl record destined to last the longest is the one where two brothers (the sons of Archie) won back-to-back games—and back-to-back MVP trophies. Peyton fired the Indianapolis Colts to a 29-17 victory over the Chicago Bears in the 2007 game, and little brother Eli did the same one year later when his New York Giants edged the New England Patriots 17-14.

It'll be a long time before that feat is duplicated. Anywhere.

Jake Delhomme of USL, who later led the Carolina Panthers in Super Bowl XXXVIII.

The "First Family" of NFL quarterbacks, the Mannings: (left to right) Eli, Payton, and dad Archie.

THE KICK HEARD 'ROUND THE WORLD

November 8, 1970
Tulane Stadium, New Orleans, La.

WWWHHHOMMMMPPP!

The sound of leather hitting leather reverberated throughout the four corners of Tulane Stadium, a noise that bounced off the half-empty steel-constructed rows of seats with a muted echo.

The thousands of New Orleans Saints fans who left early—and some of the media who left the press box and heard the excited commotion of the remaining spectators under the stands or in the elevator—missed the Kick of the Century.

Tom Dempsey had just booted a sixty-three-yard field goal—just imagine that, a successful game-winning kick with the line of scrimmage significantly short of midfield—on the last play to beat the Detroit Lions 19-17.

More than half of the 66,910 fans were gone by the time Jackie Burkett snapped the ball to Joe Scarpati for the attempt—although to hear the story relayed today not one single person left and at least a million claim to have been eyewitnesses to improbable NFL history.

The only people not to see or hear what came to be called The Kick Heard 'Round the World were the thousands making their way to their vehicles in parking lots or already tooling their way home.

But the Lions, to their chagrin, really did see and hear it. They were laughing as the Saints lined up and not really bothering to try to block the kick. After the smiles were wiped from their lips, Detroit linebacker Wayne Walker said ruefully the kick was "made by God." A fuming Lions coach Joe Schmidt said his team was beaten "by a miracle."

☆ ☆ ☆

The miracle was as much the kicker as the kick. Twenty-three years old at the time, Dempsey had been born with a malformed right hand and no toes on his right foot. He didn't let his handicap prevent him from playing sports. Wearing a modified shoe with a flattened toe area, making a square front (since banned by the NFL), Dempsey became a kicker of note.

In fact, he already held the Saints record for longest field goal, booting a fifty-five-yarder against the Los Angeles Rams—then tied for the second longest in NFL history, just one yard short of Baltimore's Bert Rechichar's record, set in 1953—during the 1969 season.

The lead-up to the kick was stupefying. At midweek, owner John Mecom had told the *Times-Picayune* no changes were imminent for the 1-5-1 team and its staff. "At this moment everybody is safe for the year. But I expect improvement," he said of the coaching staff. Hours after that paper hit the streets, the headline in the afternoon *New Orleans States-Item* read: "Tom Fears Fired by Mecom."

The Saints and Lions match-up was the first game for Coach J. D. Roberts as Saints head coach, usually the type of precursor that signaled an emotional effort for a struggling team.

☆ ☆ ☆

Sure enough, the Saints, aided by six turnovers, took the fight to the 5-2 Lions all day—a valiant effort that seemed doomed when a late Detroit drive ended in an Errol Mann field goal that gave Detroit a 17-16 lead in the fading seconds.

What left the door open for the Saints was clock mismanagement by Lions quarterback Greg Landry, who instead of running time down to four or five seconds before calling time, then kicking, asked for a timeout with fourteen seconds on the clock. That, after Mann's field goal, left the Saints with eleven seconds.

It was a fatal mistake, though understandably unrecognized by the throngs of fans by then pouring out of Tulane Stadium.

Al Dodd returned the kickoff to the New Orleans 28, stopping the clock. Then quarterback Billy Kilmer hit Dodd for a seventeen-yard gain, with the receiver stepping out of bounds. The Saints were at their 45 with two seconds remaining.

Backfield coach Don Heinrich reminded Roberts, "One play and one play only." Dempsey told the neophyte head man "I'm ready, Coach."

Looking at the Saints' 37-yard line, where the ball would be placed, and the distance to the goal line, where the crossbars stood in those days, any logical football person would have felt like the Lions: These guys are certifiably insane.

A perfect snap from the Saints' 45, a perfect hold, and the loud smack of Dempsey's modified shoe against the leather sent the ball sailing like a missile toward the goal. CBS commentator Don Criqui said as the ball neared its target, "I don't believe this . . ." Then, after it cleared the bar by inches, with the officials throwing their arms up, he exclaimed, "It's GOOD."

Even Dempsey seemed to have a hard time believing his accomplishment. "There's so much involved in kicking a sixty-yard field goal," he said. "You've got to try to hit the ball as hard as you possibly can and, yet, kicking it straight is a hard thing to do. It just so happened I hit it right and it happened at the right time."

That was the last Saints victory of 1970, but fans were so excited about their "miracle" victory that Louisiana Congressman F. Edward Hebert had the story of "The Kick'" inserted into the Congressional Record.

What wasn't saved for posterity was what happened afterward at Tulane Stadium. With a boisterous crowd outside, Dempsey would have been mobbed had he tried to leave. He killed time in the locker room with some friends, stadium security, and Saints hangers-on.

"I told them I was getting' thirsty," Dempsey said. "I could use some Dixie beer. Next thing I know a police car pulls up with three cases of Dixie. Where else but New Orleans?"

A TEAM FOR ALL SEASONS

Fall 1908
Baton Rouge, La.

It's the football team LSU fans—really, any group of fans—have been yearning for: A squad that averages between forty and fifty points a game, gives up one touchdown in the course of a ten-game season, and features a superstar ball-handler to keep the on-lookers entertained.

Except this isn't a team for the future. It was a team that ran roughshod over Dixie more than a century ago: the 1908 Tigers.

With the dazzling George Ellwood "Doc" Fenton at quarterback, the '08 Tigers put LSU on the football map.

Consider this, and remember that this was the age of horse-and-buggy football: The Tigers, averaging an unheard of 180 pounds and possessing unmatched speed, were actually close to achieving "point-a-minute" status. LSU scored 442 points in 450 minutes, and gave up one fluky touchdown and 11 total points in its 10-0-0 season. If converted to today's scoring system, the 1908 Tigers would have tallied 508 points. That's a figure that more than a hundred seasons later would still rank in LSU's top three.

George Ellwood "Doc" Fenton.

An illustration of the Tigers' potency is their thirty-four touchdowns of more than twenty yards, and eight of sixty or more yards.

Jim Halligan, a pioneer football official, flatly maintained fifty years later that, given its time and place, the '08 Tigers were the finest team ever to come out of the South. Ever.

"All the backs were big, fast, triple-threat men who handled a football like a basketball. . . . All of them were masters of the change of pace, stiff-arm, blocking on the run."

They were so good that whispers of impropriety followed. But an investigation by the Southern Intercollegiate Athletic Association revealed only that Mike Lally, while playing summer baseball, also sang at a movie house in Tonawanda, New York. When he was on the road with the baseball team, Lally paid a baritone to take his place by endorsing one of his baseball checks to the alternate singer. That check, brought before the SIAA, was the only evidence brought against LSU. Decades later the National Championship Foundation studied the season and retroactively named LSU the No. 1 team of 1908.

Fenton, too, came into posthumous national recognition. A study of football history by Sporting News determined Fenton would have been the retroactive Heisman Trophy recipient of '08, had such an award existed then. He scored 125 points that season.

"When the ball was snapped," said Auburn coach Mike Donahue, who would later also coach at LSU, "he was capable of rushing off in any direction. He was the consummate football player, born to run. He lived for, and loved, the attacking side of football."

Troy Middleton, LSU's president in the 1950s, said that during his student days at Mississippi A&M, "I saw Jim Thorpe, but Doc Fenton was a better player."

A Pennsylvanian who came by his nickname because his father traveled as a singer with an oldtime Indian medicine show, Fenton found his way to Baton Rouge after earlier playing at St. Michaels College in Canada and then at Mansfield Normal in Pennsylvania, where he played four years at end.

But he was the object of an intense recruiting battle between Mississippi A&M coach Fred Furman and LSU's Edgar Wingard. He chose LSU for two reasons: the slick-talking Wingard and the nickel beers in Baton Rouge.

When Wingard, also a Pennsylvanian, recognized Fenton's fondness for a brew on a visit to Louisiana, he reminded Doc of the blue laws back home, as well as in Mississippi.

That decision brought on the first true sunburst of football glitter in Louisiana.

For all the eye-catching offensive exploits of the Tigers, the defense was as impressive.

LSU started the season with two of what we now call out-of-conference "cupcakes," the Young Men's Gymnastics Club of New Orleans, and when Ole Miss had to cancel because of a scheduling conflict, former-athletes from Jackson Barracks in New

Orleans.

With the score at 48-0, a Tiger back named Warren Ryan fumbled near the goal line of the soldiers. A defender named Culligan scooped it up and raced the length of the field with teammates blocking the only two Tigers with a chance of catching him. In an 81-5 victory, the Tigers gave up the only touchdown of that memorable season.

Even a safety LSU gave up at Auburn was hardly earned. Years later, Fenton recounted the Tigers' closest game of the season, a 10-2 victory: "I was kicking from behind my own goal and an Auburn tackle broke through to block it. The ball was bouncing around, so I picked it up and was getting ready to run it out when a fan reached over the rope and cracked me over the head (with a cane). It knocked me cold."

The point is, the '08 Tigers were just as strong on defense as on offense, though their scoring proficiency is still staggering to the imagination.

"In 1969 we erased almost every offensive record in the LSU book," said the late Tiger coach Charlie McClendon. "Except for the 1908 records," he quickly amended. "I think those records will stand forever."

LSU's 1908 Game Results:

YMGC–N.O.	41-0
Jackson Bar.-N.O.	81-5
Texas A&M	26-0
Southwestern, Tenn.	55-0
Auburn	10-2
Miss. State	50-0
Baylor	89-0
Haskell	32-0
Louisiana Tech	22-0
Arkansas	36-4

SPREADING THE WORD

September 26, 1968
Yankee Stadium, Bronx, New York

As much as Eddie Robinson and Grambling football is a compelling story, somebody had to tell the story.

Collie J. Nicholson was as essential a part of the Grambling saga as anyone—including even Robinson—because he did tell the story, beginning at a time when not many were interested in hearing it.

In a biography of Robinson, former Southern University and Alcorn coach Marino Casem, a dear friend, said, "Collie is the one who promoted and glamorized Eddie Robinson; Eddie would not have been as big a name without Collie. The talent was there, but the motivation and the ideas weren't there. It took somebody to proclaim it."

All that Grambling achieved stood on the abilities of three men: President Ralph Waldo Emerson Jones, who doubled as the college's baseball coach and who knew a quality athletic program could open doors, personally hired both Rob and Nicholson, and had an overall vision for the school; Robinson, who put Grambling football on the map; and Nicholson, from whom the world of sports would learn the remarkable story, and who became known far and wide as "The Man with the Golden Pen."

Early on, as a youngster, Robinson was drawn to the idea of being a football coach. Nicholson, for his part, was infatuated with dreams of being a writer. He loved the way different words could be mixed to tell the same story.

He was so enthralled with the idea that, while a student at Winn Training School in Winnfield, Collie wrote the editor of the black weekly *Shreveport Sun*, eighty miles from his hometown, offering his services in writing a column for each edition—even though it would be done in longhand. Collie couldn't type yet.

Stunningly in looking back on it, the editor said to send his stuff in for the next week. Collie loved words and how they were used, but the ones with his by-line over them became keepsakes.

When he graduated, Collie matriculated to Southern, but stayed only a short time because of finances.

At this point, fate stepped in. Osiah Johnson, a former Negro League ballplayer who was serving as an assistant to "Prez" Jones, knew Collie as a good player. Finding Nicholson was back home and undecided about his future, Johnson made him an offer. If he would enroll and play baseball at Louisiana Negro Normal Institute (then Grambling's name), Collie could have a job at the school, an arrangement that included three meals a day and room and board.

Working in the business office, within six months Collie mastered the keyboard, reaching sixty words a minute on the typewriter. That skill would be the cornerstone of his career, but that first go-around at Grambling was brief. The little matter of World War II intervened.

In September 1943, Collie became one of the first black recruits in Marine Corps history, and eventually made history as the Marines' first black correspondent.

Denied the opportunity of covering combat in the Pacific Theater because of race, Collie reported on the 51st Defense Battalion, an all-black outfit, on the Gilbert and Marshall Islands. He produced a daily newsletter for the island bases and filed stories about the troops that—after review by military censors—were picked up by the Associated Negro Press for black newspapers back home.

Those newspaper editors would remember his by-line later.

Discharged in March 1946, Collie decided to finish his education in journalism on the G.I. Bill at the University of Wisconsin.

He stopped, however, at Grambling to say hello and goodbye to his old friends. The detour changed his life—and the course of football history. With a part-time job and room and board again

Before arriving at Grambling State University, Collie Nicholson was the very first African American news correspondent in the United States Marine Corps during WWII.

as bait, Prez talked Collie into completing his degree at Grambling.

The school seldom, if ever, got more out of a recruiting spiel. At a time when the job description of "sports information director" was ill-defined, Nicholson took on the Herculean task of telling the world of the exploits of Robinson and his team in the purple prose sports style so common in the '30s and '40s. America's black newspapers in particular were happy to receive copy from the reliable Collie, whom they recalled and admired from his war work, especially when other African American teams seemed far less concerned with coverage outside their areas. Eventually the Grambling stories would also begin to spill into the mainstream press.

Monroe sportswriter Nick Deriso wrote, "I've called Nicholson a shoe-leather genius because he worked in the days before computers, fax machines and wall-to-wall coverage. Collie J. used to keep stats, write the stories, then book it down (an estimated sixty miles) I-20 to the Western Union after every game, sowing these seeds of national stature through the wires to newspapers all over the country."

R. L. Stockard, who as a reporter and public relations officer of the Southwestern Athletic Conference was a close observer for a half-century, echoed Marino Casem when he said, "All the things Grambling did, Collie was the instigator."

Nicholson spread the word about the amazing collection of athletes Coach Rob was developing, which eventually forced some pro teams to start looking at them far more seriously. Collie's newspaper readers wanted to know why so-and-so didn't draft these guys, and the questions grew.

The athletes, while almost all capable, benefited from the Nicholson style. Deriso passed along a quote by Ernie Miles, who succeeded Collie at Grambling: "I remember a quarterback who was having trouble completing his passes and (worried about) how they looked. Coach told the player to concentrate on the pass. 'Do that,' Robinson said, 'and you'll be surprised how straight and pretty the ball will sound once Collie J. is finished writing about it.'"

Nicholson played a key PR role in the filming of New Jersey sportswriter Jerry Izenberg's 1967 documentary, *Grambling College: 100 Yards to Glory*. Not rare in the 1960s, there was a student demonstration underway the week the Tigers were to play Texas Southern. The game was the backdrop of the documentary, and the protestors wanted to interfere with the filming of the football team. Collie was instrumental in placating the students, who thought their actions were being filmed by some of the TV crew with the finished copy ready to be flown to New York for the network to air.

But those cameras contained no film. Grambling's homecoming, Grambling's marching band, and Grambling's choir were all shown on the coast-to-coast telecast, but nothing of the demonstrations or the National Guardsmen on campus were, saving President Jones and Eddie Robinson some embarrassment while almost instantly making the Tigers a national item.

Nicholson worked with legendary Grambling coach Eddie Robinson for over a half century.

As Stockard told Robinson biographer Denny Dressman, Collie was the marketing genius behind the "Classics" that featured Grambling against a series of black school opponents coast to coast. "He didn't hesitate to walk into (New York Yankees owner) George Steinbrenner's office and say, 'Man, we need some money.'"

Yankees president Michael Burke saw the documentary and wanted to link his historic stadium with the up-and-coming name of Grambling, if there was enough outside sponsorship for such a project. It was Collie who pounded the pavements seeking sponsors (finally getting Ballantine Beer), then set out hyping the charity game between Grambling and Morgan State.

What came of the effort was the "Whitney Young/Urban League Classic," with proceeds going to scholarships for disadvantaged New York youth.

The upshot was two small schools with enrollments of about eight thousand apiece drew sixty-four thousand to Yankee Stadium.

From there Grambling became a traveling road show, annually filling some of the most famed stadiums in America—the Rose Bowl, Orange Bowl, Soldier Field, Shea Stadium, even twice playing in Tokyo.

"We just came along at the right time," the humble Nicholson told Deriso in 2006, weeks before he died. "I tell you, the Lord was in the plan."

ALL THE NEWS FIT TO PRINT

Buddy Davis was catching flak. Mild flak, but still flak. "Don't even go there" was his standard response. "You're wasting your time."

The young sports editor of *The Ruston Daily Leader*—twenty-four years old and just two years after receiving his journalism degree from Louisiana Tech—was the object of curiosity in the northwestern section of the state with his full-fledged coverage of a predominantly black school, Grambling College.

"Anyone who didn't realize what Grambling was accomplishing at the time, 1970, didn't have the slightest concept of news," Davis recalled forty years later. "It was my job—and it turned out to also be my pleasure."

Davis was one of two Louisiana newspaper pioneers to forge paths to inclusive sports coverage. The other was R. L. Stockard. Davis was the first white sports writer to provide full coverage of a black program for a mainstream paper; Stockard was the first African American to write sports for a mainstream outlet, providing coverage of Southern University, Grambling, and by extension the SWAC for, first, the *Baton Rouge State-Times*, then the *New Orleans States-Item*.

This was an idea whose time had come long before but sadly had never been implemented in Pelican State sports.

Davis and Stockard showed the way.

Stockard's imprint is deeply pressed onto today's Louisiana sports scene. A native of Nashville, he served in Europe in World War II, earned his degree from Tennessee State, and then came to Louisiana to teach historical geography at Southern University.

While at the Bluffs, he became the first sports information director in the Southwestern Athletic Conference, disseminating the news of Jaguars' athletics across the region to black newspapers while imparting his specialized knowledge to his students—one of whom was future Hall of Fame outfielder Lou Brock. At the same time he became the first African American graduate student in historical geography at LSU.

In 1953, he boldly marched into the newsroom of the *Baton Rouge State-Times* and asked to speak to sports editor Dan Hardesty. Stockard made a case that the paper ought to increase its coverage of Southern University sports, particularly that of the football and basketball teams. He pointed out that, other than scores and who scored the touchdowns, there were no human interest stories, no background stories, and no columns providing insights on the powerful teams coached by Ace Mumford—later an inductee into the College Football Hall of Fame.

"I think he was surprised that I read the newspaper," Stockard said, "and was taken aback when I also said we were talking about a local four-year school with almost ten thousand students—approximately the same size as LSU, which got most of the coverage in the Baton Rouge media."

After taking a few days to check Stockard's observations, Hardesty agreed. As a part-time reporter, Stockard would be the eyes and ears of Southern sports to the rest of the sporting world. "But," R. L. recalled, "I had to do my own stories, my own statistics, my own game stories, my own sidebars. If I didn't do them, they just wouldn't appear in *The State-Times*. Then I had a responsibility to do the job."

Southern coverage improved as Stockard reported on the Jaguars for the next eight years—until he got a chance to teach at Southern's New Orleans branch, where he went in 1960.

The very day he moved to New Orleans, Stockard received a call from Walter Cowan, the editor of the city's afternoon paper, the *States-Item*. "I understand you used to write for the afternoon paper in Baton Rouge," Cowan said. "I could use you."

For the next decade, again as a part-timer, Stockard covered not only Southern but also Grambling and other SWAC schools as well as black high school sports.

It was in that capacity that Stockard was instrumental in putting together the first integrated game in New Orleans, the famed then-secret 1965 meeting of Jesuit and St. Augustine High Schools.

After that segment of his life concluded, Stockard became the first sports information director of the SWAC, then headquartered in New Orleans, where he also had a hand in putting together the first Bayou Classic.

"I guess," he once said, "though I didn't think of it in these terms at the time, I was kind of a pioneer."

Buddy Davis was a student at Tech and a part-time sportswriter when he accompanied Grambling to their landmark game against Morgan State in Yankee Stadium—the first of the megawatt showcases for Grambling in big stadiums across the country.

It was quite an assignment—asked for by Davis—for a daily newspaper with four thousand subscribers. It took some of the *Daily Leader*'s readers off-guard. "It wasn't said meanly," Davis recalled, "but there were those who would ask why we were wasting time and space on a predominantly black school? My stock answer was, 'It's ridiculous not to cover Grambling, a school in our own backyard that is making waves in football across the country.'"

Coach Eddie Robinson was at the height of his powers, building nationally prominent teams that would send two hundred players into pro football.

To give a sense of what Davis knew, and what his critics had no idea of, look at the quality of the teams. On the field of the 1968 Morgan State-Grambling game there were thirty-one players who would go on to play in the NFL.

Yeah, it would have been more than ridiculous not to cover this game of an area school.

When Davis graduated in 1970 he was named the *Daily Leader*'s sports editor—really he was a one-man sports department, fully covering Tech with stories and columns and high schools. Then he took on an added full-time responsibility, giving Grambling, seven miles from Ruston, equal space and coverage.

In doing so, Buddy Davis became the first white writer to cover a black sports team as a full-time beat for a largely white newspaper.

One day after a staff meeting, Buddy approached Tom Kelly, the *Daily Leader* publisher, with the idea of treating Grambling the same as any other nearby sports entity.

"I went to him after I joined the staff full-time. I said to him, 'I grew up studying sports and appreciating the history of sports. And Coach Rob and what they have done at Grambling needs to be covered. This needs to be done. They deserve it.' He said, 'Go for it. I don't have any problem with it.'"

Almost doubling his workload, just as he had for Tech, Buddy did all the pregame stories, game stories, columns—and served as his own staff photographer.

It was a fortuitous relationship. Davis—and the *Daily Leader*—had a front row seat to one of the greatest runs in college football history. In the next eleven years, Robinson coached Grambling to a 105-21-1 record (a .827 winning percentage) and won five black national championships.

Buddy had by-line stories from practically every famous stadium in the country: the Rose Bowl, the Los Angeles Coliseum, the Orange Bowl, Soldier Field, Comiskey Park, the Astrodome, the Silverdome, Detroit's Tiger Stadium, Giants Stadium, Shea Stadium, Three Rivers Stadium, Aloha Stadium, RFK Stadium, Philadelphia Veterans Stadium, and Cleveland Municipal Stadium, not to mention games played in Tokyo in 1976 and 1977.

As the only white person traveling with a black team, Davis was something of a curiosity on the road. "Coach Rob would introduce me at press conferences," he said, "and I'd have media guys coming up to me and asking, 'How is it traveling with Grambling? What's it like? You're the only white guy around.'"

Davis always answered positively and enthusiastically. "They were great guys," he said of the Tigers he covered. "Coach Rob was like a father to me," he said much later. And of the Tigers, he added, "I made special friends for life, doing what I was supposed to do—my job."

Sport writers Buddy Davis (above, with Louisiana sports legends Karl Malone and Terry Bradshaw) and R. L. Stockard (below) brought African American athletics in Louisiana to wider audiences by providing coverage for some of the Pelican State's most widely circulated newspapers.

CLEARING THE WAY

Spring 1949
Lincoln Parish, La.

Tank Younger was the first African American player from a historically Black college to play in the NFL.

Who could have known they were making history?

One evening in 1949, sitting in a car outside Ruston were Grambling College football player Paul "Tank" Younger, Coach Eddie Robinson, Collie Nicholson, the Tigers' sports information director, school president (and Tank's godfather) Ralph Waldo Emerson Jones, and Eddie Kotel, a representative of the Los Angeles Rams.

They were trying to pave the way for Younger to become the first player from an historically black college to get to the NFL—and it wasn't easy. The undrafted Younger had an exceptional collegiate career, but it took some persuasion to convince the Rams he would be a free agent worth more than just a token investment.

Because Grambling wasn't able to field a football team in the World War II years of 1943 and '44, Robinson had requested, and was granted, permission to coach Grambling High School, which had never participated in the sport. The school lost in the 1943 state finals, but won the state championship the following season.

"I found guys like Jerry Moore and Paul Younger at that little place," Robinson said later with a big smile. "They formed the nucleus of the '45 college squad. Younger played tackle, but I used him a lot on end-around plays and he scored twenty-five touchdowns. When we finally put him in the backfield, the pros discovered Grambling."

No wonder. When he played his last college game, Younger (dubbed "Tank" by Nicholson, a former Marine correspondent who said watching the 225-pound behemoth-for-the-time run reminded him of the Shermans he saw rumbling through the Pacific island-hopping campaigns of the war) had scored what was then a record sixty touchdowns. He also completed forty-three of seventy-three passes for another eleven touchdowns.

★ ★ ★

Knocking down doors or pricking the conscience of the sports world at large was never the primary mission of Eddie Robinson. Winning football games was.

But it is amazing to look back and realize how many doors were opened because of what his presence at a certain place and time meant.

Not only did Tank Younger become the first NFL player from a historically black college, but:

- Grambling defensive tackle Buck Buchanan became the first No. 1 draft choice from a predominantly black school (taken by the Kansas City Chiefs of the American Football League in 1960);
- James "Shack" Harris became the first African American to open a season as an NFL team's starting quarterback in 1974 for the L.A. Rams, and the first to start an NFL playoff game the same season;
- Doug Williams became the first African American to quarterback a Super Bowl team (the Washington Redskins in 1988).
- With Robinson molding prototypical NFL players, more than two hundred Grambling players were sent to pro football, and with the precedent set, dozens of others from other black schools also were drafted and made NFL rosters.

All those in-roads began, though, with Tank.

★ ★ ★

"We were hashing out the situation," Robinson said of that night in the car in Lincoln Parish, "and it wasn't going well." The Rams were offering $4,800, and Younger wanted $6,000. Neither would budge.

In exasperation, Kotel asked Robinson to talk sense to Younger, and explain to him that the Rams would keep him around longer at cutting time at the lower salary. "But I said, 'No, take him at $6,000 and if he doesn't do the job, fire him,'" Robinson recalled.

Tank signed for a $600-a-month contract and a $600 bonus. And he wasn't going to let his opportunity slip away. In the Rams final exhibition game that year, the rookie's only pair of beat-up old cleats, brought along from Grambling, began falling apart. But Younger, fearful of not making the team, refused to come out of the game to have the shoes repaired.

Younger was well aware of what rested on his shoulders. "The day I left Grambling," Younger said decades later, "Eddie Robinson told me I had to make it. He told me if I failed, black college football would fail."

Neither did. In those days of playing both offense and defense, Younger was exceptional at both. Part of the Rams' "Bull Elephant" backfield with Deacon Dan Towler and Dick Hoerner, Younger gained 3,640 yards rushing in his ten-year career and caught 100 passes for 1,167 yards, scoring a total of 35 touchdowns.

His success had an immeasurable impact back at his old school.

"Every fellow who came to play for Grambling College felt Tank opened a door for him," Nicholson said. "Grambling developed a certain pride other black schools didn't have."

That pride, and Robinson's molding of players into what the scouts were looking for, made Grambling a pipeline to the pros.

A grateful Younger gave back to his old alma mater, starting an honored tradition. Tank would return to Grambling each spring to help coach the players who came after him. Robinson always credited Younger with "developing the potential of a lot of kids who didn't realize what they were capable of. And the guys he helped, Willie Davis, Buck Buchanan, Rosey Taylor, Ernie Ladd, et cetera, all came back, too, to help and encourage the others. Heck, there were times I'd have to leave the field so they could get some coaching done."

There was more. After his multiple-year All-Pro career, Younger was hired as a scout and front-office executive by the Rams—the first black man to achieve those position in the NFL—and later became assistant general manager of the San Diego Chargers.

Jack Teele, a former NFL executive, said at the time of Younger's death in 2001, "Tank was really a pioneer in the Jackie Robinson mold."

THE HOMECOMING

September 25, 2006
Louisiana Superdome, New Orleans, La.

How that newly refurbished roof stayed on is a mystery. The combustion of noise and emotion that erupted beneath it was volatile enough to jettison the Superdome cover to Kingdom Come.

It had been building all day, like the rumblings before an emotional volcano. The Saints were returning to the 'Dome for the first time since Hurricane Katrina tore large strips off its roof more than a year before, displacing the team—and tens of thousands of its fans.

Now both the Saints and their fans were back.

Throngs, many wearing black-and-gold jerseys, milled around the stadium—a symbol of both what New Orleans had endured and its return—throughout the sunny day, hours before the Monday Night Football game with the Atlanta Falcons, a hated arch-rival and seen as a serious Super Bowl contender with a 2-0 record, same as the Saints. Music blared from stages set up throughout the locked down Central Business District, and tailgate revelers danced and sang to U2 and Green Day's cover of "House of the Rising Sun," with the word "Superdome" subbing for the brothel.

The seventy thousand spectators that filled the stadium were ready for some football, emotionally primed.

But that's not what nearly caused the roof to blow.

★ ★ ★

Tony Kornheiser, then a Monday Night Football analyst, tried to put things in context. "This is not housing we are talking about," he said to the national audience. "It's football.

"Housing will take years to rebuild. Football will only take a few hours to play, but you rebuild and recover a little at a time. And before you do it with bricks and wood, you do it with symbols, like a team coming back and a stadium reopening."

Before the Saints could return to their home the Superdome needed $185 million in repairs after sections of its roof were pulled loose by rampaging winds, its insides open to the torrential rains.

Everything in the Gulf region was then—still is now to a large degree—colored by the inescapable backdrop of Katrina, the winds of which ripped the city apart and whose aftermath put 80 percent of New Orleans under water. A place once musically described as a "Land of Dreamy Scenes" was transformed into a nightmarish water-world, where hundreds lost their lives and from where hundreds of thousands had to be evacuated to other parts of the country.

People could barely survive in the aftermath of the storm, much less support a football team. The Saints moved their operations to San Antonio (while their own training facility was used as a military base of emergency operations), and the club played "home" games at such sites as Giants Stadium, LSU's Tiger Stadium, and the Alamodome.

With New Orleans waterlogged for weeks and depleted of its population, the very future of the city in doubt, owner Tom Benson appeared to want to pull the plug on New Orleans and permanently move the Saints to Texas. It was then-NFL Commissioner Paul Tagliabue who basically ordered an angry Benson to stay put. Otherwise, the Lombardi Trophy might be in the showcase of the San Antonio Saints.

Yet, there are always those, much like the citizens of New Orleans, who can find the proverbial silver lining even against all odds.

As *Sports Illustrated* described, months later when safety Roman Harper, a second-round draft choice from Alabama, crossed over the Twin Spans driving into the eastern section of New Orleans, he saw a wrecked Walmart, a church missing its spire, and rooftops covered with blue tarps laid out in front of him like an ocean.

"This," he thought to himself, "is home."

Even so, things were still iffy for New Orleans. In just the immediate area of the Superdome on the day of the return game, sat a luxury high-rise hotel, an upscale shopping center, an office tower, all empty with white boards filling in blown-out windows. Just a few miles away neighborhoods of decaying houses littered the landscape, with some of those occupants holding pregame parties in their FEMA trailers.

Here was a recovering population that lost lives and homes—and had been threatened with the loss of its touchstone, its football team.

But there they were. The Saints were back, along with a new coach, Sean Payton, and a new quarterback, Drew Brees. There was reason to smile, to at least temporarily put heartaches aside.

★ ★ ★

A resounding rendition of "The Saints Are Coming" by U2 and Green Day—the memory of which *Times-Picayune* writer John Deshazier said years later still made his hair stand on end—brought the noise level to a crescendo. The final lines of "The Star-Spangled Banner," done by local legends Irma Thomas and Allen Toussaint on the piano, were drowned out by an ear-splitting roar.

But that's not what nearly caused the roof to blow.

What did was this: a minute and a half after kickoff, with the Falcons inside their own 30, Steve Gleason shot cleanly through the line, flung his outstretched body airborne, and blocked the punt coming off Michael Koenen's foot.

The ball skidded across the goal line and Gleason's teammate Curtis Deloatch recovered, then picked up the football and ran toward the stands, pointing it to the fans, as if to say, "This is for you!"

In a game thousands had been anticipating for weeks, the Saints were on the board with one dramatic play. That's what nearly caused the roof to blow.

Deshazier wrote, "Saints fans achieved a decibel level they likely never had before. The building shook and rocked from the sustained vocal pounding."

Falcons quarterback Michael Vick concurred. "I never heard such a roar," he said in admiration of Saints fans.

It was electrifying, a play fraught with symbolism. "My blocked punt signified the beginning of that trip back," Gleason said. "Us coming out and setting that tempo, and just identifying and allowing people to recognize that not only were we back as a team, but we were back as a city."

Gleason, a safety, started only one game for the Saints, but made a spot for himself on the roster by excelling in the dirty work of special teams. This was the fourth blocked punt of his seven-year NFL career, and he annually ranked among the team leaders in tackles on punts and kickoffs. Just as in high school and college, he was a team captain.

All week he had been preparing for a special punt-block alignment devised after watching Falcons' tape, one that had him lining up to the right of the center and, on the snap, going to the left of the center. Gleason had no idea if the call would come and never dreamed it would come in the opening minutes of the game.

When it did, it became not only what Drew Brees called "the biggest play of the game," but one of the biggest in Saints' history because, at 13:37 in the first quarter, New Orleans was on its way, not only to a 23-3 victory, but eventually to much bigger things.

Before the period was over, another designed play, "The Superdome Special," in which receiver Devery Henderson ran an end around, taking a handoff from Reggie Bush (and with Brees throwing a wicked block to spring him) for an eleven-yard touchdown, gave the Saints a 14-3 lead.

Of course, this was the seminal moment of Gleason's life in sports, the exclamation point to an inspirational eight-year career. "I'm the little kid that dreams of playing in the NFL, and doing something great, and tonight I did it," Gleason euphorically said.

"It was so loud inside my own head, I could have jumped outside my own skin. I felt like I was in every inch of the Superdome, up in the crowd, just so happy that I could do that for the people. I couldn't ask for anything more."

Neither could the fans. Gleason became sort of a cult hero in New Orleans, where he married and settled after football, where he continued to work in the press box helping the PR staff—and where he was diagnosed with Amyotrophic Lateral Sclerosis (ALS), the terminal Lou Gehrig disease.

He was a regular presence at Saints games as long as he could.

Of the game Gleason will always be identified with, fullback Mike Karney said, "I was crying like a baby out there. I just got caught up in the moment. I was just happy for the fans and the people of this city. I had tears in my eyes when I came out on the field. It was just a good feeling to know all seventy thousand fans were all there for you."

★ ★ ★

It's hard to separate the fairytale aspect of the story from reality, but the game meant more than just feeling good. The Saints went from there to a 10-6 record and a first-ever berth in the NFC Championship Game, where they lost to the Chicago Bears. But this was a beginning of a gilded era of Saints football.

Still, the return game will always be a part of New Orleans memories.

"As tough as it is to lose a game," said Falcons coach Jim Mora Jr., whose father was the winningest coach in Saints history, "I'd be lying if I said there isn't a little, little, little piece of me that didn't appreciate what this game meant to this city. It meant a lot."

So much so that now a statue of Gleason's block stands outside the Superdome, a symbol of what that single play did for the Saints—and for New Orleans.

It carries the title "Rebirth."

Steve Gleason making one of the most memorable plays in Saints history.

SWEET SMELL OF SUCCESS

December 30, 1962
Yankee Stadium, New York

It's the enduring image of the Vince Lombardi Packers: Jim Taylor thundering out of the backfield like a rhino behind pulling guards Fuzzy Thurston and Jerry Kramer.

Taylor was the sledgehammer in an only-the-fittest-survive offense. No one suited a role better.

With a no-neck, granite-like upper torso and legs with the resiliency of concrete, the five-foot-eleven, 212-pound fullback was the ideal battering ram.

Green Bay stormed through the National Football League during Taylor's near-decade as a Packer, winning one conference title, four NFL championships, and the first Super Bowl. Bart Starr, Paul Hornung, Forrest Gregg, Willie Davis, Thurston, Kramer, Herb Adderly, et al., formed the near-perfect football team of its day. But the slashing fullback from Baton Rouge was the offensive ignition. Taylor ran for 1,000-plus yards for five straight seasons—and this was in the era of twelve- and fourteen-game seasons—gaining 1,474 yards in 1962, a bar that was not exceeded by another Packer for forty-one years, when Ahman Green ran for 1,883 yards in the sixteen games of 2003.

Taylor retired as the NFL's No. 2 all-time rusher with 8,597 yards and 10,353 total yards, achievements that could hardly go unnoticed. He was the first of the Lombardi Packers to be enshrined in the Pro Football Hall of Fame.

But it took some of life's strange twists and turns to get there.

⋆ ⋆ ⋆

The image of Jimmy Taylor playing football is one of would-be tacklers bouncing off his sturdy legs of steel—the result of a hard childhood with an unwavering work ethic. His tremendous leg muscles were developed with two paper routes—one in the morning, one in the afternoon—bicycling what he estimated to be "a million miles" for three dollars a week to help his widowed mother. Those legs, and his awesome athletic ability, could have taken him to the top of many sports.

"Jim could have played anything and been good at it," Bat Gourrier, once the track coach at Baton Rouge High, assessed. "If you stick a tennis racquet in his hand, he would have been great. If someone had bought him a set of (golf) clubs, he could outdo you in that, too. He was just a natural athlete."

In between school and his paper routes, Taylor found time to develop into a hellacious backcourt player. "The first time I remember noticing Jimmy Taylor was when he played basketball," said Ted Castillo, the former prep editor of the *Baton Rouge Morning Advocate*. "He was an outstanding player and had a certain touch in his shooting."

Late in coming to football, Taylor blossomed two years after going out for the team, shining mainly as a linebacker, and as a senior he was selected to play in both the state football and basketball All-Star Games—a Louisiana first.

Recruiters came by the droves, but they were basketball offers. The only school that offered a football grant-in-aid was hometown LSU. That's the one he accepted, so he could stay close to his mother and help her out.

Jim Taylor while at LSU.

There was little Taylor couldn't do athletically, but he quickly ran into problems in the classroom. He had to transfer to Hinds (Mississippi) Junior College to get himself ready for major college studies, but he did and returned to LSU—after turning down even more basketball offers from Miami, Furman, and Colorado.

It took a while to learn the offense under new LSU coach Paul Dietzel, but Taylor led the SEC in scoring twice be-

Jim Taylor with Green Bay Packers legends Bart Starr and Vince Lombardi.

fore heading where his real destiny beckoned—the NFL.

★ ★ ★

"Coming out of college, I thought I was a better linebacker than a fullback, and I was told that's where I might play," Taylor reflected. "Until Coach Lombardi came to Green Bay I had only been a running back for about seventeen games. In high school I played mainly defense until I was a senior. In junior college I ran with the ball, but as a junior at LSU I didn't develop the skills necessary to become a pro running back. In college I was running from tackle to tackle, did very little pass receiving and, really, very little blocking. I wasn't utilized that much."

Not that much as a pro rookie either. The second-round draft choice mostly languished on the bench of a 1-10-1 team under Scooter McLean.

Then, as Jerry Kramer said it, "In the last two games of the year they let him play and he gained almost 250 yards for a team that didn't have much of anything."

Those two games probably saved Taylor's career. When Lombardi, who replaced McLean, studied the 1958 films, he noticed "a guy hustling his tail off," a fullback who seemed determined to make his own daylight.

"I saw enough in the movies to have high hopes that Taylor would be able to do what we had in mind," Lombardi said. "No one could have figured he would turn out to be as good as he is. That would have been too much to expect at the time."

Under Lombardi, Taylor would be utilized to the max, becoming the fullback prototype.

Taylor and Jim Brown, the premier runner of the time, are often compared, probably because they played in the same era and, ostensibly, played the same position. But Brown was strictly a runner, not asked to block, receive, or do much of anything else. Taylor, a superior blocker and receiver coming out of the backfield, played more of a do-it-all game, and relished it. Even then, in four head-to-head confrontations between the two, it was the Packer who won the statistical battles, Brown gained 72 yards to Taylor's 158 and four touchdowns in their first meeting, a 19-17 Green Bay victory. Brown finished his career with the 1965 Cleveland-Packers championship game; Green Bay won again as Taylor gained ninety-six yards to Brown's fifty. Giants linebacker Sam Huff—whose meetings with Taylor in the pits became almost mythic—said, "Brown is strong. But he doesn't hit you like Taylor does."

★ ★ ★

Huff should know. His duels with Taylor reached a fabled apex in the NFL Championship Game of 1962.

The New York temperature reached a high of fifteen degrees and the gusting thirty-mph winds made the field Siberian. Giants' defenders Huff, Rosey Grier, and Andy Robustelli knew quarterback Bart Starr would call a percentage game and took dead aim at Green Bay's most consistent weapon.

Time and time again Taylor was flung against a crack unit that knew he was coming. Each time he was stopped and slammed into the glacier-like turf, New York's chances for victory increased. Every time he was hammered into the steely ice, Huff would taunt the bloodied back: "You stink, Taylor, you stink."

At the half Jimmy's elbow had to be stitched, and in the second half his tongue was split. At the end, after thirty-one carries for eighty-five yards and two receptions for twenty yards more, Taylor could barely see through the swollen slits his eyes had become. He couldn't talk except for one shot back to Huff: After scoring the Packers' only touchdown in what would be a 16-7 Green Bay victory, Jimmy spit blood, turned, and yelled to Huff, "Hey, Sam, how do I smell from here?"

Taylor retuned to Louisiana as a member of the inaugural 1967 New Orleans Saints squad.

SMOKE GETS IN YOUR EYES

November 12, 1932
The Fairgrounds, Shreveport, La.

Homer Norton warned his team. "Next Wednesday," he said sternly a week before his Centenary College Gents would take on LSU, "I'll check each of you to see if you can hold your hands out before you without trembling. If you can, I'll wire Coach Jones to bring his team on up, that we'll be ready for them."

Turned out there were several "inspections," but after the one he held at breakfast the morning of the game, Norton said he knew the Tigers—on a streak of five shutout victories—were licked. The Gents stood when Norton entered the dining hall and, at attention, held out their hands. There wasn't so much as a quiver among the twenty-five-man squad.

The Gents were ready.

And why wouldn't they be? The real question of this game was who exactly was David and who exactly was Goliath—the little Methodist school with an enrollment of four hundred or the state university? LSU football, the favorite plaything of Gov. Huey Long, was formidable under new coach Lawrence McChesney "Biff'" Jones. But nothing that the Gents hadn't seen before. Centenary in 1932 embarked on what came to be called "The Suicide Season," with games against Texas, Texas A&M, Southern Methodist, Arkansas, and Ole Miss, along with LSU.

The Gents didn't lose any (but there was a tie with the Razorbacks a week after LSU), nor would they in 1933, though there were four more ties.

Centenary was used to taking on the Big Boys—and beating them, too.

☆ ☆ ☆

No longer a participant in football, Centenary nevertheless left an indelible mark on the sport in the 1920s and '30s. Ever since President George Sexton, who believed sports could bring renown to a school, hired Bo McMillin in 1921, Centenary came to stand toe-to-toe with some of the giants of the game.

Baylor and Iowa regularly popped up on the Gents' schedules, as did Southwest Conference opponents, usually resulting in Centenary victories. Over a three-year period between 1922 and 1924, McMillin compiled a 25-3 record and coached such luminaries as tackle Cal Hubbard, the only man elected to three major halls of fame, Pro Football, College Football, and Baseball (as an umpire).

Problem was, McMillin never actually graduated from college at his alma mater (Centre)—and he was paid an exorbitant salary—$9,000 at a time when the college president earned $2,000. As a result, in 1924 Centenary was denied accreditation by the Southern Association of Colleges and Schools because of "undue emphasis on athletics," according to the *Harvard Business Review*. The next year McMillin was out, and the college regained its academic standing.

Centenary football kept rolling along. Former Gents coach Homer Norton—a College Football Hall of Famer, as are Jones and McMillin—was rehired (in abbreviated schedules, he had coached the Gents to a 4-7-0 record between 1919-21) and Centenary continued its newly-acquired winning ways; Norton's teams went 57-15-7 over the next eight years. In the 1934 Dixie Classic, forerunner to the Cotton Bowl, Arkansas was hard-pressed to tie the Gents at 7-7.

Centenary football can still be found in the NCAA record book. On November 11, 1939, Texas Tech and Centenary played

1932 Centenary College Gents.

in a deluge in Shreveport. The game resulted in a still-standing record of seventy-seven punts (thirty-nine by Tech, thirty-eight by Centenary) and a scoreless tie. There were also forty-two returned punts, four blocked kicks, sixty-seven punts on first down, and twenty-two consecutive first down kicks by both teams in the third and fourth quarters. Texas Tech ran a total of twelve offensive plays (ten rushing, two passing) for a negative one yard. Texas Tech's Charlie Calhoun punted thirty-six times for 1,318 yards in the game.

Though Centenary certainly had an impressive record, until 1932, the school had never played the "big-time" program in its own state.

This was its chance to make a statement among the fans of Louisiana, and five thousand temporary seats were added to the stadium.

Centenary was a light team, averaging only 172 pounds and with just tackle Conway Baker—who would have a ten-year NFL career—and one reserve weighing as much as two hundred pounds. But the Gents were fast, and had a major threat with All-American Paul "Hoss" Geisler in the backfield.

LSU was not only considerably bigger, but one Tiger, center "Baby Jack" Torrance, practically dwarfed the Gents by himself, with his six-foot-five, 260-pound frame.

The teams put on a show, not because of inept offenses but because the defenses on both sides were so good.

Twice apiece the opponents threatened, the Tigers getting to the Gents' 13, with a botched pitch-out losing twelve yards and ending a serious opportunity.

Only a sixty-yard third quarter drive paid off. Gents' back Ralph Murff gained twenty-seven yards on two plays, then Manning Smith, under duress trying to pass, scrambled for seventeen yards. A piling on penalty of fifteen yards put the ball at the Tiger 1 (this was before half-the-distance penalties).

Murff scored, but the PAT was missed.

In the remaining quarter and a half, Geisler caught a pass and broke a run to the Tiger 10, but nothing more than a missed field goal came of it. LSU reached the Centenary 12, but a fumble foiled the threat—as well as the Tigers' last real chance of pulling it out.

Norton's eyes were watering after Centenary's 6-0 victory. Asked if anything was the matter, he replied, "The smoke was awful in our room. Some of it got into my eyes." His lone assistant, Curtis Parker, was also tearing up. Norton was asked if the same smoke got into his aide's eyes. "Yes," Norton nodded, "I suppose it did."

Centenary's 1932 Schedule:

41	Henderson	0
13	Texas	6
41	La. Normal	7
13	Ole Miss	6
18	SMU	7
7	Texas A&M	0
44	Southeastern Okla. Teachers	0
6	LSU	0
0	Arkansas	0

LSU coach Biff Jones.

Centenary coach Homer Norton.

STIFF-ARMED LOUISIANANS

Pelican State-bred players have finished either first or second in Heisman Trophy voting six times since the coveted bronze statue, emblematic of the best player in college football, was first awarded in 1935.

Two received enough votes to place among the elite twice.

In the first nine decades of the Heisman, which was first given in 1935, a Louisiana-raised player has finished among the finalists (top four or five) of the nationwide balloting twelve times.

Heisman Trophy Finalists From Louisiana

YEAR	PLAYER	POSITION	SCHOOL	HOMETOWN	FINISH
1951	Hank Lauricella	Tailback	Tennessee	New Orleans	2nd
1957	John David Crow	Halfback	Texas A&M	Springhill	1st
1958	Billy Cannon	Halfback	LSU	Baton Rouge	3rd
1959	Billy Cannon	Halfback	LSU	Baton Rouge	1st
1962	Jerry Stovall	Halfback	LSU	West Monroe	2nd
1972	Bert Jones	Quarterback	LSU	Ruston	4th
1977	Doug Williams	Quarterback	Grambling	Zachary	4th
1992	Marshall Faulk	Running back	San Diego St	New Orleans	2nd
1993	Marshall Faulk	Running back	San Diego St	New Orleans	4th
1997	Peyton Manning	Quarterback	Tennessee	New Orleans	2nd
2003	Eli Manning	Quarterback	Ole Miss	New Orleans	3rd
2011	Tyrann Mathieu	Cornerback	LSU	New Orleans	5th

The first Louisiana native to win the Heisman Trophy, John David Crow.

Heisman Trophy runner-up, Jerry Stovall (#21).

A THORNY ROSE

January 1, 1932
Rose Bowl Stadium, Pasadena, California

Tulane's Nollie Felts (63) clears a path for Harry "Wop" Glover (15).

Tulane was on top of its game. The Green Wave was 11-0-0 at the climax of its greatest regular season—one in which Tulane outscored its opposition 310-14—and on an eighteen-game victory streak, still the school record.

And here was the Green Wave lined up against Southern California, the No. 1 team in the land, in famed Arroyo Seco, site of the Rose Bowl, and poised to take the national championship for itself.

Never before or since—and this was eight decades ago—has Tulane football been within such easy reach of a No. 1 pennant and all the universal acclaim that accompanies such a feat.

How good was the 1931 Green Wave, which finished the regular season as the only undefeated, untied team in the country? After a 20-7 Tulane victory in the Game of the Year in the South, Georgia coach Harry Mehre called the Green Wave the best team his Bulldogs played: "Better than Yale or Vanderbilt or NYU," he exclaimed. LSU coach Russ Cohen said Tulane was "the greatest team I've seen anytime, any place, anywhere," after a 34-7 thumping.

Tulane, in that era of strait-jacket offenses, averaged an eye-catching four touchdowns a game. But, perhaps even more astonishing, was the Wave defense, which shut out nine opponents—including the first five of the season: Ole Miss 31-0; Texas A&M 7-0; Spring Hill 40-0; Vanderbilt 19-0; and Georgia Tech 33-0.

There was no question Tulane, still the only Louisiana school ever to play in the Rose Bowl, had a résumé worthy of its invitation.

This was the highest point of a "golden era" in Tulane football. In the three-year period of 1929 through 1931 the Green Wave lost one regular-season game, had an overall 28-2-0 record, won two Southern Conference titles, and shared in another. Sandwiched between an 8-1-0 record were a pair of unbeaten regular seasons—9-0-0 in 1929 and 11-0-0 in 1931—and participation in the Rose Bowl, at the time the only postseason game of consequence.

There was a certain irony in the Wave receiving its bid to the 1932 Rose. After Tulane's undefeated 1925 season, the Wave was invited to play in Pasadena, and the school turned down the overture. At the suggestion of *New Orleans Item* sports editor Fred Digby, the Rose Bowl invited Alabama, ushering in a series of games involving southern teams, ultimately including the 1931 Greenies.

It goes without saying that Coach Bernie Bierman's thirty-five-man team was loaded. Jerry Dalrymple, an end who played without a helmet, was named to every important All-American team, and tailback Don Zimmerman made several. But Bierman had several other weapons, such as fullback Nollie Felts, end Vernon "Lefty" Haynes, and halfback Harry "Wop" Glover (who was Tulane's last four-sport letterman).

So why was the Green Wave a three-touchdown underdog?

It could have been their one common opponent. USC beat Washington State 38-6; Tulane beat the Cougars 28-14. But that alone couldn't have been it.

USC, essentially playing a home game, had credentials of its own. The Trojans, under legendary coach Howard Jones, ran up 342 points while giving up 40 in going 9-1-0 in the regular season. USC lost its opener 13-7 to St. Mary's, then ripped off nine straight wins and climbed to the top rung of the polls of the day.

This was, of course, before the wire service polls, in which many qualified observers could watch and collectively evaluate all the nation's college teams. The polls of the early 1930s that had USC ranked No. 1 were one- or two-man operations, such as Helms or Williamson, or statistical junkies who worked out mathematical formulas such as Dunkel and Houlgate. So there was nothing close to an official national champion as there would be in 1935 when the Associated Press poll came into existence.

But, for what it was worth, it can be assumed that a Tulane victory in the Rose Bowl would have placed the Green Wave on top of at least one list, maybe more, although many of these polls did not figure postseason games in their calculations.

So, for the only time in its long football history, Tulane was sixty playing minutes from making a legitimate statement that it was the best college team in America.

The "Green Wave Special" headed out of Union Station on December 19 for its three-day journey to sunny California. The Tulane staff and thirty-five players occupied two Pullman cars attached to the rear of a Southern Pacific train. There were scheduled "practice stops" at El Paso and Tucson, but not necessarily on time.

"There was a train wreck outside of El Paso," lineman Louis Boasberg told New Orleans sportswriter George Sweeney, "and we were delayed ten hours. But Bierman made good use of the time. We practiced in the desert and after the workout it took us two hours to wash the sand from our body."

Once they got to Los Angeles, though, the Green Wave was swept up in the glamour of Hollywood, attending the premiere of *Hell Divers*, and meeting Marlene Dietrich, Clark Gable, and Dorothy Jordan. "Miss Jordan was from Clarksdale, Mississippi," Boasberg said, "and she told us she always pulled for Southern teams. Being a movie fan, it was a tremendous thrill for me, something you just dream about."

The Rose Bowl turned into a bad dream for the Greenies, one of those frustrating moments that occurs from time to time in every program, when what seems to be the superior team ends up on the short end of the score.

Tulane racked up more first downs (17-9) and gouged out more yards (310-230). But Southern California scored more points, 21-12.

Before a crowd of 75,562, USC showcased its famed—and odd—"spinner" play. The Trojans would come out of a huddle in a 4-4-3; that is, a front line of four, a second line of four, and a third line of three players. Then they would shift around. Seven men would go into the line and the backs moved into one of several formations. As described by Digby, there could be an end in the backfield and a back on the line, depending on the play. From that formation, USC specialized in reverses on which two or three backs and sometimes an end would handle the ball.

Sometimes the "spinner" would start like a run into the line, then the ball carrier would turn and lateral to a back in motion. It often did not give the defense time to adjust, giving the Trojans opportunities for big plays—and they got them against the Wave.

After Glover broke off a fifty-eight-yard run—Tulane's longest play of the day—in the second period, putting the ball on the USC 37, the Trojans threw the Wave back sixteen yards, then took command.

The Trojans' three touchdowns all came on variations of the "spinner." On the only touchdown of the first half, Ray Sparling, the Trojans' left end, took the ball on one of USC's hocus-pocus plays, a reverse on which the left end stepped into the backfield and the left halfback took his place on the flank. Gus Shaver, the quarterback, pitched the ball to the end on a reverse. Sparling went in from the 6.

In the second quarter, USC scored two touchdowns in the span of four plays, the first from the 29 by Ernie Pinckert. After a fumble, Pinckert went in again on the very same play from the 24 to give Southern Cal a 21-0 lead.

Finally getting its bearings, Tulane went seventy-five yards in ten plays. Glover, at 165 pounds, broke loose, being at least touched no less than ten times by Trojan tacklers as he dodged, straight-armed, and sidestepped his way thirty-three yards to the USC 16. Two plays later, on 3rd and 8, Zimmerman hit Haynes in the flat for the touchdown. Ernie Smith blocked Zimmerman's PAT, meaning the Greenies still had to score three times to win.

They almost did. After a fumble, the Wave got to the USC 10, but an interception killed the threat. Three minutes later, another fumble put the Wave in business again. A Zimmerman pass was batted in the air, but Dalrymple caught the spinning ricochet inside the 5. Glover, who gained 112 yards on 11 carries, followed a phalanx of blockers around left end for Tulane's second touchdown, its last of the 1931 season.

This defeat, looking back, was especially hurtful because the Green Wave lost its coach, too. Bierman left to go back to his alma mater, the University of Minnesota, where he coached the Golden Gophers to five national championships. The Green Wave would never win a single one.

In the decades since their Rose Bowl appearance, the Green Wave has had memorable seasons, pulled off eye-catching victories, and played in other bowl games. But Tulane never again found itself so close to a No. 1 pennant of its own.

Sad. Jim Thorpe, writing a celebrity piece for United Press, hit it on the head when he said the Trojans "deserved their victory, but a break or two for Tulane would have changed the result."

Members of the 1931 Green Wave squad.

Tulane All-American Jerry Dalrymple.

"The Flying Dutchman," Don Zimmerman.

Coach Bernie Bierman discusses the game plan with his Tulane Rose Bowl team , January 1, 1932.

SUPER SUNDAYS

January 11, 1970
Tulane Stadium, New Orleans, La.

It's one of the enduring images of Super Bowl lore: Hank Stram, strutting along the sideline like a bantam rooster, pointing with a rolled-up sheaf of paper and exhorting his team with stream-of-consciousness coaching patter.

"Way to go, boys," he chirped through cupped hands. "Just keep matriculating that ball down the field."

This was three years after the first AFL-NFL World Championship Game—which is what the title game between the two leagues was then called—and in which Max McGee, an aging former Tulane player scored the first touchdown, and in which Hall of Fame fullback Jim Taylor, who played college ball at LSU, scored the first rushing touchdown.

McGee, a reserve flanker who caught just four passes all season and was not expecting to play, finished what we now call Super Bowl I with seven catches for 138 yards and two touchdowns—all the while nursing a hangover after an all-nighter with a blonde. It's all part of the Super Bowl saga.

Louisiana is a base component of Super Bowl DNA—and has been from the start. In that first game, in which Green Bay defeated Kansas City 35-10, three eventual Hall of Fame players from the Bayou State were on the field: The Packers' Taylor, a fullback from LSU; defensive end Willie Davis from Grambling; and the Chiefs' Buck Buchanan, also a defensive tackle from Grambling. Another headliner was Kansas City's Johnny Robinson of LSU, later to be designated pro football's safety for the decade of the 1960s.

Yet another connection was the Grambling band, which put on the first Super Bowl halftime show, a performance voted one the ten best in the game's history by *Sports Illustrated*.

★ ★ ★

But this was Super Bowl IV, an extravaganza of Louisiana Who's Who and What's What, one of the most significant Super Bowls of all time, and played for the first time in New Orleans.

In a game that was a turning point of modern pro football, the two-touchdown underdog Chiefs "matriculated" their way to a thorough 23-7 "upset" of the Minnesota Vikings. Coming as it did a year after the New York Jets' stunning victory over the Baltimore Colts, this one more than put the old American Football League on an equal footing with the National Football League.

Kansas City's victory was a decisive haymaker, tying the two leagues at 2-2 in Super Bowls in the final game of the decade-long war between the pro leagues before their complete merger.

"The thing about it," Stram said later, "was we didn't have to go hat in hand, as second-class citizens, into the NFL. We went in as equals, and that was important."

In plain words, despite the Jets' upset the year before, the beatdown of the Vikings is what gave the AFL real credibility.

"While the New York Jets won Super Bowl III in part because Baltimore squandered so many scoring opportunities, the Chiefs in Super Bowl IV just flat out beat up the Vikings," former NFL official Don Weiss wrote in his book, *The Making of the Super Bowl*.

Tex Maule of *Sports Illustrated* said he had trouble writing his story on the Jets' shocker because he felt they were at least as lucky as they were good. He had no qualms giving full credit for the butt-kicking by the Chiefs, who held the Vikings to sixty-seven yards rushing.

Ed Gruver of the Professional Football Researchers' Association wrote: "To some, the Jets' victory merely allowed the AFL to gain a foothold on the beachhead that was NFL supremacy. Many felt it wasn't until the following year [1970] . . . that the AFL established equality with the NFL."

The rosters of that landmark game were dotted with seven players playing in their home state: one for Minnesota, linebacker Roy Winston (LSU), and six for Kansas City, cornerback Goldie Sellers (Grambling), wide receiver Frank Pitts (Southern), running back Robert Holmes (Southern), and center Remi Prudhomme (LSU), plus Buchanan and Robinson.

Added to that number was Stram, who was later to become head coach of the New Orleans Saints, and who was to spend the last twenty-six years of his life in Covington, across Lake Pontchartrain from the city, about forty miles from the high point of his career.

★ ★ ★

New Orleans's first venture into the Super Bowl-hosting business was a tremendous joint civic endeavor, but the efforts of the *Times-Picayune*, its editor George W. Healy, and sports editor Bob Roesler were crucial.

When New Orleans made its first pitch to host a Super Bowl in 1968, it was Roesler who whispered ominously to his boss that it was a doomed effort from the beginning. The Crescent City delegation was simply not prepared with the concrete information necessary, and the NFL owners weren't going to make such a mammoth financial decision based on vague numbers and ideas.

Roesler, though, was convinced that New Orleans was as attractive a venue as Los Angeles and Miami, sites of the first three games, and that with some work and preparation they could pull it off.

Healy was named chairman of the Super Bowl task force, with Roesler not only a member but doing most of the heavy lifting, making connections and securing business pledges. They also galvanized a united editorial front that included both New Orleans newspapers and television stations—in other words, all the opinion makers.

A year later the members of the task force went to the NFL owners' meeting in Palm Springs, California, fully prepared with facts, figures, and agreements for transportation and accommodations in hand.

Those alone likely would have been enough, but it might have been at the glitzy social function the night before the site of the 1970 Super Bowl was to be selected that New Orleans won over any lingering dissenters.

New Orleans trumpeter Al "Jumbo" Hirt serenaded the gathering, wowing the gathering before the piece de resistance: Hoagy Carmichael took the piano and accompanied "Jumbo" on Carmichael's signature composition, "Stardust," to a thunderous ovation.

The next day New Orleans was voted the site of the game, which irked the mayor of Miami, who said if he had known New Orleans was going to bring celebrities he would have brought Jackie Gleason.

Super Bowl IV was a resounding success, with the game's up-to-then largest crowd of 83,062, and the Nielson ratings putting the television audience at a then-record sixty million (excluding New Orleans, which as the game site was imposed with a seventy-five-mile blackout).

Ticket and television rights, at that time tied together as a revenue stream for the NFL, came to a record $3.8 million.

Today that figure wouldn't buy two thirty-second television ads during the Super Bowl.

But it made New Orleans a regular destination for pro football's championship game.

* * *

It was more than fitting that Stram would be the general who would pull the AFL even with the NFL. Miked for the game, the sporting world heard him chattering thoughts aloud like, "This is like taking candy from a baby," adding to his image as a dapper, jaunty, wisecracking guy on the sideline.

There was, however, another side of Stram, and perhaps the truest side—a single-minded and trailblazing championship coach who:

- guided the Chiefs to two of the first four Super Bowls (in the 1966 and 1969 seasons) and just missed a third in '71 when Kansas City lost to Miami in overtime during the playoffs in one of the longest games ever played;
- won more games (eighty-seven) and more championships (three) than anyone else in the ten-year history of the American Football League;
- helped change the game with his strategic innovations, such as the stack defense, basically the precursor of the 3-4 that came into NFL vogue in the aftermath of Super Bowl IV.

Tulane Stadium hosted three NFL Super Bowls.

Hank Stram is carried off the field after Super Bowl IV.

Author Ron Smith, in his book, *The Illustrated History of Pro Football*, compares Stram to Paul Brown, a man renowned for his forward thinking in the evolution of football.

"Stram seemed to be doing to professional football what Paul Brown had done a quarter century before," Smith wrote. "Shifting it to a higher intellectual plane, or at least developing it in the direction of an academic discipline. There was far more to learn, to practice, and to remember in Hank Stram's football than there ever had been in Curley Lambeau's or Jim Thorpe's."

Stram said of his constant football fiddling with formations, "I was like Thomas Edison. I always enjoyed experimenting, tinkering, something that would make opponents hesitate, just for an instant, before a play was run."

The moving pocket, camouflaged slot, double tight end, man in motion, stack defense, even zone defense were all components of Stram football—and all were dismissed as flimflam by NFL purists.

All of which gave Stram his answer when he was asked the secret to his team's crushing upset of the Vikings: "We just did," he said wryly, "all the things they said we couldn't do."

Super Times in New Orleans

1/11/70	Super Bowl IV	Kansas City 23, Minnesota 7	Tulane Stadium
1/16/72	Super Bowl VI	Dallas 24, Miami 3	Tulane Stadium
1/12/75	Super Bowl IX	Pittsburgh 16, Minnesota 6	Tulane Stadium
1/15/78	Super Bowl XII	Dallas 27, Denver 10	Superdome
1/25/81	Super Bowl XV	Oakland 27, Philadelphia 10	Superdome
1/26/86	Super Bowl XX	Chicago 46, New England 10	Superdome
1/28/90	Super Bowl XXVII	San Francisco 55, Denver 10	Superdome
1/26/97	Super Bowl XXXI	Green Bay 35, New England 21	Superdome
2/3/03	Super Bowl XXXVI	New England 20, St. Louis 17	Superdome
2/3/13	Super Bowl XLVII	Baltimore 34, San Francisco 31	Superdome

Pittsburgh Steelers running back Franco Harris in Super Bowl IX.

Chicago Bears running back Walter Payton in Super Bowl XX.

BAGGING THE TIGERS

December 1, 1973
Tulane Stadium, New Orleans, La.

Memories of Tulane's 46-0 pasting of arch-rival LSU in 1948 had to be savored.

A literal generation had passed since Tulane had beaten its oldest rival. In that same span—in which a child could have been born, completed a college education and then finished a tour of military service—the United States went through five presidents and fought two wars.

Looking back, Tulane's pounding of LSU in the year Harry Truman won the presidential election should have been sweet. And it was. At the time, it was the Bayou Bengals' worst Tiger Stadium defeat in history and the biggest Green Wave margin of victory in the series.

But it brought on a long, bitter drought for the silk-stocking New Orleans school. The Wave wouldn't beat the Tigers again for the next twenty-five years.

That's going quite a while without coming up for air, especially against the opponent you to beat most of all.

After coaching the Green Wave to the '48 victory, Coach Henry Frnka went 0-2-1 against LSU; Raymond Wolf was 0-2; Andy Pilney 0-7-1; Tommy O'Boyle 0-4; Jim Pittman 0-5; and Bennie Ellender 0-2 before the watershed 1973 game.

Not every LSU game was a blowout. Tulane often played well during the drought. There were close games. There were ties. And there was a constant frustration which reached an exasperating crescendo in 1972 when LSU won 9-3 in a game that ended with Tulane at the Tigers' 1-yard line.

The vexing and lingering memory of that near-miss—as well as a fine 1973 squad—fueled the fire for Tulane's next real shot at the Tigers.

Winners of eight of ten games before meeting the Tigers, Tulane's '73 pregame scenario was almost as if it had been written by the Greenies. Ellender, Tulane class of 1948, had assembled what clearly was a Tulane team with talent and ability. But the week before LSU, the Green Wave was beaten badly (42-9) by Maryland. Maybe Tulane was caught looking ahead, but no doubt it also brought on a degree of overconfidence by the eighth-ranked, 9-1 Bayou Bengals, who were two-touchdown favorites and who already had accepted an Orange Bowl invitation.

Tulane tailback Doug Bynum explodes for a 53-yard run against the Tigers.

Wave nose guard Mark Olivari said later the Maryland defeat didn't shake the Green Wave's confidence "because, unlike past Tulane teams, we could look back on the season and know we were a good team."

It was Olivari, though, who added spice to Tulane's psychological arsenal. He had heard a tape of one of General George S. "Old Blood and Guts" Patton's pre-battle speeches to his World War II troops the season before—a season when the Wave freshmen beat the LSU frosh. Part of the recording had rockets and bombs exploding in the background while the "Star Spangled Banner" played and Patton exhorted his soldiers: "Cut their guts outs! . . . We're never holding our position—we're advancing! It's the other guys that are holding on. . . ."

It inspired Olivari, and the entire week leading to the LSU game he played it over and over and over for his teammates. Sigmund Freud never conducted a more successful experiment.

Even Ellender's old coach, Henry Frnka, architect of the long, dim, and distant 1948 victory, visited practice. In addition, a very special guest would be in attendance in the person of Murphy Neal Jones, a former Tulane letterman and an Air Force pilot who had just been released after seven years as a prisoner of war in North Vietnam.

This wasn't just a football game. For Tulane, it was a crusade.

A crowd of 86,598, then the largest gathering in the history of southern football, jammed into Tulane Stadium that night with at least half (the Tulane partisans) seemingly on the verge of hysteria. The old arena was rocking under a banner which flapped gently in the breeze with a hand-scrawled message: "After 24 years—the Wave will be free in '73."

Emotion, preparation, and ability came to a boil that night as the Green Wave took the fight to the Tigers from the start and never let up.

Fierce trench warfare in the first half set the stage for some pyrotechnics after Greenies' defender David Lee intercepted LSU quarterback Mike Miley at the Tulane 30 with 1:37 remaining in the half. Terry Looney, backing up the celebrated Wave quarterback Steve Foley, saved Tulane when it looked as if intermission would arrive with a 0-0 score. But Looney, scrambling for a fourteen-yard gain on third and 10, pushed the Wave to the LSU 36 on a thirteen-yard pass to Tom Fortner.

Then Looney hit sophomore tight end Darwin Willie, who broke loose and reached for the end zone. With nineteen seconds left, Willie was buried under a sea of euphoric Greenies, and Tulane had a 7-0 lead.

Perhaps the game's biggest play came midway through the third quarter as LSU drove to the Tulane 11. Tigers tailback Brad Davis bulled his way to the 3, but LSU was penalized for illegal procedure. What would have been a first-and-goal at the 3 was transformed into a 3rd and 7 at the 16. Miley dropped back to pass, and Olivari chased him down for a 13-yard loss. Tigers kicker Juan Roca then missed a forty-six-yard field goal.

The victory was then put on ice. With Ellender's second offensive unit again in the game, tailback Doug Bynum ripped off a fifty-three-yard run through the middle to the LSU 1. Two plays later Lyndon Lasiter squiggled through the line and into the end zone. Tulane had a landmark 14-0 victory.

Ellender did not step out of his reserved character. After the raucous Wave locker room filled with media and seemingly crazed fans, Ellender asked all but the players—including the university president and athletic director—to leave. He wanted two minutes to join "his boys" in a brief prayer.

Then the pandemonium began again, only to quiet once more when a tall, graying, distinguished-looking gentleman with a cane made his way slowly through the crowd, which parted for him. It was Don Zimmerman, one of the Green Wave's truly great players, an All-American halfback on the 1932 Rose Bowl team.

Zimmerman took the hand of Ellender, whose eyes swelled with tears, kissed it and said, "Thank you for Tulanians everywhere."

Tulane players, coaches, and fans celebrate their 1973 victory over LSU. The Green Wave hadn't beaten the Tigers in their previous twenty-four meetings.

When the Lions Were Kings

Fall 1954
Strawberry Stadium, Hammond, La.

Those were the days, my friend, two years into the presidency of Ike and the dawn of Elvis's rule: 1954, the Year of the Lion Kings.

Unprecedented state attention focused on Hammond, a south Louisiana whistle stop, when the Southeastern Louisiana College Lions not only brushed through their nine-game schedule unscathed but statistically ranked with the giants of the sport.

This was a season of pure magic, one in which SLC, an NAIA program, blew away (and that's not too strong a phrase) its small-college opposition and notched one of its biggest victories ever against a rising major-college foe.

The odds of putting together a season like this are long anywhere, but the mere thought would have been labeled harebrained, given the resources of SLC (now Southeastern Louisiana University). The athletic program operated on a meager budget that didn't even provide enough funds for a fulltime sports information director to tell the story of this remarkable team. It was left to a student, Bud Johnson, to get the word out.

But to say Southeastern was the football envy of Louisiana is no exaggeration. State football was in the doldrums, including Tulane and LSU, which just a few years before had scheduled the Lions as a "breather." The Green Wave was 1-6-3 in 1954, and the Tigers went 5-6-0 after starting 0-4.

After seeing the Lions, *New Orleans Item* sports editor Hap Glaudi wrote, "The best college football team in Louisiana is the property of Southeastern College at Hammond, 60 miles north of Tulane and 40 miles south of LSU. . . . I repeat: Southeastern is the best football team in Louisiana. Its young men are unbeaten, untied and unspoiled."

Glaudi then added a challenge: Anyone who thought his words had the ring of treason, meaning authorities at Tulane and LSU, should petition the Sugar Bowl for a match to prove him wrong.

To put that landmark SLC squad in perspective, consider:

- UCLA, which was accorded a share of the 1954 major-college national championship, scored 367 points in its nine games. The Bruins allowed forty points (a 4.4 average). The Lions scored 379 points. SLC's defense, in those days of one-platoon football, yielded one touchdown in its first six games, and a grand total of forty-three for the season, yielding 4.7 points a game.

- Purdue quarterback Len Dawson led the nation's major colleges with fifteen touchdown passes. Ray Porta, the Lions' five-foot-nine, 155-pound quarterback, led the nation's small colleges with fifteen touchdown passes. No other quarterback in America that year passed for more than eleven touchdowns.

- The Lions, under thirty-eight-year-old taskmaster Stan Galloway, were unlikely champions. Twelve lettermen, fewest in the Gulf States Conference, returned from the 6-3 co-champions of 1953. The Lions were small even for the time, with an interior line averaging 208 pounds and no starting backs taller than five-foot-eleven. "I don't see how we can finish anywhere but last," Galloway said before the season's opening kickoff.

And last is just where the prognosticators picked Southeastern.

Nine games later, the Lions were not only undefeated, but in that era of three-yards-and-a-cloud-of-dust offense, Southeastern kicked up a sandstorm, with its Lilliputian backs tiptoeing their way to an average of 330 rushing yards per game.

"From the perspective of the secondary," Johnson, the student publicist, said of halfbacks Don Marino (5'8") and Larry Troxler (5'7") and fullback Tommy Bell (5'11"), "these little backs seemed to explode out of the ground. You practically could not see them until they were past the point of attack and darting through the secondary."

"Chemistry" was probably the biggest factor in the Lions' 1954 success, according to Galloway, but if there was one intangible it was Porta.

Southeastern quarterback Ray Porta and coach Stan Galloway.

"He always found a way," said Bud Montet, then the sports editor of the *Baton Rouge Morning Advocate*, who covered Porta's career as a quarterback at Istrouma High School. "Ray really wasn't that good, but when a game was on the line, he'd get the job done as well as anyone I've ever seen."

Porta originally signed with LSU, lettering as a backup in 1948 before joining the Army. Those service years added a dose of maturity to his athletic attributes, Porta said.

Galloway agreed. "I'd have to say Ray was the key to it all," the coach said. "Porta was a superior ballhandler with excellent footwork. He did not throw rockets, but set up quickly and timed his passes effectively."

Porta finished the season with Little All-American accolades and a glittering—for the time—50 completions, which covered 843 yards in 102 attempts.

It turned out there were other weapons at Galloway's disposal though.

The offensive line might have been pony-light, but it was also quarterhorse quick, a Galloway trademark. "Quickness and speed are the most important ingredients in any football team," he said, "including size."

There was no lack of good collegiate talent on the forty-man squad. Six of the Lions' top twenty-two players originally signed SEC grant-in-aids, including five with LSU. End Huey Husser, later drafted by the Chicago Cardinals, led SLC in receiving each of his four seasons; Don Peroyea was so versatile he was put at guard, tackle, and running back at LSU, but settled in at tackle for the Lions; and guard Don Fournet was the brother of LSU All-American Sid Fournet and had similar ability coming out of Bogalusa High School. Only Don's size (five-foot-eleven, 180) prevented him from receiving major-college offers. Tackle Gerald Stone and Titus Johnson, the left guard, played side-by-side for seven years, three at Bogalusa and four at SLC. Galloway was their coach during their entire football careers. There was little miscommunication on blocking assignments involving this pair. Stone later turned out to be the final preseason cut of the Cleveland Browns, then one of the NFL's powers.

Nine of the Lions' returning lettermen were in the line, which is just where any coach, given a choice, would want his experience.

★ ★ ★

Galloway wailed loudly about his teams' perceived shortcomings all the way to the opening kickoff against Northeast Louisiana. On the second play of the season, Porta flipped a quick pass to end Sal Locasio, who took off for a sixty-yard touchdown. Northeast fell 58-0.

Two decisive victories later, SLC came face-to-face with its moment of truth: Mississippi Southern (now the University of Southern Mississippi).

Southern was then at the top of its game after defeating Alabama two seasons in row, including the Cotton Bowl Crimson Tide of 1954. They had played in the last two Sun Bowls and were playing a schedule that included Memphis State and Florida State.

Southern was mammoth compared with the Lions, a man-to-man average of fifteen pounds bigger with tackles that weighed about 255 on a line that included Don Owens and guard P. W. Underwood, who would both have professional careers.

Troxler brought the overflow Hattiesburg crowd to its feet on the second play by sweeping right for forty-nine yards, setting up a twenty-yard touchdown pass from Porta to Husser—decisive in the 13-7 Lions' victory that splintered a fifteen-game Mississippi Southern home win streak.

Three games later, when Louisiana Tech went ahead 18-14, the Lions found themselves behind for the first and only time that season. But Porta galvanized his team for three fourth-quarter touchdowns, and Southeastern prevailed 35-24.

Legendary Tech coach Joe Aillet went into the Lions' dressing room afterward and got Porta out of the shower, saying, "I want to shake that man's hand."

This was long before there were postseason games on practically every street corner, and although there had been interest in SLC from some bowls, when push came to shove, they were filled by schools with more name recognition.

"On a given day we could have beaten a lot of ball clubs," Galloway later said wistfully. "Maybe not all of them, but we could have beaten some of the more prominent ones."

It was not to be. Galloway went on to coach other championship teams, though never again an undefeated one. And afterward his teams were different. They got bigger. There were no more 150-pound backs, and the lines grew noticeably, too. But, until his dying day, Galloway always did have the same one-word description of his 1954 Lions: "Special."

"WOO, PIG, PHOOEY"

January 1, 1966
Cotton Bowl, Dallas, Texas

Joe Labruzzo scored both of LSU's touchdowns in the 1966 Cotton Bowl.

The college football world had to be wondering: Who are those guys, and what the heck are *they* doing *there*?

Well, late on the afternoon of New Year's Day, 1966, the LSU Tigers were in their Cotton Bowl dressing room ripping apart a red jersey bearing the numerals "23."

In perhaps the biggest upset—and most satisfying victory—in LSU history, the Tigers were like barefoot country cousins at a highfaluting soiree: The 7-3 Bayou Bengals Tigers weren't supposed to be there. Not against previously unbeaten Arkansas, an opponent in clear position to claim a second consecutive national championship, victor of twenty-two games in a row, the highest scoring team in the country.

But the Tigers, which never seemed to hit on all cylinders throughout a disappointing season, not only crashed the party, they took it over. The Tigers pulled off the near-unthinkable.

It might be the most memorable upset by LSU in well more than a century of playing football.

It took a miracle for LSU, big losers to Ole Miss (23-0) and Alabama (31-7) to even be in Dallas, much less come out on top of an elite program.

The Tigers were highly regarded before the season, with talent that produced four future pros, including All-Americans George Rice at tackle and flanker Doug Moreau. But, continuing a four-year trend, Coach Charlie McClendon lost a starting quarterback, this time Nelson Stokley, crippling the LSU offense.

On the other hand, that circumstance also cleared the way for the high point of McClendon's early reign: the startling upset of the Razorbacks.

Because of a series of regular-season upsets and some complicated bowl politicking (this was the era before most conferences just slotted where their teams would play in the postseason), the Cotton Bowl was scrambling for somebody to play its host Southwest Conference champion. When Kentucky, ticketed for Dallas, lost to Houston, LSU athletic director Jim Corbett was on the phone selling his team.

Suddenly, LSU, with a 7-3 record, was in a major bowl against a major, major opponent—one that averaged 32.4 points a game at a time when twenty-one was an offensive juggernaut. Coach Frank Broyles had a starting tandem at running back (Harry Jones and Bobby Burnett) that averaged 7.7 yards per carry.

Also in Broyles's favor was the decision of the Associated Press to take a final poll for the first time after the postseason. The reason was three undefeated teams (No. 1 Michigan State, No. 2 Arkansas, and No. 3 Nebraska), all had legitimate arguments to be national champions.

McClendon knew, though, that at anything close to full strength, his team was not just a sacrificial lamb.

LSU, a nine-point underdog, practiced for a month with the scout squad all wearing red jerseys with the number "23" on them, the implication being obvious: The Tigers did not want to end the year as just the latest Razorbacks victim.

And, to McClendon's delight, the Arkansas fans played right into his hands. When LSU got to Dallas, the Hogs' faithful made

Quarterback Pat Screen (12) completes a pass to flanker Doug Moreau (80) in the 1965 Sugar Bowl; the pair contributed significantly to three consecutive LSU bowl victories, culminating in the 1966 Cotton Bowl win.

a point of mocking the Tigers with the smirking question, "LS Who?" As the Tigers left the hotel on their way to the buses that would take them to the Cotton Bowl, a little old woman wearing one of those silly red Porker hats in the lobby shrieked at the sight and yelled loudly, "'Look, they're actually going to show up.'"

Arkansas cut through the LSU defense for eighty-seven first quarter yards and the lead as receiver Bobby Crockett made a finger-tipped grab, then tippy-toed sixteen yards down the sidelines.

"He caught it around the 15, and there I was laying on the sideline watching him tightrope his way into the end zone," LSU cornerback Jerry Joseph said. "It was not a good feeling."

Joseph, five-foot-ten and 175 pounds, drew the unenviable assignment of taking Crockett in LSU's man-to-man scheme.

"I went back to our secondary coach, Bill Beall, and told him, 'I can't handle this guy by myself, it's just not possible,'" Joseph said. "'This guy is too good.'"

Beall immediately went to another perimeter defense, one that would "bracket" Crockett. Joseph would still have Crockett, but he would "follow" the receiver instead of trying to stay with him step for step. Safety Sammy Grezaffi—fastest man on the team—would play behind the pair to prevent a major gain.

That change was implemented,

The rest of the Tigers reacted as if cold water had been thrown in their face.

Even losing Stokley again didn't deter LSU. Backup Pat Screen picked up the torch, guiding a Tigers' offense with a slightly different look from the one Arkansas studied on film. Joe Labruzzo, a dangerous five-foot-nine, 170 pound tailback, was lined up deeper than usual so he could pick his options on the fly, depending on how the Hogs lined up.

The Tigers' offensive linemen, with Labruzzo hitting the holes behind them, took control. In nine plays Screen guided LSU eighty yards for the tying touchdown, Labruzzo scoring from the 3.

After a recovered fumble at the Razorbacks' 34 in the fading moments of the first half, Screen went for the knockout with body blows. Once LSU reached the 19, Labruzzo ran off left tackle five straight times and went in from the 1 with eighteen seconds to go until halftime. Just as important, the emotional barometer of the Tigers was changed. They weren't just trying to stay with Arkansas any more. They smelled blood.

Assistant coach Doug Hamley said he never experienced anything like that halftime.

"We couldn't hold the team in the dressing room," Hamley said. "They got up four times and tried to leave, but Coach McClendon had to hold them back because the bands were still on the field."

Beall later pointed to marks on the floor describing the way those caged Tigers pawed at the concrete as they waited for the halftime show to end.

"I knew they were ready," McClendon said. "That is, I felt if this team wasn't ready to play, I could never be sure of any team in the future."

Despite threats by both teams the rest of the way, including LSU reaching the Razorbacks' 2 in the fourth quarter where the Tigers missed what seemed to be a gimme game-clinching field goal, that 14-7 score held up to the end.

The biggest play came with 4:38 to play from the LSU 36 when Arkansas quarterback Jon Brittenum put the ball up for Crockett.

"I was guarding him on the outside," Joseph recalled, "and he got by me, so I started 'following' him—running right behind him. When he turned, I turned and . . . the truth of the matter is, the ball just hit me in the hands. It was like a dart. It was 100 percent instinct. I had no time to think. All of a sudden there was the ball, and I caught it."

Joseph didn't exactly shut down Crockett, who finished with ten receptions for 129 yards—seven after the first quarter—but did keep him contained while waiting to spring that trap. That interception took the air out of the Razorbacks' sails.

Arkansas very definitely lost not only to LSU but the national championship. Michigan State and Nebraska also lost. Decades later, Broyles said of that game, "I've never been so sick in my life."

In the final poll, the 8-3 Bayou Bengals finished No. 8 in the country—exactly where they were predicted before their rash of quarterback injuries.

In Dallas, in the roaring aftermath of the monumental upset, the whooping Tigers tore the red jersey bearing No. 23 to shreds in the locker room before Charlie Mac stood on a trunk to be heard over his shouting team, quieted them, and said what even then they must have suspected.

"The rest of your lives," Mac told them, "you won't ever forget what you did today."

LSU coach Charlie McClendon celebrates the victory with Athletic Director Jim Corbett.

THE BEST GAME POSSIBLE

February 15, 1934
New Orleans Athletic Club, New Orleans, La.

Fred Digby, proponent of a New Orleans-based college bowl game.

From the beginning, its unofficial motto has been "The Best Game Possible." For the better part of a century, the Sugar Bowl has kept its word.

It's easy now, with dozens of teams having secured national championships in the game, with dozens more high-quality teams having played in it, and with those teams having brought more than a half-billion dollars for their respective schools in the process, to think this was just a good idea whose time had come.

In the early 1930s, the timing, the financing, the circumstances—not the least of which was the dire economic condition of the world—all worked against the notion of sponsoring a once-a-year football game in New Orleans.

But, here we are, enjoying something close to the very best college football has to offer every January. For that we have primarily two men to thank: Fred Digby and Warren Miller, who came up with the same idea almost simultaneously.

★ ★ ★

Sports editor Digby was sweating out a meeting with his publisher at the *New Orleans Item*. There was a slight matter of $375 in telephone calls, no small sum in 1925, that Digby had to account for.

Tulane ran up a 9-0-1 record that season, and Digby felt the school deserved an invitation to the Rose Bowl, the only postseason game of real stature at the time. Through a series of calls to influential people around the country on how this could be accomplished, he learned the Pacific Coast representative, in this case the University of Washington, picked its own opponent.

Digby prevailed upon two friends in Seattle to present Tulane's credentials to the proper officials. Princeton got the invitation, but turned it down. Not wishing further embarrassment, Washington officials called Digby back, asking for assurances that Tulane would accept if invited. He expressed his confidence.

It was Digby who was most embarrassed. President Albert Dinwiddle's answer was no. Tulane administrators felt the train trip to California would keep its athletes out of school too long.

Red-faced and furious, Digby called unsuspecting Green Wave coach Clark Shaughnessy, who was on a trip to Chicago. Shaughnessy then called the University of Washington and recommended Alabama. The Crimson Tide, on that recommendation, became the first southern team to participate in the Rose Bowl.

Across town, in his office, a light went off for Miller, a prominent attorney. "I first got interested in the Sugar Bowl idea when Alabama went to the Rose Bowl in 1926," Miller said years later. "I thought it would be a fine thing for New Orleans to have such a game."

Digby still had to account for his telephone expenses. After a long discussion with his boss, James M. Thomson, the charges were approved. Then almost as an afterthought, Thomson asked Digby, "Why can't we have a postseason game in New Orleans?"

That suggestion became an all-consuming crusade for Digby.

★ ★ ★

It took a long time, a decade, and a lot of starts and stops, including a pair of minor football enterprises, one being a charity Doll & Toy Fund game at Loyola's stadium.

But the entire matter seemed to have reached an impasse by 1934. There were five noteworthy games on January 1 of that year: the Rose Bowl, the Dixie Classic (forerunner to the Cotton Bowl) in Dallas, the Festival of Palms (forerunner to the Orange Bowl) in Miami, the East-West Shrine Game in San Francisco, and a charity all-star game in Knoxville, Tennessee.

New Orleans had a high school game.

Within weeks, however, there was a notice of a plan by a Citizens' Committee headed by local businessman Joseph M. Cousins to create a semipro league that would play on Sundays with a championship game on January 1.

At the same time the Co-Operative Club, an organization of city executives, had decided to push for the formation of a New Year's Day bowl. Both groups were, in essence, eager to try to get the New Year's Day football concept off the ground. They would unite in the common cause.

Miller, of the Co-Operative Club, came up with a workable blueprint.

The plan was simple. At a time of massive unemployment, and when ten dollars was a substantial amount of money, a nonprofit organization would be formed, meaning not one cent would be retained above operating expenses: the associations and businesses involved would volunteer their time and labor to the workload of the project, and the $30,000 it was estimated necessary to attract top-flight teams would be derived by securing thirty guarantors to pledge $1,000 each.

That plan had to be amended because only one of the organizations, the *Item*, was able to put up that much money. A signing of three hundred guarantors at $100 apiece—no small amount in the Great Depression—with assurances of only one thing: their money back or its value in tickets—was agreed to be a more feasible plan.

A coalition of individuals and associations began putting the project on the boards.

Remarkably, the members were able to sell more than enough tickets to finance the game. Each member was given an allotment of tickets to sell to friends and associates. Even though it wasn't easy, E. Allan Smuck, who would become the last survivor of the thirty-nine founders, later said, "Everybody came through beautifully, and we were able to guarantee putting on the game. Of course, after the first game or two, as the budding classic became established, selling the tickets was easy."

On the first day of 1935, the 13th-ranked hometown Tulane Green Wave, with a 9-1 record, and third-ranked Temple, also 9-1 and the "Champion of the North," coached by the celebrated Pop Warner, played in the inaugural game. From every angle it clearly reached the stated goal of the Sugar Bowl: The Best Game Possible.

The game drew 22,026 and each team took home a check of $27,800—almost double their guarantee. Tulane won, 20-14.

In the midst of the worst economic downturn in American history, the Sugar Bowl was in business—big business.

The captains of the Kentucky Wildcats and the Oklahoma Sooners watch the coin toss before the 1951 Sugar Bowl game.

THE START OF SOMETHING BIG

January 1, 1935
Tulane Stadium, New Orleans, La.

Claude "Monk" Simons was a Tulane football hero, used to acclaim and applause. But he and teammate Dick Hardy were the unlikely heroes of the first Sugar Bowl.

They were the on-the-field firing pins of an exciting new sports enterprise—a postseason game in New Orleans that would eventually be the showcase of a multitude of national champion football teams and the annual New Year's holiday home of the Southeastern Conference champion.

In the inaugural game against Coach Pop Warner's third-ranked Temple Owls, Simons, playing one month after fracturing a shoulder in the act of a game-winning punt return against LSU, turned the tide for the 13th-ranked hometown Green Wave.

Wearing a shoulder pad made partly of rubber to protect the injury, it was Simons who made the Sugar Bowl's first memorable play, one that decades later still resonates among football connoisseurs.

Temple held the upper hand early after two fumbles, on the Tulane 10 and 18, setting up two Owls touchdowns. The much-heralded fullback Dave Smuckler had a hand in both—throwing a seven-yard pass to Danny Testa, who eased just over the goal behind a defensive back, Simons, and scoring his touchdown on a two-yard plunge.

Temple was in front 14-0, having to go a total of twenty-eight yards in six plays for its lead.

Then came the first spectacular play in Sugar Bowl history. Temple kicked off from within ten yards of the sideline to keep the return man bottled up on one side. The Wave's Johnny McDaniel took the ball on the 10 and ran up a few yards, drawing most of the Owl coverage to him. Then he lateraled to Simons, five yards behind at the 15 and running in the opposite direction. A pair of defenders were fooled just for a blink and then gave chase to the ballcarrier.

Unable to shake the pursuing Owls, Simons almost skimmed the sidelines. A block cleared the way and Monk found a convoy of Greenies. By the time he reached the Tulane 40, he was in the clear.

That play set the tone for the second half.

In the third quarter Bucky Bryan flicked a quick pass to Hardy, who leaped high between two Owls and came down with the ball in the end zone, despite one defender still clinging to his back.

In the fourth period Hardy gave Tulane the lead—and ultimately the victory—with an impromptu play. A potential interception was tipped into the air, and Hardy, the intended receiver, took the ball on the run and raced untouched the remaining fifteen yards as an Owl dove desperately and futilely at his heels.

That play provided the winning points in a 20-14 Tulane victory.

In any way football can be judged—fan interest, game excitement, financial success—the first Sugar Bowl exceeded every expectation. It heralded a future of jammed-packed stadiums, exciting games—and stunning plays.

Members of the Green Wave's 1935 Sugar Bowl squad.

New Orleans fans line up to purchase tickets to the inaugural Sugar Bowl contest, which pitted the hometown favorite Tulane Green Wave against the Temple Owls.

Tulane running back Monk Simons later served as the President of the Sugar Bowl.

Simons (47) fractured his shoulder one month prior to participating in the inaugural Sugar Bowl.

THE THIRD MAN

March 3, 1976
Louisiana Superdome, New Orleans, La.

The life and achievements of Paul "Bear" Bryant—the legendary football coach who won in the Eisenhower Age, in the Age of Aquarius, and in his own old age—was commemorated with a stamp. But the U.S. Mail was late, at least in New Orleans.

The legacy of the Bear was stamped on the Sugar Bowl long before.

The grizzled man in the houndstooth hat, who said his greatest talent was "finding the heartbeat of a football team" and who had forged college football's greatest record (323-85-17) at the time of his death in 1982, is intertwined with the history of the Sugar Bowl like no other figure since its founders.

As Mickey Holmes, the late former executive director of the game, so eloquently put it: "Coach Bryant was an extraordinary presence, and the Sugar Bowl was his stage. He had an impact far beyond that of an ordinary football coach."

Of course, Bryant wasn't an ordinary coach. In a thirty-eight-year career that spanned five decades at Alabama, Texas A&M, Kentucky, and Maryland, Bryant coached in an astounding twenty-nine bowl games. The Sugar was obviously his favorite. He coached two schools in nine Sugar Bowls, far more than any other postseason game, and won eight. Of the six national championships his teams claimed, four were showcased in the Sugar Bowl.

Sugar Bowl legend Paul "Bear" Bryant.

Two of the most memorable college football games ever played—the Notre Dame-Alabama pairing of 1973 and the Penn State-Bama game of 1979, both for the No. 1 rankings of those respective seasons—were in the Sugar Bowl.

Still, as much as anything he did on the Sugar Bowl sidelines, Bryant's influence behind the scenes was as important in the 1970s as was Fred Digby's and Warren Miller's in the 1930s in shaping the direction of the Sugar Bowl.

Conditions had changed. Every other major bowl had the insurance of tie-ins with conferences, while the Sugar remained completely "open" to all comers, which, the thinking went, was still the best opportunity to put together the best game possible. But critics pointed out that although the SEC considered the Sugar "its bowl," New Orleans had lost the SEC champion to Miami three of the four years before 1976. One Orange Bowl official confided, "We hope the Sugar Bowl keeps plodding along. We hope they never change."

When the Big Ten and the Pacific Eight conferences broke their Rose Bowl-only policies in the mid-1970s, things began to change. Champions from those leagues would continue to play in Pasadena, but the runners-up were free to play elsewhere. The SEC, which had sent as many as seven of its ten teams to bowls, now would have stiff competition for minor bowl berths.

Maybe a "marriage" between the Sugar and SEC, which had been a mutual infatuation for decades, really was the best course in this new world of college football.

Committing the SEC champion to any bowl was not in Bryant's best interest. In the mid-1970s, when the Sugar Bowl decided to try to interest the SEC in such an arrangement, Bryant's Crimson Tide was at its zenith. Year-in and year-out, he could—and would—pick where he wanted to go.

The Orange Bowl had resumed its affiliation with the Big Eight, and with the Orange likely landing national championship contenders Nebraska or Oklahoma almost every year, the Sugar Bowl realized how enticing it had become for Bryant to plan trips to Miami instead of New Orleans.

The Sugar began courting the SEC, with Bryant's close friend Aruns Callery discussing it with him. Privately some of the other coaches supported the idea, though none could commit to the tie-in until hearing from the Bear. Bryant represented only one vote but commanded such respect that no one would seriously try to tell him where his team was to play during the holidays. It was frequently only when Bryant decided where and who he wanted to play that a given year's bowl pairings fell into place.

Bryant told Callery he would not consider a tie-in, that he could go where he wanted and that he felt that arrangement was in the best interests of the University of Alabama. That put a practical end to the matter.

Months later, late in the night, Callery answered his phone and heard a growling voice slowly say, "I have to think about the rest of the conference, too," and immediately knew the Sugar Bowl was about to change.

It was an enormously unselfish gesture by Bryant, who, as with the Sugar Bowl, liked the idea of "open" bowls to let them all compete for the best pairing.

"What I'm for is all bowls to open up for everybody, nobody have a tie-up," said Bryant, who was also opposed to voting for national champions after the postseason. "If we are going to stay with the polls," he said, "take it out of the bowls. It puts too much pressure when the bowls are used for it. It takes all the fun out of bowls."

Shortly thereafter, the SEC-Sugar Bowl relationship Holmes termed "a long-time love affair" was consummated.

"The Sugar Bowl was a great bowl before Bear Bryant ever set foot in New Orleans, and it's been a great bowl since he left us," Holmes said. "But there's no question he helped shape the Sugar Bowl."

MAKING A PASS
December 31, 1973
Tulane Stadium, New Orleans, La.

It was football artistry. Unforgettable, even in a venue where more national champions have played than anywhere else. Here were two, or at least two claimants.

Played before the largest crowd (85,161) ever squeezed into venerable old Tulane Stadium for a Sugar Bowl, the fortieth renewal of the game was sheer and unforgettable drama between traditional giants Alabama, ranked No. 1 in the Associated Press poll and coached by Paul "Bear" Bryant, and Notre Dame, ranked third and coached by Ara Parseghian.

"It was one for the ages," Parseghian recalled decades after his Irish's 24-23 victory.

From the opening whistle to the game-ending horn, fans were on their feet. The lead see-sawed between the underdog Irish and the favorite Bama throughout. Notre Dame was ahead four times—taking the first lead and the last—Bama was ahead three times, and the Irish didn't nail down their victory until converting on a third and 9 from their own 2 with 2:12 remaining. Throwing from his end zone, quarterback Tom Clements hit Robin Weber—a tight end who not only hadn't practiced for two days because of a knee injury but who had not caught a pass all season.

The completion gave the Irish a first down—and the AP national championship.

Actually two "national champions" came out of the Sugar Bowl. Several years before, the AP had started voting for its final ballot after the bowls instead of after the regular season, as had been the custom, in part because of outcomes that involved Bama. (The No. 1-ranked Tide lost to Texas in the 1965 Orange Bowl, yet still kept its title because voting closed after the regular season; a year later, Alabama by beating Nebraska in the Orange jumped three teams that lost their bowl games, despite all having better overall records than the 9-1-1 Crimson Tide. On the other hand, in 1966 Bama was consigned to No. 3 despite an 11-0-0 record while No. 1 Notre Dame and No. 2 Michigan State didn't even play in the postseason.)

But United Press International, the coaches poll, continued to name its champion after the regular season, and at that point, in 1973, Alabama was No. 1. The Tide stayed there after the Sugar Bowl. In the AP, voted on by sportswriters, Notre Dame, as expected, leap-frogged Alabama.

The embarrassment caused UPI to amend its practice the next season, though Alabama continues to proclaim its No. 1 standing in that poll, ignoring the defeat.

It was an especially difficult outcome for Bryant, who coached more teams (nine) in the Sugar Bowl than any other coach and who coached more victories (eight) in the Sugar Bowl than any other.

This game, perhaps the standard by which all bowl games are judged, was his only Sugar Bowl loss.

MAKING A STAND
January 1, 1979
Louisiana Superdome, New Orleans, La.

If there is a single image that paints the Sugar Bowl picture, it's this one: Alabama linebacker Barry Krauss, seemingly shot out of a missile silo, zeroing in on Penn State's Mike Guman at the goal line.

In one of the most fabled goal-line stands in college football history, during a game between the No. 1 and No. 2-ranked teams in the land, the Crimson Tide won—and Penn State lost—the 1978 national championship. It was the final of three touchdown-saving plays that preserved Bama's 14-7 lead in the fading minutes—and this was not one of Crimson Tide coach Bear Bryant's better defensive units.

Even Krauss was surprised at his team's achievement:

"They were down there at the 1-yard line, and I had to admit I was thinking they'd probably score, go for two and try to beat us."

It was a fitting climax to a game that was a defensive classic even before the fireworks two feet shy of the Superdome end zone.

It came down to a fourth quarter for all the marbles, and the Nittany Lions' one chance to claim their first national title came when defensive end Joe Lally recovered an Alabama fumble on the Tide 19 with 7:57 to play.

On the next play, fullback Matt Suhey ran eleven yards to the Bama 8 for a first down. Then Guman took a pitch and gained two yards to the 6.

On second down, quarterback Chuck Fusina dropped back and quickly delivered a pass to Scott Fitzkee, who was flaring out near the right sideline. Fitzkee caught the pass at the 1, but before he could turn to find the end zone cornerback Don McNeal slammed him out of bounds two feet short of a touchdown. Save No. 1.

On third down, Suhey took the handoff up the middle but was wrapped up by linebacker Rich Wingo for no gain. Save No. 2.

"Fusina came out to look at the ball," Bama tackle Marty Lyons recalled, "and I was standing in the way, in between him and the ball. He started smiling. 'How much is it?' he asked. I told him, 'Bout this much.' 'Ten inches?' 'Yeah,' I said. 'You better pass.'"

On fourth down, the Nittany Lions tried to muscle it in again, but Guman was shot down by Krauss.

"They had called timeout before the fourth down, and they were trying to figure out what they were going to do and what we were going to do," Krauss said. "We thought they'd go outside or throw because they had run it on third down (to no avail), so I had given myself a little more depth so I could flow to the outside. When he gave it back to Guman, and he came back inside, there was a hole. He saw it, and I did, too."

The collision was one that, as Krauss remembers it, made time stand still.

"It seemed like he was so close," Krauss said. "He was falling, and what was actually a couple of seconds seemed like five minutes."

But Guman did come down short, and so did Penn State, which never got close again.

BIG HEARTS

December 13, 1976
State Fair Stadium, Shreveport, La.

This was not *Rocky* or *Hoosiers*, celluloid sagas in which inspired underdogs played huge favorites off their feet.

This was titled the First Independence Bowl, a game in which very few thought the depleted McNeese State Cowboys could prevail. But there they were, hanging in.

Against Tulsa, with two minutes to play, the Cowboys already had proved to a legion of naysayers they belonged on the field with the Missouri Valley Conference co-champions. After weathering a series of haymakers, they were down 16-14 with eighty yards and two minutes to go.

With no timeouts, this was going to take some doing.

The inaugural Independence Bowl was a coupling of an extremely frustrated Southland Conference and the Shreveport-Bossier City Sports Foundation, which labored hard for a postseason football game in northwest Louisiana.

Southland member Arkansas State went 11-0-0 in 1975—one of the most memorable teams ever assembled in that league—and did not receive a single nibble to play in a bowl. The seething SLC was itching to show its wares, and the fledgling Independence Bowl was ideal.

The bowl was sanctioned by the NCAA for 1976, the two hundredth birthday of the nation. That coincidence combined with a strong military presence in the area gave the event its name.

Thus, the first tie-in with the bowl was the SLC, in just its first season as a Division I league but with the capability of taking down bigger-name opponents—and a burning desire to prove it.

McNeese State, picked in the preseason as a middle of-the-pack team, was the surprise champion with a 9-2-0 record. Rutgers was the opponent McNeese was hoping to draw, for two reasons: Because the Scarlet Knights' seventeen-game victory streak was the nation's longest, and because an Eastern team would bring instant recognition to the bowl and—what McNeese was hoping for—to the team that beat the Knights.

That was not to be. Figuring it had more to lose than to win, Rutgers turned down the invitation. Not a bad second choice was Tulsa with a 7-3-1 record and victories over Arkansas of the Southwest Conference and Memphis State, conqueror of three SEC opponents.

McNeese was coached by Jack Doland, a remarkable man who played on the 1949 Tulane football team, the Green Wave's last SEC championship squad; coached a high school state championship team at Sulphur; served as an assistant on some of Charlie McClendon's finest LSU teams while working on his Ph.D; later held the office of president of McNeese; and then became a state senator.

The Cowboys would need all of Doland's purposefulness because soon after becoming the first SLC representative in the Independence Bowl, McNeese learned ten of its eleven seniors would be ineligible for postseason football (a walk-on guard being the only fourth-year player at Doland's disposal). Rule IV-II, Article II of the NCAA handbook at the time banned seniors from playing in championship events if they had been redshirted as freshmen.

Three days later things got even worse, and ugly. Six more athletes were suspended because of the presence of a female in the players' dorm.

Of the sixteen players scratched from the Independence Bowl, six were starters.

Things were looking dire for an event trying mightily for some glitter. The Independence Bowl wasn't happy, and the Southland Conference privately asked McNeese to step aside and let another school, one more capable of competitive football in a showcase setting, represent the league. Doland had an impolite suggestion of what they could do with that idea.

As it was, though, things got sticky for the bowl, which discounted some tickets to $1.50, and ended up selling just 15,542 in its 50,000-seat stadium.

Jokes abounded outside the McNeese camp about how the Cowboys would send its "junior varsity" out to meet the Golden Hurricanes. All-conference fullback Bobby Wilson was one of the players who would miss the Independence Bowl. A freshman, Oliver Hadnot, would have to fill in for him. Conley Hathorn, the Cowboy's placekicker, was out, too. Sophomore Jan Peebles would now have to kick—instead of his usual duty of holding on kicks. Both slotbacks were gone, so Doland scaled down his offense to one more basic, with more runners and fewer receivers.

For public consumption, Doland, as any good coach would, played the sacrificial lamb. "When we walk out on that field and line up against Tulsa," he said at the day-before-the-game press conference, "we're going to look like a traveling show of midgets."

Privately, Doland was pricking his team's pride, letting his players know how little respect they were getting, but confiding to his inner-circle that he had enough front-line talent for his Cowboys to make a good account of themselves. The only thing that seriously worried him was the possibility of injury, because

Quarterback Terry McFarland signals a touchdown for the Cowboys.

he no longer had enough depth for more losses not to make a difference.

It didn't take long for Doland's worst fear to manifest itself.

In a back-and-forth game, which featured two of three field goals by Peebles (of forty-two and thirty-four yards) and an early two-point conversion by the Cowboys to give them a seven-point lead at 14-7, Doland's injury concern seemed to be coming true.

McNeese's starting quarterback Jimmy Morvant went down in the first quarter with a strained knee. Backup Terry McFarland came in and played well—until he had to leave in the fourth quarter with leg cramps.

Freshman Chris Millet, who ran the scout team all season, was the only quarterback left. Before Doland sent him out, he told Millet to call "36-G." The pre-med major turned to his coach and said, "I don't know that play." Doland inquired as to what plays he might know. The youngster said he could run a dive.

Millet went in for one play before McFarland was hustled back on the field.

After Tulsa took its 16-14 lead on a field goal with 4:22 remaining, McNeese fumbled the ensuing kickoff. This could have ended its chances. But the Hurricanes were held to a field-goal attempt that missed, and the Cowboys found themselves in their do-or-die situation, two points down at their 20 with two minutes to go.

Tight end Alan Heisser caught a halfback pass from Mike McArthur to put the ball at the McNeese 48. Two running plays for four yards and an incomplete pass brought the outcome down to one play with a minute remaining. McFarland went to the air—and the pass was intercepted. But a flag fluttered down because of roughing the passer.

The fifteen-yard penalty gave the Cowboys a first down at the Tulsa 37.

Playing for a chance to kick a game-winning field goal, the job of Hadnot, the freshman fill-in who ran more like a tailback than a fullback, was to simply protect the ball and look for an advantageous spot to go down for Peebles' attempt. But Hadnot hit a crease, rocketed into the secondary, veered to the left and sprinted twenty-five yards for the go-ahead points with thirty-seven seconds to play.

"The play called was '32-veer drive,'" Hadnot said of his stunning run. ". . . I saw an opening and went for it."

"We played this one from the heart," Cowboys linebacker Bob Howell said after the epic 20-16 victory. "We just wanted it more than they did."

McNeese players celebrate victory by carrying coach Jack Doland off the field.

THE MOVING VAN

December 19, 1948
Shibe Park, Philadelphia, Pennsylvania

Steve Van Buren shot through the line, building up a head of steam until he ran straight into a defender with a sound similar to a clash of cymbals. Philadelphia Eagles teammate Allie Sherman said he never forgot the sight of the sprawled-out would-be tackler. "The only time I ever saw someone's eyes rolling around in his head," Sherman later recalled.

Van Buren was the prototype NFL power-runner—but with the added ingredients of speed and maneuverability. His Hall of Fame coach in the 1940s, Earle "Greasy" Neale, who spent thirty-four years in the NFL and played with Jim Thorpe's Canton Bulldogs early in the twentieth century, said Van Buren was a better runner than either Thorpe or Red Grange.

In his assessment, Neale said, "Grange had some ability to sidestep, but he didn't have Van Buren's power to go with it."

Philadelphia sportswriter/historian Ray Didinger wrote, "Van Buren was a player ahead of his time. He was six-foot-one, 210 pounds, yet could beat teammate Clyde Scott, a world-class hurdler, in the forty-yard dash. Van Buren's combination of power and explosive speed was more than the defenses of the '40s could handle."

As *Sport* magazine once said in a comparison with the Cleveland Brown who is generally considered the best runner in NFL history, Van Buren was "Jim Brown before Jim Brown."

To put Van Buren in context, note that in an eight-year career he led the NFL in rushing four times and also led the NFL in rushing touchdowns each of those seasons. Once, in 1945, Van Buren pulled off a rare "Triple Crown," leading the NFL in three categories: rushing (832 yards), scoring (110 points), and kickoff returns (28.7 yards per return). He also set the Eagles' single-season record (15.3 yards per return) for punt returns, but didn't lead the league. He was the first back to achieve three straight rushing titles (1947, 48, 49), and was the first back to gain at least a thousand yards twice (1947-49).

All of that achieved when seven-man defensive lines were the norm.

And he retired in 1951 as the NFL's all-time leading rusher. His 5,860 yards seems miniscule now, but remember Van Buren achieved his totals in an era when only ten to twelve games were played, counting the playoffs. Green Bay's Clarke Hinkle had been the all-time leader, but Van Buren eclipsed his record, achieved in ten years, by two thousand yards.

In the era when athletes played both offense and defense, Van Buren also had nine career interceptions.

The man had quite a résumé, one that eventually placed him in the Pro Football Hall of Fame. Which brings up the question: How could Van Buren have been overlooked for so long?

* * *

Van Buren was born in La Ceiba, Honduras, the son of a fruit inspector. But he was orphaned as a child and sent to live with his grandparents in New Orleans. As he grew up, Steve became intrigued with football. But when he entered Warren Easton High, he found he was too small. As a 126-pound sophomore, he dropped out of school and went to work in an iron foundry.

After two years of demanding labor, the boy had sprouted a few inches and his physique hardened. Steve returned to Easton and Coach Johnny Brechtel's powerhouse team, where he played well at end. He wasn't, however, Easton's best or most recruited end. Lou Thomas, who would sign with Tulane, was considered the prize Eagle at that position.

If it weren't for Oliver "Ike" Carriere, a former LSU athlete and later a prominent New Orleans judge, Van Buren's life might have been much different.

After taking in a game between Easton and Holy Cross, Carriere offered Van Buren a ride home. During their conversation, Steve mentioned he was the fastest man on his team. It also came up that his grades across the board were in the 90s. Carriere gave Brechtel a call a few days later, and the coach confirmed the statements. Immediately Carriere called LSU coach Bernie Moore, who eventually signed Van Buren.

For the next three years, though, Steve was not used as a runner. He was a blocking back in Moore's single-wing offense, opening holes for tailbacks Leo Bird and, in 1942, Alvin Dark. Not until 1943, when Dark, a military trainee in the Navy's V-12 program, was transferred did Van Buren get a shot as the Tigers' main ballcarrier. Legendary LSU trainer Marty Broussard, who served his school for six decades, recalled that when Steve learned he

LSU running back Steve Van Buren led the nation in scoring in 1942.

was to play tailback as a senior, "He worked as long and hard as any athlete I've ever known."

In a season in which only four SEC schools fielded teams due to the constraints of World War II, the opening game at Georgia provided a glimpse at what was to come. The Tigers upset the Bulldogs 34-27 with Van Buren scoring four touchdowns—the last with thirty-five seconds remaining. In the third game, though, the Texas A&M Aggies kept him contained, beating the Tigers 28-13.

At the end of the season, with LSU holding a 5-3-0 record, the Tigers were unexpectedly invited to play in the Miami's Orange Bowl—against Texas A&M. It would be the first postseason rematch in college history, and at least in part, it was Van Buren who made LSU an attraction. Though hobbled toward the end, he finished second in the country with 847 yards rushing and led the nation in scoring with ninety-eight points.

When a Miami writer asked Mickey McCann, who covered LSU for the *Baton Rouge State-Times*, about the state of the ballclub, McCann wryly replied, "Van Buren looks fine."

He looked even better on New Year's Day. Van Buren ran for 160 of LSU's 181 yards on the ground, scoring two touchdowns and passing for another as the Tigers reversed their earlier defeat, 19-14.

"He was probably the greatest running back in Southeastern Conference history," Moore would moan later, "and I used him as a blocking back until his last year. The folks in Baton Rouge never let me forget that."

Moore was not one to try to cover up a mistake. That was long before extensive NFL scouting to evaluate talent, so Moore contacted Greasy Neale, passed along Van Buren's attributes, and told the Philadelphia coach in his opinion it would be a mistake for the Eagles to pass on a back who could be just what the club needed. Not to be ignored was the fact that Van Buren was not eligible for the military because of a chronic eye problem.

With the fifth pick of the first round of the 1944 NFL draft, Van Buren was selected by the Eagles. With a $4,000 contract in hand, he set off to become one of the shining lights of the NFL.

★ ★ ★

Greasy Neale found Moore might have undersold his halfback. As a rookie Van Buren averaged 5.6 yards per carry, gaining 444 yards in nine games, and led the NFL in punt returns as the Eagles went 7-1-2, finishing second in the Eastern Conference. In 1945 he not only earned the first of his rushing titles, but he actually improved his per-carry average to 5.8.

Some might dismiss Van Buren's feats because of the continuing manpower shortage as the war wound down, but his story was just beginning to be written.

The Eagles won the NFL championship for the first time in 1948, against the Chicago Cardinals, who had beaten Philadelphia for the title the year before. The day of the '48 game a fierce blizzard blew in, snowing in much of the East Coast and blanketing Philly.

Van Buren was relaxing at home in the suburbs, expecting the game to be postponed. But the show had to go on. The NFL had sold its newsreel and broadcast rights for $33,000—this was the first NFL title game to be televised—and there was no avoiding playing even under the most adverse conditions.

Neale had to call his missing halfback to tell him to get to the stadium as soon as possible, and as best he could. Steve's car wouldn't turn over, so he had to trudge through the snow, catch three streetcars, then walk twelve blocks to Shibe Park.

The Eagles were letting in anyone for the game if they would help shovel snow off the field, and both teams had to help get the tarp rolled up. The snow kept falling, and since the borders of the field remained invisible, rope was used to mark the sidelines. The officials used the chains to mark off the goal lines as well as to measure first downs in the absence of the obliterated field stripes.

After a third-quarter fumble recovery on the Cardinals' 17, Van Buren slogged five yards through the snow and over the goal line, the only score in a 7-0 Eagles victory.

Van Buren ran for ninety-eight yards—two more than the Cardinals as a team—and was carried off the field by joyful Eagles. Then he had to dress and take the same long route on public transit back home.

The next season, with Van Buren at the peak of his career, he gained 1,146 yards in twelve games, and again the Eagles were in the title game, this time against the Los Angeles Rams. Again bad weather plagued the proceedings. Heavy rain saturated L.A., cutting the crowd to just 27,980. By game-time the field was heavy with mud.

Nothing stopped "The Moving Van." He gained a record 196 yards on thirty-one carries and Philadelphia was again the NFL champion.

Moore never got over his misdiagnosis of a major talent. Van Buren later said his college coach actually apologized to him for not recognizing his complete abilities.

"He told me he had done me a terrible injustice," Van Buren said. "I told him not to think twice about it. Everything turned out all right."

Steve Van Buren retired as the NFL's all-time leading rusher.

KING OF THE FOOTBALL WORLD

Fall 1998
Louisiana Superdome, New Orleans, La.

An elderly gentleman was effusive in his gratitude.

Clasping the hand of Shaun King as he trotted off the Tulane practice field, the man with snow-white hair and dressed in a three-piece suit, said softly but firmly, "Thank you for a gorgeous season."

The appreciation, heartfelt and universal in the coterie of Green Wave football devotees, was two-pronged: for the undefeated, untied, unexpected, and magical 1998 season, and for King, a sorcerer-at-quarterback whose sleight-of-hand skill was the most indispensable factor in the forging of the Wave's 12-0 record.

America had survived the Great Depression, four wars, and the Spice Girls since Tulane had a comparable season, 11-1 in 1931. Arguably, no single player in the Green Wave's eighty-seven-year football history at that point had meant as much to his team as King, who guided Tulane to a two-year 19-4 record—the Wave's best two-season record in almost seven decades.

Nobody would, or could, argue that Tulane was a genuine football giant that season. The Green Wave played the 96th-ranked schedule in the country, beating only two teams with winning records. But you can only play who's on the schedule, and without King, the son of a Florida preacher, the '98 season might have looked very different.

"Absolutely true," said Rich Rodriguez, then Tulane's offensive coordinator and one of the coaching pioneers of the "spread" offense. "In our system, we could only be as good as our quarterback. No quarterback anywhere could have done what Shaun did. Not (Kentucky's) Tim Couch, not (Central Florida's) Daunte Culpepper. And, remember, Shaun did it in essence with one arm tied behind his back, with a broken wrist."

Houston coach Kim Helton put those sentiments in perspective after King riddled his secondary for 316 yards and five touchdowns in a 48-20 victory, saying Tulane couldn't win five games without King. The Wave was 10-0 at the time.

In a season in which he fractured his left (non-throwing) wrist in Tulane's fourth game King:

- set an NCAA single-season record for passing efficiency (183.3), based on 223 completions in 328 attempts (68 percent), for 36 touchdowns and 6 interceptions.
- became the first player in NCAA Division I-A history to pass for 3,000 yards (3,232) and rush for 500 yards (532 and 10 more touchdowns) in an eleven-game schedule.

"Take away any of those feats," Rodriguez said, "and it would have been awfully hard for us to win every game. To us, Shaun was absolutely indispensable."

How indispensable? So much so that Tommy Bowden, head coach of that team, could not pinpoint a high point for King.

"The thing is," Bowden said after the season, "you can't be No. 1 in passing efficiency—and Shaun set an all-time record—unless you've had several back-to-back-to-back performances. In the last two years, Shaun's had (six) games in which he's thrown for three touchdowns; (eight) games in which he's thrown for four touchdowns; one in which he's thrown for five touchdowns.

"Man, he's had so many above average games it's hard to pick out one, or even just a few of his finest moments."

☆ ☆ ☆

Former coach Buddy Teevens might have been building a foundation for football respectability when he was fired after a second straight 2-9 season in 1996. That year the Green Wave lost five games by seven points or less, including two on the last play of the game.

Bowden, who succeeded Teevens, rode the talent on hand to two eye-catching seasons. Eighteen of the twenty-two starters were Teevens recruits, but at least one would not have been at Tulane had a coaching change not been made.

"Man, we were bad," King said. "I was ready to go somewhere else. I came to Tulane because I wanted to go to a college that hadn't won, to help turn things around. I didn't want to go to a program where I would sit on the bench for three years, collect three rings and not play a down."

But things weren't working out as he envisioned. He was playing, but not all that well and for a bad team.

King's first extensive playing time came on the fourth play of the fourth game of his freshman season. The starter broke a collarbone against Southern Mississippi, and King was thrown in.

"I threw my first touchdown in that game—for the other team," he recalled ruefully of a seventy-five-yard interception return, one of the Tulane lowlights in a 45-0 defeat.

King wasn't making a difference in Tulane's fortunes. By the end of his sophomore season, the Green Wave had a 4-18 record and King had passed for nine touchdowns—and fourteen interceptions.

Frustrated, he was ready to find another football team, one he hoped would make better use of his talents.

"Coach Teevens' offense was not geared for the quarterback to put up big numbers or make big plays," King recalled. "It was more of a ball-control offense. All those factors combined to make me believe I'd be better off somewhere else."

Then Teevens was fired, Bowden, son of legendary Florida State coach Bobby Bowden, was hired and King immediately ended his search for where he wanted to transfer.

"As soon as I heard the name 'Bowden,' I knew we'd be throwing the ball," King recalled. "That's all I wanted to hear. I started warming up."

The rest, as they say, is history.

★ ★ ★

King's metamorphosis in two seasons under Bowden and Rodriguez—who installed a spread suited for an accurate passer and mobile runner for when Tulane's smallish line broke down—was astounding. The lion's share of his record-setting statistics, 5,849 passing yards and sixty touchdowns passing, came in his final twenty-two games.

"I was blessed," King said. "The Lord put me in the right place at the right time. The rest was up to me."

Indeed it was. Few would say the '98 Wave represented the best Tulane team ever, or even that King was the best Tulane player ever. But the Green Wave might never have had a more valuable player, and King's 10th place finish in the Heisman Trophy balloting represented the first time a Tulane athlete was voted among the college football elite.

On the verge of Tulane's twelfth victory, against Brigham Young University in the Liberty Bowl, guard Mike Gumiela reflected, "Who could have ever imagined this finish? I was here four years ago with Shaun when we were 2-9. A lot of things had to fall perfectly in place for us to be in this position now, and the major one was the development of Shaun. He was the perfect driver."

For the perfect season.

PREP-POURRI

Here's a run that any coach would give his whistle for: In the 1960s, Shreveport's Woodlawn High was quarterbacked in succession by Billy Laird, Trey Prather, Terry Bradshaw, and Joe Ferguson. Think they got good coaching under Lee Hedges and A. L. Williams? Laird was drafted by the Patriots in 1966, Bradshaw by the Steelers in 1970, and Ferguson by the Bills in 1973. The one who didn't get to the NFL was Prather, who kept Bradshaw on the bench until his senior season and who was considered by many as the best of the lot. Prather spent a year at LSU before joining the Marines and left his football promise—and his life—in Vietnam. Ferguson quarterbacked the Knights to a 34-4-0 record in his three seasons, and he passed for 3,239 yards and 89 touchdowns, both national prep records.

Just down the road from Woodlawn at Ruston at the same time Ferguson was lighting up north Louisiana was another quarterback of future note, Bert Jones.

Under James E. "Big Fuzzy" Brown, Baton Rouge's Istrouma High flowered into a dynasty, winning eight state championships in a thirteen-year period (1950-62). His best was the unbeaten 1955 Indians spearheaded by halfback Billy Cannon, who scored 39 touchdowns and a total of 228 points. Cannon was a dual-sport superstar, excelling in track as well as football. The future LSU Heisman Trophy recipient was not only a champion sprinter, but also threw the sixteen-pound shot fifty-four feet. Brown also coached Roy Winston, who started four Super Bowls at linebacker for the Minnesota Vikings.

Holy Cross and Jesuit, who first played in 1922, have the oldest continuous rivalry in Louisiana. The schools kept it going even in the immediate aftermath of Hurricane Katrina, when the city of New Orleans was essentially shut down. Blue Jays coach Vic Eumont returned from his California refuge, and he and his old prep teammate, Holy Cross coach Barry Wilson, got enough kids together from the schools and, against all odds, put on the game. Playing at Muss Bertolino Playground in suburban Kenner, the only space available, Holy Cross won 20-6.

The 1922 Holy Cross football team.

Louisiana's longest overtime period was ninety-six hours—four days. In 1972 Neville and Brother Martin played in the state semifinals. At the end of the game, neither team had scored, and in the traditional tiebreakers the teams were also deadlocked with nine first downs and one penetration apiece. Neither Tigers' coach Charlie Brown nor Bobby Conlin of the Crusaders wanted to determine who advanced by a coin flip or go to overtime (this was before extra time became a fixture of the game), and LHSAA commissioner Frank Spruiell didn't want to move the playoffs back a week. So they played again on Tuesday, four days after the first meeting. Neville won the rematch 8-0 at a neutral site in Alexandria. Three days later—Neville's third game in eight days—the Tigers recorded their third shutout in the three games to beat Airline 6-0 for the state championship.

At Ferriday High School, fullback Donnie Daye played for towering coaching figure Johnny "Red" Robertson. During his four years under Robertson, Ferriday didn't lose a game, going 54-0 and winning four state titles. When he went to LSU, Daye played on the unbeaten (3-0-0) 1956 freshman team, then was redshirted. He came back to active duty just in time for the 11-0-0 national championship team in 1958. Daye never suited up on a losing side until the eighth game of his junior year in college in 1959. Daye's eight-year prep and college football-playing career ended with him being on four state title teams, one college national championship squad, a No. 3-ranked team, and a personal overall record of 82-6-1.

The 1936 Warren Easton Eagles, coached by Johnny Brechtel and anchored by end Billy Brinkman, shut out ten opposing teams—every regular-season opponent and one in the state playoffs. The only points Easton surrendered that entire season came in the Class A state championship game at Tulane Stadium, and it cost them. The Eagles lost to Haynesville 7-0.

The 1931 Newman Greenies—the first year the school went under the name "Newman" after originally being called Isidore Newman Manuel Training at its founding in 1904—had a banner year. The Greenies went undefeated in seven games and didn't give up a point. The year before, as Manuel training, the Class B League Greenies were 5-0-0. Newman's win streak would extend to fourteen straight victories over three seasons, but because the Greenies were not then a member of the Louisiana High School Athletic Association they couldn't compete in the state playoffs.

That the Crescent City dominated Louisiana football in the 1940s is an understatement. The New Orleans Prep League won seven state championships in the state's highest classification in that decade, an accomplishment no district has equaled before or since.

Lou Deutschmann of Holy Cross had the kind of game some dream about—and some have nightmares about—in the second game of 1952. In a 26-13 victory against Baton Rouge High,

Donnie Daye, who played on four undefeated state championship teams at Ferriday High School, as well as the undefeated 1958 LSU national championship squad.

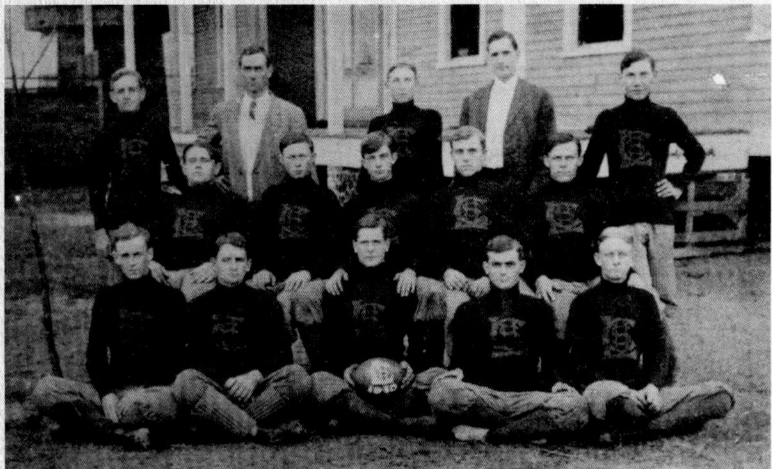

The Lake Charles High School state championship team of 1910.

Deutschmann rushed for 341 yards on sixteen carries—and had a seventy-yard touchdown run wiped out by a penalty.

John David Crow of Springhill was a man among boys in 1953 when he scored 177 points and rushed for 1,346 yards on just 83 carries—a 16.2 average. If that wasn't enough, his average had been 22.0 per carry before playing Byrd at the end of the season. Crow was held to forty-four yards rushing, and his team was down 20-6 in the fourth quarter, but the future Texas A&M Heisman Trophy recipient dropped back into a double-wing formation in the fourth quarter. He passed for 116 yards in the last period, and Springhill got out with a 20-20 standoff.

Louisiana was once home to a touchdown machine, one so prolific for his time, the late 1920s, that he was featured in *Ripley's Believe It or Not* nationally syndicated cartoon. Eddie "Touchdown" Townson of Class B Glenmora High School in Rapides Parish once scored eight touchdowns in a single 1929 game; had a total of forty-one in that single season; and a then-national record of ninety-nine for his four-year career. Counting placekicks, he scored six hundred points, heady feats for the Flapper era—especially for a five-foot-seven, 140-pound scatback. It took sixty-six years, but his state career record was finally equaled by the state's first "Mr. Football," Cecil Collins of Leesville in 1995, and then broken a year later by Anthony "A-Train" Thomas of Winnfield, who scored 106 touchdowns and 682 total career points. Thomas would go on to become the leading rusher in University of Michigan history.

Predominantly black Richwood High of Monroe broke into LHSAA football in 1970 with an eye-raising national record 513 points in eight games (64.1 ppg). That run included a 108-0 victory against Winnboro in week two, a 77-0 win against Rayville and a 7-0 defeat to Jonesboro-Hodge. Richwood reached the Class AAA title game, losing 23-12 to a Hammond team spearhead-

Eddie "Touchdown" Townson carries the ball for Centenary College. Townson once scored eight touchdowns in a single game for Glenmora High School.

ed by tailback Brad Davis. Four years later, in 1974, Richwood, coached by Eugene Hughes, won the state championship with a 12-0-1 record.

W. O. Boston High of Lake Charles, with wide receiver Robert Lavergne, broke through in 1972, taking Class AA with a 13-1-0 record after denying Haynesville a third consecutive title with an 11-6 victory. In Class A, Second Ward High, coached by Rudolph Dinvaut and quarterbacked by Terry Robiskie, won championships in 1971 and '72 with a combined 27-0-0 record.

Lake Charles is about 200 miles from New Orleans, but it is a marker in the book of Crescent City football. In 1948, Alcée Fortier under Coach Buck Seeber, defeated the Wildcats 20-0 for the state title. That was the last time an Orleans Parish public school won a state title in the twentieth century.

A decade later Lake Charles inflicted one of the cruelest defeats ever in a state championship game against Warren Easton. The Eagles held a 20-10 lead with 1:30 to go at Tulane Stadium. The Wildcats scored to cut the margin to 20-16, but only 1:22 remained to play. On the ensuing kickoff, the ball fell between two Easton backs who hesitated about who should handle it, and a Lake Charles player fell on it at the 23. The Eagles held for three plays, but on fourth down, on a halfback pass, the intended receiver and an Easton defender each leaped for the ball and it was batted away—right into the hands of a Wildcat at the 5, who made the catch and stepped into the end zone. Easton had enough time left for the kickoff and just one play. Lake Charles won 22-20. That ill-fated 1958 Easton team represented the last Orleans Parish public school to reach the state championship game in the twentieth century.

Pat Screen, the tailback in Jesuit's single-wing offense, put on a dazzling performance in yet another New Orleans-Lake Charles title game. If ever one man was the difference in a football game, this might have been it. Down 13-0 midway through the 1960 state championship game at LaGrange, Screen, who ran, threw, kicked, and caught passes that night, rallied his team to an eventual 21-20 victory. Screen had a hand in every one of the Blue Jays' points, scoring three touchdowns, running for two extra points, and passing for a third.

In 1945, just after the Japanese surrender in World War II, the Louisiana High School Athletic Association enacted a rule to restore eligibility for players whose prep careers had been cut short by military service. Jimmy Dent, all of nineteen years old, returned to Warren Easton for his high school diploma—and a last season of football—after twenty-three months of action in the Pacific. It would be hard to believe he ever saw a third and 10 as a do-or-die crisis in quite the same way his teammates might have.

The 1931 Isidore Newman team that outscored its opponents 128-0. It should be noted, however, that the Greenies only played seven games that season, three of which were against junior varsity competition.

IT'S HIS CALLING

August 15, 1969
River Ridge, La.

The inquisitive kid was persistent in wanting to know about defensive philosophies.

Looking the fresh-faced youngster up and down, the grizzled veteran of the football wars took a long pause, then asked, "Say, do you want to be a coach or something, son?"

In a nanosecond an emphatic, "YES, sir," came tumbling forth from the then-sixteen-year-old boy.

And, John Thomas Curtis did become a coach. Boy, did he ever.

Through the nearly century and a half the game has been played, with all the tens of thousands of men to have coached the sport at any level—professional, college, or prep—only one has coached more victories.

When J. T. (John Thomas, known by his initials since childhood to avoid confusion with his dad), coached his five hundredth victory in 2011, only John McKissick of Summerville High in South Carolina had coached more. And Curtis was twenty-two years younger than McKissick, who was then eighty-five and in his sixtieth season on the sidelines.

Each of their win totals dwarf those of such coaching stalwarts as Don Shula (328, most in the NFL), and Joe Paterno (409, most in major college). In that watershed season of 2011, McKissick had ten state championships while J. T. was coaching his twenty-fourth with his twelfth undefeated team.

If those facts are staggering, there are even more flabbergasting statistics: In his then-forty-three-year career, using the same option offense he used for decades, Curtis's teams had won twenty-four state championships—more than any coach in the history of the game—in three different classifications, averaged 11.7 victories with a .893 winning percentage—all this even after starting out 0-10 in his first season.

This wasn't just a fabled journey. There was almost a sense of destiny.

* * *

From the first, Curtis always seemed to be in the company of those who could further his dream, starting with his dad, John Curtis Sr., who, among other vocations, was a high school football coach. Then at East Jefferson High School in Metairie, he played under the respected Bob Whitman and Harold "Hoss" Memtsas, a New Orleans coaching legend who was briefly an assistant to Whitman—and the maven to whom young J. T. peppered the penetrating questions on the advantages and disadvantages of the "50" defense versus the "wide tackle six."

Curtis next found himself—as he blossomed, at five-foot-eleven, 215 pounds, into an All-State player, the first produced at East Jefferson—in the hands of yet another major influence: Frank Broyles at the University of Arkansas, where J. T. matriculated.

"Frank Broyles was a coach way ahead of his time," Curtis said. "His organizational skills were extraordinary. I base what I do today on what he did then. Nothing was left to chance. The coach who first talked to me about Arkansas was Barry Switzer, who was then the No. 2 offensive line coach. Nobody else at that time had two coaches handling the same unit. Today it's not uncommon, but then it was unheard of. Arkansas was at the pinnacle of college football at the time, and very clearly Coach Broyles had put them there.

"Whatever I've done, I'd have to say it was the result of what I learned from my dad, Bob Whitman, and Frank Broyles. They shaped me."

While at Arkansas, J. T. also was able to peer into the future of football. As a member of the freshmen team, when first-year athletes couldn't play varsity ball, Curtis clearly remembers a game with Southern Methodist and the coaches all instructing the Razorbacks to play back, give the Mustangs a little cushion because they had a back quick enough to make a defense pay for playing too tight. That was Jerry LeVias, the first African American to receive a scholarship in the old Southwest Conference. A few weeks later, Arkansas played a freshmen game with North Texas State, and Curtis was on the line, where he was being pulverized by one of the Eagles.

"I mean, we were Arkansas and they were North Texas State," Curtis said of the memory. "This wasn't supposed to happen. As it turned out, the guy who was manhandling me was 'Mean Joe Greene,' who would turn out to be a great pro. I didn't have a chance."

In a capsule, though, this heralded the beginning of the black athlete in the Southwest and South, and Curtis was an eyewitness.

Other forces that would shape Curtis's life were also at work.

By the time J. T. was playing his senior year, he and a certain Miss Lydia Bryant wanted to get married. She was a student at Louisiana College in Pineville, where both her father and his dad, close friends, had graduated. There was no way Lydia's dad would let her transfer from the Baptist school. J. T. switched, enrolling in the NAIA college for his last football season—and Louisiana College's, too, for some time. The Wildcats gave up the sport in the first days of Lydia and J. T.'s married life but restarted the team in 2000.

In the early 1960s, John Curtis Sr., an educator and minister as well as a football coach, founded a school in suburban River Ridge with an overarching ecumenical Christian philosophy. It was rare at a time when most religious-oriented schools were for children of one particular denomination or another.

This one was for all faiths under the Christian umbrella.

The Rev. Curtis had given up roaming the sidelines to run the school, and everything was humming along at the John Curtis Christian School—at least until J. T.'s phone rang in the spring of 1969.

It was his father.

"He told me his football coach had quit and that maybe I ought to think about coming home to takeover the program," J. T. recalled.

It was kind of out of the blue because J. T. still had nine hours—a semester's work—to go to graduate college.

That should be a snap, the Rev. Curtis advised. J. T. could come down, work with the football team during the day and take his remaining classwork at a New Orleans school at night or in the off-season.

It would take another three and a half years to get that diploma.

"I got it, though. That's the important thing," Curtis said. "As I tell the students all the time, life doesn't run on a timetable. But it's important to get important things done, no matter how long it takes."

Turned out, the dual experience at Arkansas and Louisiana College was a major learning tool.

"Arkansas was near the top of college football, and I saw close-up how things operated at a school where there was a real commitment to its program," J. T. recalled. "And I saw what it was like at Louisiana College, a school that didn't have anything like a commitment. It was a stark contrast, and I've always remembered what it was like at each one."

In any case, at twenty-two years old and without the benefit of a day's experience of being an assistant to hone his teaching skills, J. T. Curtis was a head coach.

☆ ☆ ☆

"I go to my first meeting, on August 15, 1969," J. T. vividly recalled. "I had thirty-nine notebooks and six players. I went to my dad's office and said, 'Daddy, I only had six guys here today.'

"He didn't say a word. I said, 'Daddy, what do you think I should do?'

"He finally said, 'Well, if I was you, I'd get on the phone and start calling some people.' I knew right then that he was doing his job, and I'd better start doing mine."

Enough kids were finally rounded up to field a team, but the '69 Curtis Patriots not only didn't win a game, they scored two touchdowns all season.

"I guess I was so inexperienced that I was naïve," J. T. said. "As bad as things were going, there was never a time that I didn't think we weren't going to win the next week. We never did, but I never had the sense that it was hopeless."

The next season, though, the Patriots reached the playoffs with an 8-2 record. In 1973 they reached the quarterfinals, losing to Notre Dame of Crowley 16-13.

J. T. was learning.

"That was the first time I realized that I had probably set the goals for that team and didn't realize that they probably could have gone beyond what I set for them," Curtis reflected. "So I eliminated goals from that point on. You'll never see signs up for winning this or scoring this many touchdowns. Because that '73 team probably could have won a championship, and I did not realize it."

Two years later the Patriots, without a single college prospect on the roster, won their first state title, beating the same Notre Dame of Crowley Pioneers 13-12.

"I'll never forget it," Curtis said. "They went for two after each of their touchdowns and we stopped them both times."

That was a turning point. Since then, with a staff that includes family members, brothers, sons, and son-in-laws, Curtis has molded teams that win with methodical regularity, but usually with pretty average athletes. No more than two handfuls of players, with the exceptions of a few such as Joe McKnight and Reggie Dupard, have been mega-star types.

Somebody has been doing some serious coaching.

Of course, human nature being what it is, as with anything or any person so ultra-successful, there have been cynics whispering that perhaps everything at this little private school couldn't be on the up-and-up. Too many giants were being slayed by this prep David. There had to be ulterior reasons.

"It bothered me at first, I'll admit," J. T. said. "But at some point I came to a realization that people were going to say or think whatever they wanted. All I could do was what I had been doing—the best job I possibly could within the rules."

It should be noted that all anyone with knowledge of any transgression had to do was report them to the Louisiana High School Association and they would be investigated. If anything was amiss—and proven—Curtis would be penalized.

In more than four decades, nothing of the sort ever occurred—and the Patriots have continued on their merry way of winning title after title, reaching an astounding twenty-five after the 2012 season with yet another undefeated team—with no end in sight.

So what has been the secret?

"What we want to do is raise the playing level of the average high school kid," said Curtis, who also coached six state baseball champions. "If we can do that, we can think we can compete with most other programs."

Clearly, Curtis, now also a minister as his father was, brought a special gift for guiding teams and kids to the sidelines.

"It's his calling," said Lydia Curtis on the eve of J. T.'s five hundredth victory. "We both have this intense faith and we both believe that God calls you to serve. It all revolves around your spiritual life. You've got to be happy in your heart. In my heart, I believe that he found his calling early on, and God really has blessed him."

LOUISIANA SATURDAY NIGHT

October 3, 1931
Tiger Stadium, Baton Rouge, La.

Ray Charles once warbled, "The night time is the right time," and for going on a century at LSU, it has been.

Tiger Stadium, more than any other college venue, it seems, comes to life when the sun goes down. What emerges is the essence of LSU football: purple-and-gold fervor in the stands, night stalkers in cleats on the field.

"Saturday Night in Tiger Stadium" is the most nationally enduring image of LSU sports. Fans at all corners of the sports map would identify the school most renown for playing football from twilight to the witching hour.

"It's a magical setting," sports author Mike Bynum said. "The excitement, the atmosphere, is unmatched anywhere—and I've been in stadiums from one end of America to the other. They ought to put up a statue to the guy who came up with (the idea of) night football at LSU."

That would be Thomas Pickney "Skipper" Heard, who headed the program on the October 3, 1931, evening when the Tigers played Spring Hill, a 35-0 LSU victory, under the lights.

In the vernacular of today, Heard was thinking outside the box, though he had a model for the idea: Loyola in New Orleans played Friday night football successfully for several years before LSU. The first night game in Louisiana occurred on September 21, 1929—more than two years before LSU ever kicked off after sunset—when Loyola defeated St. Edwards of Texas 18-0.

So a game under the lights was not a new idea. As early as 1897, Illinois defeated Carlisle in a game played indoors at the Chicago Coliseum.

But the concept of "after dinner" games was popularized at LSU. There were several reasons Heard experimented with such a radical notion:

- First and foremost was the shift changes of refinery workers in Baton Rouge. Many couldn't attend afternoon games, but they could in the evening, and getting off work at 7:00 p.m. allowed laborers enough time to make 8:00 p.m. kickoffs.

LSU Athletic Director "Skipper" Heard brought nighttime football to LSU.

- Competition for fans also played a role. Tulane, then in its football heyday, was playing on Saturday afternoons. A late Tigers kickoff would allow more fans to take in the Green Wave—or other teams around the state—then motor to LSU. Loyola fans, used to nocturnal football, also might be lured into supporting two teams, one on Friday nights, the other on Saturday nights. The move extended LSU's reach because an estimated 80 percent of the Tigers' crowds in those days came from within a thirty-mile radius of Baton Rouge.

- Then there was the factor—and this might have been the most important—of the scorching Louisiana afternoon heat in September. Those concrete seats could get mighty hot at mid-afternoon but were comfortable when the sun went down.

For the princely Depression-era sum of $7,500, Heard took a gamble, installed the lights, and forever changed the setting of LSU football—though contrary to popular belief, LSU continued to play some day games in November and December for years, at least until the early 1960s.

Today, due to television considerations, some of LSU's most attractive games have to be moved to daytime, meaning more money but often removing part of the mystique that makes Tigers football special. When things are going well or when the Tigers need their "12th Man," Tiger Stadium becomes a quintessential football snake pit at night, when unbridled emotion is fused with the unrelenting howl of ninety thousand zealots that often stirs the home team into pigskin feeding frenzies, needless to say, Tiger Stadium at night can be difficult for opponents. It's a fact borne out of history. In day games, the Tigers are historically about a .500 program. In night games at home, LSU is more than a .700 team.

"There's no question," former coach Charlie McClendon once reflected on the subject, "we've always been a better football team under those conditions than any other."

ESPN's Beano Cook famously said, "Dracula and LSU football are at their best after the sun goes down."

As in a movie in which an actor gives an indelible performance and it becomes difficult to think anyone else playing that role, it's hard to imagine such notable LSU moments as Billy Cannon's fabled run against Ole Miss in 1959, the "Earthquake" game against Auburn in 1988, or the 1997 beating of No. 1-ranked Florida taking place in bright sunshine. Downright impossible, to tell the truth.

LSU coach Les Miles said of Tiger Stadium, "There's a magic in the air in this place at night."

But it was McClendon who might have come up with the best description of the "Saturday Night at Tiger Stadium" aura, saying of the game-time atmosphere at the mossy old stadium, dubbed "Death Valley" by opponents, "It's like an electric wire running from the stands to the field."

Thanks to Skipper Heard, that has become the signature of LSU athletics.

"ALLONS PRO"

November 1, 1966
Pontchartrain Hotel, New Orleans, La.

NEW ORLEANS STATES-ITEM
RECORDING TODAY'S STORY OF PROGRESS
RED FLASH
VOL. 90—NO. 121 TUESDAY, NOVEMBER 1, 1966 PRICE 10c

N.O. GOES PRO!

Long-Sought Franchise Is Acquired

By PETER FINNEY

VIKINGS' TOMMY MASON . . . CARDINALS' JERRY STOVALL . . . COLTS' JOHNNY UNITAS . . . PACKERS' JIM TAYLOR
They'll be playing here . . . with other NFL stars in 1967.

Orleans Economy Scores Touchdown

By ROSEMARY JAMES

States-Item Holds Contest to Find Name for Team

$5 Per Game Ticket Cost Is Expected

Women Praise Pro Football For Orleans

"N.O. Goes Pro!" the headline of New Orleans's afternoon newspaper blared in the largest type used since Pearl Harbor.

Meanwhile, the man who made the headline appear was sitting quietly in the rear of the crowded Patio Room of the luxurious Pontchartrain Hotel, where Pete Rozelle made a point of acknowledging the forty-three-year-old entrepreneur. In front of an assembly of politicians, civic leaders, media, and hangers-on, the NFL commissioner in a salute said, "Dave Dixon has been hounding us for six years."

Rozelle, standing under a gas-lit chandelier, was in town to justify the *States-Item* headline: "Professional Football has voted a franchise to the State of Louisiana and the City of New Orleans."

The sixteenth franchise of the National Football League went to New Orleans that day almost entirely because of the bulldog tenacity of Dixon—the same major figure responsible for the Louisiana Superdome, entirely fitting since neither would exist without the other.

The events of that not-so-coincidently All Saints Day would have been largely forgotten by now if eight days later a statewide referendum to construct an all-purpose domed stadium had been voted down. The team now known as the Saints would need a place to play, and the only suitable one in New Orleans was Tulane Stadium, but the school wanted only a temporary partnership with professional football.

It all worked out, as Dixon, the workaholic visionary who inspired and guided the mission from inception to conclusion, knew it would. His hounding had not been in vain.

★ ★ ★

The man who almost single-handedly changed the landscape of New Orleans traced his involvement with sports to 1958, when Mayor Chep Morrison was trying to save the Pelicans, the city's minor league baseball team, and, at the same time, attract a major league franchise.

"I had been talking to Chep about some very informal plans he'd been talking about to build a stadium on the lakefront to catch the eye of the major leagues," Dixon said. "I told him I thought the most likely avenue for our entry into major league sports was professional football. The NFL wasn't a big deal then.

"He said, 'Why don't you do it?' I was shocked. Surprised."

Others endorsed the idea, all with the suggestion Dixon do it himself.

"That's how it got started," he said, "and then I had a tiger by the tail and couldn't let go. Always, at the point where any sane, sensible man would have given up, some little spark of encouragement—or what I would perceive as encouragement—would occur."

★ ★ ★

From the start, Dixon was aware there were hurdles to overcome, including the segregation laws of Louisiana and every other southern state as they existed at the time, as well as the strain of cynicism that more often than not colored New Orleans undertakings.

Of course, there would have to be a place to play, and Tulane Stadium, largely built at no expense to the university by the Sugar Bowl, did not want to be a venue for pro sports.

But those were problems to be overcome later. For the time being, Dixon contacted then-NFL commissioner Bert Bell for guidance (of which little was given), and, when he heard of the possibility of a new league, Dixon got in touch with Lamar Hunt, the Texas billionaire who was guiding that effort.

Dixon jumped in the deep end of the pool.

Seeds were being sown on other fronts, too. Jack DeFee Jr., the former president of the baseball Pelicans, Hector Plauche, and a committee of ten formed a group called Louisiana Professional Sports, Inc., that promoted a 1960 NFL exhibition between Green Bay and Pittsburgh at City Park Stadium. It drew more than fifteen thousand, respectable for the time.

In 1962 Louisiana Professional Sports, Inc., put on another exhibition between the Boston Patriots and Houston Oilers, featuring former LSU halfback Billy Cannon at City Park. This time Dixon was involved, helping promote the game, and having non-binding pledges passed out to gauge how many people would be interested in season tickets should New Orleans ever land a pro franchise.

The game drew 31,000 in a 26,000-seat stadium—eye-catching to the fledgling American Football League, which just two years before averaged 16,500 in attendance for its first season—and Dixon, who would shortly front his own group, New Orleans Football Club, Inc., counted more than twelve thousand pledges.

It was noticed in the NFL, too. George Halas, coach and CEO of the Chicago Bears, compared New Orleans's exhibition figures with Dallas, where the new NFL entrant drew 30,000 for its regular-season opener and just eighteen thousand for its second game.

Times-Picayune columnist Buddy Diliberto wrote, "New Orleans fans fired a $$$ shot heard loud and clear around the American Football League Saturday night . . ." The reference reflected the feeling that any new team would come from the new AFL, and, indeed, Patriots owner Billy Sullivan and Oilers owner Bud Adams immediately endorsed New Orleans as an AFL venue.

It might have happened quickly. The new Dallas NFL team, the Cowboys, and Hunt's Dallas Texans were killing each other in the competition for fans. Hunt was ready to move the Texans to New Orleans, a close-to-reality fact written about by Dixon, then-Texans coach Hank Stram, and included in a biography of Hunt. The possibility fell through because the notoriously secretive Hunt wanted any agreement with Tulane to read that the use of the stadium was for any AFL team, not his alone.

Dixon lamented later that it was an opportunity lost, and the Texans became the Kansas City Chiefs.

☆ ☆ ☆

Perhaps the most meaningful of the exhibitions came in 1963 when Dixon, whose always fertile imagination was coming up with new brainstorms, put together a doubleheader NFL pairing, with the Cowboys against the Detroit Lions and the Chicago Bears against the Baltimore Colts.

The games were significant for two reasons: Tickets were priced at eight and six dollars and the resulting $330,000 gate was the largest for an exhibition date in the history of the NFL. More important, Dixon insisted to Tulane that tickets would be sold on a first-come, first-serve basis, meaning African Americans would not be confined to a segregated area. It was a first in the South, and for the first time at Tulane Stadium seating was integrated.

It's hard to say the fifty-one thousand people had a great time, however, since in the third quarter of the first game, a deluge of 2.8 inches of rain fell in twenty-eight minutes. The games were suspended, and drenched fans—black and white together—went under the stands until play could be continued a couple of hours later. The horn went off ending the second game at about 1:00 a.m.

All told, though, the games were a resounding success on all other fronts.

☆ ☆ ☆

The good news continued. A 1964 exhibition between the St. Louis Cardinals and Green Bay Packers drew 75,229, which set the record for a preseason crowd in a non-league city.

Things were going almost too well.

The All-Star Game of the AFL was scheduled for New Orleans in January of 1965—months after the Civil Rights Act was enacted—and ticket sales were brisk, with more than sixteen thousand sold the first couple of days after they went up for sale. Then a charge of racism was leveled at the city by some of the black players, saying they were barred from some clubs in the French Quarter and were refused cab service at the airport.

The All-Star Game was switched to Houston, and all those concerned wondered if this black eye would kill any chance of New Orleans getting its spot in pro football.

It didn't. A private NFL check of New Orleans's racial situation—including stricter enforcement of the laws—was made by Buddy Young, one of Rozelle's key assistants and a former Colts All-Pro. According to Dixon, Young convinced Rozelle that New Orleans would pass any racial test with flying colors.

☆ ☆ ☆

Apparently New Orleans could pass, because the city was in the mix with Cincinnati and Seattle for an expansion franchise—though it was being considered at a bad time. With the AFL and NFL set to merge, there was a need for an antitrust exception. The chairman of the antitrust subcommittee, New York Congressman Emmanuel Celler, was in no hurry to approve the package submitted by Louisiana Congressman Hale Boggs.

Time for resolution was running short, and adjournment was

near. Without its passage, there would be no merger, and without a merger New Orleans was still on the outside looking in.

Rozelle asked for help, and got it from Boggs and Louisiana Senator Russell Long. The proposal was attached to an anti-inflation bill President Lyndon Johnson wanted passed.

The New Orleans story continued, however.

As related in a biography of Long, when the bill moved to final House passage, Rozelle called Boggs to get a feel for its chances of success. "Well, Pete, it looks great," Boggs said, then added for clarification, "Just for the record, Pete, I assume we can say the franchise for New Orleans is firm?" The commissioner hedged. "Well, it looks good, of course, Hale, but I can't make any promises on my own," he coyly replied.

Through a tight smile, Boggs responded slowly—and coolly, "Well, Pete, why don't you just go back and check with the owners. I'll hold things up here until you get back." Rozelle, taken aback, sheepishly replied, "That's all right. You can count on their approval."

President Johnson signed the bill, in essence approving the merger—and putting New Orleans into the NFL.

For the record, a quarter-century later Rozelle disputed the parts of the story about the bill. In a 1991 interview, Rozelle said, "the thing about the New Orleans franchise that intrigued me was that at the time the franchise was awarded . . . so many people thought political leverage was used here by politicians to force us to locate an expansion franchise in New Orleans when the truth was we were dying to get into the city. . . . We knew it would be a lock as a big-league franchise and it has turned out to be that."

In any case, soon there would be that gathering at the Pontchartrain Hotel, filling the Patio Room with scads of people all taking credit for the accomplishment.

Back of the room, largely hidden by the cameras and the gaggle of people assembled, was Dave Dixon and his wife, Mary. As the flash bulbs were popping and those in front were taking their bows, Mary whispered to Dave, "If all those clowns standing up at the front getting their pictures taken and taking credit for getting the franchise had helped us from the beginning, we would have had the New Orleans Saints here three years ago."

Virgil Robinson, from Grambling State University, one of many forgotten early New Orleans Saints players.
(Note that Robinson is being pursued by fellow ex-Grambling Tiger Willie Davis.)

WELCOME TO TOMORROW

August 3, 1975
Louisiana Superdome, New Orleans, La.

"THAT would be the GREATEST building in the history of man," John J. McKeithen thundered. "By God, we'll build it!"

The governor of Louisiana was bowled over by the pitch for an all-purpose stadium—the finest and most flexible in the world—by private citizen Dave Dixon, who had come hat in hand to share what he thought would be the finishing touch in securing an NFL franchise for New Orleans and in the process make the city a major destination for high profile sports and entertainment events.

McKeithen's words and Dixon's dream ultimately would transform the sports and entertainment landscape of Louisiana and create a vibrant economic engine. They also touched off a political war, a fierce firefight that cost no lives but scarred some of the combatants in the mercurial arena of Louisiana politics. For almost a decade, the fight, economic fluctuations, and changes in the size (and, thus, costs) kept the project in a state of flux.

When public opinion on the constitutional amendment to build the Superdome seemed to wane, Dixon, like McKeithen a spellbinding orator, hit the road. Stumping the state, he made an estimated seventy-six speeches in forty-six days. Some reported tongue-in-cheek that Dixon once stunned an entire Central Louisiana community when he ended a mesmerizing oration by feeding the entire gathering with just twelve loaves of bread and five bowls of gumbo.

But the miracle was that the state-wide referendum passed by 76 percent of the electorate.

★ ★ ★

On August 3, 1975, the building officially opened its doors, with the message boards sending an apt greeting: *Welcome to Tomorrow.*

This was a staggering achievement, it's anodized aluminum skin surrounding the largest unobstructed room ever built; the Battle of New Orleans could conceivably have been fought within its walls; a twenty-six-story building could fit under its roof, an egg-shaped protrusion which spans nine and a half acres.

The scope of the Superdome was so vast that its design architect, Nathaniel "Buster" Davis, conceded that no one person could have put it together on paper—computers (and remember this was the technology of the late 1960s and early 1970s) did it. It is a stupefying statistic, but the Superdome contains 125 million cubic feet of space.

Did it live up to Dixon's dream? Well, it made New Orleans a big-time sports and entertainment venue, changing the Big Easy from a hit-or-miss destination, one a little off the beaten path, and changing the Dome's $163 million price tag (a humongous figure for the time) into billions over the ensuing four decades.

The promise of the Superdome did help lure the NFL's Saints

Dave Dixon and architect Buster Curtis unveil the Superdome model.

to New Orleans. It has been the host site for seven of New Orleans's ten Super Bowls, most of any venue; held five Final Fours (including the memorable ones in 1982, when freshman Michael Jordan hit a last-minute jumper to give North Carolina coach Dean Smith his first national championship, and 1987, when Louisiana native Keith Smart hit a basket with seconds to go to give Indiana coach Bobby Knight his third title. Those games were played before some of the largest crowds in the history of basketball); there were also a heavyweight championship fight featuring Muhammad Ali; the annual Sugar Bowl, in which numerous national champions have been crowned, and where the BCS National Championship Game was regularly held; and the annual Bayou Classic between Southern University and Grambling State University. The Superdome also became the venue high school teams from around the state try to reach each year for the state football championships.

It's safe to say that more champions in more sports have been crowned in the Louisiana Superdome than any other venue anywhere.

On other fronts, the Rolling Stones, Willie Nelson, and Frank Sinatra all played the palace. The Essence Festival, bringing in big name musical acts for four days, is an annual event.

The Superdome also has been, as Dixon once famously predicted, the site where a future president was nominated. The 1988 Republican Convention met at the Dome, and George H. Bush became the GOP standard-bearer.

And the Superdome is where Pope John Paul II, not to be outdone by Michael Jordan, also sent up a prayer.

Here's a major notation about the Superdome: it's still standing and performing. In the nightmarish *Water World* aftermath of Hurricane Katrina, thousands sought asylum in the building, which served as a refuge of last resort. When winds ripped off part of the roof, leaving the stadium open to the elements, and electricity failed, leaving people without basic necessities, the Dome became a national symbol of despair.

Since then, though, the structure, later to be called the Mercedes-Benz Superdome, has gotten a do-over, improving on the original so much so that it again became a venue of Super Bowls and Final Fours.

It's still vibrant, and much more so than other facilities of its kind and period.

When the Superdome was built, the only clear model it had to compare itself with was the iconic and pioneering Houston Astrodome—which Dixon thought was essentially a covered-over baseball field. Now the Astrodome sits vacant.

The Kingdome in Seattle, and the Silver Dome in Detroit, both younger than Superdome, have been discarded.

Meanwhile the Superdome remains what it was intended to be, a magnet for New Orleans sports and entertainment, best described by, of all outlets, the *Houston Chronicle*'s Stan Redding, "It glistens like a giant dewdrop diamond on the throat of New Orleans, an awesome, skyline-crowding structure that is 'beyond tomorrow.'"

A CLASSIC GAME
Louisiana Superdome, New Orleans, La.

In 1997, then-Southern University coach Pete Richardson looked down at the man seated beside the podium and said softly, "This was his vision."

Richardson was discussing the Bayou Classic, the annual football extravaganza between the Jaguars and Grambling State, which was the brainchild of his friendly adversary, Tigers' coach Eddie Robinson, who the next day would coach his last game—in the Bayou Classic.

The game—the fiercest rivalry still played in Louisiana—has become a major social occurrence in New Orleans, a reason for reunions of families and friends, and get-togethers of just plain fans of the two universities, the professional school for the state's African Americans, Southern in Baton Rouge, and the largely agricultural and mechanical Grambling in north Louisiana.

From these diverse backdrops emerges a festive "happening" that brings together as many as two hundred thousand people for a weekend in the Big Easy, for job fairs, banquets, parties, convocations, and spirited Battles of the Bands. As many as seventy thousand attend the game.

This is how much the game has come to mean to the partisans of each school: The Bayou Classic is scheduled each year for the Thanksgiving weekend—the same weekend the NCAA's Football Championship Subdivision playoffs begin. In other words, playing each other in this venue is more important to Southern and Grambling than playing for a national championship.

So how exactly did this yearly football/social jollification come to be?

The legend of Grambling football came about largely because of Robinson and the equally legendary Tigers publicist Collie Nicholson, and they were also responsible for the Bayou Classic.

"You know, Grambling is just kind of a hamlet, and one year in the 1960s when we played Southern at Grambling, a lot of people were stranded," said Nicholson. "The two gas stations in town ran out of gas, and people who expected to fuel up after the game couldn't. We had only a small stadium (ten thousand) to begin with, so we wanted to play before more people and play more big games. We had to be creative. Real creative."

R. L. Stockard, then the media coordinator for the Southwestern Athletic Conference—and the first sports information director at Southern—concurred. Because of its remoteness, Stockard said, "Most (opponents) did not want to even play at Grambling. Nobody ever ended up in Grambling by mistake."

But that necessity was coupled with a concept that went back even further than that with Robinson, who had thoughts of a "Brown Sugar Bowl" even as a young man.

Nicholson and Robinson had made Grambling a national sporting item, with the Tigers putting together eye-catching records and Robinson sending waves of players to professional football. Grambling played football across the country, from Yankee Stadium to the Rose Bowl, and even stretched its brand overseas to Tokyo. Nicholson pointed out that Grambling's success in these promotions far away from north Louisiana, and on the field, all rested on Robinson's shoulders.

"Grambling had to win in order to be of interest," said Nicholson, a marketing genius who spread the word of the Tigers across the land. "With Rob at the helm, they did. Grambling really became a national team."

But for all its renown, Grambling was not really that big in

The inaugural "Bayou Classic" was played at Tulane Stadium in 1974.

New Orleans, the state's largest city. Southern had a much stronger following there. Grambling played a couple of early 1960s games in the Crescent City, at City Park Stadium in an ill-fated venture called the Pelican Bowl, drawing little interest and sparse crowds.

"I wanted to play in New Orleans," Robinson, who won 408 games in fifty-six years of coaching, once explained. "This is Louisiana, where we're from, and I always felt we should play at least one of our biggest games here."

That idea became an obsession with Robinson in 1964 when Grambling played Florida A&M in Miami's Orange Blossom Classic, something of a prelude to the major-college Orange Bowl.

"There were about forty-eight thousand people at that game," Robinson said, "and I just realized it really would be something special if we could do something like that in Louisiana. I talked to some of the people at the Sugar Bowl, but they were in the midst of a lot of problems at the time and just couldn't do it."

Construction of the Superdome in the early '70s revived Robinson's idea. He thought Grambling's most heated rival, Southern, would be a natural opponent for an annual game at a neutral site.

Jaguars athletic director U. S. Jones strongly disagreed.

"They had to drag Southern into this thing kicking and screaming," Stockard recalled. "Southern had a twenty thousand-seat stadium at the time, Grambling's was ten thousand. When Southern played at home they made money. They didn't want to take a chance on losing money."

Robinson eventually got his chance. Officials at the SWAC, the league in which both schools competed, informed the coach that in the alternate years when the Tigers were the home team, the game could be held wherever they wanted.

The first year the Grambling-Southern game was played off-campus was 1973, when the teams dipped their toes in experimental waters at Shreveport. The game drew forty-one thousand, more than twice as many as it could have at either of the schools' stadiums, and with a fifty-fifty split.

After more discussions with the Sugar Bowl and African American businessmen in New Orleans, Robinson was encouraged but was offered no substantial help.

"We decided to put on the game ourselves," said Robinson, who died in 2007. "We talked to the Superdome people about renting the facility. There was no problem. We hired Pace Management from Houston to promote the game and went to work."

The 1974 game was not played in the Superdome, which was not finished, but at Tulane Stadium.

"I remember standing on the sideline when all those people started coming in," Robinson said. "I remember when they announced the attendance (76,753). I said, 'WHAAAAAAT?' Nobody could believe it. Man, tears just started rolling down my face, and I started hugging people. They probably wondered what was wrong with me, but that was one of the highlights of my life."

A vision had become reality.

The Bayou Classic—much more than an annual football game.

TAKE *US* OUT TO THE BALL GAME

"Charlie Mason probably didn't know he was making history on that day back in 1883," Ted Lewis of the *Times-Picayune* wrote 111 years later.

"But when Mason went 1-for-2 for the Philadelphia Athletics in an American Association game, he became the first Louisiana-born person to play in the major leagues (the AA was considered a major league from 1882 to 1891). It turned out to be the only game in which Mason appeared, although he managed the club for part of the 1887 season," Lewis wrote.

The sport (christened "The National Game" by what was then called the *Daily Picayune* in the 1880s) left an indelible imprint on the state from its earliest days when it gained near-universal popularity after the Civil War, spread by Union soldiers from the Northeast, where the game was already a pastime that drew considerable throngs of spectators.

In fact, it is speculated that Mason, born in New Orleans in 1853, was exposed to the game by Northern troops who occupied the city during the war and the ensuing Reconstruction period. But according to Louisiana baseball historian S. Derby Gisclair, the first teams in the state were the Lone Star Base Ball Club in 1859 and the Comet Base Ball Club in 1860. The Robert E. Lees (1864) and Pelican Base Ball Club (1865) followed. A team from New Orleans called the Southerners made home-and-home visits with the Cincinnati Red Stockings (the sport's first pro club) in 1870 and 1871.

This much is not speculation: From that point, Louisiana has made an imprint on the sport.

☆ ☆ ☆

Although it wasn't until the 1920s that the state truly began finding its niche as a major talent conduit to what we now call the Big Show, since then Louisiana has been an incubator to such notable baseball figures as Mel Ott, Ted Lyons, and Lou Brock, all enshrined in Cooperstown, plus other baseball notables such as Alvin Dark, Joe Adcock, Mel Parnell, Ron Guidry, Will Clark, Vida Blue, Lee Smith, and Rusty Staub.

Pelican Stadium, home of the New Orleans Pelicans.

This is some of what Mason's trailblazing spawned:

- The youngest Louisianan to play in the majors and the youngest third baseman of all time is New Orleans's Ralph "Putsy" Caballero, who was sixteen when he played in four games for the Philadelphia Phillies at the end of the 1944 season. "I had graduated from Jesuit that year and had just finished American Legion when the Phillies signed me," said Caballero, one of the "Whiz Kids" on Philadelphia's 1950 National League champions. "Those other guys on the team looked so old to me it was like they had alligator skin. The team was in last place and all they wanted was to get it over with. But it was a big deal to me."

- New Orleanian Mel Parnell, the winningest left-hander (123-75, 3.50 ERA in ten seasons) in Boston Red Sox history, finished off his 1956 no-hitter against the Chicago White Sox with an unassisted putout of lumbering Walt Drago, the only time a no-hitter has ended with such a play.

- Shreveport's Willard Brown hit the first home run by a black player in the American League in 1947.

- More than a half-century after Brown, another Shreveport native, Albert Belle, one of the leading sluggers of his time, was the fourth player to have eight consecutive seasons of thirty home runs and 100 RBIs, joining the exclusive company of Babe Ruth, Jimmie Foxx, and Lou Gehrig. The five-time All-Star, who played with the Cleveland Indians, Chicago White Sox, and Baltimore Orioles in his twelve-year professional career, also became the first player in major league history to hit fifty home runs and fifty doubles in the same season (1995).

- Eddie Dyer of Morgan City was the first rookie manager to win the World Series when he took the St. Louis Cardinals to the title in 1946. Helping Dyer to that distinction was Orleanian Howie Pollet, who was 21-10 with a 2.10 ERA. Pollet was part of three Cardinals World Series teams in the 1940s and twice led the National League in earned run average (1.75 in 1943 and 2.10 in 1946).

- Such were his fielding skills that infielder George Strickland stayed in the major leagues for more than a decade despite a career batting average of .226. Strickland, who played at New Orleans's S. J. Peters High with Mel Parnell, anchored the infield for the 1954 American League pennant-winning Cleveland Indians, who won 111 games. In 1955 Strickland was the AL's best fielding shortstop and in 1959 was the AL's best fielding third baseman.

Mel Parnell.

- Longtime New Orleans Pelicans manager Larry Gilbert was the first Louisianan to play in the World Series (1914 Boston Braves) and had two sons play in the majors.

- Lee Smith, from the small town of Castor in northwest Louisiana, was baseball's first saves leader. He retired in 1997 with 478.

As might be suspected, there are some curiosities linking Louisiana and baseball, such as:

- The first $100,000 bonus baby, left-handed pitcher Paul Pettit of California, initially played professionally in 1951 for the Pelicans, a farm club for Pittsburgh. The Pirates didn't exactly get a return on their investment. Pettit had a career 1-2 record in the majors, though he played a decade as a good-hitting first baseman/outfielder in the Pacific Coast League.

- Speedy Matt Alexander of Shreveport had 103 stolen bases but just thirty-five hits in nine seasons in the majors. Alexander, who was 1-for-30 in 1978 with Oakland, had to go 12-for-27 in his last three seasons to get his career average up to

.217. He played on the Pirates' world championship club of 1979.

- Louisiana's second major-leaguer, John Peltz of New Orleans, led the American League in errors in 1884 with thirty-eight while playing for the Indianapolis Hoosiers. What makes that unusual is that Peltz was an outfielder.

Alvin Dark.

It was Alvin Dark, who grew up in Lake Charles, who started the rally that led to the "Shot Heard 'Round the World," one of the handful of most-remembered games in baseball lore.

Going into the bottom of the ninth at the Polo Grounds in the third and decisive game of the 1951 National League playoff, the Brooklyn Dodgers were leading the New York Giants 4-1. Dark led off and slapped an 0-2 pitch from Don Newcombe into right field for a single. Don Mueller followed with another single to right. Monty Irvin popped out, but Whitey Lockman doubled down the right-field line, driving in Dark.

Ralph Branca came in to pitch to Bobby Thomson, who popped an 0-1 fastball into the lower deck in left field, giving the Giants a stunning 5-4 victory—and an unforgettable place in baseball history.

What's that about first impressions? Sports seldom saw better debuts than that of Will "The Thrill" Clark, out of Jesuit High in New Orleans and Mississippi State in 1985. Two days after signing with the San Francisco Giants, in his first swing as a professional ballplayer in the minor leagues, Clark homered.

Ten months after that, in his first at-bat in the majors, Clark homered again—against future Hall of Famer Nolan Ryan.

Not only did the left-handed hitting Clark fashion an eye-catching fifteen-year All-Star career at first base for the Giants, Rangers, Orioles, Cardinals, and Blue Jays, in 1990 a survey of sixty-five of his major league peers said he was "the best clutch performer in baseball."

Ironically, another Jesuit graduate, Rusty Staub also earned a catchy sobriquet. When Staub, who became a major-league fixture as a teenager with the then-Houston Colt 45s, played later in French-speaking Montreal, he was branded *Le Grande Orange* for his flaming red hair.

Will Clark.

At the start of his sterling twenty-three-year career with five different clubs as a first baseman and, later, a designated hitter, Staub became only the second rookie since 1900 to play in 150 games as a teenager. He was also the only player to have at least 500 hits with four different teams. He was one of just three men to hit a home run in the majors before the age of twenty and after the age of forty; the others were Ty Cobb and Gary Sheffield.

Further, Staub and Hall of Famer Frank Robinson shared the record for homering in the most parks, thirty-two. In 1978 he became the first player to play in 162 games exclusively as a designated hitter, and in 1983 Staub tied a major league record with eight consecutive pinch hits, driving in another record 25 RBIs during that span.

Here's a Pelican State keeper: In the 1960s when Lou Brock was terrorizing National League base paths, a rookie catcher for the Atlanta Braves showed him he wasn't the only Louisianan who could play the game. On August 24, 1969, at Busch Stadium, Bob Didier of Baton Rouge threw out Brock twice in a 4-1 Braves victory. Brock stole fifty-three bases that season and was only thrown out fourteen times. These were two of them.

And the winning pitcher of that game? George Stone of Ruston.

Bob Didier was the scion of a baseball-lifer, Mel Didier, who

Rusty Staub.

Willard Brown.

is also a note in MLB history. Didier, who once snapped footballs to Y. A. Tittle at LSU, was the Los Angeles scout who tilted the 1988 World Series to the Dodgers when hobbled pinch-hitter Kirk Gibson came to the plate down by a run in the bottom of the ninth of Game 1. Didier told Gibson that should it get to that point, on a 3-2 count Oakland A's Hall of Fame pitcher Dennis Eckersley always throws a backdoor slider. It did get to that point, Eckersley did throw the backdoor slider, and Gibson sent it out of the park for a 5-4 Dodgers win. Los Angeles went on to take the Series

★ ★ ★

Babe Ruth, then and now the larger-than-life Sultan of Swat, sent towering shots out of the park in New Orleans when the Yankees trained in the Crescent City.

"Shoeless" Joe Jackson, the infamous outcast of the sport but still one of the greatest hitters in the history of the game, played for the New Orleans Pelicans in the Southern Association pennant year of 1910 before heading to the majors . . . and his eventual exile because of the notorious Black Sox scandal in which the 1919 World Series was said, but not proven, to be fixed.

Willard Brown, of Shreveport, a powerful and fast outfielder for the Kansas City Monarchs in the 1930s and 40s, was one of the Negro League's outstanding sluggers. Though his overall total is unknown, he was known as "Home Run" Brown and left such a legacy that he was elected to the Baseball Hall of Fame.

Oliver Marcell, known as "The Ghost of New Orleans," had a more than notable career in the Negro Leagues in the 1920s and '30s. A native of the Crescent City, Oliver was named as the Negro League's all-time greatest third baseman—ahead of future Hall of Famers Ray Dandridge and Judy Johnson—by the *Pittsburgh Courier*, the Bible of black baseball.

Satchel Paige, another Hall of Famer, pitched briefly in the '20s for the Negro Leagues' New Orleans Black Pelicans.

Even in semi-pro baseball, many levels below the elite, giants of the game appeared in New Orleans. In the winter league seasons of 1908 and '09, playing a handful of games in a bandbox called "Eddy's Ball Park" at the corner of Dublin and Nelson, for Manager G. E. P Murray and his team called The Eddys, was the greatest ball player of the day, Ty Cobb.

The point is, although never a major league venue, Louisiana got to see a lot of the game's greats up close.

★ ★ ★

Other notable Louisiana figures in the game:

- Ron Washington, a .261 career-hitting middle infielder in a ten-year playing career in the majors, found his stride as a manager. A resident of New Orleans even while managing in Texas, Washington rebuilt his Crescent City home piece-by-piece from the ravages of flooding and high winds of Hurricane Katrina all the while leading the Rangers to multiple World Series berths.

- Known as the "Roadrunner," Ralph Garr of the Atlanta Braves not only led the National League with a .353 batting average in 1974, but he had a record 149 hits heading into the All-Star break. To

Southern University's 1959 NAIA national championship team.

show how things can turn, the year before Garr had the ninth lowest average (.299) and lowest on-base percentage (.323) for a player with at least two-hundred hits. In college, as a senior at Grambling in 1967, Garr hit .582, and the Tigers' four-year record from 1964-67 was an astounding 103-11.

- The glittering career of James Rodney (J. R.) Richard, a right-handed pitcher from Vienna, near Ruston, was cruelly cut short by a stroke when he was thirty. He left the game after ten years in 1980 with the Houston Astros' records for most strikeouts in a season, 313 in 1979, and 1,493 strikeouts for his career.
- Another Astros pitcher with a tragic end was Don Wilson of Monroe, who pitched two no-hitters (1967, 1969). A nine-year starter, Wilson died at age twenty-nine.

The second African American signed to a contract by organized baseball was Johnny Wright, described as a "willowy right-handed pitcher." Playing for the Homestead Grays after his service in World War II, the twenty-seven-year-old Orleanian was signed less than a month after Jackie Robinson, and the two were teammates on the Montreal Royals, the Dodgers' farm club.

Wright's credentials were arguably as strong as Robinson's, who had only played one year of professional baseball and was not considered among the best at his position of shortstop in the war-depleted Negro Leagues. On the other hand, Wright had spent nearly a decade in the Negro Leagues and was an established pitching force.

"Johnny was exceptional," said George "Tex" Stephens, a longtime observer of black baseball who played against Wright as a youth. "As good as Satchel Paige," Stephens assessed. "Certainly faster (than Paige)."

Still, while Robinson rose to the challenge of breaking baseball's color barrier, Wright wilted. In three years he was completely out of the sport.

Sure, without a major league presence, Louisiana is a relative outpost in baseball. Still, the state has left its mark on the larger game.

New Orleans was the site of the first spring training excursion—in 1870 by the Cincinnati Red Stockings and Chicago White Stockings.

The New Orleans Pelicans became Louisiana's first professional team in 1887 when local businessmen secured a franchise in the two-year-old Southern League. Abner Powell, an outfielder, pitcher, and manager of the Pelicans, left a lingering influence on the game.

Powell came up with several innovations still in vogue today. Among them:

- Ladies Day, to draw on a new pool of fans. When the Pelicans lost to Charleston 1-0 on April 29, 1887, after giving the ladies "a delightful taste of the sport the men relish so much," a news account noted several hundred women attended: "They came in carriages, buggies, in street cars and on trains, charming in their spring attire, and made the cozy grandstand a bower of beauty."
- Canvas tarpaulins to cover the infield in inclement weather. Powell later said he got the idea watching stevedores cover cotton bales on New Orleans's waterfront with tarps and that he adapted the idea to the baseball field. The following year, seeing the idea in use in New Orleans, the Cincinnati Reds brought it north with them.
- The rain-check, which was a way of recouping financial losses. Accounts indicate management in the early 1900s was concerned by the fact that often when a game was halted by rain, more tickets were passed out to existing customers than had been taken in at the box office that day. Powell solved the problem with a detachable stub on the general admission ticket that remained useful in case the game was postponed.
- Powell would also claim to be the first player to steal home on a pitcher's windup.

Abner Powell.

Between 1901, when the Pelicans became part of the Southern Association, and 1959, when the franchise was sold, four future Hall of Fame athletes played for the club: Dizzy Vance, Joe Sewell, Bob Lemon, and Earl Weaver (as a manager). In 1947 the Pelicans drew more than four hundred thousand fans—outdrawing the American League's St. Louis Browns. It was a season later, though, that another golden age of Pelicans baseball began. Between 1948-56 the club was an affiliate of the Pittsburgh Pirates. Pelicans teams of that era included manager Danny Murtaugh, who would later skipper the Pirates to two World Series titles; infielder Gene Freese; relief pitcher Elroy Face; pitcher Vern Law; first baseman Dale Long; and outfielder Frank Thomas, all names that eventually would become familiar in America's sports pages.

Pelicans baseball will also forever be remembered for such local fan favorites as "Oyster Joe" Martina, Zeke Bonura, Mel Rue, and Larry Gilbert, all of whose name stands out in New Orleans sports history. An outstanding player, it was as a manager that Gilbert really made his mark. Under him, between 1923 and 1938, the Pelicans won five Southern Association pennants and two Dixie Series championships. He managed another five title teams later with the Nashville Volunteers.

The Pelicans' eighty-five-year epoch came to an end in 1960, a casualty of the convenience of watching major league games in the living room instead of spending an evening at the ballpark.

Skip Bertman led LSU to five NCAA championships.

The Pelicans, or at least their name, returned to New Orleans in 1977 when oilman A. Ray Smith planted his Triple A franchise there. The team included shortstop Tony LaRussa, who later gained fame as one of the majors' top managers. But Smith moved the club again after one season.

A successor to the Pelicans, the New Orleans Zephyrs came to town in 1993 and have made some history since then. The Zephyrs won the 1998 Triple A World Series, beating the Buffalo Bisons three games to one, with MVP Lance Berkman hitting three home runs and driving in six runs in a 12-6 clinching victory. The Zephyrs and Tacoma Rainiers were supposed to play for the Triple A title in 2001, but the series was canceled after the 9/11 attacks. The two teams were declared co-champions.

Lance Berkman.

Shreveport, which also had a long history in professional baseball, in recent decades became a nest of future World Series or pennant-winning managers: Dick Howser (1985 Kansas City Royals); Clarence "Cito" Gaston (1992-93 Toronto Blue Jays, the first African American to manage a Series champion); Bob Brenly (2001 Arizona Diamondbacks); and Dusty Baker (2002 San Francisco Giants, National League champions) all played in Shreveport.

Professional baseball in Shreveport dates to an 1895 team called the Grays in the Texas-Southern League. With only a few gaps, the city had a team for more than a century, from 1901 through the 2002 season—most of the time in the Double A Texas League. A succession of future major leaguers made their way through Shreveport.

The Shreveport Gassers (1915-24) provided the city's first Texas League championship in 1919. Four future Hall of Famers—Zach Wheat (1907), Bill Terry (1917), Al Simmons (1923), and George Sisler (1932)—were Shreveport players in the early years.

But it would be twenty-three years before another title.

Success was fleeting throughout the era Bonneau Peters owned the Shreveport Sports (mid-1930s through 1961) . Peters was considered one of the minor leagues' top independent operators, meaning he had few ties to any one major league organization. And, except for the years immediately after World War II, attendance was rarely significant.

There were playoff titles in 1952 and 1955, and a regular-season championship in 1954. Perhaps the top individual achievement in Shreveport's baseball life was the Texas League-record sixty-two home runs slugged in 1956 by outfielder Ken Guettler, a minor league phenomena who did little above Double A.

One of the significant figures in Shreveport baseball was Mel McGaha, a key player on the '52 team and manager from 1953-57 en route to a couple of major league managing jobs.

The Louisiana Legislature banned interracial competition in 1957, forcing the Shreveport franchise to leave the Texas League after that season. After a year, the Shreveport Sports returned in the all-white Southern Association (1959-61). When that league folded, the city was without pro ball until 1968 when the Atlanta Braves placed a franchise there.

By that time, integration was a reality.

Tayler Moore was head of a local ownership group that ran the team in Shreveport from 1976 through 2002, most of the time affiliated with the San Francisco Giants organization. Given a boost by the construction of the new Fair Grounds Field (opened in 1986), the Shreveport Captains won Texas League pennants in 1990, 1991, and again in 1995.

But after switching to the nickname Swamp Dragons for two seasons, Shreveport lost its organized baseball tie when the team moved to Frisco, Texas, after the 2002 season.

Since then Shreveport has fielded independent league teams in several forms and in several leagues.

No matter the level, like all Americans, Louisiana has loved its baseball.

From 1934 to 1957 the Evangeline Baseball League provided popular summer entertainment for small-town and rural residents. The league included teams such as the Houma Indians, Baton Rouge Red Sticks, Lafayette Oilers, Lake Charles Lakers, Thibodaux Pilots, Crowley Millers, Rayne Rice Birds, New Iberia Pelicans, Jeanerette Blues, Alexandria Aces, and Monroe Sports.

During the era of segregation, as far back as the late 1880s, separate leagues provided outlets and teams for African American players. The New Orleans Black Pelicans played at Pelican Stadium in the Negro Southern League from the 1920s until 1951. Other clubs were the New Orleans Eagles and the Creoles, with Herb Simpson, a superb first baseman and a native of the Crescent City.

The Monroe Monarchs played from the 1920s to 1935 at Casino Park, which was carved from the local Stovall plantation and considered one of the finest facilities in its league. In 1934 the team included the redoubtable hitter/outfielder Willard Brown. Despite the formal segregation customs of the day, the Monarchs' games were popular with both the black and white spectators of north Louisiana.

At times in the past five decades, joining the Zephyrs and Shreveport Sports in professional baseball, the cities of Alexandria and Lafayette had minor league affiliations with major league organizations.

They're still taking 'em out to the ball games in the Pelican State.

Zephyr Field.

HIGHWAY ROBBERY

September 10, 1974
Veterans Memorial Stadium, Philadelphia, Pennsylvania

He couldn't have known it at the time, of course, but when little Louis Clark Brock was assigned a research project in the fourth grade, he might have been writing his ticket to baseball's Hall of Fame.

The mischievous youngster threw a spitball in class. The target was a girl in the front of the room, but it hit the instructor. Punishment was to look into the lives of Joe DiMaggio, Stan Musial, and Jackie Robinson, giants of the game in the late 1940s, and write about them. The paper became an inspiration to a kid who realized for the first time that someone could make a living at playing a game.

"I didn't know a thing about baseball before this," said Lou, whose struggling family was living from hand to mouth. "I discovered these men not only ran after a little ball, but they got paid all that money. They made so much money I couldn't read the figures. I brought a book back to class and asked, 'What's this number?' It was something like $50,000 or $100,000. I became somewhat motivated."

That paper might have been responsible as much as anything for a career which Hall of Fame pitcher Tom Seaver says helped change the way baseball is played today, in which base running is an integral part of the strategy. Brock led the National League in steals eight consecutive seasons between 1966 and 1974, missing only 1970. He broke Ty Cobb's forty-nine-year-old record for career steals (938), and he broke Maury Wills's record for single season steals (118).

Sporting News ranks Brock as one of the one hundred greatest players of all time, right up there with DiMaggio, Musial, and Robinson.

☆ ☆ ☆

The Brocks—mother, one-year-old Lou, and eight brothers and sisters—moved from El Dorado, Arkansas, to Mer Rouge, Louisiana, in 1940. The small north Louisiana farming community was enriched with a Hannibal, Missouri, flavor. The boys grew up with slingshots dangling from back pockets and cane poles draped over shoulders.

"Mainly we played baseball," Lou said. "We'd dress in white shirts and ties and coats and leave our homes to go to church or Sunday school. We'd never get there. We'd strip to the waist and play ball. Later, we'd dress and go home. Our pants would be ripped, but our moms would look the other way."

In those days colleges didn't beat the bushes for baseball players, and Brock drew no interest despite a good high school career. But Brock was an excellent math and science student and was determined to get as good an education as he could, although he didn't even have enough money for a bus ride to the closest campus. After writing several schools explaining his dilemma and inquiring about any possible school employment, he received one response, from Southern University in Baton Rouge.

Thumbing his way the 160 miles to Louisiana's capital city, Lou was overjoyed to accept jobs as a campus janitor and grass cutter. By the first flower of spring, though, his thoughts returned

to baseball.

"I gave myself two weeks to make the team," he recalled. "But the coach (Emory Hines) never took one look at me those two weeks. I stayed on, practicing. I lost my jobs. I had no money. I began to visit friends' houses, right at mealtime. That's how I ate.

"I'd play left field, and if a ball was hit to right, I'd try to run it down. I was trying to impress the coach. He never saw me. After a month of this, I fell out. Right on the grass. Coach came over. He asked what happened. I told him I wanted to make the team. 'Ok,' he said. 'Swing a bat.' I didn't care how weak I was, I'd been waiting a month for this. They threw me four pitches. I hit four balls over the fence."

Brock hit only .186 as a freshman, but he did enough to earn an athletic grant-in-aid—necessary because of plummeting grades—for his sophomore year, when he batted better than .500. Southern won the NAIA championship that season, though, interestingly, little of Brock's base-stealing trademark was evident. "Actually," he said, "I didn't run much at all in college. I was a power hitter mostly, batted in the Nos. 3, 4, and 5 spots. We didn't play a running game—just hit the ball and circle the bases."

It was a style that suited Brock at the time. "I remember going 10-for-11 in a doubleheader over in Jackson (against Jackson State) one day," he recalled. "The fans said, 'Don't let that guy come over here again!'"

Professional scouts tripped over Brock while bird-dogging a promising Wiley College pitcher named Johnny Berry. Lou cracked a ninth-inning homer to breakup Berry's no-hitter. Berry gave up just one other hit—an eleventh inning Brock home run that gave Southern a 2-1 victory.

After his junior year, Brock took a $30,000 Chicago Cubs bonus, then, at St. Cloud, Minnesota, in the Northern League, he whacked out a league-best .361 and stole thirty-eight bases. The Cubs quickly brought the six-foot, 172-pound prize to the big club. And let it be recorded that on Friday, the thirteenth of April in 1962, Brock stole his first major league base against, of all teams, the St. Louis Cardinals.

The Cubs and Brock were a bad match. The player fancied himself a power hitter, while the club looked on Brock as a leadoff batter, someone for Ernie Banks and Ron Santo to drive home. Brock struck out 218 times that season, a statistic that forced perhaps the most infamous trade in Cubs history. Chicago swapped Brock and pitchers Paul Toth and Jack Spring for Cardinals pitchers Ernie Broglio and Bobby Shantz and outfielder Doug Clemons midway through the 1964 pennant race. Broglio, winner of twenty-one games in 1960 and eighteen in 1965, and .251-hitting Brock were the meat of the swap.

Brolio, 7-19 in Chicago, was out of baseball in less than three years. Brock batted .346 and stole thirty-three bases the remainder of 1964 as the Cards won the National League championship and beat the Yankees in the World Series—the first of three Fall Classics in which Brock would play.

Brock was credited by his teammates as the linchpin of their 1964 success, though the praise should have been shared with manager Johnny Keane, who restored Lou's flagging confidence. "This is yours," Keane told the player as the pair sauntered through left field the day Brock reported. "We know you can help us."

In St. Louis, Brock developed into an excellent hitter with more than three thousand career hits and a .293 lifetime average.

But it was on the base paths that he excited the fans. He was the first player to use film to study pitchers to get an edge in stealing, often using an 8mm camera in the dugout to study windups and pickoff throws.

"I calculate that in order to steal fifty bases, a player should reach first base at least two hundred times a season," Brock stated in 1975. Brock, who accomplished that feat twelve consecutive years, added, "Reaching first as many as two hundred times means you're going to have to hit safely, walk, or reach on an error. People always talk of Cincinnati's Pete Rose and his two hundred hits. But the fact is during the past few years I've always been four or five behind."

It was a formula for success, but it took a spur from Hank Aaron to push Brock back into the record books. A slow 1974 start had Brock in a blue funk. Aaron broke the daze. Lou watched the night Aaron hit his 715th home run, surpassing Babe Ruth's career total on April 8, 1974.

"Where am I?" Brock says he asked himself. "At the moment I didn't have one stolen base." In his next thirty-two attempts, Brock stole thirty bases. He added thirty-five more in the following two months and twenty-nine in August. Maury Wills's record of 104 single-season stolen bases was erased on September 10, 1974, against Philadelphia's Dick Ruthven, and Brock finished the season with 118.

Right after he passed Wills's record, a timeout was called and James "Cool Papa" Bell, a Negro League immortal, presented Lou with the very base he had just stolen. "We decided," Bell said, "to give him his 105th base because if we didn't, he was going to steal it anyway."

LIGHTNING STRIKE

June 17, 1978
Yankee Stadium, New York

Looking at the lithe figure on the mound hurling 96-mph thunderbolts past the California Angels, New York Yankees broadcaster Phil Rizzuto bellowed the only description that came to mind: "Louisiana Lightning."

Hot Ron Guidry was in the process of cooling off thanks to the nippy airflow of bats swishing through what seemed to be an empty strike zone. It was a performance that put Guidry in the company of such major league legends as Sandy Koufax, Bob Feller, and Warren Spahn, Hall of Fame pitchers who struck out as many as eighteen batters in a single game.

"His ball was exploding," said Ted Hendley, the plate umpire that game.

Guidry had a noteworthy career, pitching fourteen years for the Yankees as a reliever, closer, and starter. Between 1977 and 1983 he was the winningest pitcher in the game (113-57). He left a deep enough imprint for his No. 49 jersey to be retired and a plaque—alongside that of Babe Ruth, Joe DiMaggio, et al—honoring him to be placed in Yankee Stadium's Monument Park reading: "A dominating pitcher and respected leader of the pitching staff for three American League pennants and two world championships. A true Yankee."

After almost a decade and half in the major leagues, Guidry—never a serious contender for Cooperstown, though perhaps he should have been—retired with a 170-91 record, a .651 percentage, and an ERA of 3.29. Hands-down Hall of Famer Koufax, in comparison, retired after twelve seasons with a 165-87 record (.655) and an ERA of 2.76.

Not arguing pro or con, just saying. . . .

Still, Guidry will always be remembered as much for one of the most stunning seasons ever pitched, in 1978, the year he earned Rizzuto's appellation, as for his total career. Think about it: A third of a century after that 25-3 season, Guidry still owns team records (and remember we are talking the New York Yankees) for most shutouts (nine, shared with Babe Ruth in 1916); lowest ERA for a left-hander (1.74, second lowest in American League annals and tied with Koufax for lowest for a LHP since 1933); highest winning percentage (.893, the major leagues' highest in forty-four years and the best in history for a twenty-game winner); most strikeouts (248, breaking a Yankee record that stood for seventy-four years); thirteen consecutive victories at the start of a season; and sixteen complete games (five in which five or fewer hits were recorded).

Guidry became the first unanimous Cy Young Award recipient in a decade.

In Carencro, the heart of French-speaking Louisiana, Grace Guidry, reading about her son, exclaimed, "All of this is like a dream. I never dreamed it would happen. But here it is. It's happening."

So how did it happen that an undersized kid who never even played high school baseball could become one the most prominent pitchers of the sport for more than a decade?

Part of the answer is he was a natural. The first time Ron Guidry ever picked up a baseball, at age eight, he claims he threw "a seed."

"When I was ten," he said, "I could knock a sparrow out of a tree with a rock. When I was fifteen I could kill a rabbit with a rock."

These were talents that didn't particularly appeal to Grace.

"Since I was an only child," Ron said, "my mother was kind of protective. She didn't want me messing with the other kids because she was afraid I'd get in trouble."

Roland Guidry convinced his wife the boy should be allowed to play for the local park's Half-Pint team, although she was adamant it wouldn't be as a pitcher. "She didn't mind Ron playing baseball," said Roland. "But she didn't want him on the mound. She was afraid of him getting hurt, getting hit by a line drive. So he started out at eight and nine playing the outfield and first base. The boys on the team kept putting pressure on me.

They saw what Ron could do at practice, so they got me to work on my wife. Finally, it happened. He started pitching. The Half-Pints started winning. And his mother came to see him. She was amazed."

At Lafayette's Northside High, lean and agile Ron was one of the school's finest athletes. He ran a 9.8 100-yard dash and a 49-second 440, and quarterbacked a touch-football team through two unbeaten seasons. Northside, however, did not field a baseball team. The American Legion program was the sole baseball outlet for the budding outfielder/pitcher, whose fastball was beginning to attract attention.

"I was fifteen and pitching in American Legion," Guidry remembered, "when a batter squared around to bunt, and I hit him with a fastball that I was only trying to get inside. It broke his collarbone. He was a friend and it really bothered me."

★ ★ ★

Guidry's competitiveness overshadowed his still-developing talent at the University of Southwestern Louisiana (now the University of Louisiana at Lafayette).

"Ronnie was always a competitor," explained Tigue Moore, who started Guidry in American Legion. "Always wanted a challenge. He wanted to pitch against New Iberia, Lafayette's big rival. And when he got to USL, he wanted to pitch against LSU. That's where they first took notice of him. He pitched against LSU under the lights in Baton Rouge, and he threw nothing but smoke."

USL teammate Charles Bordes remembered an iron-armed doubleheader against Division II power Nicholls State.

"He asked to pitch both games. We wound up losing both . . . but Ron pitched the first one, kept warming up between games, and then pitched the second. He always loved to challenge the hitters."

Thought by most of baseball to be undraftable after his sophomore season, scout Atley Donald—a former Yankees pitcher who grew up in Louisiana and decades before played at Louisiana Tech—found out Guidry had dropped out of school and was thus available. On Donald's advice, the Yankees selected Guidry in the third round of the 1971 free-agent draft.

It was somewhat of a gamble, despite Ron's credentials, because his 7-4 sophomore record, with a 2.37 ERA, was largely built on one pitch, the fastball. New York took the chance, probably in hopes of developing a short reliever.

★ ★ ★

The biggest question was not whether Guidry's fastball was major league, but rather how someone with a five-foot-eleven frame that never carried more than 160 pounds could throw fastballs with comet-like tails.

Guidry didn't have an answer, but suspected Cajun cuisine—frog legs, seafood platters, crawfish étouffée, and sirloin—played a part.

"I've never dieted, and I hope I never do," he said. "For me, eating is like putting coals on a stove. It burns away. I'm always doing something. I don't have any one answer. What it is is a gift. Physically, I guess, it could be a number of little things. Thinness of body, length of muscles, a fluid motion, strong legs. Ever since I was a kid I was able to throw faster than the other guy."

★ ★ ★

A second part of the Guidry equation was opportunity. Because of his slight size, he didn't have the confidence of the club, including owner George Steinbrenner, who had Guidry sent up and down the club's chain. When he was with the big club, he was seldom used. In one four-game sweep, Guidry was utilized as a pinch-hitter only. The most oft-repeated story of Guidry's rise is how his wife talked him into giving baseball a last try after the disheartened pitcher turned his car in the direction of Louisiana on the New Jersey Turnpike.

That season Guidry was told, on the last day of spring training, to report to the Yankees. Then the club changed its mind, and Bonnie had to do some fast talking in order to get Ron to change the course of their south-bound auto. He was called up in May, sent down to Syracuse in July, and recalled in August.

"Before they sent Ron down," Bonnie said, "he got a chewing out from George Steinbrenner. He said Ronnie was a big disappointment. But what did he expect? The Yankees kept him idle for sixty-one days, then let him pitch three innings. He didn't pitch well. After sitting around all that time, is that surprising?"

That idle time, as it happened, proved beneficial. Veterans Sparky Lyle and Dick Tidrow took the unhappy youngster under their wings. Lyle taught Guidry the slider—a sort of half-curve, half-fastball—giving him another pitch (actually three, since he learned to throw it at three different speeds). Tidrow taught him the general ins and outs of pitching philosophy. Guidry used the spring to experiment and get in shape, but manager Billy Martin muttered darkly of an exhibition-season performance that produced a ghastly 10.24 ERA in six games. Steinbrenner wondered out loud of trading Guidry. General manager Gabe Paul said he would agree to the unloading, but with a stipulation: That Steinbrenner put in writing that the move was made over the protestations of his GM.

When Mike Torrez was late in reporting, Guidry was given the April 29, 1977, starting assignment. He shut out Seattle 3-0. Then he took a turn for the injured Catfish Hunter, and suddenly Martin realized he had found a stopper.

At the All-Star break Guidry was 6-5, but his 10-2 spurt thereafter lifted the Yankees to a World Series championship. The combination of his fastball, slider, and the experience he was now getting made Guidry an American League force.

"I was not surprised at the year altogether," Guidry said. "I knew I could pitch here."

He did wonder, though, at the vagaries of life.

"What if Sparky hadn't taken the time to show me the slider; I don't think I would have been here," he mused. "And if Dick hadn't spoken to me about pitching, I don't think I would have known what to do with the slider once Sparky taught it to me. They can claim part of my success. I've told them that already. They did it out of friendship and generosity.

"But what if Sparky had said, 'I'm not going to teach you the slider.' What if Dick had said, 'I don't want to talk to you about pitching.'"

Well, you'd have to wonder if Atley Donald was second-guessing himself for signing Guidry. When Guidry won his thirteenth consecutive game in 1978, the record he broke was the one set in 1939—by Atley Donald.

LONG SHOTS

July 31, 1954
Ebbets Field, Brooklyn, New York

Joe Bill Adcock is practically a one-man trivia quiz.

Here are several major-league teasers to which Adcock is the correct answer: (1) Who is the first player to total eighteen bases in one nine-inning game?; (2) Who was the first (and one of only three ever) to hit a home run to the mammoth center field bleachers of New York's Polo Grounds—483 feet from home plate?; (3) Who hit a memorable shot over the right-center field fence of Milwaukee County Stadium but was credited with a double?

For a guy who had never played organized baseball until entering LSU on a basketball scholarship, that's leaving quite an imprint on the game.

Adcock, a native of Coushatta, retired after seventeen seasons in the major leagues as the twentieth most prolific home run hitter of all time and with the third highest career fielding percentage (.994) for a first baseman.

An overview of Adcock's extraordinary career brings up the most perplexing question of all: Where exactly was the high point?

★ ★ ★

In the first inning of a game in Brooklyn, Adcock, batting cleanup, dug in. "Don Newcombe tried to jam me," he recalled decades later, "and there wasn't a man made who could jam me."

He must have been right. Certainly he was on that day in a game between the Dodgers and Adcock's Milwaukee Braves. Using backup catcher Charlie White's bat because he broke his own the night before, Adcock hit a first-inning shot down the left-field line that threatened to hook foul, but ended up in the stands.

In the third inning, the Braves first baseman came up twice against reliever Erv Palica. Adcock doubled and homered.

There was one on when Adcock came up against Pete Wojey in the seventh. He again sent the ball out of the park.

Leading off the ninth against twenty-one-year-old left-hander Johnny Podres, Adcock again homered to pick up his seventh RBI of the game.

In that 15-7 win, the Braves put on the greatest offensive performance in major league history to that point. Adcock homered four times against four Dodgers pitchers and amassed an astounding eighteen total bases.

Dodgers trainer Don Wendler recalled that game years later, awestruck.

"That double went over the scoreboard and into the screen in right-center, and it looked as if it were taking off when it hit the wall," Wendler said. "One of Joe's homers that night was over the roof in left-center in old Ebbets Field. That was no cheap home run."

Talk about a record for the ages, and the story gets better. The day before, Adcock had a homer, a double, and a single, giving him twenty-five total bases in two games, tying a record set by Ty Cobb in 1925. It got better yet. In a third game, in his first at-bat, Adcock hit another double, giving him twenty-six total bases in ten at-bats.

"All it would take to break my record (for a single nine-inning game),"Adcock deadpanned twenty-five years later, "is for some hitter to get up and poke four homers and a triple. That would be nineteen total bases and that would do it."

Sure enough, somebody did eventually surpass Adcock. Shawn Green of the, ironically, Los Angeles Dodgers collected nineteen total bases in 2002 against, ironically, the Milwaukee Brewers, on four homers, a double, and a single.

Only took forty-eight years.

★ ★ ★

In the 1945-46 basketball season, Adcock was the leading scorer for the LSU Tigers, averaging 18.6 points a game. In the 1946 baseball season, in a game he had never really played, Adcock was a hard-hitting first baseman for the SEC champion Tigers.

Everything Adcock did on the diamond, then and later, came

Former LSU Tiger Joe Adcock in the locker room after hitting four home runs in a single game, which is still tied for the MLB record.

about because of Red Swanson, an LSU assistant coach in football, basketball, and baseball, who saw something in the fluid-moving, six-foot-four, 220-pound athlete that simply said "baseball."

Swanson, who took over baseball duties when Coach Jess Fatheree was called into the service, asked Adcock to give the game a try.

Adcock would later say, "Coach Swanson told me to come out for the team because we had some good road trips coming up. But I had never played high school baseball. All we ever played on the sandlots up home was 'One-Eyed Cat.' Heck, I didn't even have a baseball glove."

Swanson told his regular first baseman (Sinclair Kouns) to take Adcock out and teach him the rudiments of the position. "Sinclair still says he taught me how to play first base," Adcock said, "and lost his own job."

Three years later Adcock had his choice of which sport he wanted to pursue as a professional. The right-handed batter was drafted by the Cincinnati Reds. The New York Knicks of the NBA also offered him a contract, but the Reds paid him a bonus to stick strictly to baseball.

If he hadn't agreed, the sport might have missed out on some of its most memorable moments.

★ ★ ★

By 1953, his first season with the Braves, Adcock served notice that he was growing into a formidable power hitter. Early in the season, on April 29, he belted a home run of epic proportions in New York's Polo Grounds.

Years after the fact, Adcock said, "I can still see the pitch I hit in the Polo Grounds bleachers off Jim Hearn of the New York Giants." Probably so could any one of the 3,927 fans in attendance. It was that awesome.

He not only sent Hearn's fastball an estimated 475 feet from home plate, but the center-field wall in the Polo Grounds had a fence and screen that was nine feet high. The ball reached the tenth row of the ball park, making spectators' jaws drop at the ball park and causing screaming headlines the next day. A fan named Bob Eidelman retrieved the ball and, after the 3-2 Braves win, swapped it for two warmup balls and a $25 check from Milwaukee manager Charlie Grimm.

The mammoth home run in a park built in 1911 had never been done, and would be accomplished only two other times—by Henry Aaron and Lou Brock—before the stadium was demolished in 1964.

★ ★ ★

Harvey Haddix of the Pittsburgh Pirates was pitching major league baseball's greatest game ever on May 26, 1959. Against the defending National League champion Braves, in twelve innings, Haddix mowed down every one of the thirty-six batters he faced.

In the thirteenth inning, however, Milwaukee's Felix Mantilla reached first on an infield error, ending the quest for a perfect game. Mantilla moved to second on a sacrifice bunt, then Hank Aaron was intentionally walked. Up came Adcock.

Damp, foggy night winds were swirling around Milwaukee County Stadium, but Adcock said when he looked at the ramparts, "That flag was still as a mouse."

On Haddix's second pitch to him, Adcock caught a high slider and sent it out of the park, obliterating Haddix's magnificent performance.

That wasn't the end of things, though.

As Adcock trotted around the bases, Mantilla scored. But Aaron had a brain freeze. Thinking the ball had hit the fence instead of going into the stands, Aaron cut across the diamond to the dugout.

Because of the blunder, National League president Warren Giles ruled that Adcock's home run was a double and that Mantilla was the only run that scored. Officially the game is listed as a 1-0 Braves victory.

Still, it satisfied Adcock. His team had won, and he had proved—again—a point to himself. Adcock said to his dying day in 1999, "I never felt there was a pitcher I couldn't hit."

SUNDAY SPECIAL

August 21, 1929
Fenway Park, Boston, Massachusetts

A 2010 blog made an insightful and valid list of five "Amazing Baseball Records" and drew an intriguing response.

"I still marvel at Ted Lyons at the age of forty-one completing all his starts (twenty) in 1942 and leading the American League with a 2.10 ERA," wrote Tal Smith, then-president of the Houston Astros. Obviously in awe of a feat that has nearly disappeared from the sport, Smith added: "For his (twenty-three-year) career, Lyons completed 356 of 484 (73.6 percent) of the games he started."

Lyons was rarely in the baseball spotlight most of his years in the big leagues, toiling for the woeful White Sox during what Chicagoans called their "Snowball in Hell" stretch in the aftermath of the Black Sox Scandal. Sixteen of the twenty-one years before World War II, the Sox finished in fifth place or lower (never higher than third) in an eight-team league; had only five winning records; and wound up an average of thirty games out of first place.

Yet, Lyons always shone through the Sox's darkness. Three times during that period (1925, 1927, 1930), the right-hander won twenty or more games. In 1925, he won twenty-one games, tops in the American League, pitching for a fifth-place team. In 1929, Lyons threw an AL-leading twenty-nine complete games and 297 2/3 innings for a team that finished 62-92. He had a 22-15 record. In 1934 Lyons threw forty-two consecutive innings without giving up a base on balls.

In Lyons's last years manager Jimmy Dykes began using him only in Sunday afternoon games because he was the only gate attraction the Sox had to lure decent crowds. That earned Lyons the moniker "Sunday Teddy," and he made the most of the situation, winning fifty-two of eighty-two games in that scenario.

After coming back from the Marines in World War II, Lyons retired with what seemed a so-so 260-230 career record. But his peers knew better.

"If Ted Lyons had pitched for the Yankees," exclaimed Joe McCarthy, manager of the Yanks during most of Lyons's career, "he would have won four hundred games." Bob Feller ranked Lyons among his top ten of all time. In the late 1930s, Babe Ruth, then retired, showed up for a Yankees-White Sox game, not, he said, to see the Yankees play, but to see Lyons pitch.

In a powerful assessment, Hall of Fame player-manager Tris Speaker said, "If I had the choice of any pitcher for a clutch game, the guy I'd pick is Ted Lyons."

And Ted Williams said the more someone came to plate against Lyons the worse things got for the batter: "He'd learn more about you by playing those little pitcher-batter thinking games, and he'd usually out think you."

A barometer of how highly thought of Lyons was came in the Hall of Fame balloting of 1955. Only three other pitchers were elected in the entire decade of the 1950s, and when Lyons was inducted at Cooperstown, he received 86.45 percent of the vote—second only to Joe DiMaggio's 88.84 .

Lyons, born in 1900 and five foot eleven, two hundred pounds in his prime, first played the game as an eight year old with a broomstick and a sock sewn into a ball in Vinton, in southwestern Louisiana.

In Donald Honig's oral history *Baseball When The Grass Was Real*, Lyons said he occupied himself all summer with baseball.

"I was a ninety-pound second baseman in high school," he said. "I used a big Joe Jackson bat . . . and I had to choke it up maybe two-thirds of the way and kind of push at the ball. A few years later I got up to 135 pounds, and I started pitching. I was sixteen years old then."

A multi-sport athlete at Baylor University, Lyons was spotted twice as a baseball prospect. Connie Mack's Philadelphia Athletics trained in Lake Charles, about twenty miles from the Lyons's hometown. Seeing Lyons on the mound, Mack offered to pay his way through school if he signed with the A's. Ted turned him down. Then, as a senior at Baylor, the White Sox were working out near Waco. A newspaperman, looking for an angle for a story, got Lyons to pitch to Sox catcher Ray Schalk.

"I had a pretty good fastball back then, and I let him know it," Lyons recalled. "After the workout Schalk and some of the other fellows came over and said there was a possibility they might contact me. That pleased me because the White Sox were one of my favorite teams when I was a kid. At the end of the school year in June (1923), after I graduated, I signed up. I got a $1,000 bonus. I took it and bought myself a Ford car. A brand new Model T. That was my first car. Cost me $428. What would you say a new Ford would cost today?"

Lyons motored to St. Louis, where the club was playing the Browns. He never spent an inning in the minor leagues.

It was the start of a notable career, highlighted by a 1925 game in which he held the Washington Senators hitless until two were gone in the ninth inning, then a 1929 no-hitter against the Boston Red Sox.

Lyons threw five straight balls to open the game and saw out of the corner of his eye a reliever warming up. A line drive was caught at shoetop level, and the baserunner was thrown out by center fielder Johnny Mostil at first. Only one other runner reached base, on an error, and Lyons completed the 6-0 no-hitter in the phenomenal time of sixty-seven minutes—but perhaps fitting for a pitcher whose average game over two decades lasted one hour and forty-five minutes.

Before 1931, Lyons was the master of the "sailer," a cut fastball. An arm injury caused him to retool his weaponry, and he started using a knuckler, curve, and changeup to great effectiveness.

"He lost his fastball pretty early," said retired *Chicago Sun-Times* baseball writer Ed Munzel in 1992, "but developed a knuckler and had such great control that he might not throw more than eighty-five, eighty-eight pitches in a game."

In his era, long before free agency, Lyons never got the chance to move to a pennant contender. And the White Sox were not about to give up their most popular and valuable player, even though he had high trade value.

"I didn't find it frustrating," he said at the end of his career. "It would have been nice to win a pennant, just one, to see what it's like, but Chicago is a wonderful town with wonderful fans."

Lyons perhaps isn't that well-remembered among Hall of Famers, even in his home state. But that isn't the case in Chicago, where his career has been compared to the Cubs' Ernie Banks, who also spent his career in the Windy City on teams that were seldom in contention.

Lyons moved back to Louisiana to help with a sick sister and eventually began experiencing medical problems himself. In 1983, the White Sox wanted to retire Lyons' jersey, but he resisted invitations to return to Chicago, citing his sister's illness.

"His sight was gone, and he had a lot of trouble with his legs," said Chuck Comiskey, grandson of White Sox founder Charles Comiskey. "I think he was embarrassed because someone would have had to help him onto the field. He had that kind of pride."

Lyons's No. 16 was finally retired in 1987, one year after his death in a Sulphur, Louisiana, nursing home.

Ted Lyons with fellow Hall of Famers at Yankee Stadium for old-timers day, August 1, 1955; (left to right) Joe DiMaggio, Gabby Hartnett, Ted Lyons, Dazzy Vance, Ray Schalk, and Home Run Baker.

MASTER MELVIN

August 1, 1945
Polo Grounds, New York

Forget the fact that Mel Ott hit 511 home runs—an achievement that at the time of his retirement was the highest for any National League player, and surpassed only by two others, American Leaguers Babe Ruth (714) and Jimmie Foxx (534).

Ott was much more than just a home run hitter. He was a total ballplayer.

To put Ott in true context, answer this multi-layered trivia question about some Hall of Fame titans:

What baseball player had more career hits than Babe Ruth (2,876-2,873); a better career batting average than Willie Mays (.304-.302); a better career slugging average than Mike Schmidt (.533-.527); and more career bases on balls than Stan Musial (1,708-1,599)?

Of course, the answer to all of the above is Ott, the fresh-faced kid who reported at the tender age of sixteen to John McGraw, the prickly and legendary New York Giants manager. At a time when the main concern of his contemporaries back home at Gretna's McDonoghville-Jefferson High School was the popping of pimples and/or planning for the prom, Ott suddenly was involved in on-the-job training to solve major league pitching.

Did McGraw's tutelage take? Well, when Ott retired twenty-two years later he left the National League records not only for home runs and bases on balls, but also for runs scored (1,859), RBIs (1,860), total bases (5,041), extra base hits (1,071), extra bases on long hits (2,165), and most double plays for an outfielder in a season (12)—a record that still stands. He set a total of twenty-three club and league records; he hit thirty or more homers eight times and led the NL in that category six times; and nine times he drove in one hundred runs or more.

Any reasonable observer might have to say, yeah, something seems to have clicked in this unlikely journey to Cooperstown.

* * *

"Mr. McGraw," the boy muttered shyly in the Giants manager's office, "I'm Mel Ott."

Those words in September 1925 ushered in an era at Coogan's Bluff, the home area of the New York Giants.

But New York, with its gigantic skyscrapers and polyglot population, isn't the West Bank of New Orleans, where Ott was supposed to be finishing his senior year of high school. How did he ever get to the bustle of Gotham from sluggish Gretna, across the mighty Mississippi from the Crescent City?

Ott was a catcher when he and teammate Lester Rouprich worked out with the New Orleans Pelicans of the Southern Association, hoping to draw interest from the club. Manager Larry Gilbert said later of his first look at the teen, who threw right-handed and batted left, "He was just a kid, but one of the greatest natural hitters I ever saw. His catching was like that of any high school catcher, but his hitting was something to see."

Owner Alex Heinemann, however, felt the boy was too small and much, much too young.

Harry Williams, millionaire sponsor of a summer semi-pro team in Patterson, Louisiana, about ninety miles from New Orleans, wasn't as choosy. Williams, a lumberman and the husband of silent movie actress Marguerite Clark, needed a player. "I told Harry," Gilbert said, "that I wanted Rouprich right back, as we were sending him to the Cotton States League, but he might want to keep Ott up there."

With an unorthodox batting style from which he drew unusual power for a smallish player (five foot nine, 160 pounds in his prime), the left-handed hitting Ott would raise his right foot and point it toward the mound on the pitcher's delivery.

"I really don't know when I started doing it," Ott once said, "but I found that when I tossed my right leg up, it threw all my weight into my swing."

If it looked peculiar, the results were impressive. The stance spawned a gorgeous, effective swing.

In a short time Mel was the hottest thing going in the semi pro league. His reputation swelled so that Heinemann had a change of heart and offered Ott twice the $150-a-month plus room and board Williams was paying. He called McGraw, a personal friend, who telegrammed Ott to report for a tryout.

With Williams heading for a European vacation and not on hand, Mel thought the cable was a prank by the sometimes eccentric businessman.

"What are you doing HERE?" shrieked Williams upon his return. Although his mother felt the boy should go back to school, Mel's father convinced her this was a not-to-be missed opportunity.

Ott, still plump with baby fat, walked tepidly into the Polo Grounds, spikes over his shoulder and suitcase in one hand, catcher's mitt in the other, to find what fate had in store.

★ ★ ★

The following day, with Ott taking batting practice, McGraw whispered excitedly to Frankie Frisch, "Did you see that?" Mel was firing screamers off the outfield wall. "He's just like one of those golfers," McGraw marveled. "His whole body moves but his head doesn't. I don't give a damn about that crazy kick (but) that's the best natural swing I've seen in years!"

Wanting no one to tamper with Ott's pure swing, after signing the boy to a $400 bonus and a minimal contract to simply sit next to him and learn the game, McGraw determined he would not be sent to the minor leagues. The manager also realized Ott had no future in catching. "Did you ever play the outfield?" Big John asked. "Yes, sir! When I was a kid," Mel answered. "Good," McGraw retorted with a laugh. "Next spring at Sarasota you can start all over again."

Ott credited McGraw's "desire for perfection" with making him a good right fielder, working Mel tirelessly on playing the tricky, angled wall in right field.

Thick leg muscles made Ott susceptible to cramps, and he also had to put in hours of work in learning the fundamentals of base running, a skill in which he was woefully weak. A New York track coach, Bernie Wefers, was sent to Florida to instruct Mel on the essentials of running. "It's a good thing I could hit," cracked Ott, thinking back on his early deficiencies.

"He'll never go to the Olympics," McGraw assessed, "but at least he'll be able to come in on a ground ball."

Mel played in thirty-five games in the 1926 season, primarily as a pinch-hitter. On May 2, on his second at-bat, he got his first major league hit.

"I'll never forget the first time I saw Ott in the National League," said umpire Cy Pfirman. "He was pinch-hitting, and when he stepped to the plate, only seventeen years old, I thought we had a kindergarten league. But when he smacked that ball I changed my mind, quick."

On his first starting assignment, on August 21, against St. Louis and Grover Cleveland Alexander, the United Press identified Ott as ". . . an eighteen-year-old boy." Mel was seventeen, but the reporter thought McGraw was pulling his leg and had given him the wrong age.

In 1927 Ott played in eighty-two games, batting .282. Chicago's Hal Carlson had the distinction of giving up Mel's first home run, an inside-the-park screamer that skidded under Hack Wilson's glove. Homers became habit-forming. To a pull hitter like Ott, just the sight of the Polo Grounds' 257-foot right-field fence must have been mouth watering. Of Ott's 511 home runs, 323 were sent whistling out of the Polo Grounds.

A major factor in three Giants' World Series appearances, Ott went four-for-four against Washington in the 1933 Classic, including a four hundred-foot home run that staked New York to a 2-0 lead in what was eventually a 4-2 victory. In the fifth and deciding game, Ott hit a tenth-inning title-clinching homer (originally ruled a double after the outfielder got his glove on the ball before disappearing from sight after toppling over the low center-field fence. The decision was overruled, and Ott was the Series hero).

On Augusr 1, 1945, when Ott was player/manager of the Giants, he set the bar for National League sluggers. He reached five hundred home runs with a shot against Johnny Hutchings of the Boston Braves.

★ ★ ★

The first year he was eligible, Ott was elected to the Hall of Fame with 87 percent of the vote, meaning there was never any doubt about his worthiness. For all his achievements, however, he seems almost a forgotten superstar. In part, perhaps, because his home runs are downgraded because of the short right field of the Polo Grounds, and also perhaps in part because he was quiet, non-controversial, and seen as a genuinely nice guy—which is what he is remembered for today as much as anything.

In 1946, when Leo Durocher was the fiery manager of the Brooklyn Dodgers and Ott was managing the Giants, broadcaster Red Barber commented that Leo the Lip should make an attempt at being more of a nice guy.

"Nice guy," Durocher snorted. "Being a nice guy gets you nowhere. Absolutely nowhere! Look over there," Leo bellowed, pointing to Ott in the opposing dugout. "There's one of the nicest guys in the world. Is it doing him any good? He's in last place. That's where nice guys finish. Last!"

That outburst has found a permanent niche in American parlance.

Ten years later, when forty-nine-year-old Ott was killed in an automobile accident, it was Durocher who said from the heart, "That was nicest guy ever to put on a shoe."

It was a tribute to the man. The record book stood in mute testimony to an all-around great ballplayer.

SHOWING THE WAY

June 2, 1984
Rosenblatt Stadium, Omaha, Nebraska

It was a perfect baseball scenario. Mark Higgins belted a grand-slam in the fourth inning and freshman pitcher David Lynch had command, striking out nine in his seven-plus innings.

The University of New Orleans was cruising past the University of Michigan 11-3.

This wasn't just any college baseball game. This was the College World Series.

It's not uncommon now for Louisiana schools to make, compete in, and even win the CWS. Tulane, UL Lafayette, and LSU have been there. There have been times when multiple Pelican State teams have made it to Rosenblatt Stadium, the former mecca of the college game, at the same time.

But, under the Johnny Appleseed of Louisiana college baseball, Coach Ron Maestri, UNO was the first of the "big" schools to get there.

Although Maestri's Privateers had made the Division II College World Series in 1974, when UNO competed in the small college ranks, thirteen years after he took over the program—originally having to sow the field, cut the grass, coach without assistants, and work on the design of a new stadium (built without state appropriations)—he now had his team on the sport's biggest stage.

To say Maestri—and the Privateers—did it the hard way would be an understatement.

On the field, the 46-26 Privateers had to win the South II Regional at Mississippi State, the college standard bearer of the area at the time, and a field that included heavyweight South Carolina. They did, beating the Bulldogs 6-3 in a game that meant more to Maestri than he ever let on.

Knowing a challenge when he saw it, Maestri came to New Orleans in 1972 when baseball at UNO, then a satellite campus in the Louisiana State University system, was two years old. At the time an assistant at Bradley in Peoria, Illinois, the Braves' head-coaching job would have been his in a year when Coach Joe Stowell retired. A chance meeting at a basketball tournament at Gulf Coast Junior College with UNO's first basketball coach and athletics director Ron Greene, who also attended Bradley briefly, set things in motion.

The job at first required Maestri to serve as an assistant basketball coach, although he went seven years before he had a baseball assistant himself. Tom Schwaner, a former high school coach who eventually succeeded Maestri, was the first UNO baseball assistant and got the job because he worked for nothing.

Taking on the upkeep of the field himself and coaching wasn't all Maestri did. He talked the administration into letting him manage the concessions at Privateers events to subsidize his meager budget.

It became a solid program built on Maestri's back, though he was always quick to point out that Homer Hitt, the founding chancellor of the school, was always supportive and that he got immeasurable help from such people as Herman Farley, a florist who in his spare time helped Maestri build the original field.

It became a program that excelled on sheer determination and grit. Although working with six scholarships—less than half of the NCAA allotment of thirteen—and a lean budget, Maestri's teams went to three NCAA tournaments in his first eight seasons, including the small college World Series.

Lenny Yochim, special assignment scout for the Pittsburgh Pirates, marveled at the accomplishment.

"When you travel around the country and you look at the facilities and money other schools have, and you look at what he's done . . ." Yochim said, "it's amazing. The guy's a magician."

In 1979, Hitt got Maestri some land on the east campus, near the current site of Lakefront Arena, and Maestri moved the Privateers into a new facility and gradually improved the park until it became a million-dollar showcase—again without any state money or help. The new field was—and is—a result of Maestri's boundless energy. He designed it, conceived the advertising program to make it financially feasible, and meticulously oversaw its grooming.

"I did what was necessary," he said.

☆ ☆ ☆

What Maestri did altered the course of the college sport in Louisiana, which had always been kind of a casual spring pastime. UNO started beating teams across the region and making a name for itself against the so-called Big Boys.

"This was clearly an up-and-coming program," recalled a University of Miami assistant of a game between the Hurricanes and Privateers in 1977. "They were well-coached," said Skip Bertman, who later also would have an influence on baseball in Louisiana.

Bertman also agreed that Maestri was a Pied Piper of college baseball in the Pelican State, where the game always has been played well but at a lower lever of intensity and interest than today.

Tulane generally had been a fair program but was forced to ratchet it up a notch because of the sudden presence, and easy comparison, with a neighbor reaching heights never before seriously envisioned for Green Wave baseball. LSU also had been an up-and-down program, but when UNO and Tulane got better, the Tigers had to as well. They did, and because of LSU's extraordinary success, other state schools began putting resources into baseball, to the point that Louisiana now has a half-dozen quality programs.

"When you think of it like that," Bertman mused, "Maestri had a lot to do with it."

The perfect ending to a fairytale story would have been for UNO to win the national championship.

Didn't happen.

Beating powerful Mississippi State, with Orleanian Will Clark and Rafael Palmeiro in the Bulldogs' lineup, in the regional to get to the CWS might have been the high point of the season. The Privateers, with three future major leaguers (Higgins, Wally Whitehurst, and Jim Bullinger) in the lineup, lost to eventual champion Texas 6-3 in its first Series game, then belted Michigan before losing 8-7 on a walkoff home run to Oklahoma State.

It was a more than respectable showing for the Privateers.

But it was the memory of beating State to get to Omaha that Maestri truly relished.

"Years before," Maestri said, "when we were first getting the program off the ground, we had just gotten our old field in somewhat playable condition, though the infield wasn't settled yet when we played Mississippi State. They were really the model program in the South at the time, the one everyone tried to emulate. We were just trying to reach respectability."

When Mississippi State arrived, Maestri asked if the Bulldogs could do the traditional pregame hitting practice off the infield, as UNO was doing, in order to save wear on the tender area for the game. "Coach Paul Gregory was a real gentleman and had no problem with it," Maestri said, "but one of the assistants lit into me. He was yelling about what a great program they had and here they were, reduced to playing this rinky-dink outfit."

Later, after State thumped UNO, a despondent Maestri retreated to a shed, located on the uneven and spongy ground where hard-hit balls sometimes died without so much as a bounce, and reflected on the affront. Realizing how far his program had to go, he almost cried.

"It's not something I dwelled on," Maestri said, "but when we beat Mississippi State to reach the College World Series, I did think about it."

UNO Privateers Coach Ron Maestri.

THE SHOWSTOPPER

June 16, 1996
Rosenblatt Stadium, Omaha, Nebraska

There it was, in the situation that all kids imagine at playtime, "two out in the ninth inning, trailing by a run . . . and I step into the batter's box. . . ."

We all know how that plays out in every youngster's mind: with a game-winning home run.

Warren Morris lived that dream for real, and to say he simply rose to the occasion is an understatement.

The shot—Morris's first of the season—gave LSU a 9-8 victory over the Miami Hurricanes, the 1996 College World Series championship, the single most memorable moment in the Tigers' storied baseball history, and it made a Louisiana folk hero of Morris, a Tiger who not only missed a major portion of the season with an injury but wasn't even on the team as an athlete on grant-in-aid.

He was at LSU on an academic scholarship.

Skip Bertman built a baseball dynasty at LSU, coaching the Tigers to five national championships in a ten-year span, and making thirteen College World Series appearances in his eighteen years at the helm. Paul Maineri followed suit with another title, giving the program championships in 1991, 1993, 1996, 1997, 2000, and 2009.

And Morris's feat isn't the only do-or-die LSU drama ever to be played out at venerable Rosenblatt Stadium. In 2000, Brad Cresse's RBI single in the bottom of the ninth brought home the winning run for a 6-5 victory over Stanford, as the Tigers rallied from a three-run deficit.

But, maybe because it involved an improbable homer, Morris's heroics are what immediately pop into the minds of fans when the subject turns to LSU baseball, much like Billy Cannon's famed eighty-nine-yard punt return is the signature play of Tigers football. And perhaps people also remember Morris's game because it was such an unlikely outcome after a series of self-inflicted wounds.

- In the fifth inning, a two-out fly to left field that Chad Cooley appeared to catch was ruled a two-run triple, putting Miami ahead 5-3.
- The Hurricanes notched two more runs in the sixth when the Tigers mishandled three straight bunts, two of which were ruled as errors.
- LSU base-running mistakes cost the Tigers a run in the third inning and another in the fifth.
- When the Tigers scored twice in the eighth, erasing a four-run deficit and tying the score at 7, reliever Patrick Coogan surrendered two hits with two outs in the top of the ninth to put Miami back in the lead, 8-7.
- Bertman went out to the mound with the intention of taking Coogan out. "He challenged me," Coogan said. "He asked me if I really wanted to be in the game. I said, 'Hell, yeah.'"

He retired Miami's next batter on a weak fly to center field, setting the scene for the Tigers' ninth.

Morris, nicknamed "Mercury," put his status on the team in perspective when he said with a wide grin: "I'm pretty much a freebie."

As a prospect at Alexandria's Bolton High School, Morris was unnoticed—and unrecruited—by LSU. Morris had never so much as been offered a free ride at LSU. Not even a partial scholarship.

He did his hitting on an academic scholarship, and his grade-point average of 3.728 in zoology was even more impressive than his batting average of .455 in the '95 SEC divisional tournament.

Morris, who was a left-handed batter but a right-handed thrower, was a preseason All-American at second base, so he wasn't exactly an unknown quantity.

In October 1996, however, he broke the hamate bone in his right wrist. He tried to play through the pain and participated in twenty games, but the discomfort became too intense. Morris consented to surgery in April, knocking him out of thirty-nine games. He couldn't even take batting practice again until the week the Tigers reached the NCAA regionals.

Still, he wasn't fully recovered and the lingering pain restricted his power. Morris was relegated to the ninth spot in the batting order—which is where he was slotted in the fateful ninth inning with LSU down a run and down to its last out.

Designated hitter Brad Wilson was the first man up. Wilson was 1-for-12 in the College World Series and was 0-for-4 with three strikeouts against the Hurricanes. He belted a double down the left-field line off reliever Robbie Morrison. A groundout to second by Justin Bowles moved Wilson to third, but Morrison got Tim Lanier to strike out.

As the dejected Lanier passed Morris in the on-deck circle, he made a plea to his teammate: "Pick me up." Morris would reflect later, "I wasn't trying to hit a homer. I was just trying to keep the inning alive, tie the game, and let somebody hit me in."

Seconds later Morrison's first pitch to Morris was a high curve, and he cracked a liner to right field. Wilson came in to tie the score while Morris raced around the bases, waiting for the ball to drop. But the ball stayed up just high enough to reach the stands, landing in the third row.

"I didn't think I could hit it that far," he said afterward. "I think I hit it part of the way and the guys on the bench blew it the rest of the way."

The game was over. It took seconds to realize what had happened. Several Miami players fell despondently to the ground, and rounding second, Morris threw up a finger signifying "No. 1" before being buried by jubilant teammates as he jumped on home plate.

An unlikely athlete was the linchpin of an unlikely LSU national championship.

To put Morris's feat in context, consider that it remains the only walkoff, championship-winning home run in CWS history. It is also the only two-out, ninth-inning walkoff homer to determine a title at any collegiate or professional level.

ESPN further showcased the moment when it gave Morris its "Showstopper of the Year" award.

But the clearest perspective was the notation that while Morris was laid up with his injury, LSU put together a very respectable 30-15 record. In the games with him in the starting lineup, though, including the one for the championship, the Tigers were 22-0.

In the preseason of 1996, Morris was asked to evaluate himself as a player. His prescient response: "As a batter, I guess the best description of me is that I'm a tough out."

REACHING FIRST

June 6, 1970
Meador Park, Springfield, Missouri

Nicholls State Coach Ray Didier.

Not LSU, not Tulane, not UNO, not UL Lafayette. None of those College World Series participants were the first Pelican State school to seriously contend for a national baseball title.

That was Nicholls State, then an eleven-year-old program that in 1970 surprisingly found itself on the doorstep of an NCAA Division II College World Series title. Four years before UNO made the elite small-college field, the Colonels were one game and two runs short of hoisting No. 1 banners along the banks of Bayou Lafourche, which traverses through the quaint Cajun town of Thibodaux.

Nicholls sitting atop the college baseball world would have been fitting. In the days when college baseball was perceived as an afterthought at most athletic programs, Nicholls State had it going under Ray Didier, a coach with a Midas touch.

★ ★ ★

Didier, who came from a famed athletic family in Baton Rouge that included a brother, Mel, who would become a noted major league scout, another brother, Gerald, who was a minor league infielder, and a nephew, Bob, who was a catcher in the majors, started coaching at Southwestern Louisiana Institute (now UL Lafayette) in 1948.

In nine seasons Ray's SLI teams won five Gulf States Conference championships. He also coached football at Southwestern for six years, winning one league title. In 1957, Didier moved to LSU where the Tigers went 104-79 under him and won the 1961 Southeastern Conference championship. He also served as an assistant on Paul Dietzel's 1958 national championship football team.

In 1963 he went to Nicholls State, where he coached the Colonels to 217 victories between 1964 and 1971 when he gave up baseball to concentrate on the school's athletic directorship duties.

Didier retired with an overall 458-311-3 baseball record, a .647 percentage.

★ ★ ★

Just reaching the title game was a good story. After a 25-13 season and a second-place Gulf States Conference finish in 1969, the Colonels had set a realistic goal of winning the 1970 league title. Nicholls State spent the season flexing its muscles, beating non-conference opponents LSU (twice), Southern Miss, and Ole Miss.

But, as it turned out, winning the conference would be a bit

Nicholls State shortstop Mike Davis.

harder. In order to take the GSC crown Nicholls State needed to sweep Southwestern and then Northeast Louisiana (now ULM) in back-to-back doubleheaders.

It would not be an easy task. Southwestern sent a young sophomore left-hander named Ron Guidry to the mound—to start *both* games. The Colonels beat the future Cy Young Award recipient each time, 2-1 and 3-0. "They needed to beat us, so they threw their best pitcher," Mike Davis, then a sophomore shortstop, said to *Houma Courier* sports editor Brent St. Germain four decades later in recounting the journey to the precipice of Nicholls' finest athletic moment. "He threw two complete games and we beat them both times."

The next day Nicholls State took NLU in the first game 5-1, but lost the second game 2-1, giving NLU the conference championship.

Still, with a 29-16 record in the days when colleges generally played fewer than fifty regular-season games, the Colonels seemed certain to make the tournament field as an at-large entry, if not the NCAAs, then the NAIA. Nicholls State was a member of both. Didier gave his players the choice, and they decided they would go to whichever sent an invite first. That was the NCAA.

The Colonels were sent to the Mideast Regional in Bloomington, Indiana, where they promptly lost their opening game to Southern Illinois-Edwardsville, then needed a miraculous ninth-inning rally to stay alive.

Trailing Union University 3-0 in the ninth, Nicholls was down to its last strike but mounted an unlikely rally for a 4-3 win.

The comeback came as a shock to team bus driver "Big Sam" Levy, who left in the ninth to get the bus warmed up for the long trip back to Thibodaux. When he got back, Davis recalled, "We are jumping up and down all excited and he is wondering what is going on. He missed the greatest comeback I guess you will ever see."

Subsequent wins over Illinois State and SIU-Edwardsville (twice) sprang the Colonels into the Division II College World Series in Springfield, Missouri. There they won their first two games, 3-1 over Springfield College (Massachusetts) and 8-5 over Missouri State.

Now the Colonels had a clear shot at the national championship. In the double-elimination tournament, Nicholls State just had to win one game. San Fernando Valley State (now California State-Northridge) had already lost one CWS game and would have to beat Nicholls twice.

Winners of six of their seven postseason games, the Colonels had to be feeling confident of their chances. For San Fernando to prevail it would have to become the first team in history to come through the losers' bracket, meaning at the end it would have played a tournament-high seven games in the CWS.

San Fernando breezed in the first game, 9-4, setting up a second game that same afternoon for the championship.

From the Colonels' perspective, heartbreaking is the only way to describe the outcome. With Nicholls ace Gene Duhé (11-5) on the mound, San Fernando scored just two runs—but that turned out to be enough. In the 2-1 defeat, the Colonels appeared poised to bust the game open in the seventh inning with the bases loaded and no one out.

But two strikeouts and a harmless grounder ended the threat—and for all practical purposes put an end to a memorable season.

The Colonels finished with a more-than-respectable for the day 35-19 record—but fell two runs short of hoisting any No. 1 banners along the banks of Bayou Lafourche.

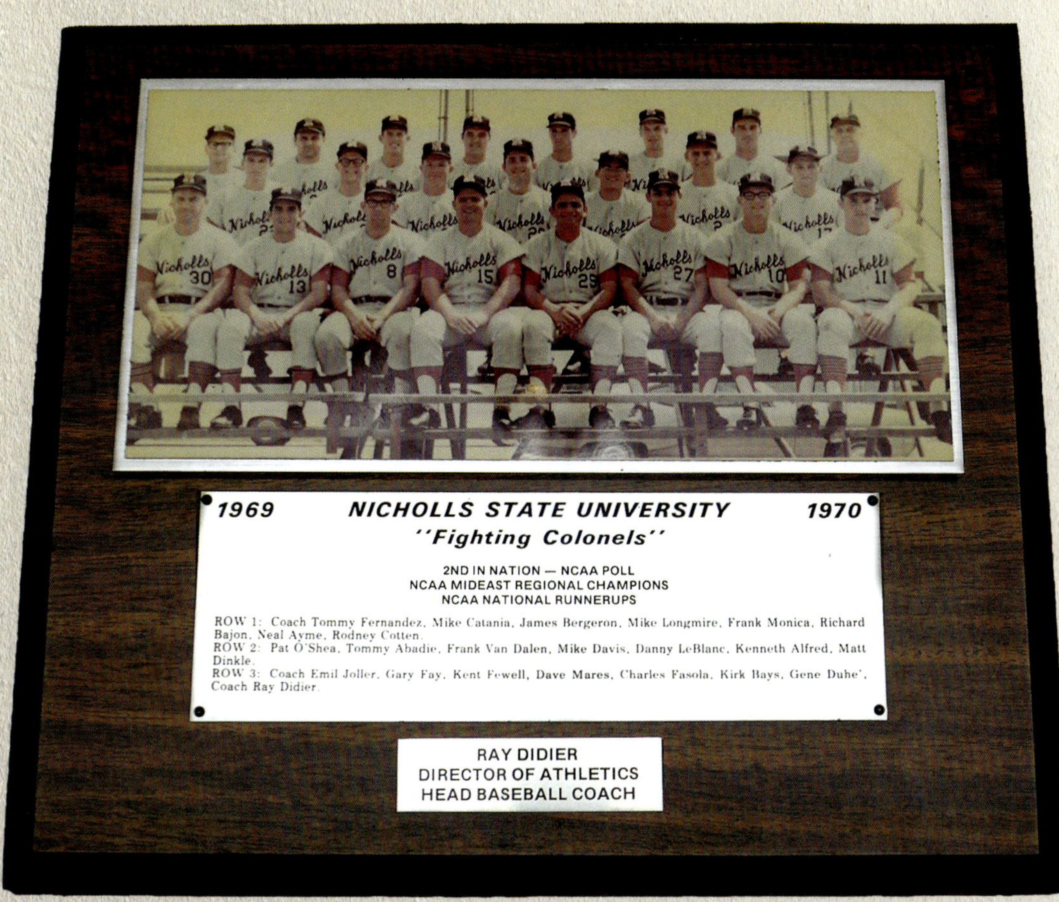

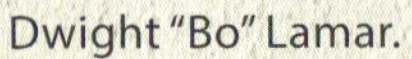
Dwight "Bo" Lamar.

Bob Pettit.

Avery Johnson.

Shaquille O'Neal.

Pete Maravich.

Robert Parish.

HOOP DREAMS

There's a lot of truth in Louisiana to the news of a "bouncing baby boy."

Think about this: when the National Basketball Association, celebrating its half-century anniversary in 1996, listed its fifty greatest players, seven—fully 14 percent—were born within the borders of the Pelican State.

New York, with a population of fifteen million more than Louisiana, was the only state that produced more of pro basketball's elite—eight.

Bob Pettit, Willis Reed, Robert Parish, Elvin Hayes, and Karl Malone all took their first breath within the state's perimeters, then developed and showcased their talents at Louisiana high schools. Two others, Bill Russell and Clyde Drexler, left at early ages.

To further press the issue, Pete Maravich and Shaquille O'Neal are not native Louisianans, but made their names in the state and are still closely associated with LSU, and Pistol Pete played his most productive pro years in New Orleans, where he spent the rest of his life.

Joe Dumars, also born in Louisiana, joins the others in the Basketball Hall of Fame.

★ ★ ★

Louisianans in the highest pantheon of basketball include:

Robert Parish – A dominant seven-foot center who could shoot from the outside, block shots, and play brick-wall defense, Parish played on four NBA title teams (three with the Boston Celtics, one with the Chicago Bulls). "The Chief," who went to college at Centenary, played during a golden age of the Celtics. He and teammates Larry Bird and Kevin McHale became known as "The Big Three." Parish retired after having played 1,611 NBA games over twenty-one seasons, the most of any pro basketball athlete. The Celtics, one of the most storied franchises in American sports, retired Parish's 00 jersey.

Elvin Hayes – One of the NBA's all-time greats, "Big E" will always be remembered for one of the most important games in college basketball history—UCLA vs. the University of Houston at the Astrodome in 1969. Hayes and Don Chaney of Baton Rouge were the first two African Americans to join Coach Guy Lewis's UH juggernaut of the 1960s. Undefeated No. 1-ranked UCLA put its forty-seven-game win streak on the line against the unbeaten Cougars. Hayes scored thirty-nine points and had fifteen rebounds playing against the renowned, but injured, Lew Alcindor, who was held to fifteen points in a 71-69 Cougar victory. It was the first regular season college basketball game ever nationally televised. Hayes went on to a star-spangled pro career, retiring with 27,313 points and 16,279 rebounds.

Joe Dumars – The cornerstone of Coach Chuck Daly's 1990s Detroit Pistons' "Bad Boys." After playing at McNeese State, Dumars was an NBA All-Star six times, All-Defense four times, and the 1989 Finals MVP. Detroit won two championships with Dumars playing both point and shooting guard. He ended a fourteen-year playing career with 16,401 points, 4,612 assists, 2,203 rebounds, and 902 steals. He was the recipient of the NBA Sportsmanship Trophy, which has been renamed the Joe Dumars Trophy. He is now the president of the Detroit Pistons.

★ ★ ★

There are many more nuggets in Louisiana basketball lore.

Dwight "Bo" Lamar of the University of Southwestern Louisiana was the author of one of the game's most phenomenal achievements when he led the nation in scoring (36.0) for the 1970-71 season when the Ragin' Cajuns were a small college power. The following season USL (now UL Lafayette) moved up to major college competition, and Lamar again led the nation in scoring (36.3).

Bob Hopkins finished his college career at Grambling with 3,759 points—ninety-two more than Pete Maravich's major college record. Hopkins had four years of college competition, Maravich three.

Hopkins, Lamar, and Maravich are not the only Louisiana-based athletes to lead the nation in scoring. Bill Reigel of McNeese State averaged 33.9 points a game in 1955-56, the year he paced the Cowboys to the NAIA championship.

Perhaps the most well-rounded player from the Pelican State may have been Calvin Natt, who averaged twenty-three points and eleven rebounds during his career at Northeast Louisiana University (now ULM) before embarking on an eleven-year NBA career.

To get Frank Bryan, whose athletic career at LSU was sandwiched around World War II, the Anderson, Indiana, Packers in 1947 matched the salary of the highest-paid player in the National Basketball League—George Mikan. Bryan got $7,500 and was a league All-Star seven times in his nine pro seasons.

Tulane's Warren Perkins, also a WWII vet, had the distinction of playing in the NBA's first-ever game. On the night of October 30, 1949, the Tri-City Blackhawks played the old Denver Nuggets at Wharton Field House, a high school gym in Moline, Illinois. The game drew a crowd of 3,450.

Nat "Sweetwater" Clifton played only one season of basketball at Xavier University in New Orleans before Pearl Harbor changed the course of his life, but he still holds a special position in Louisiana sports. Clifton was the first African American to sign an NBA contract, with the New York Knicks. He became one of the first three black players to play in the league, the first to appear in the NBA Finals, and at age thirty-four became the NBA's oldest first-time All-Star.

The No. 10 jersey of Southern University's Bob Love was the second ever to be retired by the Chicago Bulls (Jerry Sloan's was the first). Love, who led the Bulls in scoring for seven straight years, and whose triumph over a severe stuttering problem was inspiring to teammates, friends, and fans, later became an executive with the club.

George Johnson made it to the NBA and Marlbert Pradd played in the old ABA. But Billy Ray Hobley may have been the most famed Dillard Blue Devil of all. Known as "Supertrotter," Hobley went from the Gentilly campus in New Orleans to the Harlem Globetrotters, for whom he played—and clowned around for—for twenty-two seasons. In February of 2011, nine years after his premature death, Hobley became the twenty-ninth recipient of the Globetrotters' "Legends" award.

Two of the most startling upsets in NCAA Tournament history involved Pelican State schools. In 1993 Jervaughn Scales scored twenty-two points as thirteenth-seeded Southern University beat fourth-seed Georgia Tech, 93-78. A last second shot from the corner in 2006 gave fourteenth-seed Northwestern State a scintillating 64-63 victory over third-seed Iowa. Both teams lost their next games.

Even a faraway and storied franchise as the Boston Celtics has a touch of Louisiana gilt in its record book. On March 12, 1985, playing at the University of New Orleans's Lakefront Arena against the Atlanta Hawks, Larry Bird set the Celtics' single game scoring record with sixty points. The game took place there because, in the absence of a pro team in New Orleans after the Jazz left for Utah, the Hawks, having attendance problems, scheduled twelve regular season games in the Big Easy. This was the tenth of those twelve games, and before a crowd of 10, 079—near capacity—Bird scored twenty-three in the first half, then nineteen and eighteen points (including Boston's last sixteen) in the third and fourth quarters. He finished with 22 of 36 from the field and 15 of 16 free throws in the Celtics' 126-115 victory.

After twenty-five years, Dale Brown retired from LSU in 1997 as the SEC's second-winningest basketball coach with 448 victories. He also left as the SEC's losingest coach with 301 defeats. Sixty-eight of those defeats came in his last four seasons, all losing ones in which his Tigers never finished higher than eighth in the conference.

One of New Orleans's fondest basketball memories is that of the Bucs, in the old American Basketball Association. Featuring home-grown talent such as Louisiana Tech's Jackie Moreland and Grambling's Jimmy Jones, plus crowd pleasers—and future renowned coaches—like Larry Brown and Doug Moe, the Bucs advanced to the first ABA championship series, losing four games to three to the Pittsburgh Pipers. Playing at small Loyola Fieldhouse, the Bucs averaged 2,337 paying customers a game and stayed in New Orleans just three seasons (1967-1970).

The New Orleans Hornets (later changed to "Pelicans," the old-time baseball mascot), the city's newest NBA franchise, competing with superstar guard Chris Paul, wore Bucs throw-back uniforms for four games during the 2009-10 season in honor of the fortieth anniversary of the ABA team.

PREP-POURRI: Not just one, but the two highest scoring players in high school basketball in America came from Louisiana. Greg Procell, a five-foot-eleven guard at Noble Ebarb High School in Sabine Parish, scored 6,702 points in his four-year career. As a senior in 1969-70, an era when there were no restrictions on the number of games played, he averaged 46.7 points in lighting up the scoreboard for another national record 3,173 points in sixty-eight games. He broke the then-record for points in a season, held by Harold Ray Strother of Plainview, Louisiana, by five hundred points. Of Choctaw-Apache Indian heritage, Procell once hit for a state-record one hundred points in a single game.

Demond "Tweety" Carter of Reserve Christian School outside New Orleans scored 7,457 points, which technically makes him the highest scorer in high school basketball. But Carter played varsity basketball six years, from the seventh through twelfth grades, and the National High School Sports Record Book only recognizes ninth through twelfth grade statistics.

When Procell was putting up his mind-numbing numbers, he was shooting to catch other Pelican State shooters. At the time Bruce Williams (5,814) of Florien and Jackie Moreland (5,030) of Minden were the only players to crack the five thousand-point barrier. Another Louisiana sharpshooter, David Cambre, of French Settlement, was the first player to score as many as five thousand points, 5,367 in a career that ended in 1955. But that total included 753 he scored as an eighth grader, and like Carter's pre-ninth grade points, they were not recognized by the Federation.

Joel Hawkins is the measuring stick of Louisiana high school basketball coaches. He coached Southern Lab in Baton Rouge to eleven state championships in a thirteen-year span. Counting his time at G. W. Griffin and Lake Providence, Hawkins compiled a 1,071-263 record, (a .803 winning percentage) and twelve state titles—best in state history.

One of the most memorable games in the championship tournament—then the Top 24—came in 1979 in Alexandria when homestanding Peabody, paced by future Tulane stalwart Paul Thompson, played Redemptorist of Baton Rouge and future LSU Tiger Howard "Hi-C" Carter. A crush of Peabody fans who were unable to secure tickets to the sold-out Rapides Parish Coliseum stood at least ten feet deep at each gate trying to catch a glimpse of the game. Thompson triggered a thriller, upsetting Redemptorist 55-53. Redemptorist rebounded with the championship in 1968, and went on to win seventy straight games.

In 1967, undefeated LaGrange (35-0) downed equally unbeaten Baton Rouge High 62-57. LaGrange's James "Poo" Welch and BRHS's Al "Apple" Sanders each scored thirty-two points. Baton Rouge came back the following season with a 31-0 record.

During a two-year stay in Lake Charles, the Top 24 was the stage for the end of one long victory streak and the catalyst for another. In the 1977 AAAA finals Rummel upset nearby DeRidder with All-Everything Mike Sanders, 52-48, snipping the Dragons' wins at forty-one straight. Rummell returned a year later with not only a 35-0 record, but on a forty-nine-game victory streak. The Raiders beat Fair Park 83-64 in 1978. That year Rummell, Newman, and Country Day each won, giving the Crescent City three titles in one season for the first time.

Jimmy Jones.

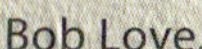
Bob Love.

Wayne Perkins.

Billy Ray Hobley.

PLAYING THE BIG HOUSE

March 29, 1982
Louisiana Superdome, New Orleans, La.

Coming from whom it did, this was a mouthful. "At the time," Michael Jordan said, "it was the biggest moment of my life."

His Airness was recalling his first splash on a big stage—and this was on the biggest stage college basketball had ever been played, the first Final Four held in the Louisiana Superdome.

In a glimpse of future Hall of Fame gatherings, North Carolina coach Dean Smith sent out Jordan and James Worthy with their teammates against Georgetown's Patrick Ewing and his fellow Hoyas, coached by John Thompson.

There were 61,612 spectators in the Dome, the first live mega-crowd to witness the NCAA's "One Shining Moment."

And, in a Final Four crowning that others could be measured by, Jordan gave them the finish of a lifetime. The Tar Heels' freshman hit a sixteen-foot jumper with fifteen seconds remaining, which after Worthy (the MVP) received an errant Hoyas' pass, gave UNC a 63-62 victory—Smith's first NCAA championship after three previous trips to the title game.

Smith would add to his résumé in another trip to New Orleans eleven years later.

The term "Final Four" by itself connotes dramatic championship basketball. It's the nature of the beast with superior athletes and teams rising to the occasion practically every season. But it's hard to envision any venue providing as many pyrotechnics as the Final Four in the Superdome.

Five times the event has been staged in the Big Easy, and four times memorable, spine-tingling, down-to-the-wire hoops have been played.

Five years after the heroics of Jordan and Worthy, Indiana's Keith Smart—from Baton Rouge—scored twelve of his team's last fifteen points, capped by a sixteen-foot jumper from the left baseline with ten seconds remaining to give the Hoosiers a 74-73 victory over heartbroken Syracuse. A crowd of 64,959—the Final Four record for many years—watched as Coach Bobby Knight garnered his third national championship.

Syracuse coach Jim Boeheim was so devastated by the one-point defeat in 1987 that he had never even watched film of the loss to Indiana.

Baton Rouge native Keith Smart releases the winning shot of the 1987 NCAA championship game.

In 1993, before a crowd of 64,151, Dean Smith picked up his second title in one of the event's most memorable finishes. The North Carolina-Michigan game, won by the Tar Heels 77-71, was sealed by a completely out-of-the-ordinary play: In the fading seconds, Michigan's Chris Webber, his team's leading scorer with twenty-three points, was double-teamed and instinctively tried to call timeout—when Michigan's allotment was already depleted. The technical foul sent UNC to the free-throw line for the final points.

Boeheim got a second shot for his title in 2003, against Kansas. Freshman sensation Carmelo Anthony, despite being shut out in the final thirteen minutes, scored twenty points in an 81-78 Orange victory—removing the burden of never having won a title in almost three decades of coaching off the shoulders of Boeheim, an above-average basketball mentor.

Boeheim's biggest moment in the sun was viewed in person by 54,524 fans—a good crowd, but significantly smaller than the 70,913 in the renovated, expanded, and newly renamed Mercedes-Benz Superdome who saw Kentucky and Anthony Davis stave off a furious Kansas surge in the final minutes of the Wildcats' eighth title run, 67-58, in 2012. The attendance in that particular game dwarfed even the Michael Jordan game that opened the era of live gates numbering in the tens of thousands.

So how did the Superdome became the cradle of "Big Arena Basketball"?

James Worthy, MVP of the 1982 NCAA Final Four.

★ ★ ★

For all its versatility, before 1982 there was a fear that a building such as the Superdome could be completely unsuitable for basketball, though the NBA Jazz successfully used it for three seasons.

Because of movable stands, the Superdome had a series of configurations, including the normal basketball setup of 19,463. Other stands, which sat farther out, could double the basketball seats and were offered to the NCAA when Superdome officials bid for the '82 Final Four.

But when they first surveyed the building, NCAA officials immediately envisioned the vast potential of a Superdome Final Four and went one better: they wanted to open still another section, the east side terrace, against the judgment of stadium officials.

The NCAA, realizing what a tough ticket the Final Four had become, decided to "stretch" the Supderdome basketball limits from forty thousand to sixty thousand. With twenty thousand seats considered excellent, twenty thousand considered good, and twenty thousand stamped "distant vision," the NCAA went to extraordinary lengths to warn ticket buyers of seat locations which, from the top row of the east terrace, were 425 feet away from the court.

But it is important to note that the twenty thousand more seats of "distant seating" were available to persons to whom it was important to attend.

"They were correct," said Bill Curl of the Spectacor Management Group, a company specializing in venue operations. "It (the NCAA decision) satisfied far more fans than it irritated. I think the observation of the fan who was asked about sitting so far from the court—he said if they were playing in a twenty thousand-seat arena, he wouldn't be there—spoke for the majority. To be honest, we expected more problems, more gripes on some of the distant seating, but we received far, far less than we anticipated."

Certainly there is a loss of basketball "intimacy," but Dean Smith, who was hesitant to comment on the Superdome as a tournament site in 1982, became a booster.

"You might give up some of the intimacy," Smith said, "but more people can see the game live."

An euphoric Curl said after the pioneering 1982 championship, "The spectacular final game was frosting on the cake. You heard no complaints of lighting, seating, playing conditions. Neither team had a problem shooting in an arena not built specifically for basketball.

"I tell you what, we were delirious. We proved a big house was not too big."

Michael Jordan's first taste of stardom came at the "Big House."

That Championship Season

April 13, 1935
New Jersey Auditorium, Atlantic City

Long before they started singing "One Shining Moment" at the Final Four, LSU had one.

The college basketball crown of the 1934-35 season was worn, sort of, by the Tigers, the unlikely national champion for the only time in the history of the program.

Basketball was four years from an NCAA Tournament and three years removed from the advent of the National Invitation Tournament.

There were no conference tournament after the regular season, no postseason bids to sweat out, and no grueling gauntlet of dangerous opponents on the road to the throne. There were a total of fifteen games played—including a one-game, winner-take-all shootout.

But the Tigers were No. 1. Sort of.

Just off the famed boardwalk of Atlantic City, New Jersey, LSU staged a fiery comeback to defeat Pittsburgh 41-37 and secure the only national championship trophy given out that year.

"To tell you the truth," said Buddy Blair, who broke the backs of the Panthers and the hearts of their fans with a stirring performance, "I don't think we thought that much about a national championship, either before the game or afterward. We just knew we had an extra game to play."

The Tigers, though, left an impression on the five thousand-plus spectators at the Atlantic City Auditorium.

"They came, we saw them and took them to our hearts," wrote Mal Dodson of the *Atlantic City News* of the Tigers after their victory. "We shall not forget them for years to come, for they gave us more thrills than any basketball team ever thought of giving before."

Heady praise, to be sure.

The Tigers, in the description of the day, were loaded in that season in the midst of the Great Depression. Malcolm "Sparky" Wade, a brilliant performer and considered the best ballhandler in the land, was LSU's first All-American and team captain.

Wade, who stood five foot seven, entered LSU four years earlier with an exceptional class of basketball talent that included Jack Harris, Ben Journeay, and Blair, who was himself a remarkable athlete. Blair was the winning javelin thrower on LSU's celebrated 1933 national champion track team and later played a major league season for the Philadelphia A's before a knee injury ended his athletic career.

But LSU basketball still almost had to make its mark without Sparky.

Sparky's carried an old bandana filled with sandwiches made by his beloved mother when he got off the bus in Baton Rouge in September of 1931.

Soon, though, he was back on a bus headed for Dallas and Southern Methodist University, which had also heavily recruited him after a spectacular high school career at Jena High School. He had locked horns with Tiger coach Harry Rabenhorst over an unknown issue.

When Gov. Huey Long, the consummate Tiger fan – and meddler, called Rabenhorst to find out how the team was progressing with their coveted new addition, he became livid upon learning Wade had left.

In short order, an SMU teammate in the athletic dorm told Sparky he was wanted on the phone. When Wade asked who it was, his incredulous teammate said, "He says he's the governor of Louisiana."

With some trepidation, Sparky took the phone and softly said, "Yes, Governor." Through a string of expletives, the Kingfish informed the player he had 36 hours to get back to LSU, and that if he did not, a bulldozer would be dispatched to Jena to cut the road in front of the Wade household so wide that Mrs. Wade would have to swim to get out of town.

Sparky was soon back with the Tigers and on the road to Atlantic City, and eventually the game they would be forever remembered for.

That team ran through a fourteen game regular-season schedule, in which LSU played eleven games in the Gym-Armory on campus, and two at Tulane, eighty miles away in New Orleans. The other was in Houston, at Rice.

In other words, the schedule was favorable for the formidable team assembled by Coach Harry Rabenhorst.

Rabenhorst always put a premium on defense. In an era when there was a center jump after every point, no time constraint in getting the ball upcourt, and no violation for planting a defensive specialist in the lane—all factors in a slow and low-scoring game—LSU was a regular scoring machine. The Tigers averaged an eyebrow-raising 48.5 points a game. Only twice did opponents register as many as forty points.

Wade, who dazzled the South with an 11.0 career scoring average, outdid himself as a senior with a startling 12.5-point average. His total of 197 points in the sixteen games was an SEC record. It has since been eclipsed.

Wade, who dazzled the South with a 11.0 career scoring average, outdid himself as a senior with a startling 12.7-point average. His 197 points set the SEC record.

The one LSU misstep came in the fourth game of the season, at Rice where the Owls jumped out 15-0, and beat the Tigers 56-47.

Because of the Great Depression, the Southeastern Conference discontinued its end-of-the-season tournament, so things ended a bit disappointingly since LSU and Kentucky did not meet. The Bayou Bengals were 13-1, 12-0 in the SEC. The Wildcats were 19-2, 11-0. A co-championship was declared, and the teams packed it in.

Then fate took LSU by the hand. Harry Costello, a war hero, author, and Washington, D.C., newspaperman, was hired as the LSU sports information director. From his East Coast sports contacts, Costello knew a promotion group in Atlantic City was attempting to put together a basketball spectacular—called the American Legion Bowl—involving the two best teams in the country. Immediately after being hired, Costello got in touch with the appropriate officials and made a compelling argument that, indeed, his new employer was no worst than the second-best basketball team in the land.

Weeks after LSU's last game with Tulane, Rabenhorst gathered his team together and told them they could play one last time—against Coach Doc Carlson's 19-5 Panthers, a team which scored 878 points (a 36.5 average) in winning the Eastern Intercollegiate Conference championship for a third consecutive season. And they would play this game in a part of the country none of them had been to before.

"Heck, we were just a bunch of country boys," Bill Leathers said. "We had traveled before, but about as far as LSU scheduled games."

Not only would the Tigers have to get back in basketball form, they would have to do it the hard way. They could not practice in usual surroundings because the Gym-Armory was being used for functions held for LSU's seventy-fifth anniversary jubilee. So the team practiced in available high school gyms around Baton Rouge.

Blair was able to practice sparingly because of his participation in the Texas and Southwestern Relays and other track meets. Wade wasn't in top form after he broke a knuckle on his left hand.

Still, Rabenhorst was confident. "When these guys get hot," he said bravely, "they'll beat any team."

Lloyd Lindsey, at six-foot-two LSU's tallest starter, recalled the Tigers arrived in New Jersey after a train ride of several days, during the middle of a northeaster—a cold, nasty storm. "The

Sparky Wade, star of the 1935 LSU team.

next day they had a parade," Lindsey said. "That was in the heyday of Huey Long, of course, and everybody we met wanted to discuss the Kingfish."

Blair was given the most crucial assignment of the game with Pitt: defensing All-American guard Clair Cribbs. "He was an exceptional player," Blair said. "It didn't look easy."

Pitt came out fired up and making LSU look as if it had never seen a ball that was round before. Less than eight minutes into the game, the Panthers led 13-3 and were cruising.

"They used a figure-eight offense against us," Blair said, "a lot of motion, and we hadn't seen it before. It took us a while to figure it out."

LSU started slowing the Panthers on defense and that allowed the Tigers to make some inroads. The Tigers' fast break became devastating. Blair had scored five points at the half, when Pitt led 26-17, but he put the cuffs on Cribbs, who finished with ten points and began getting frustrated. "He was so angry because he couldn't shake me," Blair said. "I think he wanted to shoot me."

Blair also got hot, hitting second-half bank shots that pulled LSU into position to win. Pitt was double- and triple-teaming Wade, who countered by backhanding the ball to Blair and Lindsey. Blair's seventh field goal gave LSU its first lead at 35-33, and the Tigers never again fell behind.

Blair finished with twenty of LSU's forty-one points, and scored nine of the Tigers' sixteen field goals—four more than any other player in the game—as well as doing a superb job on Pitt's main threat.

Lon Jourdet, coach at the University of Pennsylvania, was awestruck at the comeback.

"I thought I had seen all the basketball I wanted, but LSU opened my eyes. When the Tigers got (the ball), they were always dangerous."

Blair said the magnitude of the victory didn't hit the Tigers until long after the game was played. "We just went back to class, and, in my case, track. That much just wasn't made of it at first," he said.

Rabenhorst always was proud of the feat, though he didn't believe LSU played its greatest game against its greatest opponent. He said afterward, "I thought we could win by ten points."

Coach Harry Rabenhorst watches his 1935 Tiger squad warm up.

Pressing the Issue

March 19, 1945
Municipal Auditorium, Kansas City, Missouri

Jack Orsley's instruction to his Loyola Wolfpack was clear: "I don't want to see any daylight between you and your man."

The implication was obvious. If the smaller, slower 'Pack didn't play air-tight defense, they had no chance of winning what up to that point seemed like a pipe dream—a national championship.

Loyola was in the finals of the 1945 National Intercollegiate Basketball Tournament, the forerunner of the NAIA, against the Pepperdine Waves, the 30-2 team observers said was the class of small-college basketball that season.

The Wolves had to contend with a much taller opponent, including Nick Buzolich, a six-foot-seven center, an imposing collegiate player. Even by the standards of the 1940s, Orsley's Wolfpack was short. His tallest player was backup center Joe Gurievsky at six foot four. The tallest starter was Jim Bonck at six foot two and a half inches in the pivot.

After getting a look at Pepperdine, Orsley said of the thirteen-point favorite Waves, "There wasn't a doubt in my mind what we had to do to have a chance: We had to press them from the start and never stop."

That Loyola, 24-5 going into the title game, was in this position at Kansas City's famed Municipal Auditorium, a mecca of championship basketball, was astounding in itself.

Basketball was the only sport sponsored by the New Orleans Catholic university. Five years before administrators had decided to drop football, track, and boxing and to put in a physical education program with basketball the only competitive sport. They hired Orsley, a former New Orleans prep coach and ex-football/basketball athlete at the University of Illinois, to guide the program.

In the ensuing five seasons, Loyola went 88-21, claiming three Dixie Conference championships and one Southern AAU title. The Wolfpack now was on the verge of a national championship.

And Orsley accomplished all that with players who grew up within a streetcar ride of Loyola's St. Charles Avenue campus. The five men he sent out against Pepperdine all came from New Orleans high schools: Leroy Chollet of Holy Cross and T.J. Whittacker of Jesuit at forward, Bonck of Jesuit in the middle, and John Casteix of Jesuit and Jim Hultberg of Warren Easton at guard.

"It sure didn't cost anything to recruit that bunch," Orsley said wryly.

The way things turned out in the thirty-two-team tournament, after beating Phillips College and Central Norman College to reach the semifinals, Loyola's biggest test on the national stage came against Southern Illinois. In a game that was tied for the third time in the second half with fifty-eight seconds remaining, Casteix, the Wolfpack captain, won it 37-35 in the fading seconds with a long, one-handed shot from the corner.

That set up the championship game.

Loyola's full-court press was airtight. Hardly a beam of light sliced through the Loyola defenders and the Waves on offense. Slowly, Pepperdine became unraveled, throwing the ball away and seeing passes intercepted. Ahead 27-23 at the half, the Wolfpack, still pressing, slowly pulled away, building a lead that reached nineteen points.

With a couple of minutes remaining in what would become a 49-36 Wolfpack victory, Pepperdine coach Al Duer came over to the Loyola bench and shook Orsley's hand. "Can you imagine that happening today?" Orsley said decades later.

Chollet led all scorers with eighteen points, while the towering Buzolich was kept in relative check with twelve points.

The Wolfpack defense had followed instructions to a "T," holding Pepperdine to its lowest output of the season.

It was a special moment for more than one reason. This was the first national basketball title in the age of postseason tournament play ever won by a Louisiana school, and remains the only one ever won by a New Orleans college. Also the NIB tournament was established by none other than James Naismith, the inventor of basketball in order to recognize an annual national championship for smaller colleges and universities. Receiving the Maude Naismith Trophy (named for Naismith's wife) remains the high-point of Loyola sports history.

JUST OUT OF REACH

April 1, 2006
RCA Dome, Indianapolis, Indiana

It's sort of like being fitted for the green jacket at the Masters. Except it's navy blue, and presented annually to coaches who guided teams to what is called the "Promised Land" of men's college basketball—the Final Four.

"It's like being admitted to a club," John Brady said, "the Final Four Club. You don't get it for winning, you get it for making it that far. That's just how hard of an accomplishment it really is."

Brady is proud to have one, and, no, he didn't win a Final Four. But he's proud that his résumé says he reached one.

In 2006, Brady's LSU Tigers got to Indianapolis by beating No. 1 seed Duke (62-54) and No. 6 seed Texas (70-60) in the NCAA Tournament's Atlanta Regional, before losing 59-45 to UCLA in the semifinals, ending a surprisingly good run.

Brady's predecessor as LSU coach, Dale Brown, who has two Final Four jackets, said one of the highlights of his career was standing on the court at Philadelphia's Spectrum hours before LSU's semifinal game with Indiana, looking around the lighted arena and thinking that this was the highlight of his career.

"Winning is the ultimate prize, of course," Brady said, "but the achievement of getting there in the first place isn't diminished when a team comes up a little short. When a school is mentioned as a 'Final Four team,' it is made as a designation of something special, an achievement that puts you in the company of many great coaches."

Point well taken. Just the term "Final Four" provides any program with instant and long-lasting recognition as a factor in the sporting world.

To put it in perspective, the four teams that make it, surviving the regular season and grinding tournament competition, represent just 1.3 percent of the more than three hundred schools that make up NCAA Division I basketball.

That's what's called survival.

★ ★ ★

When it's going right for LSU basketball, the Tigers play on a high plateau. Between the men's and women's teams, and under a combined seven coaches, LSU has reached the Final Four a hard-to-believe total of nine times.

That's pretty high cotton, especially at a place with a reputation as strictly a "football school."

That is, of course, a back-of-the-hand description meant to indicate the sport is a stepchild in the pantheon of Tiger sports. LSU basketball, a program founded in 1908, has more SEC championships (ten, as of 2012), than any other school in the league, except for the sport's standard-bearer, Kentucky. And, in the same time period, LSU has been to more Final Fours (four) than any charter member SEC school except the perennial-contending Wildcats (fifteen).

But, with all that pre-Final Four success, once they get there, the Tigers have none. Once they get to the game's biggest arena, the Tigers seem to succumb to stage fright. LSU is a cumulative 0-11 in Final Fours. To rub salt in the wounds, three of the men's defeats and one of the women's came at the hands of the eventual national champion.

Bob Pettit, a force in early 1950s basketball, was the glue of Coach Harry Rabenhorst's 1952-53 squad that won the SEC with a

23-1 record—then dropped two in a row (in the days when teams played two games in the Final Four), 80-67 to Indiana, the team that would ultimately win it all, and 88-69 to Washington.

Twenty-eight years later, Brown, the second-winningest coach in SEC history with 448 victories in twenty-five seasons, had the Tigers in contention again with a 31-3 regular season and early tournament record. But Isiah Thomas and Indiana overcame Rudy Macklin and Ethan Martin and not only prevailed again, 67-49, but again won the title. Then Ralph Sampson and Virginia beat the Tigers 78-74 in the last Final Four consolation game ever played.

Ricky Blanton and LSU caught fire in the final stages of the 1985-86 season, winning five of their last six games, giving the Tigers a 27-11 record when they were paired up with Louisville. The Cardinals thumped LSU 88-77 before taking the championship.

In their last trip to the Big Show, LSU, under Brady and with future NBA players Glen "Big Baby" Davis and Tyrus Thomas, won the SEC, finishing with a 27-8 record—until the season ended with a thud when UCLA took the Tigers apart 59-45.

Give LSU kudos for its long history of climbing to within two steps of the ultimate basketball crown. But that brings up a question LSU fans have wrestled with for generations: Is the shine taken off a season when a team reaches the Final Four and loses, or is being in position to win something 99 percent of the basketball-playing schools in America fell short in attempting an accomplishment to be cherished?

"It's something to take immense pride in," Brady, a proud member of the Final Four Club, said unequivocally.

Future NBA players Tyrus Thomas (left) and Glen Davis (right) led LSU to the 2006 NCAA Final Four.

Mail Delivery

August 10, 1992
Pavelló Olimpic de Badalona, Badalona, Spain

For Karl Malone, no games were ever tougher, more demanding, more intense.

Not the ones with thousands of screaming fans and scores being kept. He was talking of the ones with just the players and coaches in empty gyms. No pencils, no stat sheets, no other people.

"The most competitive and most challenging thing I ever did was the practices," Malone said to Jody Genessy of *The Deseret News* in Utah where Malone's pro team was located. Of the "Dream Team" that won the basketball gold medal in the 1992 Olympics, he said of practice, "It was truly off the charts. Once the games started, we all felt that was fun."

In the first Olympics in which the U.S allowed the use of active NBA players, Malone was a member of a transcendent squad that included Michael Jordan, Larry Bird, Patrick Ewing, and Clyde Drexler—all superstars at the top of their games.

Jerry West, once a preeminent guard himself and then the general manager of the Los Angeles Lakers, characterized the contingent as less of a Dream Team for opponents and more of a "Nightmare Team." And he was right.

The U.S finished its 8-0 run through the best of the rest of the world with a 117-85 dismantling of the talented Croatia squad and an average tournament margin of victory of 43.8 points.

Dubbed "The Mailman" long before by Keith Prince, Louisiana Tech's sports information director, because "he almost always delivers," Malone was America's third leading scorer with 104 points (a 13.0 average) and tied with Ewing as the leading rebounder with 42 (a 5.3 average).

In other words, on perhaps the most formidable team ever assembled, Malone delivered.

He almost always did.

★ ★ ★

At north Louisiana's Summerfield High, where he averaged 26.3 points and 12.3 rebounds a game, Malone was a three-time selection as the Outstanding Player in Class C.

In a three-year career at Louisiana Tech, he earned All-American and All-Southland Conference honors and finished among the top scorers and rebounders in school history.

And in the NBA, Malone had a stellar nineteen-year career in which he stamped a near-unarguable claim as the game's greatest power forward ever.

"I don't think you're going to get much arguing over that," former Grambling and New York Knicks Hall of Famer Willis Reed said. "When you speak about the great power forwards in the game, the roll call begins with Karl."

The figures don't lie when placing Malone among the game's best ever. His 36,028 points are No. 2 behind the 38,387 of Kareem Abdul-Jabbar. In all but two of his nineteen seasons in the NBA, Malone averaged more than twenty points per game. Ironically, the exceptions were his first and last years, and he had a career high of 31.0 in 1989-90. He averaged more than ten rebounds per game in ten of his seasons.

It wasn't just God-given talent. "Karl was renowned for his work ethic and that's what separated him from so many players," Utah Jazz teammate John Stockton said. "Nobody could outwork Karl. It was amazing how he trained and conditioned himself to be the best player he could possibly be."

★ ★ ★

Steve Welch spoke of how his eyes bugged out the first time he saw Malone on the court.

"Actually, the first time I ever saw Karl play was when Summerfield was playing Shady Grove, which had a great player named Terry Martin," Welch, then an assistant coach at Louisiana Tech, recalled. "It was Karl's junior year, and I went to see Terry. But after seeing that game, I told Coach (Andy) Russo that Terry Martin was good, but Karl Malone was a full running stud."

That he was.

Dominant inside and with a powerful six foot nine, 256-pound physique that helped shatter two backboards at the Thomas Assembly Center, Malone averaged 18.7 points and 9.3 rebounds in 92 games at Tech. Russo's entire offensive system revolved around Malone. With a deadly fade-away jumper, he connected on nearly 60 percent of his field goals, and his wide frame proved a formidable obstacle for any would-be defender.

In his junior year, he got the Bulldogs to within a whisker of an NCAA Elite Eight appearance. Only an eleventh-hour, rim-rounding shot by Oklahoma's Wayman Tisdale kept Tech from advancing out of the regionals at Reunion Arena in Dallas and to—who knows?—maybe even an eventual date with the Final Four.

It was about at that point that Malone's near-unlimited potential started becoming more than apparent. Former Tech guard Dave Simmons, then a graduate assistant coach, became convinced Malone's star was destined to shine in the NBA after seeing him compete against the likes of Hakeem Olajuwon of Houston, Keith Lee of Memphis, and Tisdale.

"After we played Oklahoma, I'm thinking that if Tisdale is a first-team All-American, then Karl is just as good and can have a great career at the next level," Simmons told Buddy Davis of the

Ruston Daily Leader.

Former Tech teammate Rennie Bailey recalled, "We had a game in Karl's junior year where we were down at Beaumont against Lamar and they were up about two points on us with three or four minutes remaining. As captain of the team, I called a timeout, huddled us up and told everyone that for the rest of the game we were getting the ball inside to Karl. Every time we got it, we were going to get it in to the big man. And we did. On every possession during those final minutes, Karl was touching the ball—and scoring.''

The Bulldogs wound up winning, 68-65.

Others noticed, too.

Super scout Marty Blake critiqued Malone to the fullest. "Karl and the Tech team had this game down at McNeese State when he and Joe (Dumars) played," Blake recalled. "It created quite a stir with the NBA scouting fraternity. Here you had two of the best players in the country on the same court, and both of them were certain to be playing at the next level.

"When I walked into the gym that night, there were about thirty scouts sitting on press row. You knew when you walked out you had just seen two future NBA players."

Blake liked what he saw, noting on his scouting report that "Malone has the potential to be one of the top power forwards in the NBA."

Yes, indeed.

☆ ☆ ☆

Malone opted to pass up his senior season, and the Utah Jazz made him its No. 1 pick (No. 13 overall) in 1985.

Over the course of his next eighteen years in the sport, he would wear the Jazz jersey and become the team's most popular and successful player ever. Teaming up with Stockton, a point guard, the duo made the "pick-and-roll" an art form.

Karl earned thirteen trips to the All-Star Game, twice was named its MVP, and was also twice named the NBA's overall MVP. He powered the Jazz to two NBA Finals, too, though in each case Jordan's Chicago Bulls prevailed. He also was again a key component in a second gold medal-winning Olympics in 1996 in Atlanta.

Malone always said all that success flowed directly from his mother, Shirley, who showed through example what hard work could achieve.

Karl, the hardest-working man in basketball, would acknowledge without hesitation that she was his role model. He said, "Mom was my greatest inspiration."

RIDE 'EM COWBOY

March 16, 1956
Municipal Auditorium, Kansas City, Missouri

Bill Reigel and Dudley Carver took turns driving for layups—the coffin nails as McNeese State hammered home its most memorable men's basketball season—and the NAIA championship.

With a 50-43 lead in the closing minutes, the Cowboys were in their possession mode, just holding the ball, until Texas Southern came out of its zone. Then McNeese would zip through the defense for uncontested baskets. The last four came in this fashion, with Reigel and Carver each collecting a pair in the 60-55 victory.

That duo, along with Frank Glenn, were mainstays on a team that only lost three games all season and won its last eighteen to reach the mountaintop of small-college basketball.

It was one of Louisiana's memorable basketball odysseys.

In his distinguished career, Ralph Ward never coached anything like a one-man team. But Reigel was obviously McNeese's most indispensable player.

Reigel, a six-foot-five forward with a deadly turnaround jumper, led the nation in scoring with a 33.9 average during the regular season, and set an NAIA record with 158 points in the five games of the tournament.

The *Kansas City Times*, covering the NAIA Tournament, said it best: "He has every shot in the book, and hits on all. He's a southpaw and his touch is soft as a bride's kiss. . . . Reigel hits from everywhere but the bench."

Those shooting skills, along with the defensive strategies of Ward, made the Cowboys a force in the mid-1950s.

It was simply a matter of good fortune for Reigel to be in Ward's program. Reigel failed to even make his high school team until he was a senior at Monaca, Pennsylvania. A growth spurt and his rapid athletic development led to a scholarship to Duquesne University. He transferred to Duke, then was drafted into the U.S. Army.

It was in the service that Reigel met Charles Kuehn, McNeese's first basketball All-American and a former Cowboys assistant coach. Kuehn suggested Reigel might want to finish out his last two college seasons in Lake Charles.

But McNeese was no one-man team. Reigel's teammates, the six-foot-five Carver (with a 15.4 ppg scoring average) and six-foot-two Frank Glenn (13.6 ppg), filled in additional scoring and essential defensive duties and were pillars on a team that won 91 percent of its games.

★ ★ ★

Ward's Cowboys of 1955-56 were the odds-on favorite for the Gulf States Conference championship, despite the graduation of a two-time all-league player in Roy "Toddy" Moore, who held school career scoring records.

Even with the proverbial target on the backs of their jerseys, the Cowboys delivered on every level. Their only defeats in thirty-six games were in the early season to New Mexico A&M 75-71 at home and midseason road games at Lamar Tech 61-60 and Northwestern State 78-66.

Then McNeese ripped off eighteen consecutive victories, with its closest shave coming in the opening game of a best-of-three series with Centenary College for a berth in the NAIA Tournament. The 'Pokes were behind by nine at the half, when Reigel had just three field goals. He put in eleven baskets in the second half, though, and McNeese went ahead with free throws in the final forty-four seconds, two by Ruble Scarborough, one by Glenn, and two by Reigel, who set a Haynes Memorial Gymnasium record with forty-three points in the 76-72 victory. In the second win, at Lake Charles, Reigel was limited to eighteen points, but his teammates picked up the slack, and McNeese won 74-64.

Making it to Kansas City, the Cowboys must have been a revelation to the thirty-two-team field. One rival coach dismissed them as "the smallest, the scrawniest, and most undernourished looking team in the tournament."

Shooting 48 percent as a team and playing what was described as the best defense in the tournament, scrawny McNeese went on a brawny tear, beating Georgetown (Kentucky), 88-65; Central State (Ohio), 87-74; Tennessee A&I, 76-68; and Pittsburg Teachers (Kansas), 78-72, setting up the championship game with Texas Southern.

★ ★ ★

This matchup looked to be almost too much to ask of the smaller, scrawnier Cowboys. Texas Southern sophomore center Bennie Swain was six foot ten, a full five inches taller, and with a reach estimated as a foot longer than Carver, who had to try to shut him off in the middle.

With the Tigers doing a good job of defending Reigel, and Swain controlling the middle with five in-close baskets in the first half, Texas Southern took a 35-34 lead.

Carver ratcheted up his defense in the final twenty minutes. Between him and Glenn, Swain was frequently outmaneuvered from his comfort areas near the basket. He was held to one field goal in the second half. With Swain shut off, the Tigers were forced to an outside-shooting mode, which was not enough to offset McNeese's main threats.

Reigel had twenty-one points on nine of twenty-one shooting, but Glenn had fourteen points (and seventeen rebounds), and Carver added eleven points to go with his stupendous defense.

Six minutes into the second half, Glenn hit a two-handed shot, and McNeese went ahead 44-42 for the first time. When Reigel and Scarborough hit on a couple of driving field goals to make the score 48-43, the Cowboys were ahead for good. Down the stretch the Tigers came within three points three times, but the 'Pokes held them off with their delay tactics that opened up the Tigers' defense.

The scoring by Glenn and Carver offset Texas Southern's defense on Reigel, and Glenn's rebounds—sixty-eight for the tournament—consistently gave McNeese second shots and frequently limited the Tigers to only one.

Still, in the aftermath of the 60-55 victory, it should be noted Reigel had 1,001 points in the regular season, and he added 219 in the seven postseason games for a total of 1,220—the second-highest total in small college NCAA history at that time. He was named the NAIA's Player of the Year.

With the joy of a championship, there were also repercussions back in Louisiana. The politicos were already in an uproar because of the presence of black University of Pittsburgh fullback Bobby Grier in the 1956 Sugar Bowl, and now McNeese's last three games in Kansas City were against predominately African American schools (Tennessee A&I, Pittsburg Teachers, and Texas Southern).

Four months later, the unexpected consequence and long-lasting impact of that combination of events was the enactment of state segregation laws that forbid athletic competition between blacks and whites for almost a decade.

McNeese's Bill Reigel led the nation in scoring during the 1955-56 season.

HAWKING A TITLE

April 12, 1958
Kiel Auditorium, St. Louis, Missouri

This was it, do-or-die time. The St. Louis Hawks had squandered a lead they had held almost all game, ten points in the third quarter and six to open the fourth. Now in the early moments of the last period, the Boston Celtics were in front, 86-84.

They were playing Game 6 in the NBA Finals, and a Hawks defeat would even the series at 3-3 and send the deciding game to Boston Garden, where the defending champions would enjoy more than the usual home court advantage—and a probable second straight title.

Bob Pettit already had left a fingerprint on the series. Now he would have to put a deep, indelible dent in the Celtics' nascent championship express. The Hawks couldn't put distance between themselves and Boston, despite Pettit scoring nineteen points in the first half and six in a row to open the second. The Celtics, playing with a hobbled Bill Russell, kept coming, putting a cloud over the St. Louis crowd of 10,218.

Despite being double- and triple-teamed, Pettit—known to pro basketball fans as "Big Blue"—took complete command at crunch time, cementing what would become his legendary status. He sank basket after basket, keeping the Hawks in the game practically single-handedly. With a little more than twenty seconds to go, Pettit drove the lane and softly arched a shot just over Russell's outstretched hand for a 108-105 St. Louis lead.

Tommy Heinsohn, the principal defender on Pettit, hit two free throws with sixteen seconds remaining to keep Boston in it.

With defenders draped all over Pettit, Hawks guard Slater Martin took an errant shot. Pettit came through the forest of Celtics surrounding him and tapped the miss into the basket.

The Hawks won 110-109, and Pettit scored fifty points, including nineteen of St. Louis's last twenty-one.

"Pettit was a madman," said Boston guard Bill Sharman. "He was going up in the key so high that six foot ten Arnie Risen couldn't stay with him. In the huddle we were asking each other, 'How can we stop Pettit?' We tried sagging on him, then two-teaming him when he made his move. We tried to stop the Hawks from passing to him. We even tried using Tommy Heinsohn to guard him face-to-face when he didn't have the ball. We might as well have tried to bribe the guy to take it easy."

Pettit had gained sweet revenge for Boston's Game 7 victory the previous year when he missed a tap-in at the buzzer that would have won it for the Hawks. Instead, it was just another Celtics' victory in Boston's Golden Age.

This one was different. The Hawks' notable 1958 victory, though, had exhausted Big Blue.

"After it was over," recalled Pettit, "all I could do was sit on the locker bench with my head in my hands, gasping. I have only a hazy memory of the last few minutes. I don't have any idea of how I got to the dressing room, I was so exhausted."

But while his teammates pounded his back and shook his hand, Bob answered a reporter's question with one of his own: "How can you feel any better than this?"

* * *

Joe Dean, who watched the college careers of Pete Maravich and Shaquille O'Neal from a close vantage point, is adamant that his old teammate is the best LSU basketball player ever.

He has a case. In 1974, the Southeastern Conference's fortieth anniversary and twenty years after his last game as a Tiger, Pettit was voted the best in the history of the SEC.

It was a remarkable rise for a man who said the only game he excelled at as a youngster was marbles.

As a freshman at Baton Rouge High School, Pettit was cut

from the football, baseball, and basketball junior varsities. As a sophomore he decided to concentrate on basketball, but Coach Kenner Day cut Pettit again. It was a move Day would never live down, but one Pettit staunchly defends.

"We were five over the roster limit, and I really wasn't good enough to make the team," Pettit said. "He knew it and I knew it."

The hurt of rejection in adolescence can scar some people, but Pettit wouldn't allow it. Determined to improve his skills, he joined a church league and spent every spare minute working on his game. He hung a bent clothes hanger on the garage door and shot tennis balls through it for hours at a time.

His father once recalled that his son "put two large reading lamps in the window, turned them toward the basket and practiced at night. He'd made up his mind he was going to make the team."

At the time, Bob, scrawny and awkward, stood five foot eleven.

By the time he enrolled for his junior year, Pettit had sprouted to six foot four and was playing basketball as he had only dreamed about before. Day also coached the football team, so until that season ended he had a senior player oversee basketball practices. Pettit said teammate Charlie Roberts told him Day was aghast when he heard Pettit was practicing at center.

But that season Pettit made the All-City squad, and the following year he was a six-foot-seven All-American on the state championship team.

Still, college coaches were not bowled over. Harry Rabenhorst offered Pettit a scholarship at LSU, which was fortunate because few other schools came calling.

"Tulane, Loyola, some of the state schools, and later DePaul and Western Kentucky came around, but I guess no more than six or seven actually recruited me," Pettit said. "Coach Raby took me out for a steak one night—that's how you recruited in those days—and said, 'Well, we've got a scholarship for you if you want to come,' and I accepted."

For LSU, which hadn't made much of a basketball splash since Sparky Wade boosted the Tigers to what was then a mythical national championship of 1935, it was a fateful decision. Pettit's career yielded a three-year record of 59-15 and two NCAA appearances, including the first Final Four appearance for any SEC team other than Kentucky.

Pettit developed into an imposing six foot nine presence—a center who could play facing the basket, with a soft shooting touch accompanied by a wicked hook. Renowned trainer Alvin Roy worked out a weight program for Pettit to improve his strength. At the end, once Pettit got a hand on the ball, few could take it away.

He had transformed himself into a major basketball force.

"His work ethic was incredible," said lifelong friend and LSU teammate Ned Clark. "That is what eventually showed up on the court. Nobody in the SEC, and very few anywhere, could fake and drive around the basket, put up a hook, or hit a medium jumper the way Pettit did."

★ ★ ★

With all his accomplishments as a collegian, it was as a pro that Pettit left his biggest impression—although he wasn't sure he wanted to go in that direction.

"Pro basketball didn't have the glamour it has today, and I came very close to signing with an amateur team, one of the teams where you work for the company and played for the company team," he said. "The salaries were close to the NBA's then, and each year some of the top players went that way. But it was a year-round job. I wanted to come back to Louisiana and go into business."

Picked second by the then-Milwaukee Hawks, Pettit asked for a $15,000 contract, a bold proposal at the time for an untried rookie with $100 to his name. Hawks owner Ben Kerner counter-offered $9,500, a salary which equaled the highest amount ever given a first-year player. The parties agreed to $11,000, but Bob had to report to Milwaukee a month ahead of schedule to help sell tickets.

On the court Coach Red Holzman transformed Pettit into the game's first power forward.

How did it work out?

When he retired after a star-studded eleven-year career, Pettit had:

- scored 20,880 points, then the highest career total in NBA history;
- pulled in 12,851 rebounds, the second highest total in NBA history;
- scored the most field goals (7,349) and the second highest number of free throws (6,182) in NBA history;
- been named All-Pro ten consecutive years, Most Valuable Player in four of the eleven All-Star Games he played in, and the NBA's Most Valuable Player twice.

Still, he'll always be remembered for that scintillating Game 6 performance in 1958.

Heinsohn said he never heard the end of it from legendary Celtics coach Red Auerback, who constantly reminded his old Hall of Fame player, "We would have won ten straight (championships) if you had held Pettit to forty-eight points!"

HOT AS A PISTOL

January 31, 1970
The Cow Palace, Baton Rouge, La.

The "Pistol" with dad/coach, Press Maravich.

Swis-h-h-h-h-h.

That's the whine of the shot heard 'round the basketball world, still reverberating through the years.

"Pistol" Pete Maravich put up a high, arcing shot over an Ole Miss zone that whistled through the net seventeen feet away, catching nothing but the silk cords. The basketball equivalent of the sound barrier—Oscar Robertson's career scoring record—had been shattered.

"All hell broke loose in the instant that shot went in," said Jay McCreary, who was on the LSU bench as a Tigers assistant coach that night.

Every one of the eleven thousand crammed into the Cow Palace (the John M. Parker Agricultural Center, where LSU then played its games, with an official capacity of 9,500, including the horde of photographers and reporters who ringed the court), it seemed to McCreary, suddenly flooded the floor trying to get to the new scoring king, who was hoisted onto the shoulders of his teammates.

"The whole time Pete kept pointing to the scoreboard, pointing out we still had a game to finish," McCreary said. There was 4:43 remaining in what would be a 109-86 Tigers victory. Maravich entered the game needing thirty-nine points to tie Robertson. He finished with fifty-three points—and twelve assists.

Maravich was a seminal figure in the history of Southeastern Conference basketball. He almost singlehandedly focused attention on a sport that was a decided stepchild to football in the South. The excitement Pistol Pete generated with his mesmerizing ballhandling skills and prodigious scoring was the cause of full houses across the league for the very first time. In his aftermath practically every school in the SEC, including LSU, constructed bigger arenas for basketball.

His detractors often point out that Pete never played on a championship team. But they miss the point. The season before he donned an LSU varsity uniform the Tigers were 3-23. He never played on a losing Tigers team, and at the end of Maravich's senior season LSU was 22-10 and finished second behind Kentucky in the SEC. That was a .700 percent improvement and catapulted LSU into a championship-contending program.

Jeff Tribbett started in the backcourt with Maravich, who died in 1988 at age forty. Tribbett came to LSU after a high school career in Lebanon, Indiana, where he played with Rick Mount, probably the nation's most sought-after prospect as a prep senior.

"He (Maravich) was probably the greatest guard who ever lived, and a great scorer," Tribbett said twenty-five years after the record-setting night. "But Pete was more than that. In my mind he was the greatest ballhandler that ever lived. He changed the game in that, from the NBA down to junior high; now you see people trying to do what he was criticized for doing: behind-the-back passes, between the legs assists. Pete showed those could be effective offensive weapons. But his scoring is what caught everybody's attention."

Robertson's record of 2,973 career points at the University of Cincinnati had been set a decade earlier. But from the first basket of Maravich's forty-nine points in his sophomore debut against the University of Tampa to a long-range basket in the National Invitation Tournament against Marquette, the sport has never seen a more voracious scorer.

Pistol Pete left LSU with 3,667 career points—a 44.2 career average—694 more than the great Big O, which is amazing in itself. It has to rank with Joe DiMaggio's fifty-six-game hitting streak in standing for so long, decades for both. No one has seriously challenged either, and in Maravich's case that is despite enormous changes—and advantages for offensive players—in college basketball.

The 3-point shot, a shot clock, and four-year varsity careers have become part of the sport since Maravich's last LSU season of 1969-70. Several athletes had opportunities to splinter Maravich's record, though it would have taken four seasons. Chris Jackson scored 1,854 points in two seasons at LSU before turning pro. Doubling his total, which would have required a continuation of his scoring average of thirty points, would have given Jackson 3,908 points.

Basketball giant Larry Bird, who lost a season of eligibility because of the transfer rule, scored 2,850 points in three seasons at Indiana State. Bird reasonably could have been expected to score 950 more points—for a total of 3,800—had he played a fourth season.

That conjecture, of course, is a long way from that evening at the Cow Palace when LSU fans filled the rafters in anticipation of seeing basketball history in the making.

With the Tigers trailing 14-11, Maravich launched a seventeen-point surge with a fallaway jumper that brought the fans out of their seats, then in quick order whipped out four dazzling assists that put the crowd in a frenzy—and put LSU in firm command, 28-14.

Pistol made a jumper with 8:49 left for his thirty-seventh point. With 7:58 to go, he banked in a twenty-five-footer over the Ole Miss 2-3 zone, his thirty-ninth point, which tied the record, though Pete thought it was the record-breaker. A chant went up from the crowd: "ONE, ONE, ONE!"

Five more times he came down and got his shot, and five times he missed, once on a twisting drive up the middle, the ball rimming in . . . and out.

"They were shots Pete would make 80 percent of the time," Tribbett recalled. "They weren't forced."

Then came the basket everyone came for, and a startled Maravich was overrun, then lifted by his teammates to the glee of the roaring crowd.

"I thought I broke it on the basket that tied it," he said. "But then I heard the crowd start up again. . . . I knew something had happened when I saw all those guys rushing at me with flash bulbs."

Some of the admiring fans in attendance that night might have been annoyed had they known what the sometimes puckish Maravich was contemplating. Asked about the missed shots before the record, he said: "Maybe I was worried subconsciously (about the record), but I also knew I had thirteen more (regular-season) games to do it. Actually, I thought it might be fun to average three points and twenty assists the rest of the way to keep everyone in suspense."

Pete Maravich being carried off the court after breaking the record for most points scored in a college career.

Shooting Down the Knicks

February 25, 1977
Louisiana Superdome, New Orleans, La.

"Pistol" Pete Maravich spent a career mesmerizing basketball fans with his Houdini-like ballhandling skills and sometimes outrageous scoring binges.

College basketball's all-time scoring leader was the face of the expansion franchise New Orleans Jazz when he stupefied a Superdome crowd with a sixty-eight-point outburst against the defensively sound New York Knicks.

In the era before 3-point field goals, Maravich went 26-of-43 from the field, a 60.5 shooting percentage, in a 124-107 victory that left the eleven thousand spectators slack-jawed.

At the time it was the most proficient scoring game for a guard in pro history, five points better than Jerry West's standard of fourteen years earlier. With the Knicks "trying everything we could to stop him," according to New York coach Red Holzman, the Jazz All-Pro hit in every conceivable manner.

Maravich scored his sixtieth point after streaking baseline and taking a pass. Defensive pressure caused him to lose his balance, but he was somehow able to get airborne across the lane and make a left-handed reverse basket under the hoop.

The shot that tied West's record, the sixty-third point, started with Pete positioned low against Butch Beard. He grabbed a bounce pass and flipped in a six-footer over his head with his back to the basket.

The sixty-fifth point came at the end of a twenty-five-foot jumper that arched over the outstretched arms of two defenders—what would be a 3-pointer in today's game.

An amazed Holzman explained in awestruck tones afterward, "He played just a great, great game. I'd hate to think where they'd be without him. He was just marvelous. His performance was the best I've ever seen for a guard."

Maravich scored seventeen, fourteen, seventeen, and twenty points by quarters and could have had more. One basket was erased after a referee ruled that he stepped out of bounds. A sequence of photographs by the *New Orleans Times-Picayune* later showed Pete was forced out of bounds by Beard, meaning the Jazz should have retained possession. Then Pistol Pete fouled out—for the only time that season—while hitting a bucket with 1:18 remaining. Taking the ball to the basket, Maravich was whistled on a hairline charging call. "It could have gone either way," he said later. "Another ref and it could have been a 3-point play."

Certainly, with that much time remaining, Maravich would have had the opportunity to get off three or four more shots, meaning seventy-five points was a distinct possibility—a possibility that haunted the roundball perfectionist. Pistol Pete didn't sleep that night, going over the game and wondering what he could have done better.

Though he didn't buy it, the answer was nothing.

Refusing to Wilt

May 8, 1970
Madison Square Garden, New York

Willis Reed (left) battles Wilt Chamberlain.

Willis Reed knew what his task was: He didn't have to out-score Wilt Chamberlain, didn't have to out-rebound him. What he had to do was just minimize the seven-foot-one Chamberlain, perhaps the greatest—certainly the strongest—center in pro basketball history.

This was no small assignment for Game 7 of the 1970 NBA Championship Series. In their last meeting, without an injured Reed, Chamberlain owned the paint, scoring forty-five points and pulling down twenty-seven rebounds in a 135-113 rout as the Los Angeles Lakers evened the series at 3-3.

The first legitimate shot at a title in the Knicks' twenty-four years as a franchise might well have rested with Reed—and he could barely walk.

The compelling story of the title game actually began in Game 5, when in a first-quarter drive to the basket against Chamberlain, Reed suddenly lay writhing on the floor with an intense stabbing pain emanating from his right hip.

"I was sick when I saw Willis," said Dave DeBusschere of his teammate in a twisted shape under the basket.

"My knee had been bothering me," Reed said later, "and I was supposed to take a shot (of medication) before the game, but I refused. When I went to make that move on Wilt, I pushed off on the right side. It was too much stress. I tore the muscle fibers and I went down."

The rectus femoris muscle, which extends the length of the thigh, was badly strained.

New York, after a halftime speech by Coach Red Holzman mimicking an old Ronald Reagan script, imploring his team to win it for Willis, actually did, 107-100. But Chamberlain found the Knicks easy prey in the next game, setting up Game 7 for the title.

Reed could still barely walk, but DeBusschere pleaded for a miracle. "Try to make it just half a game," he urged. "Just come out on the court Friday, and we'll be champs."

Willis vowed to himself, "I'll play if I can crawl."

Knowing this was a moment not to be passed, the six-foot-nine, 240-pound Reed said, "All my life I waited to play in an NBA championship game; that was where I wanted to be. If I could just walk, I was going out. When it comes to the seventh game for an NBA championship, there was no way that team was going on the court without me. If it meant the end of my basketball career, so be it."

It was determined by team physicians that the leg couldn't be damaged any worse by playing, though a great deal more treatment would be needed to put Reed on the court. Heat and whirlpool treatments were to be accompanied by the injection of a six-inch needle of cortisone several hours before playing. Thirty minutes before tip-off another shot, of Carbocaine, was necessary.

Phil Jackson watched the injection of the second shot and became ill.

While the Knicks warmed up, Reed rested in the locker room. Five minutes before tip-off, he got up and limped through the tunnel and into the arena. Chamberlain and Lakers teammate Keith Erickson caught sight of the hobbling figure and traded this-is-going-to-be-easy smiles.

But the entrance changed a forlorn New York crowd into an enthusiastic fan base howling with emotion, and it carried to the Knicks. It was as if a lost cause was reversed on the emotion of the moment.

"It came at exactly the right time," Bill Bradley said. "We were high when we came out to warm-up; we settled down toward the end of the warm-up. Then he came out, and it brought us up sky-high."

☆ ☆ ☆

Almost anyone seeing a thirteen-year-old wearing size thirteen shoes, or a ninth-grader standing six foot five could guess

Grambling coach Fred Hobdy with Willis Reed (right) and teammates.

where he might be leaning as a career choice. Lendon Stone, the basketball coach at Westside Consolidated High School in Bernice, Louisiana, blinked, pinched himself, then walked over to introduce himself.

A natural shooter, Willis averaged twenty-eight points as a senior when Westside won the Class C state championship. But he was also an All-State end, and football was his first love.

Things began to change a bit when young Willis was at a Ruston bus stop waiting to get back to Bernice. Grambling College basketball coach Fred Hobdy was also there, waiting to pick up Charlie Hardnett, later a Tigers All-American.

"I was only a high school sophomore," Reed said, "but Coach Hobdy introduced himself and we talked a good while. When I had to leave he said he would have a scholarship to Grambling when I was ready. He had never seen me play, though he did later, of course."

Hobdy said, "In my business you make it a point to get to know a kid that tall."

Hobdy's strongest recruiting opponent, when it came time for Willis to decide which direction he was going to go was none other than Tiger football coach Eddie Robinson. "Not this one, Eddie, please," Hobdy begged.

Coach Rob gave in.

Three of Reed's collegiate years he made All-American. He scored 2,335 points and lifted Grambling to the 1961 NAIA national championship. Hobdy was right; this one had all the makings of a great basketball player.

The Knicks picked Reed in the second round of the 1964 draft, a slight that irked him. "I was ready to play when I finished Grambling," he later bristled, "and I knew there weren't eight guys better than me. (General manager) Eddie Donovan called after the Knicks picked me and explained they thought I could help at center, although they had picked 'Bad News' Barnes in the first round at center. I thought to myself, 'I don't think I like these guys for some reason.'"

Donovan would later say he saw Reed when he was ill and was unimpressed.

In his first season, Reed averaged 19.5 points, broke the Knicks' rebound record with 1,175, made the All-Star team, and was the NBA's Rookie of the Year.

His trademark was his picks. Reed was a master of beautiful and jarring picks, effective even against taller and heavier players. They were unshakable, and every Knick scored behind them.

It's interesting to note now, in these days of stratospheric salaries, that for that outstanding rookie season, Reed was paid $14,000, plus a bonus.

A forward in his second season, while Walt Bellamy held down the middle, Reed averaged twenty points. Over the course of the next few years, the Knicks began assembling such future luminaries as Dick Barnes, Bradley, Walt Frazier, and DeBusschere. A trade of Bellamy in 1968 freed up Reed for fulltime duty at center, setting the stage for the 1970 championship.

Reed was the heart of the Knicks. He played a pinwheel center, spinning both the offense and defense out of the pivot. Everything revolved around him.

After a 60-22 regular season, the Knicks defeated Baltimore in seven games and Milwaukee in five to gain the NBA Finals. For Willis, it was a matter of Wes Unseld and Kareem Abdul-Jabbar down, Wilt Chamberlain to go.

"I think people are at their best when the challenge is the greatest," he would say later.

Dragging his leg behind him as he made his way to the court for Game 7, Willis was about to answer his greatest challenge.

On this night, he was no longer an intimidator. He was an inspirator.

In less than two minutes after the start of the game, Reed hit on two jump shots that gave the Knicks a 5-2 lead, an advantage they never relinquished.

He worked to do one thing: outmaneuver Chamberlain. He kept Wilt from having his way. If Wilt wanted a spot on the floor to set up, Reed denied him that spot, forcing Chamberlain farther away from the basket than he wanted to station himself.

Did he do his job? Depends on how you look at it. Chamberlain finished with twenty-one points and sixteen rebounds, not bad in anybody's book. In cold black and white, Reed's own stats were pedestrian—four points, three rebounds, one assist.

But Chamberlain had twenty-four fewer points and eleven rebounds fewer than he had in Game 6. His danger zone was neutralized, which allowed the other Knicks to clamp down on the other Lakers. Los Angeles scored 99 points on ability. The Knicks scored 113 on pure inspiration.

"He showed so much guts that you had to gut it out with him," Dave Stallworth marveled. "You got to go mad when a man who ought to be in a wheelchair comes out there."

An emotional Bradley said, "His courage is incredible. I had chills before this game."

Reed played just twenty-seven minutes that night, but he was the unanimous MVP of the first title team in New York Knicks' history.

It was the performance almost everyone referred to when Reed's No. 19 became the first jersey the Knicks retired.

THE IMPOSSIBLE DREAM

March 14, 1973
Municipal Auditorium, Kansas City, Missouri

The headline in the *New Orleans States-Item* said it all: "Xavier Does the Impossible."

The team representing the unique little school in the Gert Town area of New Orleans was the toast of small-college basketball that day, a giant-killer after jarring undefeated and No. 1-ranked Sam Houston State.

Impossible? Of all the people who saw the Bearkats brush aside Wartburg College 88-62 without breaking a sweat the night before in the NAIA Tournament in Kansas City, only a small contingent sitting in the 10,500-seat arena gave Xavier the remotest chance. Sam Houston State, with All-American James Lister in the middle, was bigger, and unquestionably, of the thirty-two teams in the tournament, had the most raw talent in its starting lineup with three future NBA draft picks.

Sporting a 27-0 record, the Bearkats were the odds-on favorite to breeze to the national championship.

Only the small band of Gold Rush players and Coach Bob Hopkins, who was already formulating a game plan, had a sense the Bearkats could be heading for a fall.

Senior guard Donald "Slick" Watts put the task in context: "It's all in the mind. If you can be sure in your mind that you can play with (high-caliber teams), you can beat them. But if you go into the game thinking you are outclassed, you will be."

Xavier, flying under the radar but with impressive credentials of its own, was certain it could compete.

The Gold Rush had rallied the night before from a four-point halftime deficit to beat Marist College 81-65, which advanced them to a tournament's next round. After the victory Coach Hopkins congratulated his team and then sent them back out to the court to see their second round opponents, the Bearcats, totally destroy Wartburg.

As imposing as Sam Houston State's front line was, with six-foot-nine Robert White, six-foot-eight Gary Moss, and six-foot-eleven Lister, who four decades later is still the Bearkats' all-time leading scorer (2,304 points, 21.9 average) and rebounder (1,682, 16.0 average), that was exactly where Hopkins wanted to direct his attack. He wanted to play the guards tight and prevent good looks from the outside, defend and box out on the inside to prevent second and third offensive shots.

After watching Sam Houston State from the stands, while everyone else was ohhhhing and ahhhhing, the confidence of the Gold Rush grew, especially after hearing Hopkins' game plan.

"Play well defensively on the perimeter and we'd have a chance," guard Greg Berniard recalled, "because their big men couldn't handle the ball. We noticed this watching them play the night before."

The Gold Rush had a sense the touted Bearkats really could be beaten—and that they were just the ones to do it.

☆ ☆ ☆

Younger, comparatively undersized, and not nearly as renowned as its opponent, Xavier was a team on the rise, bristling with athletic talent but smart enough as a group to know talent alone often isn't enough.

Sophomore forward Bruce Seals and Watts would go on to play in the NBA. Forwards James "Shirt" Williams, Sammy Young, and Berniard were solid college players, heavily pursued by bigger programs, as was defensive specialist Dale Valdery.

Under Hopkins, a former professional himself, the cousin of Hall of Fame great Bill Russell, and once the college game's all-time leading scorer with 3,759 points in four years at Grambling, the Gold Rush was a disciplined and honed outfit. Xavier lost two of its first three games that season, then ran off ten victories in a row before bringing a 21-5 record into the meeting with Sam Houston State.

This was a special group, one with unusual cohesiveness.

"If ever there was a team with what you might call 'charisma,' that team was it," said Dr. Norman Francis, president of Xavier and a fervent basketball fan. "They had style to match their talent."

And no player had more style than "Slick" Watts. Bald because of a childhood accident, he played with eye-catching headbands.

"It was an incredible team, not only because there was a lot of talent," said Valdery, who would later become head coach at his alma mater, "but because it was made up of talented individuals with clearly defined roles—and the willingness to play those roles."

Part of their smooth play was because the sophomore core of the Gold Rush—Seals, Williams, Berniard—had played together for six years, going back to their first season at New Orleans's Booker T. Washington High School, one of the preeminent programs in the state under Coach Ted Washington and where Seals was Louisiana's MVP in 1971.

The three were close friends, off the court and on, but were all set to continue their basketball elsewhere. Seals was headed to Cal-Berkley, Williams to Tulane, and Berniard to Creighton. Then the three attended a party in August, and realized they were starting to miss each other already. Seals, who had already moved to California, came down for the shindig. Homesickness and a persuasive talk with Hopkins changed his mind. Williams wanted to major in accounting, and, after some investigating, was satisfied that Xavier's program was excellent. After thinking it over, Berniard realized that maybe "playing before the hometown people I'd get more notice."

Their party brought the three together again, at least for a couple of years.

Xavier is a singular institution, the only Roman Catholic college founded specifically for the education of African Americans in North America.

It excelled in its mission both in the classroom and on the playing fields. "We were like a Black Notre Dame," is the way former athletic director Felix James once described Xavier, which was founded in 1925. "We excelled across the board."

An area near the back of the campus housed the athletic complex (football field, track, gym) called "Gloryland" in the 1930s and '40s when mainstream newspapers largely ignored black sports.

Famed Olympian Ralph Metcalfe began to coach track and field at Xavier immediately after the 1936 Games in Berlin, and at one time twelve of the Southern Intercollegiate Athletic Conference's sixteen track and field records were held by Xavier.

The basketball program produced perennial champions, with the Gold Rush winning thirty-six consecutive games at one point in the 1940s. Nat "Sweetwater" Clifton, the first black to sign an NBA contract, played at Xavier before World War II intervened.

Sports at Xavier were always conducted with a certain decorum. Dr. Francis was a freshman in 1948, and he recalled, "The Sisters of the Blessed Sacrament, who founded Xavier, always had a saying that if we did something, we should do it well," Francis said. "We certainly did with academics, and I think we did with athletics."

Francis remembered with a smile how the team would often change uniforms at the half because the sisters wanted the players to look a little neater than they did in sweaty jerseys.

But, in 1959, rising expenses forced the school to disband athletics. A decade later, in 1968, limited sports were brought back in the form of basketball. In the three years after Hopkins arrived from Alcorn State, he rebuilt the Gold Rush with records of 9-11, 19-10, and now 21-4.

Against the Bearkats, with a lineup standing at 6'11", 6'9", 6'8", 6'2", and 6'1", Hopkins sent out 6'8" Seals, 6'6" Young, 6'4" Williams, 6'2" Watts, and 6'1" Berniard.

There was a real sense in the Kansas City Auditorium that the Gold Rush were like sheep being led to slaughter. And the start of the game looked like that, too. Sam Houston State jumped to a 7-0 lead in the first three minutes. It took the Rush, with Seals skyrocketing into the air blocking shots, nearly twelve minutes to gain its equilibrium—and take the lead. Xavier went into the locker room with a one-point edge, 32-31, and no one in the auditorium could believe it.

The second half began as a see-saw battle with the Bearkats going back in front with sixteen minutes showing. Then Seals and the Rush began to tighten up defensively, and the crowd sensed the kill. With six minutes left Xavier retook the lead 53-52 on two Berniard free throws, and the Gold Rush, with Seals hitting from the outside, took complete control with twelve unanswered points to make it 65-52 with just 2:10 remaining.

Just as Hopkins drew up, Sam Houston State was in foul trouble throughout the second half as Xavier continued to work inside against the taller Bearkats—and force them to commit fouls. The Bearkats' three big men—Lister, White and Bob Moss—all had four fouls before midway in the final period.

Seals stole the show with thirty-two points, ten rebounds, and a dozen blocked shots—five against Lister, who finished with twelve points and seven rebounds.

Xavier had done the impossible. But the Gold Rush didn't win the NAIA championship. It was upset the next night by eventual champion Maryland-Eastern Shore.

However, the 67-60 victory over Sam Houston State was still a watershed moment—the only time in the long sports history of the city that a New Orleans school beat a No. 1-ranked basketball opponent.

Xavier's Bruce Seals drives the lane.

PLAYING BEAT THE CLOCK

February 26, 1978
Charlotte Coliseum, Charlotte, North Carolina

At tip-off time, not one person in the arena could have suspected they were about to witness an historic game.

At the end of the Sun Belt Conference Tournament championship game between the University of New Orleans and the University of South Alabama, what most of them knew is what they had witnessed was b-o-r-r-r-i-i-n-g.

And at least one interested observer, Sun Belt commissioner Vic Bubas, knew something drastic had to be done.

That night UNO and South Alabama met in a game that would play a role in fundamentally altering college basketball. It was an impetus to introducing a shot clock to college basketball.

Before the advent of the clock, a team could hold the ball until it got a high-percentage shot or as long as it maintained possession to keep opposing offenses in check. It was a tactic, famously utilized by North Carolina coach Dean Smith, which was coming under increasing criticism for ho-hum play.

But South Alabama coach Cliff Ellis, thinking his team's best chance at the league title was to contain UNO's six foot ten center Wayne Cooper and that the best way to do that was to employ a slowdown strategy, put the ball in deep freeze—all game long. Cooper finished with four points and four rebounds, but the plan blew up on Ellis when Privateers guard Nate Mills hit a twelve-foot jumper at the buzzer for a 22-20 UNO victory.

After halftime, when UNO led 7-6, Bubas could practically hear television sets across the region being clicked off.

Pro basketball had used a shot clock for decades, and women's basketball had had a thirty-second clock since 1971. Only men's college basketball was played without a clock, and scoring averages had declined in the past decade.

Bubas petitioned the NCAA to let the Sun Belt experiment to give the college game a boost.

"I probably wouldn't have made that case if we were talking about the Big Ten or Pac-10, established conferences," Bubas said. "But this was the Sun Belt, three years old, a young league trying to develop as a basketball entity and trying to cultivate fans. We were asking our schools to play in bigger arenas, trying to make Sun Belt Conference basketball into a big-time event. Games like we saw that night was not the way to do that."

Bubas, formerly an esteemed coach at Duke University, was given the okay for the 1978-79 season—though the clock operation was not quite what we know today. A forty-five-second clock was used by the Sun Belt, but it was turned off with four minutes to play, ostensibly to finish every game under the same conditions teams might have to play under in the NCAA Tournament.

How did it work out? The Sun Belt was used as an example four years later when *Sports Illustrated* made a pitch for a universal college shot clock. SI pointed out that:

- In the time span of its experiment, no SBC team had been able to win a conference game without scoring at least fifty points;
- Scoring in the SBC for both teams per game in the 1981-82 season was 141.8 points, an average of about twenty points more than in leagues such as the Big Ten and Atlantic Coast;
- Of the 17,085 shots taken in 164 conference games that season, 95 percent were put up in the first 29 seconds of possession;
- And the clock did not force pell-mell offense. In all those league games, only nineteen clock violations were called.

In 1986, the rest of the NCAA followed suit with the forty-five-second clock, and in 1993 it was reduced to a thirty-five-second clock. The Sun Belt experiment was an idea whose time had come.

The loss in the 1978 Sun Belt tournament final brought out Ellis's detractors and defenders. His reasoning, though, was sound. The Jaguars had won several games during that season with stall tactics, and he thought that's what was required against UNO. Both Bubas and Privateers coach Butch van Breda Kolff defended Ellis, saying a coach should do whatever is within the rules for his team to win.

Afterward in the locker room, Ellis was nearly in tears. His team not only let a tournament championship slip away, but he felt the game might have put a damper on an upcoming autograph party. An instructional guide by Ellis had just been published. It was entitled *The Complete Book to Fast-Break Basketball.*

SILENT KNIGHTS

February 27, 1965
Jesuit Gym, New Orleans, La.

The squeaking of sneakers on the hardwood, the thump-thump of the ball, and the occasional shrill whistle were the only sounds bouncing off the walls of the field house, a near-empty shell of its usual game-day self.

There was no roar of the crowd that Saturday morning. In fact, there was no crowd to speak of.

The quintessential Clash of the Prep Titans—a game that would have packed most area college arenas, between the two best basketball teams in the state—was played covertly. Only a relative handful of people, in an area where thousands would have been interested, got to see history in the making, or even knew of it.

St. Augustine High, 30-0, was playing Jesuit, 26-1, each ranked No. 1 in Louisiana, the Purple Knights in the then blacks-only league, the Blue Jays in the then whites-only association.

It seems strange now, when it's commonplace for athletes of all shades to compete with and against each other, but this was 1965, less than a year after the Civil Rights Act passed, and no integrated game had been played on the high school level in Louisiana before.

There had been integrated sporting events in Louisiana previously, perhaps most famously the 1956 Sugar Bowl between the University of Pittsburgh and Georgia Tech, and this was less than three months after Syracuse and LSU played a "mixed" Sugar Bowl, games that bracketed the restrictive segregation laws enacted after the mid-1950s game that kindled a black vs. white sports ban that cut across the spectrum of pro and amateur athletics.

But feelings on both sides were running high, particularly because St. Augustine, of the Louisiana Interscholastic, Athletic, and Literary Organization, was already pushing to play with New Orleans's other Catholic schools in the Louisiana High School Athletic Association, which oversaw the state's white sports.

Ironically, one of St. Aug's strongest allies was Jesuit.

★ ★ ★

St. Augustine was a powerhouse school from its beginning in 1951, both on the field and in the classroom. One of its founders, Father Robert Grant of the Josephites, the religious order that runs the school, was principal in 1965. "Excellence in All Areas" was the motto he brought to St. Aug, and all areas meant scholastics, band, debate, sports—every single thing St. Augustine was involved with. The school produced an inordinate number of National Merit and Presidential Scholars and sent its best students to the nation's most prestigious universities.

As a high-achieving all-male college preparatory school, St. Augustine was a mirror-image of Jesuit. The main difference: One was all black and the other predominantly white.

That main difference was a major source of irritation for Father Joseph Verrett, St. Aug's assistant principal, who strongly objected to the school's basketball team being ignored by New Orleans's morning newspaper, the *Times-Picayune*.

In twenty years of coaching the Purple Knights, George "Nick" Connor compiled a 384-141 record, winning five district championships and two state titles. So St. Augustine was a proven basketball commodity. And the 1964-65 St. Aug team was one of Connor's best.

But in the 1960s, it was a struggle just to get so much as a box score from a Purple Knights basketball game in the paper—or that of any other black school either. "That was a real sore spot with us," said Harold Sylvester, then a six foot five sophomore rebounding machine for the Knights and later the screenwriter of *Passing Glory*, a largely fictionalized television movie based on the real game between St. Aug and Jesuit. "It was like we weren't good enough to even acknowledge that we'd played."

It should be noted that the afternoon paper, *The States-Item*, did have a part-time black sportswriter, R. L. Stockard, who did weekly roundups on the African American schools.

But the *Picayune* was by far the dominant news outlet, and Fathers Grant and Verrett not only felt their students were being slighted, but that the *Times-Picayune*'s blanket of silence limited knowledge of potential prospects from college recruiters.

★ ★ ★

While the defending black state champion Purple Knights were compiling their impressive record away from the eyes of the mainstream press, Jesuit was also on a roll, going 87-4 over three straight state championship seasons. The 1964-65 Blue Jays, coached by Dick Francis, were being proclaimed Louisiana's "Team of the Century."

And every one of Jesuit's box scores got in the paper, usually with the lead prep story of the day.

The two best programs in Louisiana were mere miles apart, but, according to the laws of the day, prohibited from playing.

Sitting in Father Grant's office one afternoon, Stockard planted a seed in the principal's mind: the regular seasons were over, and both schools had more than a week before their respective state tournaments would begin. Why not play each other: (1) to stay sharp; and (2) to see who is really the better team?

According to Stockard, Grant dismissed the idea, saying Jesuit would never agree. To which Stockard said he responded, "You never know until you try."

Grant picked up the phone and talked to Rev. Donald Pearce, S. J., the priest who served as Jesuit's athletic director. Pearce mulled over the proposition and said he'd get back.

Jesuit was in a predicament. With the possibility of being suspended by the LHSAA, the Jays couldn't schedule an "official" game, and given the climate of the times, there were political considerations to take into account.

Father Verrett said later there was another nuanced, subtle factor. "It might have been harder for a Catholic school to refuse to do the just and Christian thing, particularly when it involved another Catholic school," he reasoned. "If those boys couldn't get on the floor together, what does that say about Christianity?"

Pearce called Grant back, and he did agree, but only if certain conditions were met—all in Jesuit's favor: The game must be held at the Jays' gym; it must be officiated by refs chosen by Jesuit; it was to be kept under wraps before and after no matter what the outcome; and the only spectators would be a few administrators from the schools.

Stockard believed decades later that Jesuit thought St. Augustine would decline, feeling the deck was being stacked against the Purple Knights.

But Jesuit didn't have all the cards. The Knights said they'd be there, but three of the Blue Jays, including two starters said they would not, choosing not to participate.

Not just school personnel were present. Behind the locked doors, some family and friends of both schools attended (meaning it would be impossible to keep quiet). In a gym with a capacity of three thousand, a total of forty to sixty people were in the stands—though not Father Verrett, who was offended by the secrecy. But sitting near the bench was a reporter. Stockard walked into the gym passing as an assistant coach.

☆ ☆ ☆

"It was a strange game," said Billy Fitzgerald, one of Jesuit's mainstays. "No crowd noise, no emotion from the stands. Just kind of . . . quiet. We wore game uniforms, but it was like a scrimmage."

Sylvester agreed the game's setting was odd, but said St. Aug played with stronger-than-usual intensity. "To Jesuit," he reflected later, "it was just a basketball game. But for St. Aug, this was the game of our lives."

And the Knights played like it. With 2:10 left in the first quarter, the Knights had a fourteen-point advantage and were never seriously threatened after that in what turned out to be an 81-59 St. Aug runaway. Superstar senior center Isiah King had his way in the middle and scored twenty-six points.

The absence of the missing Blue Jays starters can't be dismissed. Fitzgerald acknowledged the game almost certainly would have been more competitive with them. "I don't know if it would have made much difference, closer perhaps. Win, I don't know. St. Aug was really good."

Two years later, such games began being almost commonplace. St. Augustine won a federal lawsuit that allowed not only the Purple Knights into the LHSAA, but also every other black school in the state.

In 1965, though, Jesuit went on to win the second of its three straight LHSAA championships, while St. Augustine lost in the first round of the LIALO playoffs to Scotlandville, an opponent it had beaten 66-63 in triple overtime in the regular season.

Connor wasn't happy with the way things turned out, saying his team seemed to lose focus after the "secret" game (the news of which got out just about the time the final buzzer sounded). He said later, "I would have preferred losing that scrimmage to Jesuit, and winning the 1965 LIALO state championship."

Fitzgerald and Sylvester, the first African American to receive a basketball scholarship to Tulane, would later be college teammates. But both said the subject was never a topic of discussion between them.

It obviously stayed in Sylvester's thoughts for decades. He said, "It was the day we proved we could play with the guys with the names in the box scores."

Purple Knight Harold Sylvester became the first African American to receive a basketball scholarship to Tulane University, where he was teamed with Jesuit standout Billy Fitzgerald.

BELLES OF THE ROUNDBALL

Queen Brumfield.

It's surprising because for some reason it's never been a major topic of sports conversation outside the immediate areas where it's being played, but Louisiana women have always been at or near the top of basketball. Not just the Lady Techsters or the Baskin Lady Rams, but around the state.

One of the state's most compelling stories is that of Queen Brumfield (Nard) playing through serious distress to score twenty points to help clear the way from her pivot position for a 92-76 Southeastern Louisiana University victory over Phillips University of Oklahoma for the 1976 AIAW national championship.

The game at Cal State-Pomona had to be stopped ten times for Brumfield's shoulder to be popped into place. She rose to the occasion, making that game the summit of SLU basketball history, women's or men's.

She left Southeastern as the school's leading scorer with 2,972 points and top rebounder with 1,586.

Records, of course, are made to be broken, but the most dazzling statistics of Brumfield's SLU career very likely won't ever be approached. In her four seasons at the Hammond school, the Lady Lions were 117-16—a 94.7 percentage.

* * *

Sports might never have had a more consistent champion, not only in women's basketball but in athletics generally, than Kim Mulkey of Tickfaw.

As a player, the pigtailed guard led Hammond High to four state titles, then went to Louisiana Tech where she directed the Lady Techsters to two national championships.

She also picked up a gold medal in the 1984 Olympics, and then picked up another title at Tech as Leon Barmore's assistant coach. Since then Mulkey coached the Baylor Lady Bears to multiple national titles, thus becoming the first

Sheila Thompson-Johnson.

woman in NCAA history to win national championships as a player, assistant coach, and head coach.

★ ★ ★

Sheila Thompson-Johnson made a mark at Louisiana College, both as a player and as a coach, leading the Lady Wildcats to the Final Four (NAIA Division II) in both roles.

She played at LC from 1977 through '81, and coached there from 1985-89.

A two-time All-American, Thompson-Johnson spearheaded a spot for the Lady Wildcats (21-9) in the 1980 Final Four field, where they finished fourth in only the fourth year of the existence of the LC program.

Her teams were 75-43 in her four years as head coach, and she guided the Lady Wildcats to third place in the NAIA national tournament in 1986. Later, Thompson-Johnson became the school's first female athletic director.

★ ★ ★

Lin Gamble was a scoring machine for Central of Grand Cane High School, averaging 37.4 points as a junior and 48.2 points as a senior. In one memorable tournament at Shreveport's Haynes Gym, Gamble scored sixty-four points one night and sixty-five points the next.

Louisiana had no women's programs when it was time for college, and Gamble went to Ouachita Baptist in Arkansas, where she was a three-time All-American in the late 1960s. Ouachita Baptist finished second nationally twice and no worse than fifth in her four seasons.

Gamble represented the United States in the 1971 World University Games and in the Pan American Games, where she scored twenty-eight points against Cuba in the game that gave the USA the silver medal.

★ ★ ★

Five consecutive trips to the Final Four would look good on any program's résumé. But the LSU women, with superstars Seimone Augustus and Sylvia Fowles in the lineup at different times, have fared no better than the LSU men once they've achieved Final Four status.

Neither have gotten further than the semifinals.

In 2003-2004, Hall of Fame coach Sue Gunter molded one of her best teams. Gunter took sick, though, about two-thirds of the way through the season and assistant Pokey Chatman took the 27-8 Lady Tigers the rest of the way. Perennial power Tennessee edged LSU 52-50 in the NCAA semifinals.

A year later, Baylor, the ultimate champion, whipped a 33-3 LSU squad under new coach Chatman 68-57 in the semifinals.

In 2006, Duke thrashed LSU 64-45, again in the semifinals.

Chatman was removed from her position during the 2006-07 season because of allegations of inappropriate behavior. It was a year in which the Lady Tigers went 31-4 and assistant Bob Starkey took over in the last five games, winning four. Then LSU was beaten in the semifinals by Rutgers 59-35.

Van Chancellor was named permanent head coach and again LSU enjoyed regular-season success, going 31-6 in 2007-08. The Lady Tigers again got to the Final Four, but dropped a heartbreaking 47-46 game to Tennessee.

★ ★ ★

Although they have little relationship to the game as it's played today, New Orleanian Clara Gregory Baer authored the first published rules of women's basketball in 1891. Hired to establish the first physical education department at Sophie Newcomb College, Baer put the rules of the game she called "basquette" to paper. There was no dribbling, no guarding, and no stealing of the ball, and no two-handed shot. The game was played in seven divisions over the court.

Any mention of women's basketball would be incomplete without Eun Jung Lee, who left her homeland of South Korea to play at Northeast Louisiana University (now ULM), and team-

Kim Mulkey.

mate Lisa Ingram. Both All-Americans, they combined for a memorable basketball epoch, leading the then-Lady Indians to a four-year 102-15 record, and were the catalysts for NLU reaching the 1985 NCAA Final Four. Ingram left with a 23.0 career point average, and Lee left with career averages of 18.8 points, 7.5 assists, and 2.5 steals.

One of the best women's teams to ever come out of New Orleans was the 1983-84 Dillard Devilettes led by Jackie Franklin. Dillard finished 33-4 overall and in the NAIA Final Four, where the Lady Blue Devils won three of their four games, losing only to eventual national champion North Carolina-Asheville 81-64.

PREP-POURRI: Edna Tarbutton is not the only superstar coach in Louisiana women's basketball. Carrice Russell Baker ran up an astonishing 972-191 record (an .836 percentage), and eight state championships at Winnsboro and Jena (four at each school), and finished second four more times. Jelly Pigott coached Jena to a record twenty-three appearances in the Sweet 16/Ladies 28 tournaments, even though most of her success came before the establishment of the state tournament in 1969. Her teams won six state championships and finished as the runner-up three times during her eighteen seasons at Jena, where she coached from 1952-70. During that period her teams averaged thirty-five victories, losing no more than five in any season.

Southeastern Louisiana University Lady Lions, the 1976 AIAW National Champions.

Sue Gunter.

Seimone Augustus.

Clara Baer.

Wind Beneath the Wings

1940s-1950s
Baskin Gym, Baskin, La.

As soon as the group would enter the gym, walking single file in their distinctive white coveralls, the whispering and pointing would begin: "Here comes Baskin."

Even players from the game in progress would stop and stare.

"Sometimes," Frances Lyles recalled more than sixty years later in an interview with Ted Lewis of the *Times-Picayune*, "I think we intimidated some people so much we had them beat before we ever went on the floor."

Could be.

From 1947 through 1953, the Baskin High School girls basketball team compiled a winning streak unsurpassed in the history of the sport at any level—218 straight victories.

Unfazed by a loss, the Lady Rams reeled off another seventy-one in a row before losing again. And they capped that 1955 season with their eighth consecutive state championship.

How impressive is that?

Well, the No. 2 winning streak in high school girls basketball is 154 games by Monetta, South Carolina, from 1933-40. The boys prep record is 159 by Passaic, New Jersey, from 1919-25.

In college basketball, the top marks are 131 by Wayland Baptist (before women's sports were sponsored by the NCAA), ninety by the University of Connecticut women, and eighty-eight by the UCLA men.

In the NBA it's thirty-three by the Los Angeles Lakers. Tops in the WNBA is fifteen by the Houston Comets.

That only leaves the Harlem Globetrotters, and beating the Washington Generals 2,495 consecutive times hardly counts.

Baskin usually didn't just scrape by either. The average margin of victory during the winning streak was thirty points, 54-24. Scores such as 60-10, 33-9, and 49-6 dot the list.

The most remarkable thing is that this monumental achievement was not accomplished by a large school with plentiful players and resources or by a selectively recruiting entity whose raison d'être is its basketball team.

Rather, this was a small school in a single caution-light community in rural Franklin Parish whose players primarily came from farming families in the area, hardly the likely incubator for such success.

In fact, Baskin High School no longer exists, having been consolidated along with former rivals like Ogden, Crowville, Fort Necessity, and Winnsboro, which stopped the winning streak, into Franklin Parish High in 1998.

But what Baskin did have going for it was its coach—Edna "Tiny" Tarbutton—whose single-minded dedication to discipline and fundamentals had her players both fearing and loving her.

"She'd whip off her belt and get you," said Dixie Baskin Jackson, whose feat of never playing in a losing game earned her a spot in *Ripley's Believe It Or Not*. "And she knew our parents stood behind her 100 percent."

Even worse was the dreaded threat, "I'll take your ball suit."

That approach certainly got her players' attention.

"Miss Tarbutton (the players never called her 'Coach,' and certainly never 'Tiny') had a knack of watching a team and figuring out how to stop them," said Lyles, who was a sophomore at Baskin when the winning streak began. "Then she knew we had confidence in her, and whatever she told us, we'd execute it."

That extended to always entering the gym the same way, especially during tournaments, which were a staple for most programs in those days.

"We didn't make a sound," Lyles said. "Miss Tarbutton would point to where she wanted us to sit. You didn't get popcorn and stuff and especially didn't talk to boys. Maybe after the game we could visit a little bit, but before then she wanted your undivided attention."

The coveralls were purchased at cost from Haddad's Men's Store in Monroe and had "BASKIN" stitched across the back and "GIRLS BASKETBALL" across the front.

"We were the only team with anything like that," Lyles said. "They set us apart.

"Miss Tarbutton made sure we had them clean and starched. She said we were going to be ladies."

Behaving like "ladies'" was important in girls sports in those pre-Title IX days.

★ ★ ★

Girls basketball was a much different sport in those days as well.

When Tarbutton, who grew up near Monroe and played at Ouachita, began her coaching career after graduating from Northwestern State in 1943, it was a six-on-six game, or, more properly, three-on-three with forwards and guards restricted to half of the court.

A player could dribble only once before either passing or shooting. That was increased to two dribbles in the late 1940s and eventually to an unlimited number, although the three-on-three concept remained in force in some states until the 1970s.

Tarbutton was no full time coach, teaching three social studies classes each day along with three physical education classes.

She did like to use two of the PE classes to scout out potential talent as young as ten years old. The other PE class was the final period of the day and reserved for practice so that the players could catch the bus to get home.

Her coaching supplement when she started was $10 a month, and she never had an assistant, although Marquerite Franks, her longtime scorekeeper, acted as an unofficial aide, especially when it came to dealing with the players' problems.

Still, girls basketball was a big deal in Baskin. Fans filled the three hundred-seat Baskin gym. Sometimes for big games, the gym windows would be cracked open and crates stacked outside so more fans could watch.

The road trips were special, too, even if the team rarely traveled more than a hundred miles away. "That's why they wanted to be on the team because it was something to look forward to," Tarbutton said in an interview before her death at age eighty-seven in 2009. "This was a rural area and not very prosperous.

"Most of their families didn't have cars. If they played basketball, they got to go places."

★ ★ ★

Baskin's basketball fortunes began to decline after the mid-1950s, although following four seasons in which the Lady Rams won a total of nine games, Tarbutton closed her career with twenty- and twenty-two-win seasons in 1975 and '76, giving her a final record of 654-263-2.

The honors rolled in after that—the Louisiana High School Hall of Fame, the Louisiana Sports Hall of Fame, the National High School Hall of Fame, and, finally, in 2005, the Women's Basketball Hall of Fame.

At first, Tarbutton resisted such attention. But Lyles said, as she grew older and she saw the affection her players had for her long after their high school days were past, Tarbutton mellowed, although she always emphasized that the accomplishments were her teams', not hers.

One special occasion came when players from her state championship teams, a total of nine, purchased banners to commemorate each one for the old gym, which is still in use at a junior high.

Tarbutton initially wanted just one banner without her name on it. But eventually she was won over.

"When she was presented her ring, someone sang 'Wind Beneath My Wings,'" Lyles said. "I think it was the first time I ever saw tears in her eyes.

"I think that at that point she finally realized how special it was to take a bunch of farm kids and mold us into champions and ladies."

Ladies First

March 28, 1982
The Scope, Norfolk, Virginia

Sonja Hogg and Leon Barmore led the Lady Techsters to multiple national championships.

Leon Barmore was heaping praise on Cheyney State, the team his own Louisiana Tech squad had just beaten 76-62 for the 1982 national championship—the first women's basketball title crowned under the auspices of the NCAA. "Give credit to Cheyney State," Barmore, Tech's associate head coach, said. "They and Southern Cal are the two best teams in America, other than us, of course. And I don't mean that in an arrogant way."

Didn't matter if he did. It was the truth.

Louisiana Tech was at the pinnacle of women's basketball. The Lady Techsters not only had won the first NCAA championship, but the year before beat Tennessee in the title tournament of the AIAW, the first association to sponsor women's college athletics. Tech also made the championship game in 1978, losing to Old Dominion and finishing with a 34-4 record.

The Lady Techsters were just heating up. During the two seasons of 1980-81 and 1981-82, Tech went 69-1—34-0 and 35-1.

How dominating was Tech in that era? Well, the head coach of the Techsters was Sonja Hogg, and her assistant was Barmore. Among the players were Janice Lawrence, Pam Kelly, and Kim Mulkey. Everyone of those people have been inducted into the Women's Basketball Hall of Fame.

To put Louisiana Tech women's basketball in focus, consider: as of 2011, the Lady Techsters have won three national championships, reached thirteen Final Fours, twenty-eight Sweet 16s, and twenty-seven Division I NCAA tournaments. Tech has produced three Wade Trophy recipients (Kelly, Lawrence, and Teresa Weatherspoon), emblematic of the best woman player in the country in a given season, and five Olympic medalists. Tech also has an all-time record of 1,000-212, a .825 winning percentage that ranks as the best of any Division I program.

So how did such a colossus of women's basketball spring up in the red clay hills of north Louisiana?

No fiction writer could sell such a simple-minded scenario.

The unlikely seed of the program was planted when Tech president F. Jay Taylor called in a twenty-eight-year-old physical education teacher at Ruston High School, whose main connection with sports was overseeing the pom-pom squad. Sonja Hogg had no previous playing or coaching experience above the intramural level, but Taylor asked her if she would be interested in starting the school's first women's athletic program.

"I was confident and young," Hogg later told Buddy Davis of the *Ruston Daily Leader.* "I didn't know what I didn't know."

She took the job, and the two agreed the program was to run along a certain model.

The president didn't just want an appendage of the Louisiana Tech Bulldogs, the men's program, and he insisted the women carry themselves with class on and off the court, which is probably why he first thought of Hogg, an elegant woman and a Tech graduate.

When she agreed, Hogg got a $5,000 budget, the right to design the uniforms, to change the school color for those uniforms—and to change the name of her team.

From the start Hogg's team wore baby blue unis—as opposed to Tech's traditional dark blue—with sleeved jerseys.

"Back then they didn't have sports bras," Hogg said. "I didn't want us out there playing with bra straps hanging out."

She also would not allow the players to wear knee or elbow pads. Too unladylike.

The fans who would eventually flock to see Tech's women grew to view the girls the way they would their daughters. "What we did was right for Ruston," Hogg said. "It's a very conservative town, and it was important that we have a team that looked nice and conducted themselves like young ladies. Now we wanted to be competitive too—ready to knock somebody's head off. But it was also important how they presented themselves."

And they would not go by Tech's men's teams' name. "A lady Bulldog is a bitch," Hogg said. So, eventually, the most famed of Louisiana Tech programs would be known as the "Lady Techsters."

Barmore once said of Hogg, a woman who dressed to the nines, "She looked like she stepped out of a magazine." Hogg was color-coordinated: She drove a white Cadillac, often wore a white fur coat on recruiting trips, and frosted her coiffed hair to match. She used all that as an example for her girls to always look their best because that would help them do their best.

"I told my team before we ever played my first game," she recalled saying, "'Miss Hogg is dressing for your basketball game the way I expect you to play.' And I was decked out."

Tech played well but lost its first game at Southeastern Louisiana 59-55. But in their first home game the Lady Techsters were decked out, too, undressing LSU 97-83.

That first Hogg team, featuring a five-foot-nine center, played four home games, and produced a not-bad-at-all 13-9 record.

Hogg could recruit, and she could promote. The Lady Techsters eventually started outdrawing the men. "Sonja was all about raising the awareness of women's basketball," said Tennessee coach Pat Summitt. "She wasn't just a great recruiter, she was a great promoter. She could sell an Eskimo ice."

Part of what she put to good use was advice from an old friend at Ruston High, close to the Tech campus. Barmore, the dour-looking but highly successful boys coach at Ruston High, was accessible and willing to share his thoughts and considerable expertise. Hogg used to run over to the high school during Barmore's early afternoon free period and pick his brain.

Hogg did pretty well on her own, stitching together three winning seasons and a 54-28 overall record with a roster of players all coming from within a hundred miles of Tech. She knew, though, that to go further the Lady Techsters needed help.

Barmore was a coach clearly destined for something more than high school basketball, and Hogg recognized that. She asked Taylor for permission to hire Barmore for the princely sum of $13,000 a year. He was to be what was in reality Hogg's co-head coach. "I could see we were on the cusp of having our program explode," Hogg said. "But I had to be able to recruit all over the country, and we needed someone who could give the kids the Xs and Os they needed. There aren't many people in the country that know the game like Leon Barmore."

★ ★ ★

Barmore, once an all-conference guard at Tech, came on board in 1977. From then on, Hogg began concentrating on recruiting and public relations. Barmore was left with what he was most comfortable doing: coaching.

"At first I read all these books on the psychology of women," Barmore said. "But finally I said 'enough.' I'm just going to be me. With the women I suppose that out of ten comments I make I'll want nine to be positive, and the one negative to really work. With the guys everything would be negative."

Whatever it was, it turned out to be near-perfect.

"It was just a great confluence of events," Hogg said. "We'd been doing things first class from the start because we had the support of our president. And because of Leon, our players were always determined, focused, and serious about their business. You couldn't ask for a more wonderful situation."

Hardly. In two years the Lady Techsters reached their first AIAW Final Four, two years after that Tech won its first national championship, and a year after that the first NCAA title. That was in the midst of a run of six straight Final Fours.

Three years later Hogg decided to pursue other opportunities. She left Tech with a 307-55 record and the two national titles. But she knew the Lady Techsters remained on the solid footing of Barmore's coaching. He would take Tech to nine more Final Fours, and another national championship in 1988.

When he retired from Tech in 2002 Barmore had a record of 576-87, a winning percentage of 86.9—highest in the history of the game, men or women.

Throw in his totals when he was Hogg's co-head coach, and Barmore was 739-105 with an even higher victory percentage of 87.6. His career was highlighted by five national championship game appearances, a national title, nine berths in the Final Four, and twenty consecutive trips to the NCAA tournament.

Of course, the names of Hogg and Barmore will be intertwined forever in Louisiana Tech sports history. "I don't know if there's been a relationship in coaching quite like ours," Barmore said. "I doubt if there's been one with the kind of success we had."

RINGSIDE
Sec. D6
Row 11
Seat 4
$200.00 Taxes Incl.
ENTER ANY GATE
LOUISIANA SPORTS, INC.
presents
THE BATTLE of NEW ORLEANS
NO REFUNDS
WORLD HEAVYWEIGHT CHAMPIONSHIP
LEON SPINKS vs MUHAMMAD ALI
PLUS TWO CHAMPIONSHIP BOUTS AND UNDERCARD
FRIDAY, SEPT. 15, 1978-6 P.M.
SUPERDOME - NEW ORLEANS, LA.
World Heavyweight Championship
RINGSIDE
Sec. D6
Row 11
Seat 4
$200.00 Taxes Incl.
Fri., Sept. 15, 1978
6 P.M. - SUPERDOME
NEW ORLEANS, LA.
JOE BROWN
EVERLAST
Pete Herman
FORMER BANTAM-WEIGHT CHAMPION OF THE WORLD
Sports Illustrated
LEMA ON LONG IRONS
LIGHT HEAVYWEIGHT
WILLIE PASTRANO
Ready to defend his title
WORLD'S CHAMPIONSHIP FIGHT
MUN. AUDITORIUM - MON, APRIL 29 - 8:30 P.M.
NEW ORLEANS BOXING CLUB, INC.
Presents WORLD'S JR. MIDDLEWEIGHT CHAMPIONSHIP FIGHT
DENNY MOYER
DENNY MOYER, CHAMPION
15 ROUNDS - VS - 15 ROUNDS
RALPH DUPAS
RALPH DUPAS, No. 1 CHALLENGER
HIGH CLASS PRELIMINARIES
Popular Prices, Tax Included
Balcony $3.50 - Unreserved Main Floor $5.50 - Reserved Ring & Boxes $7.50-$10
Buy Your Tickets Now
Tony Canzoneri
TONY CANZONERI
NEW ORLEANS
FEATHERWEIGHT CHAMPION

The Clang of the Bell

When the arms of Muhammad Ali went up, the roar from the sixty-three thousand-plus spectators was deafening.

The self-proclaimed "Greatest" had just beaten Leon Spinks in a unanimous fifteen-round decision to regain his heavyweight championship—for an unprecedented third time.

No one, of course, at the time knew what a historic moment that was—the last time Ali, one of the most popular and charismatic athletes of all-time, would ever throw up his arms in victory.

New Orleans again found a way to be linked in the record books.

That evening of September 15, 1978, in the Superdome was going to be remembered in any case. The redoubtable Muhammad Ali headlined a Carnival of Champions, which drew an indoor record for a crowd that not only filled the seats, but that paid more than seven million dollars—the biggest gate in boxing history. The Superdome card also presented three other title bouts.

★ ★ ★

One of the most remembered fights in the latter years of the twentieth century—not for its artistry but for its perplexing finish—was also held in the Dome. The "No Mas" bout of November 26, 1980, in which Sugar Ray Leonard reclaimed his World Boxing Council welterweight belt when Roberto Duran suddenly quit in the eighth round, stunned viewers.

Duran, peppered with left jabs and combinations, was befuddled by Leonard's style. When the frustrated Duran, known as "Hands of Stone," couldn't get his offense going, rather than continue, he threw up his hands in disgust. It was scored a TKO, and the State Boxing Commission fined Duran $7,500 for the way in which the fight was terminated.

★ ★ ★

Smokin' Joe Frazier left an imprint on New Orleans—and on Terry Daniels—at the Rivergate Auditorium on January 15, 1972, the night before the Dallas Cowboys beat the Miami Dolphins in Super Bowl VI at Tulane Stadium.

Frazier floored Daniels twice in the third round, then bounced him into ropes and face down on the canvas in the fourth for the KO. Daniels, who wouldn't quit, said memorably afterward, "I felt like shaking the ref's hand."

★ ★ ★

Louisiana's own kings of the ring include:

- Joe Brown, often overlooked but with a smooth style combined with a KO punch. The native of Baton Rouge won the world lightweight championship in a fifteen-round decision over Bud Smith after breaking his hand in the second round. He successfully defended his title eleven times. Brown was *Ring* magazine's "Fighter of the Year" in 1961 when he was thirty-six. "Old Bones" retired in 1970 at age forty-five with a 116-47-13 record, many of his defeats coming in the eight years after he lost his title to Carlos Ortiz.

- Pete Herman is considered one of the greatest bantamweight world champions. The New Orleanian first won the championship in 1917 by beating Kid Williams in a match in which the challenger allowed the champion to pick his own referee, Bill Rocap. But Herman won the decision in twenty rounds, and Rocap said "I can sincerely say that Herman beat him because he was the better fighter."

  Later Herman became the first bantamweight to regain a title, beating Joe Lynch in 1921, months after Lynch took it from Pete, in Brooklyn before a crowd of twenty thousand.

In his last fight, against Roy Moore in Boston's Mechanics Building, Herman was almost totally blind. He was missing so badly from the outside the referee warned him about carrying his opponent. But when they went toe-to-toe and Pete was able to fight by instinct and sound, he gave Moore such a fierce pounding that Moore was begging him to ignore the referee's warnings.

Herman won his last fight and retired with a 71-12-10 win-loss-draw record to go with fifty-seven no-decisions, pro fights that did not factor in a win-loss or draw record.

- Tony Canzoneri, at five foot four, fought in twenty-one world championship bouts in four divisions—fluctuating between 118 pounds as a bantamweight, 126 as a featherweight, 135 as a lightweight, and 140 as a light welterweight—from 1925 until 1939. Born and raised in Slidell but fighting out of New York, Canzoneri won the world featherweight title in 1928 by beating Benny Bass. He knocked out Al Singe in 1:40 of the first round for the lightweight title in 1930, becoming one of an exclusive group (Barney Ross and Henry Armstrong) to hold two world championships simultaneously. In 1931 Canzoneri beat Jack Berg to win the junior welterweight championship, a rare fighter to have held titles in three or more divisions. He retired having held a total of five championships with a 137-24-10 record that included forty-four knockouts.

- Willie Pastrano, an early sparring partner of the young Cassius Clay, won the light heavyweight championship on a razor-thin decision from Harold Johnson in Las Vegas in 1963. A protégé of trainer Angelo Dundee, famed mentor of Muhammad Ali, Pastrano defended his title twice before being knocked down for the only time in his career in a TKO defeat to Jose Torres.

  Taking a beating in that bout, Pastrano was asked by a ringside physician if he knew where he was, and he famously replied, "You're damned right I know where I am! I'm in Madison Square Garden getting the shit kicked out of me." That was Pastrano's last fight. He retired with a 63-13-8 record.

- Ralph Dupas, dubbed the "Native Dancer" in New Orleans for his elusive will-o'-the-wisp style in the ring, fought across several divisions. He was the top-ranked light heavyweight in the world but was knocked out by Joe Brown. As a welterweight he defeated future middleweight champion Joey Giardello but lost to Emile Griffith.

  Dupas also lost a close decision to Sugar Ray Robinson. He won the light middleweight championship by beating champion Denny Moyer in a unanimous decision in 1963. Dupas retired with a 106-23-6 record.

* Bernard Docusen deserves a special mention as he is often described as the "uncrowned champion" of the 1940s and early '50s. *New Orleans Times-Picayune* boxing expert Waddell Summers staunchly maintained Docusen was one of the best of his era. The first protégé of legendary New Orleans trainer Whitey Esnault, who also started Dupas and Pastrano, Docusen won thirty-seven consecutive bouts. In 1948 he fought Sugar Ray Robinson in Chicago—then at the height of his considerable powers—for the welterweight championship and lost a close decision. At that time there were only eight divisions and only one champion for each division, and Docusen never got another shot at a title. He retired in 1953 with a 70-10-6 record.

☆ ☆ ☆

Perhaps the finest amateur to come out of Louisiana was Eddie Flynn, who came under the tutelage of New Orleans's famed coach Tad Gormley while a student at Loyola. Flynn rang up a 144-0 record as an amateur and defeated Erich Campe of Germany for the welterweight gold medal in the 1932 Olympics. It would be twenty years before another American boxer would win a gold medal.

Louisiana was the first state to legalize boxing with gloves in 1891. But long before that, the state was the first venue of a world championship bout. Briton Jem Mace beat American Tom Allen in Kenner, just outside New Orleans, in 1870. A statue commemorating the event now stands near the river in Kenner's Rivertown.

The longest bout in the history of the sport was held in New Orleans in 1893. Jack Burke and Andy Bowen fought 110 rounds for seven hours and nineteen minutes without a winner. It was a draw.

Eddie Flynn, of Loyola University, won an Olympic gold medal in 1932.

THE BATTLE OF NEW ORLEANS

September 7, 1892
Olympic Club, New Orleans, La.

John L. Sullivan (above) and Jim Corbett (below).

The sound of leather smacking soft flesh echoed through the din of the roaring crowd. John L. Sullivan, whose name was synonymous with swaggering victory in late nineteenth-century America, pitched forward, unconscious and defeated.

Gentleman Jim Corbett had done the near-unthinkable by beating Sullivan and beating him easily in the ring of the New Orleans Olympic Club.

The world heavyweight title passed to Corbett. And with it a boxing era passed into history.

The watershed match—fought in a boxing ring of sawdust and canvas-covered dirt and enclosed by barbed-wire security in an arena equipped with electric lights—was the first championship bout fought under the Marquis of Queensbury rules, meaning with gloves. It was also a fight in which speed, youth, and boxing savvy prevailed over the traditional slugging and power tactics of the day.

Reflecting on the clear historical overtones of the fight, the lead story of the *New Orleans Times-Democrat* the next day read: "James J. Corbett was the Wellington of a pugilistic Waterloo last night and John L. Sullivan must have felt the fearful faintness of heart with which Napoleon gazed upon the old guards' last and fruitless charge upon the British Squares."

Another newspaper, the *New York World*, pondering the enormous popularity of the Great John L., wrote disparagingly of Corbett, "He has robbed the country of a very striking individuality. If he had gone to Switzerland with a shovel and dug away Mount Blanc, he could not have hurt the feelings of the Swiss more than he has damaged the feelings of thousands of Americans."

The bout, the third of a three-day boxing extravaganza in which Jack McAuliffe beat Billy Myer to retain the lightweight title and George Dixon knocked out Jack Skelly in the eighth round to win the vacant featherweight championship, was the object of much interest, owing to Sullivan's larger-than-life stature and the fact that this was his first title fight in three years.

There was unparalleled press coverage for an 1800s sporting event. Correspondents from across the country came to tell the story of another conquest for Sullivan, whose personal motto—and the title of his autobiography written before the Corbett match—was *I Can Lick Any Son-of-a-Bitch in the House.* He backed up the boast with a 42-0-3 record before the match with Gentleman Jim, who was 16-1-4 with one no-decision.

There seemingly was no quenching the interest in the combatants, personal and professional, contrasts that were tailor-

made for sports writers.

Sullivan was a muscle-bound braggart who once told the Prince of Wales: "I've heard a lot about you. Do you ever put up your dukes?" On the other hand, Corbett was a fashion plate and intelligent athlete who took a definite brains-over-brawn approach to boxing.

Dispatches went out to all points of the country, and accounts were read in music halls and gambling resorts in New York, while thousands jammed streets in Chicago and San Francisco straining to catch the bulletins on Sullivan, the Boston Strong Boy who trained on beer and pretzels, and Corbett, the gentlemanly young bank clerk from San Francisco.

In the three years since he defeated Jake Kilrain at Richburg, Mississippi, in history's last bare-knuckle bout, Sullivan had fought only exhibitions, including one with Corbett, in between performances of the play *Honest Hearts and Willing Hands*, a melodrama that was performed all over the world and in which he played a leading role.

Never a great trainer, Sullivan was thirty-four, weighed a flabby thirteen pounds more than his announced 212 pounds, and probably had lost his hunger in the ring, if not at the dining table.

"I hereby challenge any and all bluffers to fight me for a purse of $25,000 and a bet of $10,000," Sullivan proclaimed in the nation's newspapers. "The winner of the fight will take the entire purse. . . . First come, first served. . . . The Marquis of Queensbury must govern this contest, as I want fighting, not foot racing, and I intend to keep the championship of the world."

Corbett beat everyone to accepting the challenge and the posting of the $10,000 side bet. The bout was set at the Olympic Club because it was the only one that could make the $25,000 guarantee and was in one of the three states where boxing was legal.

The stipulation of fighting with gloves was a concession to growing public outrage at the brutality of bare-knuckle boxing. Indeed, an 1882 Louisiana law prohibited "personal combat with fists." However, in New Orleans, boxing with gloves under the auspices of a club was legal, Louisiana being the first state to legalize gloved fights in 1891. Sullivan and Corbett fought with five-ounce gloves.

★ ★ ★

Corbett, who turned twenty-six a week before the fight and was always in good condition, immediately started training hard for what he realized was the fight—and the opportunity—of his life.

Sullivan, a devastating puncher who believed he could beat Corbett without being razor-sharp, couldn't get himself into fighting condition.

"I could not get the big fellow to do one-tenth enough road work or any other work to prepare him thoroughly," trainer Phil Casey said. "He would not work, and the only thing left to do was to fix him up the best way we could. Many a time when he would start out of his quarters for a long road jog, he would not go more than a couple of miles."

When he did jog, it was generally in the company of Miss Clara Tuthill, described as a fetching beauty.

★ ★ ★

The night of the fight, Corbett played one-upsmanship, staying in his dressing room until the last minute, then standing in the aisle to deny Sullivan's prerogative as champion—that of entering the ring last.

Called to the center of the ring by referee John Duffy, Sullivan looked paunchy with his excess weight while Corbett seemed trim and fit at 187 pounds. After the instructions were read, Corbett glanced up, reached over to Sullivan's throat, pushed a forearm to John L.'s Adam's apple and asked, "Do you mean this is a foul?" Sullivan glared at his opponent.

Sullivan rushed from his corner at the bell and started throwing haymakers. Corbett bounced around, neither fighter hitting or being hit. Corbett's tactics went on through rounds two and three, before the crowd started booing him and hissing the word "Sprinter" at him.

Corbett turned his back to Sullivan and asked the crowd to give him "a chance for a few rounds."

"Most of the crowd thought I was running away," Corbett told sports writer Grantland Rice four decades later. "But I merely wanted to see what he had and how he worked. I finally decided to start something in the third. I first broke his nose with a left, and then I slugged him across the ring. That was the tipoff to the crowd that a real fight was on—that those 5-1 odds were not as safe as they had looked to be."

Sullivan's lack of conditioning was apparent after several rounds of throwing roundhouses, but Corbett knew he was still dangerous. He continued to play a waiting game but began getting more and more punches in.

A bombardment in the twentieth round left Sullivan's face soggy with blood.

Another assault in the twenty-first had Sullivan reeling.

"I saw he was badly jarred," Corbett recalled, "so I let go with another right and left to the head. I followed this with a right to the jaw, which carried everything I had left—and he fell to the floor."

At the count of ten the crowd let loose an ear-splitting cheer in appreciation of Corbett, which irritated him because those same fans had done the same for Sullivan at the start of the fight.

After Duffy threw up Corbett's arms in victory, he went to Sullivan's side, placed his arms around John L.'s waist and helped his seconds place him in his chair.

"All I have to say," Sullivan sighed groggily "is that I came to the ring once too often, and if I had to get licked, I am glad it was to an American."

Uncharacteristically, Corbett refused the congratulations of one well-wisher, not even allowing the man in his dressing room, filled with euphoric well-wishers. Eventually the man climbed to the transom and yelled out his congratulations.

The well-wisher was Robert Fitzsimmons, who five years later would post a fourteenth-round knockout in Carson City, Nevada, to take the title away from Gentleman Jim.

Corbett (left) with Sullivan (right) several years after the great fight.

Crowds at the New Orleans Fair Grounds Racetrack.

Risen Star won two legs of the 1988 Triple Crown, the Preakness and Belmont Stakes.

And They're Off

Like a shooting star, he flashed across horse racing's horizons, then disappeared.

But that brief light was bright enough to make railbirds squint.

"Spectacular," is the one word description of Risen Star offered by Fair Grounds cognoscenti Ronnie Virgets, who has watched them run since the 1950s.

Risen Star, a colt who stands on the highest pantheon of thoroughbreds ever to call Louisiana home, was the top three-year-old of 1988 and winner of two of that year's Triple Crown races. The colt was put into context by Virgets, who added, "He was memorable, one of the very best—anywhere and at any time."

Fifteen years after Secretariat captured the hearts of sports fans across the globe with his Triple Crown run to horse racing glory one of his sons emulated similar star power.

Owned and trained by one of the sport's oddest couples, quiet and reserved New Orleans lawyer and bank president Louis J. Roussel III and ebullient Ronnie Lamarque, a singing auto dealer, Risen Star's own run was spectacular. And brief.

As recounted in Bob Roesler's book *The Fair Grounds: Big Shots and Long Shots*, Roussel, an experienced trainer on a local level, had seen Risen Star's dam, Ribbon, win a stakes race at Jefferson Downs and was impressed by her hard-working ways. When he saw her foal, the big (seventeen hands) dark bay colt in Kentucky, it was love at first sight. "He had a way of carrying himself the way good horses do," Roussel recalled. "He had that look of an eagle. He had a lovely head. I'd never buy a horse with an ugly head because I'd have to live with him."

Roussel, who had survived throat cancer in 1977, gave the colt his name for religious connotations. His fiancée (Vicky Bayley) thought of the name Risen Star when they attended Christmas services. "The Star of Bethlehem showed the Three Wise Men where Christ was born," Roussel explained. "On Easter Sunday, we celebrate the resurrection of Christ after his death on the cross. The angel at the tomb told the women, 'He has risen.' That's how we got 'Risen Star.'"

Risen Star won his first race at Jefferson Downs, then his first two at the Fair Grounds. He lost the Lecomte Handicap, finishing second to Pastourelles by a length and a half. He got his revenge by beating Pastourelles by a length in the Louisiana Derby.

Believing the colt showed major potential, Roussel made him a symbol of charity. He promised an order of nuns, the Little Sisters of the Poor, ten percent of Risen Star's winnings. The sisters' coffers for good works immediately started growing. In Risen Star's first eight races he notched six wins and two places.

When the time for the big stage arrived, Risen Star came from dead last in the Lexington Stakes to beat Kentucky Derby favorite Forty-Niner by a head. In the Derby, with Cajun jockey Eddie Delahoussaye aboard, he finished third in the mile-and-a-quarter race, behind Winning Colors and Forty-Niner, beaten by a neck and three lengths.

As *Times-Picayune* columnist Peter Finney wrote, "He ran wide all the way. He probably ran a mile and a half in a mile and a quarter race."

Still, Roussel was not discouraged. Entered in the mile and three-sixteenths Preakness, Delahoussaye saved ground along the rail then, at the five-sixteenth pole, he steered Risen Star inside of Forty-Niner and Winning Colors, and held off charging Brian's Time for the victory.

In the third round of the Triple Crown, the mile-and-a-half Belmont Stakes in New York, Risen Star had a dinked front leg. But it was determined not to be so serious that it would hinder or hurt him.

In a field of six, smallest in a decade, Delahoussaye looked ahead to the pace-setter, Winning Colors, and thought to himself it was going to take a very special horse to catch the leader. Then Risen Star seemed to realize it was time as he raced into the turn for home.

"He was just galloping. He was just pulling me out of the saddle," Delahoussaye said. Star was flying to the finish line, increasing his lead with every stride.

Risen Star won by fourteen-plus lengths over Kingpost in 2:26 ⅖, at the time the second fastest Belmont time ever. The record of 2:24 flat was set in 1973 by his daddy, Secretariat.

"That goes to show how great he was," Roussel said. "He won the Belmont by fifteen lengths despite the injury."

That was Risen Star's last race. The leg continued to bother him, and the owners decided he should be retired. Only three years old, he left as a champion. He ran just eleven races, and never finished out of the money with eight wins, two places, and one show.

His feats were noteworthy. When Risen Star was named the Eclipse Colt of the Year, he became a third-generation recipient. His grandsire, Bold Ruler, was recognized in 1957 and his father, Secretariat, in 1973.

Risen Star's career winnings of $2,029,849.00 meant the nuns—and the poor they serve—made out all right, too.

How important has horse racing been to the sports scape of Louisiana, a state where it has been a part of the culture for well more than two centuries?

Author Ed McNamara, in his book *Cajun Racing: From the Bush Tracks to the Triple Crown*, makes the case that Acadians were steeped in a horse culture even before their exile from Nova Scotia to Louisiana in 1755, and it has carried on. According to legend, Cajun irreverence for authority was illustrated by a custom at Sunday mass of the men sometimes stepping outside during the sermon to run their horses around the church. The upshot is that, irked priests aside, the races may have lured to the services wayward members of the flock who otherwise may have stayed in bed.

Regardless, horses and racing have been a part of Cajun Louisiana in the southwest portion of the state from its earliest days, on every kind of animal that moved but especially on what developed to be a breed called quarter-horses (named for their short sprints)—and created some of today's most recognizable jockeys.

Cajun Country can produce diminutive people who ride tall in the saddle, and in the latter stages of the twentieth century, natives of Southwest Louisiana became household names for consistently reaching the winner's circle. Such familiar names on Louisiana tracks as Delahoussaye, Robby Albarado, Calvin Borel, Kent Desormeaux, Mark Guidry, Craig Perret, and Randy Romero, became forces on ovals across America. Marlon St. Julien gets special mention for riding in the 2000 Kentucky Derby. St. Julien was the first African American jockey to ride in the Run for the Roses since Henry King in 1921—seventy-nine years before. His mount, Curule, finished seventh behind winner Fusaichi Pegasus.

Each of these jockeys have left a mark in the sport's premier races, and all got their starts racing bush tracks in south Louisiana.

In an intriguing story, Native Dancer with Cajun jockey Eric Guerin of Maringouin, was seriously bumped off stride by Money Broker early in the 1953 Kentucky Derby and finished second to Dark Star. Guerin steered 'Dancer to subsequent victories in the Preakness and Belmont. The horse retired with twenty-one victories and one second in his twenty-two career races, all but one with Guerin in the saddle.

One of the giants of state and national racing was John Franks of Shreveport, who set a near-impossible standard as the recipient of a record four Eclipse Awards as an owner and breeder.

Franks was the leading owner at Louisiana Downs in Bossier City for eighteen consecutive years, 1982 through 1999. He led the nation in races won seven times (1983, '84, '86, '87, '88, '89, and '94), and in earnings five times (1983, '84, '86, '93, and '94). Franks's best years were 1993, when his horses won $5.6 million, and 1989, when his horses won 225 races. In 1986 Franks's horses won thirty-two stakes races at seventeen tracks.

Franks was also the owner of Answer Lively, the 1998 Breeder's Cup Juvenile winner who was voted American Champion Two-Year-Old Colt. But his favorite day came in 1991 at the Fair Grounds when four horses he bred won stakes races.

A dozen of Franks's horses won one million dollars or more.

There was a time when New Orleans was the epicenter of the sport. In 1850, New York's *Wilkes' Spirit of the Times*, the country's leading turf and sporting journal, reported that "New Orleans was 'the national center of thoroughbred racing.'"

In *New Orleans: A Pictorial History*, Louisiana author Leonard Huber wrote, "In 1847, when the Mexican War broke out, New Orleans was the leading horse-racing center of the United States. The city boasted four tracks . . . and the newspapers gave about equal coverage to the doings at the tracks as to the War with Mexico."

For much of the span of the nineteenth and twentieth centuries there were as many as five major parimutuel tracks in operation in the Bayou State—the Fair Grounds in New Orleans, Evangeline Downs in Lafayette and Opelousas, Delta Downs in Vinton, Louisiana Downs in Bossier City, and, for many years the now-defunct Jefferson Downs in Kenner.

Racing was such a part of the lifestyle that tracks came and went in the early nineteenth century, including one built a few miles south of what was then the boundaries of New Orleans on the plantation of General Wade Hampton in 1814. Another, built by François de Livaudais in 1820 on his Live Oak plantation, was located near what is now the intersection of the city's Washington and St. Charles Avenues.

Nearby Race Street is named in commemoration of that track.

There were also the Jackson Course, which opened in Chalmette (1826); the New Orleans Course (1828); the Eclipse Course, on the present site of Audubon Park (1837); the Louisiana Course (1838); and the Bingaman Track in Algiers (1847).

Perhaps the most fashionable and prominent was the Metairie Race Course, built in 1838, which came to be considered the most important in the United States at the time. The rules that governed the site were "generally accepted throughout the Union and were adopted by all the other Southern courses in circuits," according to the 1884 edition of *The Historical Sketch Book of New Orleans.*

"Life on the Metairie."

In a notable feat, the last stakes race at the Metairie Race Course before it closed in 1872 was won by Monarchist, a son of the famed Lexington. Ten days later, the first stakes race run at the Fair Grounds, which would become the foremost track in New Orleans, was won by Monarchist. Three days later he also won the Louisiana Stakes.

The Fair Grounds is the third oldest track in America, behind Saratoga (1864) and Pimlico (1870), but is the oldest site in the country on which racing has been continuously operated. It is really a combination of two tracks. In 1908 the Fair Grounds bought the City Park track, dismantled the grand stand, and moved it to Gentilly where the Fair Grounds now sits.

Opened originally in 1852 as the Union Race Course, its name was soon changed to the Creole Race Course. But in 1859 the Mechanics and Agricultural Fair was held on the site, and the public started referring to the area as the "Fair Grounds." The name stuck.

★ ★ ★

Among the multitude of luminaries to have raced at the Fair Grounds were Pan Zareta, who became the winningest and greatest weight-carrying mare in the annals of American turf. In 151 starts from 1912 through 1917, she won seventy-six times, with thirty-one seconds and twenty-one thirds. Pan Zareta carried more than 130 pounds twenty-eight times and 140 pounds seven times. She set or equaled eleven track and American records and was so beloved in New Orleans that when she died in 1918 Pan Zareta was buried in a place of honor in the Fair Grounds' infield.

John Henry raced eight years starting in 1977 at Jefferson Downs where he won his first race by a nose. He later ran at Evangeline Downs and the Fair Grounds where he lost nine starts. Shipped out to the West Coast, the gelding suddenly became quite formidable. In 1984, his last year of racing, he won six of nine starts, and he earned more than two million dollars in purses. He retired with thirty-nine victories, fifteen seconds, and nine thirds in eighty-three starts—all of which brings to mind John Henry's first finish at Jefferson Downs after his jockey fell off.

★ ★ ★

Like more than a few track people, Allen "Black Cat" LaCombe was an unforgettable Runyonesque character. He typified the sport, and to an extent a New Orleans sub-culture. This was a man who threw a party for his draft board when it called him to service in World War II. A promoter of boxing matches and beauty contests, during his army time in Persia LaCombe rounded up some animals and promoted camel races. He once set up a card headlining Egypt's King Farouk's favorite heavyweight—his bodyguard. Sgt. LaCombe made sure his own fighter was not the winner that night, filling him with food and drink before he entered the ring.

A chronic loser, LaCombe always maintained he couldn't pick his brother out of a crowd of Orientals. A handicapper by avocation, he set up headquarters at the Fair Grounds when his vocation turned into publicity director there after an ill-fated run to become governor of Louisiana. That may have been his longest shot considering he publicly endorsed another candidate.

LaCombe's fondest wish was to be buried in the infield at the Fair Grounds, along with the remains of the immortals Pan Zareta and Black Gold. After his passing in 1989, he had to settle for a leisurely drive in a hearse around the old track, lined with hundreds of friends, patrons, and touts, a trek that started with a bugler fittingly playing the tune that defined his life, *Call to Post.*

Allen "Black Cat" LaCombe.

HE'S MY BROTHER

April 8, 1854
Metairie Race Course, New Orleans, La.

There's nothing quite so fierce as a sibling rivalry, and this one took on legendary proportions.

Champion thoroughbreds Lexington and Lecomte had the eyes of the sporting world riveted on New Orleans's fashionable Metairie Course for more than a year. In that span the previously unbeaten half-brothers each lost for the first times in their respective careers to each other and the series produced two world-record times.

Both were offspring of the redoubtable racer and sire Boston, the lord of bluegrass racing. Lexington was widely considered the premier racehorse in the world; Lecomte was born and bred at the stable of Thomas J. Welles, owner of a plantation near Alexandria in central Louisiana.

Their meetings would be the high points of their lives, but in a story that would end in sorrow.

The acclaimed colts met for the first time in the Great State Post Stakes in New Orleans, a famed match race get-together where turf enthusiasts from all points across the South came to compete against Louisiana favorites.

That type of racing was vastly different from what we think of today. In the 1850s a match race was a grueling test of speed and endurance run in four-mile heats over two races, with the best time determining the winner. If the races were split, a third heat would be run. In other words, each event was really a series of two or three separate races (the heats) but counted as just one race.

Between these two thoroughbreds a third heat had never been necessary. In four match races, the renowned Lexington had never seen the heels of another animal at a finish line. Lecomte had five victories in five races.

Each of the owners put up $5,000 for a purse of $20,000, and four horses were entered in this race, though there was no question the attraction was Lexington, representing Kentucky, and Lecomte, entered for Mississippi despite his rearing. Highlander represented Alabama, and Arrow entered for Louisiana.

They came to the post in front of a crowd of twenty thousand that included former president Millard J. Fillmore, who was one of the judges. "There is no way I would miss this great sporting event," an enthusiastic Fillmore said.

Lecomte's jockey was Abe Hawkins, a slave and one of the first black professional athletes to gain national prominence. Lexington's jockey that day was Creole rider Henry Meichon.

Lexington emerged victorious by winning two straight four-mile heats, but with major competition from Lecomte, who led the second heat by as many as eight lengths before being literally nosed out as the near-exhausted animals hit the finish line.

The *New Orleans Daily Picayune* described the second heat thusly: ". . . the race was an excellent one; its varying chances, its uncertain termination up to the last minute, the severity of the contest, the amount of money at stake and immense number of people in attendance, will render it a brilliant event in the racing annals of the country."

That, however, was not the end of this saga.

The Great State Post Stakes had been run in wet, heavy conditions made tougher because of a strong wind. The Lecomte camp publicly called Lexington a "lucky mudder," and declared that the outcome was a fluke. They challenged for a rematch.

Richard Ten Broeck of Lexington's syndicate wished to accept, but his partners did not, wanting to rest the colt. Ten Broeck immediately bought them out (for $5,000, it was later revealed), and Lexington and Lecomte were paired again, along with an aged gelding, Reube, in the $2,000 Jockey Club Purse a week after their initial meeting.

At the tap of a drum, Lecomte rushed to the early lead, with Lexington hard on his heels. Reube trailed badly from the start. The horses held those positions for three miles. At that point, the pace increased as Lexington made lunges for the lead, forcing Lecomte to higher speeds in order to stay in front.

The *New Orleans Times-Democrat* described the race as the horses entered the fourth mile: "Lexington partially closed the gap that Lecomte had opened on him, and attempted to out-foot him. The attempt was immense, but it was ineffectual. The spur was freely used to induce him to do what his friends claimed for him—that he was the fastest horse in the world at a brush, but Lecomte baffled all his efforts, kept the lead and (won), amid deafening shouts, by six lengths, in much the quickest time ever made in the world—7. 26!"

As an aside, it apparently had no bearing on the outcome but Meichon pulled up and jumped from his mount after three miles when someone leapt the fence waving him down as though signaling he had traversed four miles. He quickly took off again, but Lexington was already far behind and considered already beaten at the time of Meichon's faux pas.

In the second heat, Lecomte held off Lexington in the stretch and was again the winner, this time in 7:38 ¾. Lecomte's victory represented the only race Lexington ever lost.

★ ★ ★

The defeat shocked, then rankled Ten Broeck, him owning the world's greatest horse and all. Now it was his turn to challenge, for a "rubber" match. Welles wasn't interested.

In order to secure another duel, Ten Broeck offered to run his horse against Lecomte's record time, and added a bet of $20,000. As side inducements, according to the *New Orleans Bee*, more than $500,000 was wagered.

Almost a year after the Great State Post Stakes, on April 2, 1855, Lexington ran against no opponent but the clock, though not under normal circumstance. The outcome was so important to Ten Broeck he brought in the nation's leading jockey, Gil Patrick (later the rider aboard the winning Ruthless in the first Belmont Stakes), for the run against the clock.

Lexington was aided by a running start, and by two other horses (Arrow and Joe Blackburn) entered to push him.

It was a strategy that worked to perfection. Lexington completed the first mile in a blazing 1:47 ¼, the second in 1:52 ¼, the third in 1:51 ½, and lapped the four miles in 7:19 ¾, shattering his half-brother's record by more than 6 ½ seconds and setting a record that will stand forever. That form of horse racing soon gave way to shorter distances.

★ ★ ★

After that smashing run, Lecomte's owners could hardly turn down the challenge of another go with Lexington. The date was set for two weeks afterward, on April 14, 1855.

It was an ill-fated decision. Lecomte came down with a serious case of colic and was violently sick for days.

Still, he cantered to the post. "When the blankets were stripped from the horses," wrote the *Daily Picayune*, "and their magnificent combinations of blood, heart, and muscle stood glistening and flickering in the sun, the crowd . . . could not resist a burst of admiration, at which Lecomte stepped coquettishly about, showing his beautiful chestnut coat and branching muscles, while the darker Lexington, with a sedate and intelligent aspect, looked calmly around, as if he felt the sensation was quite expected and deserved."

From the start the outcome was not in doubt. Lexington shot to the lead and easily ran down the greatly weakened Lecomte. The winner came in a time of 7:23 ¾.

Seeing his horse in such distress, Welles withdrew Lecomte from the second heat.

It was a last hurrah. In short order, Lecomte died. Lexington was going blind, just as their father, Boston, had, and was retired to stud in which he was a prodigious success. He became America's leading sire sixteen times, producing 236 stakes winners, including 3 in the Preakness, named for one of his sons, 348 second-place finishers, and 42 coming in third.

Today the half-brothers are still remembered. Lexington, the near-perfect thoroughbred, was properly mounted and for more than a century his skeletal remains were on display at the Smithsonian Institute. The name of Lecomte lives on through a town located south of his home of Alexandria that was named in his honor, even though it was misspelled—Lecompte.

Must be a Louisiana thing.

Lexington.

Lecomte.

A Heart of Gold

May 5, 1924
Churchhill Downs, Louisville, Kentucky

A plebeian colt once ruled the Sport of Kings. Only Al Hoots, a half-Irish, half-Native American rancher from the Oklahoma Indian Territory, saw it coming.

An equine thunderbolt the color of onyx flashed across the Kentucky landscape, galloping amid the sound and fury of flying hooves and the ringing roar of a record crowd in a heroic Run for the Roses.

Hoots had a vision of a foal from his beloved filly winning the Kentucky Derby, and, long after his death, that's exactly what happened. Black Gold, a horse from the wrong side of the stables, and the son of Hoots's Useeit, won the 1924 Kentucky Derby, years after Hoots's death but just as he saw it.

An enduring—and endearing—legend was born.

Black Gold, according to race historian H. P. Robertson, is "the hero of racing's most romantic true story."

Jet black and small as thoroughbreds go, about fourteen hands high, Black Gold possessed the unmistakable heart of a champion. As a two-year-old running in the Bashford Manor Stakes at Churchill Downs, Black Gold fell to his knees in a collision, got up, and went on to win in a stunning victory.

Oh, how that must have irked the Kentucky bluebloods. Black Gold was not one of their kind. He was a thoroughbred without a pedigree and tasting his dust was degrading. "The offspring of an outlawed dam and the half-brother of several bums of the turf," was the description of Black Gold by one anonymous racing writer.

But Black Gold was a towering figure on the sporting scene of New Orleans, where he scored his first victory, was stabled, did most of his running, and was looked upon as an adopted son. Known as "The Indian Horse," Black Gold was the only winner of both the Louisiana and Kentucky derbies, but he also won the Ohio State Derby and Chicago Derby in 1924, the first racehorse ever to be champion of four derbies—a feat unequaled until Smarten won derbies in Ohio, Pennsylvania, and two in Illinois in 1980—fifty-six years later.

In the saga of Black Gold, though, this is putting the tailhead before the nose.

☆ ☆ ☆

Useeit was owned—and loved dearly—by Hoots, part Osage Indian, who first saw the mud-brown filly in losing a close race to a much bigger, more powerful animal. Hoots was smitten with the horse after the courageous performance and traded eighty acres of grazing land to get her.

She also came from mixed blood, a part quarter-horse who was almost unbeatable in sprint races in the country fairs around Oklahoma and on the quarter-tracks and bullrings of the Far West.

Bill Keefe, the late sports editor of the *Times-Picayune* in New Orleans, where Useeit and especially Black Gold would make impressions, once wrote: "Useeit raced here many times and, while she was looked upon as nothing but a sprinter, she showed rare staying powers and was as game a little trick as ever looked through a bridle."

Her record showed it. Useeit won thirty-four races, though she couldn't beat her nemesis, Pan Zareta, in six races. She won enough, however, to keep Hoots and wife Rosa afloat. Useeit had mixed, but not dismal, results as a broodmare. A disappointing yearling named Tulsa was the result of a union with Ivan the Terrible, but a year later Useeit had a foal named Tuscola who performed reasonably well as a race horse.

Hoots loved the horse so much that he entered a "gentleman's agreement" at a claiming race in Juarez, Mexico, that nobody would claim his filly. The agreement wasn't honored and a man produced the $1,500 claiming price. Hoots excused himself for a few minutes and came back brandishing a shotgun. That settled the dispute, but Hoots and Useeit were both banned from racing and the filly's name was stricken from the thoroughbred registry.

Three years later, Hoots was dying. He begged his wife never

to sell Useeit, even though they barely made ends meet. Hoots told Rosa he had a vision that Useeit would someday have a foal who would grow up to be a Kentucky Derby champion. Hoots asked for Rosa's promise to keep, and breed, Useeit. "If you will promise to do this for me," he told his wife, "I will die a happy man."

Hoots did die a happy man.

An illustration of how bad Hoots's luck was running came not long after his death with the discovery of oil on the Osage Indian lands. Rosa came into money, and with part of it she saw to it that Al's vision had a chance for fruition. She sent Useeit to Kentucky to be bred to the fashionable Black Toney.

A foal, named Black Gold, for his father, for his ebony coat, and for the rich crude that allowed the first step in Hoots's vision come to pass, was born in 1921 in a field near Col. E. R. Bradley's Idle Hour Stock Farm near Lexington, Kentucky.

A part-Cherokee named Harlen Webb, a former Oklahoma deputy sheriff and friend of Hoots, was hired to train Black Gold. For the colt, that might have been the best—or it might have been the worst—possible choice. Webb, a severe alcoholic, was apparently abusive to the animal. Shipped to New Orleans, Black Gold developed by being run in the cold, in rain, and in knee-deep mud, and often was left out in the elements without even a blanket. No wonder Black Gold became a fractious and ill-tempered animal.

Whatever the reason, he did, however, develop into a runner. Quite well.

Black Gold ran—and won—his first race at New Orleans's Jefferson Park, with J. D. Mooney, son of a New Orleans riverboat captain, aboard. In the same racing style for which his mother was famed, Black Gold was in front from start to finish.

And he kept running. As a two-year-old he had eighteen starts, won nine, placed five times, and came in the money twice.

Hitting his stride as a three-year-old, Black Gold won the Louisiana Derby, "in a canter," according to the *Daily Racing Form* chart. In a muddy wire-to-wire victory, Black Gold covered the mile and an eighth in 1:57 ⅗. That same season he won the Ohio Derby by ten lengths, and then came from forty lengths back to win the Chicago Derby.

Somewhere, though, a sore right forefoot began bothering Black Gold, and the injury was aggravated when a nail lodged in the same foot. Webb rejected serious veterinary treatment, and his limp was evident when Black Gold came to post at the Derby Trial three days before the 1924 Kentucky Derby. There were no evident effects of the injury at the bell, however, as Black Gold fired out on a slow track and hit the wire eight lengths ahead of Wild Astor.

This was the Golden Jubilee Run for the Roses, the fiftieth Kentucky Derby. The winter book had made "the Indian Horse" racing out of New Orleans a 50-1 shot at Churchill Downs, but the impressive Derby Trial opened some eyes. When several Eastern "name" entrants withdrew, Black Gold was suddenly the odds-on 9-5 favorite for the Kentucky Derby, then run on the third Saturday in May.

Louisville was filled with Native Americans for the race that weekend, all pulling and wagering heavily on "The Indian Horse" looked down upon by the bluebloods, but the one with which they so strongly identified.

The vision was so close to being fulfilled, Rosa Hoots couldn't leave Black Gold's presence. Being close to him now was like being close to her husband, and, despite Black Gold's querulous disposition, she spent the night before the Derby in a tack room near Black Gold's stall.

So certain the dream was about to come true, Rosa boldly brought a box of expensive cigars for Col. Matt Winn, the general manager of Churchill Downs, to be presented after the victory.

Before eighty-one thousand, then the largest crowd to witness a Kentucky Derby, and, for the first time, to the strains of *My Old Kentucky Home*, Black Gold took the field along with eighteen other thoroughbreds

Breaking from the rail, Black Gold tracked the early leaders. Mooney had to check him after interference, and was in sixth place at the half-mile pole. By the stretch, Black Gold held third place. Leaders Transmute and Bracadale weakened, then Transmute fell back, and Chilhowee rushed past them all to lead Bracadale by a head.

Then Mooney made his move, asking for everything Black Gold had, and he responded like black lightning, streaking over the track. They passed Bracadale, they passed Chilhowee; they crossed the finish line a half-length ahead of the field.

Al Hoots's vision had come true.

"Black Gold's dash down the stretch was a spectacle that can never be forgotten by those privileged to witness his triumph," read one account of the race.

Mooney put up a splendid ride, getting his horse out of a terrible logjam. When Black Gold shot across the wire a winner, the Churchill Downs course presented a picture that has never been equaled in any track in America. The crowd, becoming hysterical, lifted the winner's name in a mighty tribute and began to stampede around the judges' stand, where Mrs. Hoots, the triumphant jockey, and trainer Webb were called to receive their honors.

The foot injury eventually caused Black Gold's retirement to a life of ease and breeding. But he was not proficient as a sire. Three years later, in bad physical shape, he was back at the New Orleans Fair Grounds.

On January 28, 1928, in the Salome Purse, as the field neared the sixteenth pole, everyone waited for top-weighted Black Gold to make his move.

At that point he couldn't. He stumbled and nearly fell. Jockey Dave Emery stood up in the saddle trying to stop his mount. A bone in his foreleg had snapped, but with the heart of a champion Black Gold refused to stop. He crossed the finish line on three legs, his other foot dangling.

Bill Keefe's report the next day read: "Jockey Emery quickly pulled him up in front of the stand. Black Gold was led back of the paddock and, still shaking his proud and perfect head in resentment at the tight hold taken on him by an assistant, flinched as the needle of destruction pierced his skin, tossed high his head and pricked his ears even as the needle was withdrawn, and the next fraction of a second dropped dead."

Black Gold was buried in the infield of the Fair Grounds, facing Oklahoma. In more than a century of thoroughbred racing at the Fair Grounds, only one other horse was given that honor. In the other Fair Grounds grave is buried Pan Zareta, the only horse who ever outran Black Gold's mother, Useeit.

In Memoriam !

—WITH HIS FORELEG BROKEN "BLACK GOLD" HOBBLED AFTER THE FIELD BEFORE HE FELL. A THOROUGHBRED TO THE LAST!

THE MAN WHO'LL MISS HIM MOST. WEBB, THE INDIAN, WHO TRAINED HIM FROM A COLT.

BLACK GOLD, 1924 DERBY WINNER, MAY BE GONE BUT NOT FORGOTTEN

Lies Buried Beside the Track on Which He Made His First Bid for Fame

Teeing Off

The cradle of modern golf, St. Andrews in Scotland, in an indirect way played a role in the flowering of the game in Louisiana, too.

George Turpie was born a chip shot from the famed St. Andrews course in 1880 and naturally became a lifelong addict of the sport—though never anything close to being a champion. In 1895, at the age fifteen, he once caddied for early golf giant Harry Vardon, who won the Open Championship six times, a feat still unequaled. More than seventy years later Turpie, who died at age eighty-eight, spoke of that to Peter Finney of the *Times-Picayune* as one of the highlights of his long life.

Not long afterward, Turpie left for America, saying he wanted to "look into things across the water," settling first in Chicago, then New Orleans. It was Turpie who gave the game its first major impetus in the Crescent City, designing the first course in City Park, then at New Orleans Country Club, still largely the layout used today. Eventually Turpie served as the pro at three different New Orleans clubs.

His influence didn't end there. On a trip back to St. Andrews in 1901, Turpie's wife delivered a child, daughter Marion. Fate or Turpie wouldn't have had it any other way, because Marion became one of the sports' premier women's amateurs, winning the Southern Amateur three times (1926, 1928, 1931) and collecting titles across the land, including the Women's Western at St. Paul's, Minnesota, and the New York State Women's Amateur, both in 1937.

Marion was so hooked on her father's game that when she married in 1929 she decided the happiest way she could spend her honeymoon was playing in the Pan-American tournament in Biloxi, Mississippi, where she shot 77 on the last day of a losing effort.

Winner Marion Turpie, of New Orleans, is congratulated by runner-up Ruth Raymond, of Baton Rouge, upon winning the 1931 Women's Southern Amateur Golf Championship.

* * *

When Hal Sutton was on his game, he could cut the best down to size. It was a long time between drinks of water, but in moments when the tournament was on the line, he did what seemed unfathomable—staring down possibly the two greatest golfers in history with tournaments squarely on the line.

Both times, he held off his opponents with dramatic irons shots.

Sutton, who grew up in Shreveport, won a major and did it with no less than the Golden Bear, Jack Nicklaus, stalking him.

Sutton, a graduate of Centenary, won the 1983 PGA Championship at famed Riviera Country Club in Los Angeles, with the hard-charging Nicklaus in position to snatch it away. Sutton led wire-to-wire, but Nicklaus had made up six strokes on the last day to trail by one on the seventy-second hole.

The Golden Bear breathing down the neck of any twenty-five-year-old would be enough to buckle the knees of most. But Sutton gathered himself, and on his second shot, from the middle of the fairway, he unsheathed his five-iron, took his swing, and arched the ball to the flag 201 yards away. It came to a rest twelve feet away and slightly uphill of the hole.

All he had to do was lag the ball closer, then tap in a putt from four inches away.

"I've got a pretty good average on four-inchers," he cracked later of his one-stroke victory over Nicklaus.

Seventeen years later, in the Players Championship at Ponte Vedra Beach, Florida, after a rain delay pushed the last seven holes to Monday, Sutton led by a stroke over Tiger Woods.

On the exacting 440-yard eighteenth, Woods missed the green with his approach shot. Sutton swung his six-iron at the flag 179 yards away, then, with the ball in the air, shouted, "Be the right club today!"

It was, the ball landing eight feet from the hole. Woods caught Sutton's eye and with a wry smile gave him two thumbs up. Sutton two-putted to nail down the one-stroke victory.

Sutton was 1980's College Player of the Year at Centenary, the PGA Tour's Rookie of the Year in 1982, played on four U.S. Ryder Cup teams, and was the non-playing captain of another.

But it's hard to imagine any bigger golf thrills than, with a tournament on the line, going head-to-head with the Golden Bear, then Tiger. And beating both.

No one else ever did.

Golf has spawned other Louisiana landmarks, such as LSU's four national championships (1940, 1942, 1947, 1955), and the oddity that four of the state's golf protégés won their only majors in the PGA Championship. Lafayette natives Lionel Hebert (1957) and Jay Hebert (1960) became the first brother combination to both win the same major since Scottish pros Willie and Alex Smith won the U.S. Open in 1899 and 1906. While Hal Sutton won the PGA in 1983 and David Toms in 2001.

Among the luminaries who left a Pelican State imprint on the game of golf are:

- Nelson Whitney, one of the foremost amateurs in the first two decades of the twentieth century, won the Southern Amateur five times between 1907 and 1919 and finished second three times. Bobby Jones, considered the greatest golfer of the time, only won the tournament three times.

- David Toms, from Monroe, La., prevailed by two strokes over Phil Mickelson in the 2001 PGA tournament. Toms also beat Mickelson by a stroke to take that year's Compaq Classic in New Orleans for his fifth PGA Tour victory. He has double-digit tour victories, and has spent a considerable amount of time in the Top 10 of the Official World rankings.

- Jay Hebert, a mainstay on LSU's 1947 national title team and, before that, a Marine veteran of Iwo Jima, left an indelible mark on pro golf. In his first ten years on the tour he won seven tournaments and finished second sixteen times. He also played on the U.S. Ryder Cup teams of 1959 and 1961 and served as Ryder Cup captain in 1971.

- Lionel Hebert, at age twenty-nine, was the Rookie of the Year in 1957, finishing fifteenth on the money list (with $10,968). Hebert would only win four tour tournaments, though one was a major. But his biggest contribution to the sport might be his role as one of eleven veteran golfers that pushed for the establishment of the senior tour. Lionel was chairman of the PGA tournament committee in 1962-63 and 1972-73.

- Clifford Ann Creed qualified at the age of eleven for the 1950 Louisiana Women's Amateur tournament. Then she kept going. She won Southern Amateur titles in 1957 and 1962. Creed also won the North and South Amateur and the South Atlantic Amateur in '62. Then she helped a U.S. Team score an 8-1 victory over Britain and Ireland in Curtis Cup competition. She won eleven tournaments in her pro career.

- Jimmy McGonagill, a native of Texas, won five consecutive Louisiana State Amateur championships. After turning pro, he won the Louisiana Open pro championship in 1938 and 1940. Regaining his amateur status, McGonagill won a total of nine State Amateur championships. McGonagill once played thirty consecutive rounds at the par-71 Shreveport Country Club in an average of 67 strokes—a total of 120 under par. At one time he held records at thirty-seven different courses, including all the courses in Caddo and Bossier parishes.

Jay and Lionel Hebert of Lafayette, the only brother duo to win the PGA Championship.

A Bolt of Lightning

June 14, 1958
Southern Hills Country Club, Tulsa, Oklahoma

Tommy Bolt was nicknamed "Thunder" Bolt for his volcanic temper, for wrapping clubs around trees, or throwing them in creeks. He was known as much for his tantrums as for his golf, and Bolt was one of the sport's finest ball-strikers.

"If we could've screwed another head on his shoulders," the legendary Ben Hogan once said, "Tommy Bolt could have been the greatest who ever lived."

Bolt, a Hall of Famer who won fifteen tournaments on the PGA Tour in the 1950s and '60s, learned the game on public courses around Shreveport. He almost completely integrated his emotions and abilities at the 1958 U.S. Open, the world's most prestigious tournament, when he virtually ran away with the crowning victory of his career.

That year the Open was played in Tulsa, on a cutthroat course, Southern Hills. It called for a precision game, and the course was further toughened by Robert Trent Jones.

"It was a good test of golf to start with," Bolt recalled of his conquest of the 6,907-yard layout, "and they really let the roughs grow. The fairways, and I'm not kidding, were thirty yards wide. We almost had to walk single file."

Ninety-degree temperatures had shots skidding on the three-sixteenth growth on the greens, and the pin placements had the field in near mutiny. Gene Sarazen complained the course was "ridiculous," and that the man "who placed those cups ought to be hung." Hogan suggested that a protest committee be sent to the U.S. Association of Officials. Not one of the 162 entrants equaled par on opening day, though the winner had already been crowned.

"I birdied the very first hole on about a fifteen-foot putt," Bolt said, "and the instant it fell in the cup I knew those other guys were playing for second place. It just felt that way. All I had to do was keep the clubs in my hand and finish. That's just how complete the control was on my emotions and how happy I was with the world. That's the way you have to be."

Everything, even the heat and twenty-five-mph winds worked to his advantage.

"I love hot weather," Bolt said. "I've got a bit of arthritis in the upper part of my back and neck, and hot weather relieves it. So while everybody else was sweltering and falling by the wayside, boy, I just kept grinding."

The twelfth hole, which devoured the rest of the field, opened the gates for Bolt. The par 4, 445-yard dogleg allowed no one but Tommy a birdie. In his four rounds he had three and a par on that hole. "We played thirty-six holes the last day, too," he recalled joyously, "and I just ate 'em up."

A string of six birdies in seven holes of the morning round the final day put all the pressure on Bolt's immediate challengers. The gallery went slack-jawed and wide-eyed as Bolt's putting produced scores of 3-3-3-5-3-3 from the tenth to the fifteenth holes. A six-foot putt on the tenth, a four-foot putt on the twelfth, and eight-footers on the fourteenth and fifteenth demonstrated an almost uncanny oneness between golfer and course.

No one but Bolt escaped Southern Hills without at least one 75 on the par-70 course. Bolt's highest round was 72.

"I had complete concentration and composure from the moment I teed it up every day," he said. His total of 283 beat Gary Player by four strokes.

The gallery saluted Bolt with cheers as he made his way up the eighteenth fairway. He waved his brown straw hat in acknowledgment and announced, "I am a man of peace." After playing the hole he retired to the press tent and immediately launched into a verbal assault on a reporter.

The sportswriter's morning story said the forty-year-old Bolt was nine years older. The reporter apologized, explaining it was a typographical error. "Typographical error, hell," Tommy shot back. "It was a perfect four and a perfect nine!"

TAKING A CHANCE ON LOVE

August 19, 1945
Chickasaw Country Club, Memphis, Tennessee

Freddie Haas was thinking a two-stroke lead against Byron Nelson on the last day of a tournament was not nearly enough to make anyone predict a PGA Tour victory.

This was August 1945, days after the shooting of World War II stopped, and Nelson was scorching the pro circuit with a still-hard-to-fathom eleven consecutive wins. But here at Chickasaw Country Club where the Memphis Invitational was being held, there was Haas, a twenty-nine-year-old amateur from New Orleans wearing Bermuda shorts, actually leading Lord Byron in the final round.

Fifty-six years later, Haas, who died in 2004, told Peter Kessler of *Golf Talk Live* that a bad break when Nelson just missed the hole on the sixth with a seven-iron, the ball hitting the flag, then rolling forty feet away, opened the door for him.

"Whoa," Haas said he thought, "he didn't make a hole-in-one. Let's see what I can do." Haas hit it within six feet.

Nelson's chip shot rimmed the cup, then rolled five feet past.

"Now he's hit the cup twice and he's laying 3—and I've got a six-foot putt. I don't know how the ball went in, but it did," Haas recalled, "and then he lipped out again and makes 4. Now I've picked up two strokes."

That day, two days after shooting a course-record 64, Haas shot 68 to give himself a comfortable lead.

That sixth hole, though, spurred Haas to his most memorable moment, the one for which he'll always be remembered, although he was always quick to note he didn't exactly stop Nelson. Lord Byron finished fourth behind Haas, who shot an 18-under 270, George Low Jr. (275), and another amateur, Bob Cochran (275). Nelson shot 276.

★ ★ ★

Haas would have had a place in Louisiana sports history had he never played as a pro.

Growing up in Demott, Arkansas, the son of a golf pro, young Freddie developed his game on a six-hole, sand-grass course that he helped his father build. Dividing his time between the links and basketball, Freddie won Arkansas state golf titles in 1932 and 1933, earning a grant-in-aid to the University of Arkansas.

But when his dad became the pro at Morehouse Country Club in Bastrop, just across the state line, an uncle, Louisiana state senator Leo Terzia, took Freddie to the state amateur tournament in Baton Rouge. In an exciting duel, Haas reached the finals, eventually losing to LSU freshman Bobby Anderson.

In the gallery that day was none other than Louisiana's Kingfish, U.S. Senator Huey Long, who envisioned the two finalists bringing a national championship to LSU.

As Haas remembered the story decades later, Long told the seventeen-year-old athlete to "forget your scholarship to Arkansas, and get the recruits we need to win the national championship here."

Young Haas's advice to Long was to first find a suitable golf course, pointing out an area near the football stadium where there were cows grazing. Long blanched at the thought.

"LSU is an Agricultural and Mechanical school," Long reminded the boy. "If I moved those cows (for a golf course), the farmers would be very upset."

In 1937, two years after Long was assassinated, Haas won the NCAA national championship at the famed Oakmont course in Pittsburgh, beating his LSU teammate Paul Leslie for the title—the only time up until that point that two golfers from the same school had reached the individual finals.

It should be noted, years later LSU would build a course on campus—right where Haas suggested.

★ ★ ★

That Haas was one of the premier golfers of his day is apparent in his 125 amateur titles, including the 1934 and 1937 Southern Amateur championships, the former impressing none other than Bobby Jones to extend a personal invitation for Haas to play in the first Masters.

In those days, though, pro golf didn't pay much and Haas, with a growing family, was doing fine financially as an insurance salesman. Still, he never lost that itch to try the tour.

In 1945 he told his wife Paula he was going to play in three tournaments just to see how he'd fare, and if he did well, he wanted to go pro.

The Memphis Invitational was one, and became synonymous with Haas, and the legend of Byron Nelson.

★ ★ ★

Talk about earning your spurs. After joining the tour, Haas's first victory came in the 1948 Portland Open where he won in a playoff—beating Ben Hogan and Arnold Palmer.

Eventually, he also became the first golfer to play on both the Walker Cup (for amateurs) and Ryder Cup (for pros).

He would win only five tournaments as a pro. Still, Haas's time on the tour paid off. He ended up with listed career earnings of $154,000 (which only go back to 1950), but he continued with his insurance business. His golf connections helped Haas go into group insurance in a big way, said his son, Ted.

"I know he sold insurance like gangbusters," said *Times-Picayune* columnist Peter Finney, whose daughter married Ted. "It's hard to say which was his sideline business."

Freddie Haas won the 1937 NCAA individual golf championship as a senior at LSU.

Follow That Birdie

May 16, 1965
Lakewood Country Club, New Orleans, La.

There stood Dick Mayer, a stroke behind and thirty-five yards from the flag on the eighteenth hole. The green was surrounded by twenty-thousand fans waiting to see the new champion of the Greater New Orleans Open crowned.

Bruce Devlin, the leader whose ball was five feet from the hole—and the victory—was waiting on the green with Billy Martindale, tied with Mayer, and Jack Nicklaus, two strokes back.

Days after discarding the new pitching wedge he'd been using the last few PGA Tour tournaments, Mayer pulled out the beat-up old one he was using so successfully in this tournament. He was at the precipice of the most memorable shot of the New Orleans Open, first played in 1938, and of his own two-decades-long PGA career.

The Greater New Orleans Open was the sixth richest in the world with a $100,000 purse. And Mayer could certainly use the $20,000 winner's share.

Since winning the U.S. Open and the World Tournament in 1957, when he was the PGA Player of the Year and earned a tour high of $65,835, the star of the hard-living, chain-smoking Mayer had fallen. Fast. A year later, Mayer earned $4,448; in 1959, $7,691; and a grand total of $87.50 in 1960, when he finished 243rd on the money list.

From 1961 through 1964 he fluctuated from 91st to 135th on the money list, and picked up a total of $14,000 in those four years—barely enough to cover caddy and entrance fees.

"It was the exhibitions that went with the world title—fifty of them for $1,000 a crack," Mayer said of his abrupt drop in the PGA, where he won six tournaments between 1953 and '57. "They were a disrupting influence on my game. Those one-night stands, and the partying, turned out to be real concentration-breakers . . . in fact, they broke me."

Starting on his comeback trail at age forty-one in '65, Mayer, a slightly built native of Samford, Connecticut, had won only $562.50 in six starts—$200 of which he picked up the week before when he shot a 70 in the final round of a rain-delayed Colonial, which wasn't finished until Tuesday because of the monsoon-like weather in Fort Worth.

"That 70 did a lot to lift my spirits," Mayer said. "I didn't see the Lakewood course until I teed off Thursday and depended a lot on my caddy getting me around. My 72 (in the first round) was wobbly, but that 67 on Friday really got me thinking of a high finish.

"On the practice tee before the final round, I was making the ball do what I wanted. I didn't know whether I could win, but I felt I'd play well. It was the first time I had real confidence in a long time."

So, a chip shot away from a finish among the leaders, it's hard to believe the plight of his game the last few years didn't cross his mind as he pulled back his club.

Mayer picked right up from where he left off since the start of the tournament. He had three birdies already on the day—a ten-foot putt on the sixth, an eight-footer on twelve, and a five-footer on fourteen—to go with fourteen birdies (and just four bogeys) leading up to Sunday.

But heading to the final hole, he looked to be in trouble, pulling his tee shot into the trees and leaving his four-iron second shot a good thirty-five yards short of the green.

The rest is history. The first phase of the most electrifying

PGA Tour victory ever played in Louisiana came when Mayer flicked away his burning cigarette butt, stood over the ball and measured the distance, then hit a pitch-and-run which rolled straight toward the hole. Then, plop, it rolled in and put Mayer a stroke ahead.

Crediting his old wedge and all-around short game, Mayer said, "When it got about six feet from the cup I thought it had a chance. . . . Every thing I used today, I was not worse than five feet off the pin." Mayer finished with a final-round 68 and 15-under 273 for the tournament.

The second phase came when Devlin stood over his short putt to send the tournament into a playoff. He blew it, rolling the ball past the hole, sending him to a frustrating fourth second-place finish that season.

"I played my best round today," the Australian explained of his round of 70 and final score of 274, "but a couple of three-putt greens killed me."

Mayer, perhaps thinking of his own recent woes, said "God, I was happy when that shot went in, but when Bruce missed his putt, I felt badly for him."

It was the last tournament Mayer would ever win.

The memorable histrionics, though, were summed up by Nicklaus, who finished in a three-way tie for fourth at 275. He shook his head and murmured, "It was simply fantastic."

(Clockwise from right) Rod Milburn, Tad Gormley, Artis Davenport, Hollis Conway, Emment Toppino, and the 1981 Northwestern State University 4x100 meter relay team (center).

MAKING TRACKS (AND FIELD)

Of all the illustrious athletes produced in Louisiana, Rod Milburn ranks in the forefront. Raised in Opelousas, where he couldn't compete in anything because of asthma, Milburn became a champion hurdler at Southern University and eventually set a bevy of world and Olympic records.

In the 1972 Munich Games, Milburn set the Olympic record in the 110-meter hurdles in 13.24.

Known in the track world as "Hot Rod," Milburn also set world records in: (indoors) the 50-yard hurdles (5.8); the 55-meter hurdles (6.8); the 60-yard hurdles (6.7); the 120-yard hurdles (13.3); (outdoors) the 120-yard hurdles (13.0); and the 110-meter hurdles (13.2).

"I got so comfortable running the hurdles," Milburn once explained, "it was just like a ballet going out there and going through the routines."

Between 1970 and '71 he won seventy-eight consecutive races, and he was selected the World's Outstanding Athlete in 1971.

Milburn was ranked No. 1 in the world three years in a row, from 1971 through 1973, a streak that broke a six-year run by another Southern hurdler, an ex-paratrooper from Ohio named Willie Davenport.

☆ ☆ ☆

Among the most scintillating Louisiana track feats ever was Northwestern State's 4x100 NCAA championship of 1981, the Demons' first Division I title.

Two notable football players, Joe Delaney, who went on to a short but eye-catching career with the Kansas City Chiefs before his premature death, and Mark Duper, called "Super Duper" as a Pro Bowl receiver with the Miami Dolphins, were part of the relay team along with Victor Oatis, who also played in the NFL, and Mario Johnson.

That June 6, 1981, night at steamy Bernie Moore Track Stadium on the LSU campus, the NSU unit lined up against crack relay teams from Georgia, Tennessee, Arizona State, San Jose State, Florida State, Arizona, Oklahoma State, and Baylor in the final.

Among the world-class sprinters running against the Demons that night were Georgia's Melvin Lattany and Herschel Walker, Tennessee's Willie Gault and Jeff Phillips, Arizona State's Ron Brown and LaMonte King, and San Jose State's Virgil Torrence.

The Demons' 39.32.2 time, 7.1-tenths of a second ahead of Georgia, set a stadium record.

A plaque near the NSU track in Natchitoches commemorates the achievement.

☆ ☆ ☆

For many years, Northeast Louisiana University was an incubator for track champions. Using a fiberglass pole, John Pennel, a tremendous all-around athlete, became the first man to ever pole vault seventeen feet in 1963, the season he broke or tied the world record four times—and was named the world's "Athlete of the Year."

At the time of running on cinder tracks, in the late 1950s and early '60s, Northeast's Don Styron lowered the 220-yard low hurdles world record to 21.9 seconds, and two years in a row *Track and Field News* selected him as the world's best triple hurdler, combining the 120-yard highs, 220-yard lows, and 440-yard intermediate hurdles. His twin, Dave Styron, was also a world-class athlete with personal bests of 9.3 for 100 yards, 10 seconds flat for 100 meters, 45.7 for 400 meters, 25-plus in the broad jump, 6-6¾ in the high jump, and 14-1 in the pole vault.

Though he didn't quite reach the heights he aspired to, Shreveport's Hollis Conway, who competed for Southwestern Louisiana (now UL Lafayette), left a legacy as a high jumper. He retired in 2000 as the only American to win two Olympic high jump medals (silver in 1988 and bronze in 1992). Conway was the No. 1 high jumper in the U.S. for seven consecutive years (1988-94) and set the NCAA records for both the outdoors (7-9¾) and indoors (7-9¼) jumps.

Lafayette's Walter Davis, a two-time world champion in the triple jump, was a major factor in LSU's 2002 NCAA title when he won national titles in the long jump, triple jump, and 4x100 meter relay. In 2006 he was the recipient of the Jim Thorpe Award, given to the nation's outstanding male athlete in field events and decathlon.

Coach Pat Henry led twenty-seven national championship teams at LSU between 1988 and 2004.

USL's Harold Porter ran on the U.S. Track & Field Federation's national championship 400 meter relay.

In the summer of 1992 some of America's greatest athletes—including Carl Lewis, Gail Deavers, and Michael Johnson—competed in what is arguably the most significant summer sporting event ever staged in New Orleans, the Olympic Trials. The ten-day event drew 137,262 spectators from around the world to see who would represent the USA in the Barcelona Olympic Games.

One was the most decorated athlete in LSU sports annals, Esther Jones, a sprinter who won six national championships, six SEC titles, and an Olympic gold medal with the U.S. 4 x 100 relay team in Barcelona. She was a twenty-one-time All-American at LSU between 1988 and 1991.

No Louisiana track figure stands taller than Pat Henry, who coached twenty-seven national championships (men and women) at LSU between 1987-2004, including both the men and women's titles in 1989 and 1990.

LSU's "five-man track team" was truly amazing, especially for the Depression era. It included hurdler Glenn "Slats" Hardin, a four-time NCAA champion who also won a silver medal for the 440-meter hurdles in the 1932 Olympics and a gold in 1936; world record shot putter (52'10) Jack Torrence; and high hurdler Al Moreau, who ran a world-record 14.2 as the runner-up in the NCAA's 120-meters event.

Dr. Artis Davenport accomplished more with fewer resources than practically any college coach in track history. As head coach of both the men's and women's teams at Southern University of New Orleans, and with stints at Dillard and Alcorn State, Davenport was NAIA Coach of the Year four times. In his forty-two years as a coach on the collegiate level he won seven national championships, led three national championship runner-up finishes, and coached forty-eight individual track champions and 178 All-Americans. These were accomplishments achieved without benefit of a paid assistant, limited scholarships, and virtually no budget. He developed six Olympians at SUNO representing four different countries.

The most renowned orthopedic surgeon in the sports world, Dr. James Andrews, was an SEC pole vault champion at LSU in the early 1960s. As a prep athlete at Homer High a few years earlier, he was encouraged at a state meet at LSU by another Tigers trackster, champion sprinter and shot-putter Billy Cannon, who took the kid aside and told him he had great potential if he kept working and developing. Andrews said he was inspired by Cannon's interest. How many athletic careers were saved over the decades because of that moment, one has to wonder?

Loyola coach Tad Gormley was truly a molder of men. He trained and sent four athletes to the 1932 Olympics. They included gold-medal winners Emmett Toppino and boxer Eddie Flynn. The others were long jumper Rolland Romero and boxer Dennis Flynn. Toppino moved Grantland Rice to hyperbole at the Games where the quartet of Bob Kiesel, Toppino, Hector Dyer, and Frank Wykoff ran the 4x100 relays in a world record 40.1. Rice described Toppino's second-leg effort as "running like a prairie fire fanned by a tornado."

In 1935, Loyola's Romero, with a leap of 50 feet, 4⅞, broke the national AAU meet record in the hop, step, and jump (now called the triple jump), set by world-record holder Dan Ahearn twenty-three years before. Romero wasn't able to medal in two Olympics, though. In three consecutive Olympic Games (Amsterdam in 1928, Los Angeles in 1932, and Berlin in 1936), eight of the nine U.S berths in the hop, step, and jump were filled by Louisiana athletes. Between 1932 and 1943, Louisiana athletes won ten of twelve national AAU titles in the event. But Hammond High's Sid Bowman, who first jumped in the 1928 Games, and Orleanian Romero were the only American triple jumpers to make the Olympics twice during that period.

PREP-POURRI: The national javelin throw record was set in the spring of 1966 at the City Meet at Bossier High School. The throw of 244 feet, 11 inches became the first taste of national notice for the young, blond-haired athlete who heaved it, a Woodlawn High School senior named Terry Bradshaw.

Triple jumper Billy Brown of Baker High won the 1937 national AAU title with a leap of 49-7¼, a mark that stood as a national interscholastic record for twenty-six years. Later, at LSU, he set the American record in the 1941 national AAU meet with a jump of 50-11. Sportswriter Jerry Byrd noted this was an especially remarkable achievement considering the fact the event wasn't held in college meets and Brown trained for it for only a week or two each year before he went to the national finals.

LSU women's track and field teams won ten consecutive outdoor national championships between 1988 and 1997.

SETTING THE BAR

June 17, 1933
Soldier Field, Chicago, Illinois

Only in Hollywood would this story have been scripted. With a national championship resting on the last event of a meet, and a scrawny boy having to pole vault a half-foot higher than he ever had before to tie the world-record holder, the lad, armed with advice from an old competitor, jackknifes over the barrier.

He brushes the bar on the way down. It shakes slightly, but holds.

The crown is secured, as is the everlasting legend of the team—and the athlete.

Here is where the closing credits should roll.

Except this wasn't the silver screen. This was real life.

Matt Gordy, a five-foot-eleven, 135-pound senior pole vaulter, was the unlikely hero of LSU's long-shot 1933 NCAA Track and Field championship squad. LSU now has more national Track and Field titles (men's and women's) than any other Division I school, but this was the first the Tigers ever produced—the famed, if erroneously named, "Five-Man Track Team."

The legend is that a five-man squad all scored points and beat the rest of the sporting world. Not entirely true. Because of Depression-era economics, Coach Bernie Moore brought ten athletes—plus himself, an assistant, and a trainer—to Chicago in three cars to the meet. All fifty-eight of LSU's points came from just five of those athletes. Hence the misleading moniker.

Despite the presence of several elite athletes on the team, including Olympic hurdler and world-record holder Glenn "Slats" Hardin, Moore moaned that LSU "will be lucky to place as high as fifth" but hastily added he fully expected at least five Tigers to score points. But Matt Gordy, who weeks before finished third in the Southern AAU meet behind Don Zimmerman of Tulane and Bill Roy of Loyola, didn't figure in his equations.

Gordy was a product of his environment. He grew up in Abbeville, where years before a citizen had made a trip to Japan and returned with a can of bamboo shoots. One of the only two bamboo groves in the United States eventually sprang up there, and kids who grew up in that area began chopping the sticks and cutting them into vaulting lengths.

That was the start of Gordy's athletic career.

★ ★ ★

A bad break for Ohio State's Jack Keller aided the Tigers' cause. Keller, a world-class hurdler, crashed into a barrier in the 120-yard high hurdles and was eliminated from that event and the 220-yard low hurdles. It was Hardin who gave spectators something to remember by setting a world record in the 220-yard low hurdles, 22.9 seconds. He also won the 440-yard dash in a meet record of 47.1 seconds. Weight man Jack Torrance also set a world record in the shot put with a heave of 52-10, almost three inches farther than the previous record, and also placed third in the discus. Al Moreau placed in each of the hurdles, and Buddy Blair was fourth in the javelin.

In what had become a two-team competition, LSU found itself leading Southern California 49-47 for the national title. The outcome would depend on the pole vault, throwing the spotlight on Gordy and USC's Bill Graber, who held the world record of 14 feet, 4¼ inches—nearly a foot higher than Gordy's personal best.

This was a different Gordy, however, thanks to Zimmerman, the Tulane athlete who beat him in the Southern AAUs. Zimmerman, who fell out of contention in the NCAA Championships after clearing thirteen feet, had previously advised Gordy to cut the size of his bamboo pole. "I decided to try it out," Gordy said. "So I cut off the heavy knob of the pole, then took off three feet more at the top. This cut my pole down to twelve feet, six inches instead of eighteen feet, six inches."

Pole vaulter Matt Gordy led LSU to its first national title in any sport.

The shortened pole, Gordy found, helped immensely. It "produced better form and was much easier to handle in coming down the runway," Gordy said, adding, it also provided "perfect pull under the chest and better balance in the air."

What more could anyone ask for? Gordy, at last, had an answer.

Graber had set the meet record by vaulting 13 feet, 11 ⅟16 inches—more than five inches better than Gordy had ever cleared. It would be a far-fetched finish, but if Matt could just equal Graber's mark LSU would outpoint the Trojans.

Steeling himself for his last attempt, with the national championship at stake, Gordy shot down the runway with all the speed he could muster. Posting his pole, he launched himself. Up, up, up. Gordy jackknifed himself over the bar, brushing it. It wobbled, and a breeze was blowing, making it appear the bar might fall. But it didn't.

Gordy had equaled Graber.

Moore had been watching from the top of the stadium, but Gordy said the coach might have outraced any of the athletes at the meet in reaching the vault area. "I hadn't picked myself out of the pit before he was there grabbing my hand," Gordy said.

Thanks to the unlikely vaulter, the final standings read: LSU 58, USC 54, Indiana 27.

And LSU had left its first mark on a national stage.

LSU coach Bernie Moore.

Matt Gordy clears the bar.

LSU's 1933 National Championship squad.

BURNING DESIRE

August 6, 1948
Wembley Stadium, London, England

1948 US Women's Olympic Track and Field team.

That she was from New Orleans is almost beside the point, for when Audrey "Mickey" Patterson stood amid a flourish of flags and anthems in London she became the first African American woman to earn a place on the winners' platform of the Olympic Games.

It was a memorable moment in black history. Louisiana sports history, too.

Once dubbed "a female Jesse Owens," Patterson won a bronze medal that day, eight-tenths of a second short of gold. Still, her journey to the high point of her career as a world-class sprinter was nothing short of scintillating.

Patterson lined up and ran for years without ever finishing behind another competitor. Where did she ever get this drive, this love of a sport that can be grueling, especially for a girl who didn't get much familial encouragement?

It was sheer happenstance that Xavier University is located in the area of the Crescent City where Mickey grew up. Had her family settled anywhere but South Genois Street Mickey's whole life might have been different.

She became interested in track as a child while watching the Xavier squad practice at a nearby field. Talk about starting young, Mickey began running as a third-grader at Daneel Elementary School, although her dad didn't particularly like the idea.

"I was an only child, and my parents wanted me to become involved in every aspect of school life," she explained decades later. "But I think Dad kind of thought sports were for boys, at least at first," Mickey added, giggling.

So she became involved. By the time Mickey was halfway through high school at Gilbert Academy, she was an accomplished dancer, sang contralto, performed in the band, and was an honor student. She played on the girls' basketball team, and her track abilities developed beyond anyone's expectations.

Leonidas Epps, a former Xavier athlete, guided her in track. He had Mickey working with—and against—boys in order to condition her for stronger competition. It was good strategy, apparently, because Mickey went unbeaten in high school.

After her senior year, Mickey became the object of an extensive recruiting efforts by most of the South's black colleges. She chose Wiley College in Marshall, Texas. Within a year Mickey, at five foot seven, 113 pounds, became a national sprint champion. In her first three meets as a freshman Mickey won three 100-meter races and three 200-meter runs, which propelled her into the National AAU Women's meet. She was again victorious in the junior 200-meters. Her coach, Fred Long, is the one who made the comparison between Jesse Owens and Mickey.

A semester later he lost her talents to Tennessee State.

"There was a student strike planned at Wiley because of some grievances, and as soon as my father heard the word 'strike,' he yanked me out of there," Mickey recalled. "He was an old-fashioned man, and he had no use for any nonsense in school."

In any case, the little firebrand began doing for Tennessee State what she had been doing for Wiley, completing another unbeaten season, and breaking the American and meet records in the 220-meter race with a time of 26.4 in the National AAU Women's Indoor Track and Field Championships.

Many felt Mickey had a lock on an Olympic berth, but the opportunity of a lifetime almost got away.

The morning of the qualifying heats, she burned her leg with a hot iron. Despite the injury she ran and won the 200-meter race. Then she retired to the ladies dressing room. By some inexplicable circumstance, she got locked in and was unable to report as her name was being called for the finals. A concerned Coach Tom Harris began a search for her and located his weeping star just in time.

Undaunted by the narrow escape, Mickey reported immediately, lined up and recorded a victory in 25.3. Later she finished a step behind Mabel Walker in the 100, the first time Mickey had finished as low as second since entering high school. But she earned her Olympic berth.

Patterson finished a close third in the 100-meter dash semi-finals in the London Games, eliminating her from the event, but she won the fifth heat in the 200 to gain the semis, then ran second and entered the finals.

"Francina Blankers-Koen of the Netherlands (a thirty-year-old athlete dubbed 'The Flying Housewife,' who won four gold medals in the London Games) won the finals in 24.4," Mickey remembered of her Olympic performance. "Audrey Williamson and I finished in a virtual tie for second, but they gave her a 25.1 and placed me third at 25.3. I'm still not convinced Audrey beat me, but I was only eight-tenths of a second behind the winner and I'm very proud of my performance."

Audrey "Mickey" Patterson (right) won a bronze medal in the 200-meter dash at the 1948 Olympics.

LAGNIAPPE

Located on Chef Menteur Pass east of New Orleans, the Tally Ho Club was founded in 1815, making it the oldest hunting and fishing club in the United States.

A NET GAIN

June 27, 1951
Centre Court, Wimbledon, London, England

Ham Richardson (center) receives an NCAA award.

It's hard to imagine any world-class athlete starting out with a bigger handicap than Hamilton "Ham" Farrar Richardson.

As a career-long amateur in the pre-Open format, he had an amazing tennis career, ranking first in the U.S. twice and in the top ten nine other years before he had to devote more time to earning a living.

Starting as a champion in the national juniors, Richardson later played on seven U.S. Davis Cup teams, once being the youngest captain at nineteen, and amassed a personal 20-2 record, still the event's highest victory percentage. He combined with Alex Olmedo to win the 1958 U.S. National Doubles title; was the first four-time Southeastern Conference singles and doubles champion (an achievement still not equaled six decades later), and twice won NCAA singles titles.

With a 58-2 cumulative record at Tulane, four NCAA titles wouldn't have been out of reach either except that SEC freshmen in the 1950s couldn't compete in the college nationals seniors with three previous varsity seasons were similarly banned by the NCAA. As a sophomore and junior, however, Richardson proved to be college tennis's best. Only Cincinnati's Tony Trabert and Texas's Sammy Giammalva, a pair of formidable names in the scrolls of the sport, ever broke Richardson's spell on the collegiate courts.

★ ★ ★

All this was accomplished while Richardson kept his diabetic condition under control—no easy task with a dire illness that fosters extreme fatigue and requires constant monitoring to balance sugar in the body. Daily injections of insulin can allow a somewhat normal lifestyle, but not, according to medical theory of the late 1940s, the strain of athletics.

"The first physician we went to," said Richardson, who was fifteen when diagnosed, "said I could not play competitive tennis again. So I went to a second doctor. He said the same thing, so I went to a third. When I finally found one who said I wouldn't have to give it up, my tennis picked up right where it left off." Much easier said than done, and requiring an iron discipline.

During the 1950 French Junior Championship, which he won, Ham spent nights at a Paris hospital so doctors could try to stabilize his fluctuating blood-sugar levels. The evening before the finals of a 1951 Newport, Rhode Island, tournament, Ham passed out. The next day he won in a five-set match.

Living in Baton Rouge, Roger Richardson, Ham's father, was a tennis-smitten oil research executive, who first brought his son to the courts as an eleven-year-old. A coach, Jim Bateman, provided guidance in the sport after the bug took hold. Bateman schooled the boy in fundamentals. One scant year later Ham was playing competitively with contemporaries and a year after that was a member of the national boys doubles team.

The skinny little blond, it could and would be presumed, was one of those phenoms who could only have been made in sports heaven.

"No, I don't think so," Ham once reflected. "You have to remember I was a damn good athlete. I was a good baseball player at University High, and captain of the basketball team when I was a sophomore. I loved the traditional games boys play, too. And I could play pretty well."

His talent on the court began to overtake every other sports interest, though.

"There's nothing so much fun as winning," Ham said, saying he began concentrating much more on groundstrokes than stroking grounders.

★ ★ ★

No one in the Deep South was better at developing tennis talent than Emmett Paré at Tulane. The 1929 national clay-court singles champion, Paré had played with some success against his era's finest players, including Ellsworth Vines, Wilmer Allison, Bitsy Grant, and even Bill Tildon.

The Richardsons agreed Ham merited the opportunity to learn the game at the knee of the master.

"I'd catch the bus every Saturday morning at seven o'clock and go down to New Orleans," Ham recalled. "I'd get to the station about nine thirty, catch a streetcar to my aunt's house to change clothes, then get over to the New Orleans Lawn Tennis Club, where Coach Paré taught. He was a tough taskmaster who made his students work very hard on the fundamentals. He'd drill, drill, drill until a player was comfortable with a shot. That, I think, was the secret to his success."

Richardson made his first major splash Emmet Pare in 1949, when he made the national junior finals. He was fifteen pounds underweight as a result of his diabetes, but it was the best showing for a Louisianan in thirty-five years.

Jim Bishop, president of the United States Lawn Tennis Association, gushed, "He's the best prospect in a quarter-century" while watching Ham become the state's first national junior champion in 1950. He also won the River Oaks juniors, the Western juniors, and the Heart of America juniors.

Ham demonstrated an ability to step up in class and still hold his own. The teen defeated Davis Cup veteran Ted Schroeder in straight sets in an exhibition. Earl Cochell, then one of America's finest players, was pressed by the now six foot, 158-pound newcomer at Houston. Herb Flam averted a defeat after Ham came within one point. In the National Interscholastics, Richardson required only thirty-six minutes to prevail in the finals.

★ ★ ★

Cary Richardson took her boy to England in June 1951 to compete at the holy ground of the sport, Wimbledon.

"Britain in those days," she recalled later, "was still on rations. We had to go to the U.S. Embassy to get Ham milk, and I had to have meat sent over from home. It was kind of difficult with Ham's diabetes. We were staying at the same hotel as Budge Patty, the defending champion, who was Ham's doubles partner and singles opponent in the second round. Ironically, the limousine picked all of us up, Ham, Budge, and myself. Well, Budge, just making small talk, asked Ham if he thought there would be any good matches that day. It was an innocent remark, but it just about floored Ham. He replied meaningfully, 'At least one!'"

The brash youngster numbed the Wimbledon crowd by stopping Patty, 4-6, 6-3, 4-6, 10-8, 6-4. Using what was universally described as a brilliant backhand and cool head, the freckle-faced Richardson forced the fourth-seeded Patty into a fidgety game. Grim and head-bowed after misses, Patty roamed the court, gritting his teeth at his rival's upstart effort. Completely demoralized by the final game, Patty lunged and literally fell in a vain attempt to reach Ham's winning shot, a backhand, cross-court shot that hit the net and bounced just over Budge's racquet.

The headlines screamed, "Invalid Boy Beats Patty" and "Sick Lad Advances."

The papers returned to more familiar names in a few days. Ham enjoyed another victory, then fell to Brazil's Armando Vieira, although he and Patty advanced to the doubles semifinals.

★ ★ ★

At Tulane, Ham excelled in the classroom as well as on the tennis courts. Missing weeks of school at a time because of tennis, he often took enormous academic loads, as much as twenty hours, taking his books with him on the road. He whizzed through college with a degree in economics in seven semesters, failing to a make a superior grade only twice in thirty-five courses. That achievement earned him a Rhodes Scholarship to Oxford and membership in Phi Beta Kappa.

Ham Richardson was no dumb jock.

So what were the only two courses he received grades as low as B?

One was Conversational French. "Ham was out playing tennis (in the Davis Cup) and that hurt his work," said instructor Eve Worris. "Constant presence is required in a grammar course." The same semester Ham was awarded the Alcée Fortier Memorial prize, given to the best French student at Tulane.

The other B subject? Phys ed, a first aid course.

Alas, with those academic "lapses," Ham's cumulative Tulane grade-point average dipped to 3.92.

Ham Richardson, the only person to ever win four SEC singles and four SEC doubles championships.

MARSH MADNESS

1945-2008
Louisiana's Great Outdoors

Whether sitting in a blind in the wetlands awaiting the birds, reeling in bluefin on the offshore waters of the Gulf, or hunting quail, woodcock, or deer near the Atchafalaya, Grits Gresham felt he was in paradise.

Louisiana. The Sportsman's Paradise.

At one time perhaps the best-known outdoorsman in the world, Gresham was a fisherman, hunter, conservationist, and serious journalist, who spent decades telling the rest of the country of Louisiana's wildlife riches and warning of the dangers—now impending—of not taking care of the bounty given his adopted state.

With all that, Claude Hamilton "Grits" Gresham Jr. with his trademark mutton-chops sideburns and Stetson hat with a roll on either side, always acknowledged that any claim he had to fame skyrocketed when he became a television fixture, spending more than a decade showing the country celebrities at play in the waters around Louisiana on *The American Sportsman*, then as a pitchman in jocular Miller Lite commercials with other famed sportsmen and athletes.

"You work all your life trying to get a few (important) messages across," Gresham once reflected, "and in thirty seconds (of horseplay before a camera) you're famous."

Still, if ever a man enjoyed his lot in life, it was Gresham, completely at home in the great outdoors.

"It was the diversity he loved," his son Tom said. "Grits loved the variety of the fishing, which ranges from the lakes and rivers, where you can catch bass, crappie, catfish, and others, to the inshore waters teeming with red fish and speckled trout, to the largely overlooked offshore fishing for tarpon and billfish—some of the best in the world. He loved hunting, too, waterfowl, squirrel, rabbits, deer are all in abundance in Louisiana. He loved educating people about Louisiana's bounty, and I think he loved being a part of a unique domain.

"Grits hunted and fished all over the globe, but he continued to love the variety and quality of Louisiana's outdoors. Through his writing and television shows, he took this message to the rest of the country."

★ ★ ★

He got both his nickname ("Little Grits" when he was a youngster in South Carolina) and a love for the outdoors from his father, a sportswriter and minor-league baseball player.

But it all might have begun when "Little Grits" got his first air rifle as a Christmas gift at the age of five. "I slept with my gun," Gresham said. "There was a big window next to my bed, and we lived right on the edge of the woods. Most mornings I'd wake up and there would be a fat ole rabbit sitting right outside that window. I'd roll over and pop him before I even got out of bed."

He seems to have inherited some of his dad's athletic ability, hitting .590 on his high school baseball team and .440 as a freshman at the University of North Carolina.

Then came World War II.

After serving four years in the Army Air Corps, by now married, he decided on a career in his greatest interest: wildlife management. He transferred to LSU and got his undergraduate degree in forestry, then a master's degree in wildlife management. For his masters, he studied under Dr. Leslie Glasglow, spending time in the marshes and growing to love the expanse and diversity of Louisiana's outdoors.

After a bit of wandering with the United States Fish & Wildlife Service after graduation, Grits returned to the Pelican State forever. He was editor of *Louisiana Conservationist*, and nested his own little flock of wife and three kids in Natchitoches along the Cane River, never to leave until his passing more than a half-century later, in 2008.

★ ★ ★

Getting out of a taxi in Madrid, Spain, as relayed in Shreveport sportswriter Jerry Byrd's book, *Louisiana Legends*, Grits heard someone booming out his name. It was actor Rip Torn, whom Grits had taken on a duck hunting trip in Louisiana with Burt Reynolds six years before. When Torn's wife, actress Geraldine Page, asked how he was able to recognize Grits so far away, and so far away from home, he replied, "Nobody else in the world has a hat like that."

That particular hunting expedition was the debut of *The American Sportsman*, a weekly outdoors venture co-hosted by Grits and famed baseball/football broadcaster Curt Gowdy. For thirteen years, Gresham hunted woodcock with the likes of Andy Devine, geese with Andy Griffith, Mexican doves with Bing Crosby and Phil Harris, Mearns quail with Mel Tillis, and alligators with Bruce Jenner.

The one constant was Gresham getting in a word or two about the importance of conservation, of making sure nature's resources were always being replenished.

He did the same thing in his weekly outdoors column in *The Shreveport Times*. Finally, the editor called Grits and said, "If you keep writing editorials, we're going to have to put you on the editorial page." That suited Grits just fine. It expanded his audience in the state to go with the tens of thousands of the readers of his nationally syndicated column.

☆ ☆ ☆

Gresham's studies of Louisiana's vast marshlands, which receive massive migrations of waterfowl funneling down the Mississippi Flyway, and his appreciation for the delicate nature of the largest estuary in the world, made him a very early student on the loss of the wetlands and the potential catastrophe awaiting the state—and the country as a whole.

Decades ago he was writing about coastal erosion, correctly identifying the cause as diversion of water flow—the results of levees and channelization projects.

The dichotomy of the state's riches were voiced in the *Louisiana Sportsman* in 2012 when it editorialized:

> With speckled trout and red fish action that is unrivaled in the country, with clouds of ducks filling the skies most winters, with near-shore waters that teem with cobia, dolphins, and snapper, Louisiana is rightly dubbed the "Sportsman's Paradise."
>
> But the marsh that serves as the very foundation for those staggering fish and game stocks are disappearing, and in many places it's totally gone. Unless serious costly, and painful steps are taken, in (a few) years the Sportsman's Paradise will become Paradise Lost.

It's a warning Grits Gresham sounded long ago.

A STAR IS BORN

August 12, 1932
Los Angeles, California

Gilbert Gray took a long, circuitous route to the inaugural Star class sailing event in the 1932 Olympics in Los Angeles.

But, in the end, New Orleans sailors Gilbert and crewmate Andrew Libano Jr., sailing under the auspices of the Southern Yacht Club—founded in 1849 and the nation's second oldest—struck gold.

Gilbert was known world-wide in sailing circles, having had first place finishes in the 1927 Midwinter Championship in Cuba and the 1928 International Star Championship.

On *Jupiter,* a two-man sloop-rigged craft from which, for purposes of balance and breeze conditions, crewmen often would hang low off the windward side with only their lower legs inside, Gilbert and Libano won five of seven races and were never seriously threatened—not even by the favorite, Britain's *Joy,* skippered by the renowned Colin Ratsey and Peter Jaffe.

The Star class was originally supposed to be an Olympic exhibition, but at the last minute was inserted as an Olympic event—and is now the longest-tenured sailing competition in the Games.

Just getting to sail down the California coast was an ordeal. This was at the lowest point of the Great Depression, and Gray—who joined the SYC little more than a decade before as a teenager, not specifically to sail but to be able to swim there and go to weekend dances, usually attended by a cluster of single young ladies—was not a wealthy man. The treasury of the SYC was depleted, and the club was accumulating more debt daily.

Click Schreck, Buddy Fredrichs, Barton Jahncke.

It was Charles Tessier who finally rescued the venture when things seemed darkest. Tessier, the SYC's Commodore, volunteered to personally underwrite the venture, and the Luckenback Steamship Line offered to ship the *Jupiter* to the West Coast.

Then in the Olympic Trials, while the boat was docked in San Pedro Harbor, vandals ripped apart its mast, tiller, and rudder, along with those of several other boats, forcing a postponement of the trial's second day of racing.

From then on, though, Gray, known as a "scientific" tactician of modern sailing, took absolute command of the Star class competition. He steered the *Jupiter* past the fleet of seven sloops twice around the six-mile triangle course in 2:38.42, five minutes faster than the *Joy.*

Jupiter was so dominant that even in the sixth race, in which it finished third, Gray and Libano tightened their grips on the gold medal. The French sloop *Tramontante* and the *Swedish Star* hit each other. The finish was *Tramontane, Joy,* and *Jupiter.* But because of the brush, the French boat was disqualified, and the *Jupiter* was accorded second place.

In the end, *Jupiter* accumulated forty-six of a possible forty-nine points, and the USA picked up its first gold medal in Star class sailing.

★ ★ ★

SAIL ALONG: Almost four decades later, in the 1968 Games, another Orleanian sailed to a gold medal.

George Shelby "Buddy" Fredrichs, a New Orleans stockbroker, and his crew of Barton Jahncke (sales manager of a steamship company) and Gerald "Click" Schreck (a sailmaker) sailed the Dragon class *Williwaw* to a resounding victory. Like most ventures, the victory rested on the shoulders of others behind the scenes. Nathaniel "Buster" Curtis, who would later have a hand in even more Louisiana history as the major architect of the Louisiana Superdome, and was an accomplished sailor himself, had been elected Commodore of the Southern Yacht Club in '68. As the concerted effort for the Games began, Curtis deeded his Dragon, *Dixie Doodle II*, to the Olympic Sailing Association, backing the enterprise. *Dixie Doodle II* became the *Williwaw.* The Orleanians were the pre-race favorites after a string of international championships over the previous three years, including two North American titles, the European title, and the World Championship of 1967. With the support of the SYC, the *Williwaw* won seven races on the triangular-type Olympic course near Acapulco, Mexico. With sails designed by Schreck, the *Williwaw* finished 2-6-1-1-2-1-1 to easily defeat its nearest competitors, Denmark and East Germany.

These were not, however, Louisiana's only sailing Olympians. Gene Walet III sailed in two Games, in 1956 at Melbourne, Australia (where he was the youngest American competing at age twenty-one years, eighty-seven days, and his crewman-father, Eugene Walet Jr., was the oldest at fifty-five years, sixty-four days) on the *Spirit III*, and the 1960 Rome Olympics, finishing ninth and tenth, respectively.

John Dane III, who as a young man sailed against Gilbert Gray and Fredrichs in the Sugar Bowl Regatta on Lake Ponchartrain, became America's oldest Olympian, sailing in the Beijing Games at age fifty-eight in 2008. He and his son-in-law Austin Perry competed in the Star class. Another Orleanian, Johnny Lovell, with crewmate Charlie Ogletree, are astoundingly four-time Olympians (1996, 2000, 2004, 2008), and brought home a silver medal in the 2004 Athens Games in the Tornado class.

So why would so many sailors from a relatively small area, all of whom perfected their sailing skills on the same water, Lake Pontchartrain, just north of New Orleans, reach Olympian proportions?

Lake Pontchartrain is 630 square miles with a mean depth of ten to sixteen feet. "The winds out on the lake are shifty and because the lake is so shallow," Dane said, "the water conditions can range from flat to rough and choppy, which all forces one to adapt."

Lovell said, "I think the lake is one of the most challenging places to sail in the U.S. You have a strong north breeze with a steep chop or a light shifty southerly (wind). Also, of course, placement can change the dynamics of racing on the lake because of the land effects.

"I guess the biggest quirk would be the fact that the lake is so big and yet so shallow, creating choppy conditions that are difficult to sail in, especially in light air."

1932 – 1940
GRAY AND LIBANO WIN THE STAR OLYMPICS

Gilbert Gray skippered and Andrew Libano, Jr. crewed aboard JUPITER to win the Olympic gold medals in the Star class at Newport Harbor, CA. Upon their return to the city, their amazing performance was accorded a resounding welcome by the entire populace.

THE FACE OF THE WILDCATS

March 15, 1994
Alex Box Stadium, Baton Rouge, La.

"Hey!"

The voice ricocheted around the near-empty arena, momentarily freezing Billy Allgood from his task of picking up his team's towels after an afternoon shoot around.

"Don't you know nobody is supposed to come in here and do that?" the arena custodian bellowed from several rows up in what seemed to be a show of authority.

Allgood didn't know he was doing anything out of order. But he spent a long career doing what others said he couldn't.

He did it that 1978 night, too, coaching his Wildcats from little Louisiana College, a Baptist-affiliated NAIA school to a 55-54 victory over Texas-El Paso and its Basketball Hall of Fame coach Don Haskins.

Any coach worth his whistle has a signature victory—a win the fans and/or alums can point to years later and still get goosebumps thinking back on it.

Allgood had two. On another night, in another sport, on another foreign field, Allgood left a blot on the record of another Hall of Fame coach, LSU's Skip Bertman. In 1994, Louisiana College, starting five freshmen, defeated the nationally ranked Tigers 7-5 in Baton Rouge—the first time an NAIA team beat a reigning NCAA Division I baseball national champion.

In other words, at small Louisiana College, a school not generally thought of as an athletic powerhouse, Billy Allgood put some mighty big skins on the wall. It's the reason Allgood, a coach who had to make the most of what skimpy resources he had to work with at the school in the central portion of the state, remains the enduring face of a program long after retirement.

☆ ☆ ☆

Allgood always knew what he was supposed to do. He coached the Wildcats to 328 basketball victories, a total that included such other Division I victims as Tulane, Mississippi State, and University of New Orleans.

"I was just never impressed that the outcome of basketball games was really all that important, although I tried my best to teach my teams how to win. That was my job," he once reflected.

> But I really just wanted to work with young people and hoped I could help in some way build people who left Louisiana College with character and purpose, and who could successfully use what they learned here in their lives. Winning could be nice, but it was not the most satisfying part of the job to me.
>
> I think the thing that pleases me the most when I look back on it, is that in my twenty-six years as basketball coach, only four players did not graduate. That's a rate of better than 95 percent, and I'm pretty proud of that.

Allgood spent thirty-nine years at Louisiana College with varying lengths of tenure as athletic director, basketball coach, baseball coach, assistant football coach, and instructor in the physical education department.

In basketball, his record was 328-331. Allgood estimated he coached more than one thousand baseball games, but no one at the school kept records. Allgood was a "builder," a man who coached respectable teams at a school without the resources to sponsor respectable teams.

Two years after the state took away the school's baseball field for construction of an expressway, Allgood built a new baseball park—literally by himself. The program, reinstated in 1970, now plays at Billy Allgood Field, where the Wildcats have won—and continue to compete for—conference championships.

But the athletic high point of Allgood's career came in that memorable baseball game against LSU in 1994—a game in which Allgood, as usual, drove the team bus as well as the team.

"That was the most phenomenal victory I was ever involved with," Allgood said, still amazed decades later at what his kids pulled off against an opponent that would again finish its season in the College World Series.

"I'm not foolish enough to think Skip or LSU was pointing to us," Allgood said. "At the same time, it wasn't a fluke. LSU scored three unearned runs in the eighth inning."

★ ★ ★

Allgood's legacy, however, probably is the physical mark he left at Louisiana College. For example, he didn't just cut out a field for the baseball team. He made fourteen additions to Billy Allgood Field, including a press box, weight room, new bleachers, lights, restrooms, and bullpens. He also lent his expertise to building baseball facilities at Pineville High, Alexandria Senior High, and several other central Louisiana schools. Allgood also raised the funds for the Lady Wildcats' locker room and was instrumental in several other projects.

Still, it was his coaching acumen that caught enough attention that he was courted by several so-called "big-time" schools, including LSU. In the mid-1960s, Tigers athletics director Jim Corbett asked Allgood to come to Baton Rouge to interview.

Allgood said he was flattered and excited, until he realized there were several kids on his Wildcats team to whom he had promised he would be the Louisiana College coach as long as they were there. He called Corbett back to decline the invitation to interview for the job that went to Press Maravich.

"It was just as well," Allgood said in reminiscing. "I think I was already where I was intended to be. We didn't have the most eye raising records, and we didn't have kids that were the most recruited around. But we did have kids with some fiber about them, and I was pleased to be around them. And I really believe in what this school is all about, its religious orientation."

"I think I was right where the Lord wanted me, doing what I was meant to do."

A GRAND SLAM

December 28, 1946
City Park Stadium, New Orleans, La.

The motto still resonates in the halls of New Orleans's Jesuit High School: "Pick up all the tricks in '46."

The words were uttered by a poetic assistant coach at the school, Willie Brown, who in January of that golden year was thinking the Blue Jays could be more than just good across the board in their upcoming sports.

Seldom has there been such an on-the-mark prophecy covering multiple games in multiple sports played over the course of multiple months.

Not in the school year of 1945-46, but in the calendar year of 1946, Jesuit had a sports run that was unprecedented in Louisiana—maybe anywhere. The Blue Jays not only won four state championships, a sweep of the so-called major sports, but came within a hair of being unbeaten in every sport. Only a four-point defeat in a dual track and field meet with defending champion Holy Cross, which would finish second to the Blue Jays in the state meet, marred their record.

It was a time, in the afterglow of victory in World War II, when anything seemed possible. Still, this was a staggering feat—though arch-rival Holy Cross did win three state titles the year before (football, basketball, track).

Compared to today the schedules seem abbreviated, but they were the norm, and competing in Class AA, then the highest classification in the state, the Jays swept to crowns in basketball (15-0), track (five-of-six meet victories), baseball (13-0), and football (13-0-0).

In between the two school years, the Blue Jays added another state title—and a national championship: the American Legion team winning the Little World Series—Jesuit's fifth championship of 1946.

It wasn't until almost seven decades later that another school took a spot on that lofty tier with Jesuit. John Curtis Christian School in 2011-12 won six state championships (football, boys basketball, girls basketball, indoor track, outdoor track, and softball), and in the same school year. The only difference in these notable achievements is Jesuit did it in the highest classification—and notched a national title on its résumé. When Curtis won the AA championships there were three levels of competition above them.

★ ★ ★

At a time when athletes played multiple sports instead of the specialization they are steered to today and the coaches coached more than one sport, Jesuit had a pool of outstanding players such as champion sprinter John Petitbon, later a football All-American at Notre Dame; Harold "Tookie" Gilbert, a basketball and baseball player who would get to the major leagues; and Hugh Oser, who would finish his high school career with thirteen letters. He won four of them in '46 as an All-Prep center in basketball, a triple jumper in track, an All-Prep pitcher in baseball, and an All-Prep end in football.

"The reason we were so successful," Oser said later, "is that we had several guys who lettered in more than one sport." In other words, they had athletes who could do more than one thing, and usually pretty well.

They were coached by talented mentors such as Gernon Brown, Willie's brother, who would mold sixteen Jesuit teams into state champions in a twenty-year career, in football (five), basketball (one), and baseball (ten); and Eddie Toribio, who coached the track team to the '46 title and the Legion team to the Louisiana and Series championships.

When they returned to school in the fall of '46, the Blue Jays embarked on a demanding football odyssey, including four out-of-state opponents, in which no opponent came within two touchdowns of Jesuit.

JESUIT
14
11
JESUIT
12

Gernon Brown was a three-letter coach (football, baseball, and basketball), a brilliant teacher, and astute motivator. When Brown, the school's athletic director, found himself without a basketball coach at the start of that season, he appointed himself, though he had no experience in the sport. He said, "I just read a basketball book, got the best kids, and we won." The joke was, if you hid the book, he'd call off the practice.

If Gernon Brown was a basketball novice, so was Toribio as a baseball coach. A star football and track athlete at Jesuit in the early 1930s, Toribio returned to his alma mater as track coach in '46 and immediately the Blue Jays took state.

He inherited the American Legion team because of a rule that barred major league scouts from coaching in the Legion program. The rule eliminated Gernon Brown, who bird-dogged for the Giants.

Toribio's Legion team was not given much of a shot, even on the state level, because several players from the championship roster of the spring were missing with other summer pastimes. It did have excellent pitching, though, and the glue of the team, shortstop Don Wetzel—who would later change the daily lives of almost all Americans. Wetzel, captain of the Legion champions, would leave Jesuit to go on to a distinguished business career—and invent the ATM machine.

Wetzel was described as "spectacular" in the field and fueled the Jays with a .450 batting average in the Little World Series, a summer run that ended in Charleston, South Carolina, with a 3-1 victory over Trenton, New Jersey.

Toribio always said Wetzel was more responsible for winning the national championship than anyone. Today his bronzed spikes hold down an honored place in the Blue Jays' trophy case.

When the autumn arrived, all that remained was football. Jesuit was gunning for its fourth title of the decade in the sport, having won state championships in '40, '41, and '43.

The football superstar that year was Petitbon, a single-wing tailback. A few months earlier, in the spring of '46, as a fourteen-year-old sophomore, he was a champion sprinter in the quarter-mile.

By that fall, as a 165-pound junior, Petitbon sparkled on one of Louisiana's finest high school teams ever. The Jays handled their chief city rivals impressively, beating St. Aloysius 13-0, Holy Cross 32-0, and Warren Easton 27-6. In the state final it was Jesuit over Jennings 48-14.

The Jays' defense was stellar. Only two opponents put as many as fourteen points on the boards. Offensively, Petitbon did most of the damage running off tackle behind double-team blocking. The Jays mixed the air game with two accurate throwers, one being Petitbon at his tailback spot, the other a wingback.

Oser was a glue-fingered end, a stand-out on defense, and also handled the punting.

In a memorable season, one of the most lasting of those memories came with a 55-0 fourth-quarter lead against Nicholls. Gernon Brown grabbed his third-string tailback, Maurice "Moon" Landrieu, later the mayor of New Orleans, by the pads, looked the little bench-warmer in the eye, and sent him into the game with the order: "Get in there, son, and open up the offense."

The only close call came in the state playoffs against Istrouma when, with the Jays leading 13-6, the Indians drove to the Jesuit 2.

"We called time and got together," Petitbon, who was later a member of the defensive unit on Coach Frank Leahy's 1949 national championship team at Notre Dame, relayed to schoolmate Peter Finney, a sportswriter. "We promised, if we held, we'd all go to Mass (every day) for the next month."

Jesuit did hold, and Petitbon said the team kept its vow.

It all came to an end in the CYO Classic, a four-year-old post-season game which annually tried to pair the best New Orleans Catholic school against the best parochial school from elsewhere in the country. In 1946 the Jays were matched against Gonzaga High, another Jesuit school from Washington, D.C., with a 9-0-0 record and at the time riding a fourteen-game victory streak.

Jesuit not only won 19-0, they held a 13-4 advantage in first downs against the Purple Eagles, who never got past their own 43-yard line.

Oser, who blocked two punts, was the game's MVP.

At that point, poet-prophet Willie Brown, reflecting on the stunning achievement of the past twelve months, sighed, "There will never be another year like this."

JAYS SOAR

24	Pensacola (Fla.)	6
41	Baton Rouge	14
13	St. Aloysius	0
20	Boys High (Atlanta)	0
31	St. Stanislaus (Miss.)	6
55	Nicholls	0
41	Peters	6
32	Holy Cross	0
20	Fortier	7
27	Warren Easton	6

State Playoffs

19 Istrouma (South La. Championship) 6
48 Jennings (State Championship) 14

CYO Classic

19 Gonzaga (Washington, D.C.) 0

THE NAMES IN THE GAMES

The instant he heard it, Russ Faulkinberry said he knew "Ragin' Cajuns" was the perfect nickname for a team in Louisiana.

In 1963, Faulkinberry was the football coach at the University of Southwestern Louisiana, then playing with the nickname "Bulldogs," to which he secretly objected.

Why and how schools adopted their team identifications is fascinating—none more so than the one in the middle of the largest pocket of the state's Cajun population, the college now known as the University of Louisiana at Lafayette.

Faulkinberry, a history buff who grew up in Tennessee, was sensitive to the indignities forced on the early people of Acadiana, the region where he now lived and coached. The British, he knew, drove the oppressed Acadians out of Nova Scotia two centuries before, sending them on an odyssey that eventually led them to Louisiana. That bothered Faulkinberry.

"There we were," he said, "playing in English red jerseys, and with an English bulldog for our mascot. That just didn't fit in Cajun Country."

One spring evening, Faulkinberry was to speak at a Kiwanis Club meeting for USL boosters. Members were going to kick off a season-ticket drive. The meeting moderator, from the south Louisiana town of Kaplan, divided the boosters into two "teams," each charged with selling more tickets than the other. He yelled to one group, "Give me the Roarin' Cajuns," and to the other, "Give me the Ragin' Cajuns."

Faulkinberry's ears picked up when he heard the latter. He thought, "Man, that's what I'm looking for."

After the meeting, Faulkinberry went to his office and made notes. He ordered Bob Henderson, USL's sports information director, to start using 'Ragin' Cajuns' instead of 'Bulldogs' in all references to the football team. It worked particularly well for that sport because forty-three of Faulkinberry's forty-five players were from Acadiana, the region where the largest population of the once-displaced Cajuns settled. It was a natural connection.

By the early 1970s, the school officially had adopted the moniker for all its athletic programs. It's a near-perfect reflection of the culture of the people, food, music, and good times of Louisiana—undeniably one of the best nicknames in the Pelican State. Maybe anywhere else, too.

★ ★ ★

It wasn't tigers roaming the wilds of Louisiana that gave LSU its nickname. There weren't any. It was soldiers.

Louisiana soldiers whose fighting style was so fierce, they were called "Louisiana Tigers."

College sports are littered with nicknames that at first glance appear odd. No hurricane, golden or otherwise, has hit Tulsa. Wolverines aren't naturally found in Michigan. And tigers, of course, are not indigenous to Louisiana.

LSU, then a quasi-military school, played without a nickname for its first three football seasons, though the team was called the "Baton Rouge Boys" by the New Orleans papers that covered the 1893 LSU-Tulane contest in the first college football game played in Louisiana.

By 1896 the team had its first mascot—a greyhound named Drum, the pet of the LSU commandant of cadets, a Lt. Gallop—and a growing identification with a native Louisiana bird, the pelican.

Justin Daspit, a member of the 1896 Tigers, explained in a 1929 interview with Maud O'Bryan of the *New Orleans Item-Tribune* that as LSU entered the 1896 season, the team was being called Pelicans and even had insignias of the fisher-bird sewn on its jackets.

That particular team was a fighting bunch, the first exceptional LSU squad and one that played with uncommon ferocity. LSU finished with a 6-0 record and outscored its opponents 136-4.

Fans were taken with the team, and it wasn't long before some made a double-barreled connection with history and likened the LSU team to the Louisiana Tigers.

The original Tigers were fighting men of the Civil War, Louisiana brigades in Robert E. Lee's Army of Northern Virginia, of which one officer was Major David Boyd, a professor of ancient languages at LSU, then located in Pineville and known as the State Seminary of Learning.

Through the exploits of some, all of the Louisiana units became identified with the name. Only a few outfits, though, left for the war with the official designation of "Tigers." One that did was the Washington Artillery of New Orleans, which marched behind the unit's logo of a snarling tiger head.

None, however, gained more fame than a colorful band of New Orleans-based volunteers under the command of Major Chatham Roberdeau Wheat. This was the only company of Wheat's battalion to adopt the Zouvave uniform, which had a distinct French-North African look of baggy trousers, braided jackets, and tasseled fez for the head. Their marching orders were barked in French.

The tide of battle was turned at Bull Run to an overwhelming Confederate victory assured in large measure by Louisiana Tigers made up of the Zouvave troops and Donaldsonville Cannoners.

It was written by Northern soldiers who fled to Washington,

D.C., after Bull Run that the words "Louisiana Tigers" served as an adequate explanation for what happened. "Damned devils, every one," was the description of the Tigers by one retreating Yank.

More fame came throughout the conflict with their ferocious fighting, particularly at the Battle of Shenandoah Valley and to the decisive Southern defeat at Gettysburg.

Boyd came out of the war to become the second superintendent of the Louisiana Seminary of Learning, by then in Baton Rouge, and surely would have been receptive when in 1896 fans began referring to the team as "Tigers," the honored namesake of his old fighting unit.

It was an intriguing line: "The 'Great Rolling Green Wave' lived true to its name when it washed over Mississippi A&M."

That was from the *Times-Picayune* on November 15, 1920, two days after Tulane claimed its fifth victory in seven games.

Just a few days before, "Green Wave" was not Tulane's nickname. Nobody in the mainstream sporting public had ever even heard of it.

In all the decades since then, the words "Tulane" and "Green Wave" have been so linked they are almost interchangeable.

Tulane fans owe a major debt of gratitude to E. Earl Sparling, at the time a student, part time sports writer—and a pretty lame poet. But it was Sparling who started Tulane on its way to its enduring identification and away from early, unofficial nicknames of "Olive and Blue" and "Tulanemen."

Change had been in the wind for a while. In 1919, the *Hullabaloo*, the Tulane student newspaper, started referring to the dark-shirted Tulane team as the "Greenbacks." Eventually the moniker came into general usage and became the school's first formal athletic identification.

In the October 29, 1920, issue of the school paper, however, as Tulane prepared for its first intersectional football game at the University of Michigan, Sparling wrote a convoluted poem entitled "The Rolling Green Wave," which was displayed at the top and in the center of the front page.

The fourth verse, in which the then-nicknames for Georgia Tech and Alabama are mentioned, seems to get to the heart of the matter:

> Now Tech's got a Gold Tornado,
> Alabama's a thin red line,
> But we've got a Rolling Green
> Breaker
> That'll cover 'em every time.

The same issue of the *Hullabaloo* stated that the "great green wave rolled toward Michigan." But after a long train ride to Ann Arbor, Tulane lost 21-0.

Two weeks later, as 4-1-1 Tulane prepared for unbeaten Mississippi A&M, a story with no byline appeared in the *Hullabaloo*, saying that the LSU football team, returning from a game at Alabama, and, of course, an upcoming Tulane opponent, would attend the A&M contest. "When Tulane's 'Green Wave' goes into action against the Mississippi A&M machine," read the short article on November 12, 1920, "it will be under the watchful eyes of the LSU team."

That was first use of "Green Wave" in the mainstream press.

Two days later, in sports editor Bill Keefe's *Times-Picayune* account of Tulane's 6-0 victory, he said of Tulane holding A&M at the 10-yard line, "The Green Wave stopped (A&M) there." Fred Digby, sports editor of the *Item* and Sparling's boss, opened his Monday morning review of the game, "Tulane's Green Wave is still one of Dixie's undefeated elevens . . ." (meaning it hadn't lost to a Southern team).

What really welded "Green Wave" to Tulane, though, was a catchy fight song, written five years after Sparling came up with the name. Marten ten Hoor, dean of Tulane's College of Arts and Sciences, and Walter Goldstein, associate professor of music at Tulane's women's college, Newcomb, collaborated and came up with "The Olive and Blue March," for which the composers received one hundred dollars.

No small trick, but the rhythmic, light, and fun-to-sing tune manages to include all of Tulane's nicknames. Various lines are: "Here's a song to the Olive and the Blue;" "Here's to the Greenbacks who never will say die;" and "Roll, Green Wave, roll them down the field."

It's registered on sheet music by two different titles: "The Olive and Blue March" and "Roll On, Tulane."

Even with that, the song is more commonly referred to by a third title: "Roll Green Wave."

Unlike at Southwestern Louisiana, even before Louisiana Tech fielded a team, there was a deep attachment in Ruston to the tag of "Bulldogs."

In the autumn of 1899, five Tech students found a homeless and hungry bulldog. After they gave it something to eat, the skinny animal followed them to the home they shared, where he was allowed to sleep the night in their kitchen. Hours later, the students were awakened by the barking dog, who ran from room to room to alert them that the house was on fire.

After getting the occupants up and nudging them outside, the dog seemed to realize one of the boys was missing and reentered the smoke-filled building. The student had made his way out through another exit, but the attempt to find him cost the dog its life. When the fire was extinguished, the students found the heroic animal lying in an unburned corner of one room, dead from the smoke and heat.

His newfound and grateful friends covered him in two jackets, one red and one blue, and buried him at the place they first found him.

The story spread, and when Tech fielded its first football team two years later, it was an easy decision to choose a nickname that honored the dog that embedded himself in Tech's heart.

How did Louisiana's other four-year school get their nicknames? Here's a brief history:

- Centenary College: Since 1921, the school's moniker has stood as a reminder of what is expected of its student-athletes. That season the football team got into a fight with another team, upsetting then-president George Sexton. He took the unusual step of gathering his team before the next game and sternly setting down an iron-clad rule "From now on," Sexton warned his athletes, "you will act like gentlemen." Since then Centenary athletes of both genders have competed as Gents and Ladies.

- Dillard University: The first football squad in the mid-1930s must have been possessed of an impish sense of humor. When asked to vote on what the relatively new Methodist-affiliated school, merged from two other historically black New Orleans universities, wanted to be known as, the team voted for Blue Devils. Dillard no longer plays football, but now its athletic teams are referred to as "Bleu Devils."

- Grambling State University: The Tigers are so named because the founders of the school, many from the Baton Rouge area, wanted their programs to emulate that of LSU.

- Louisiana College: The school's first athletic director, Simon Tudor, was from Kentucky and a huge University of Kentucky sports fan. So about 1915, when Louisiana College started a sports program, he adopted the UK mascot (Wildcats) and primary school color (blue). Orange was added to the school's color scheme later.

- University of Louisiana at Monroe: Originally named for the Ouachita tribes who live in the northeastern corner of the state, in the politically correct atmosphere at the turn of the twenty-first century, ULM had to change to a name perceived to be less offensive to some, going from Indians to Warhawks.

- LSU Shreveport: Dubbed the Pilots, the athletic teams of LSUS are named for the riverboat navigators that traverse the Red River, which flows near the city.

- Loyola University: Wolves have long been associated with St. Ignatius Loyola, a knight, priest, theologian, and founder of the Catholic order of intellectual clerics in the 1500s. Prominent in the crest of his Basque family is a golden pot and a pair of wolves, which symbolizes the attribute of generosity—sharing one's bounty even with the wolves.

- McNeese State University: Cowboys might seem like an odd nickname for a Louisiana school, but McNeese comes by it honestly. Namesake John McNeese was a ramrod on the first cattle drive across the Sabine River.

- University of New Orleans: Privateers became the name of UNO teams in the 1960s after four elections, beating out such designations as Dolphins, Ospreys, and Tigersharks. Such a seafaring name fits because UNO's is located on Lake Pontchartrain and a privateer, Jean Lafitte, played an important role in the history of New Orleans. Interestingly, a secondary name, Bucs, also came into common usage for UNO. But it has the exact opposite definition. A privateer is a crew member of private ships commissioned to legally sail against enemy vessels of commerce, warships or navy. Bucs is short for buccaneers, another word for pirate—some of the very people privateers were sent to fight against.

- Nicholls State University: The school is named for Francis T. Nicholls, a former governor of Louisiana and colonel in the Confederate Army. Hence, the name "Colonels."

- Northwestern State University: Louisiana might have missed out on the most memorable name in college sports when Northwestern chose to become the Demons in 1922. Two students split a ten dollar prize for the winning suggestion in a contest. One of the other proposed nicknames was Cyclops.

- Southeastern Louisiana University: The school adopted the name "Lions" in 1931 when Southeastern was a junior college. The name came from the suggestion of one of its athletes, Elmer Sanders. In 1962 businessman Clifford Ourso donated a live lion mascot to SLU and named it Roomie for Roomie Wilson, a longtime SLC trainer.

- Southern University: This much is certain—Southern's teams originally were called the Bushmen. According to Dr. Everett Baker, a historian associated with the school, Southern changed the name to Jaguars in the early 1930s. The reason for the change, Baker said, doesn't appear in any of the records.

- Southern University-New Orleans: Originally the Black Knights with black and red as its colors, SUNO changed to just Knights when it later changed to blue and gold colors, the same colors as its parent school Southern University.

- Xavier University: The catchy name Gold Rush has been in use since the athletic program was launched in 1928. When the women's program started, its teams were dubbed the Gold Nuggets.

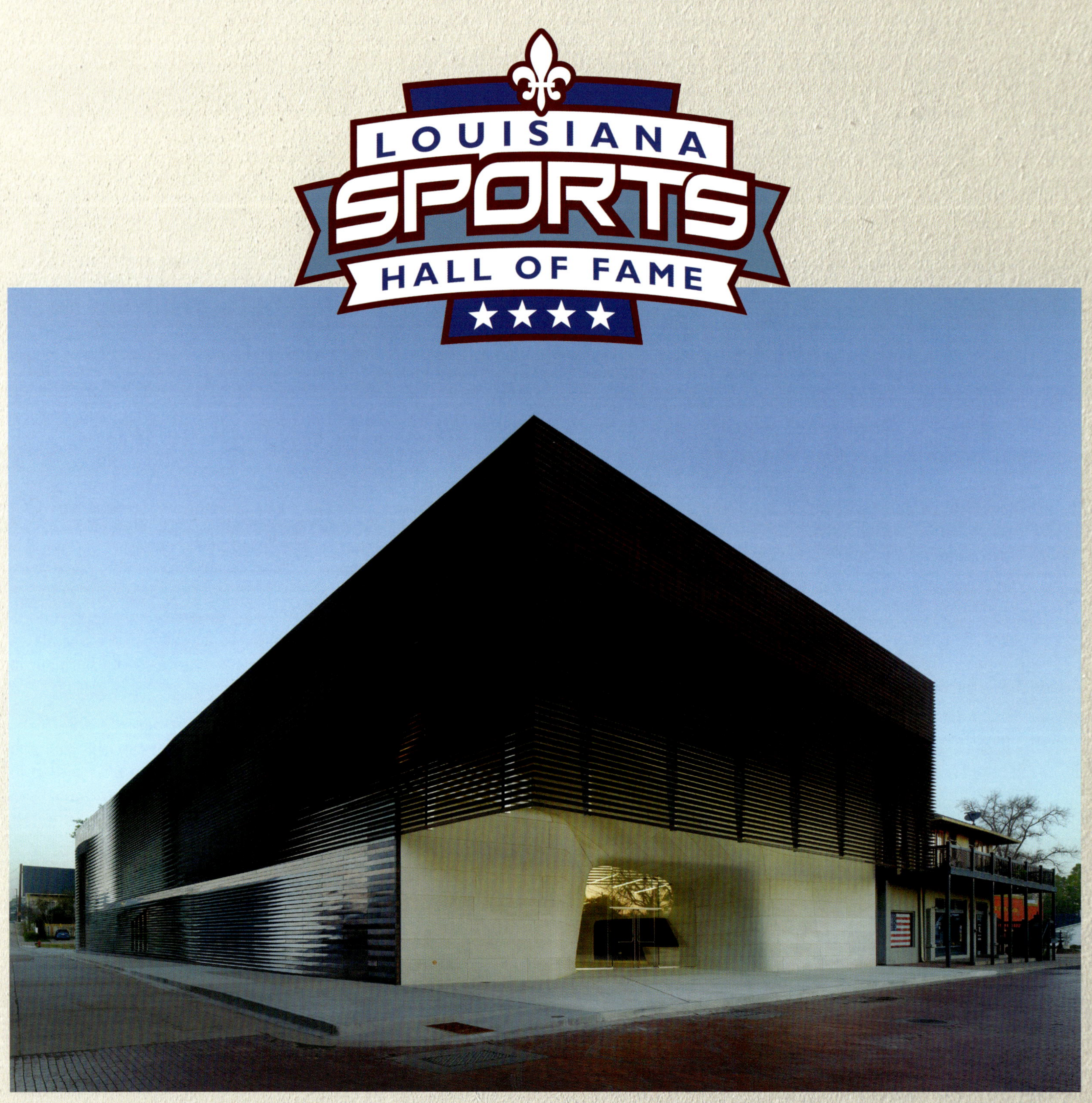
LOUISIANA
SPORTS
HALL OF FAME

Postscript

by Doug Ireland

La. Sports Hall of Fame Museum

June 28, 2013
Natchitoches, La.

Sports provides so many lessons. Hard work pays off. Unselfishness does too. Teamwork puts you over the top. Adversity can be overcome. It's important to dream, and in a big way.

You've noticed those themes, and countless others, in these pages, artfully authored by the incomparable Marty Mulé.

They ring true when reflecting both on how this spectacular collection of legendary Louisiana sports stories has come together, and on an even grander scale, the opening of the magnificent Louisiana Sports Hall of Fame Museum in beautiful, historic Natchitoches.

First, a few words about this book. Mulé has already cited many of the team players who contributed to *Game Changers*, which like the Hall of Fame is a product of the dreamers in the Louisiana Sports Writers Association. All involved, and everyone who reads it, celebrate his skillful composition, his relentless research, and his pure passion to make this project a fitting testament to the LSWA, to the Hall of Fame, and to Louisiana sports fans and sports heroes.

We owe immense gratitude to his fortitude in seeing this through when we were well past halftime and had no idea how or where this wonderful work would find its way into print. There were some noble efforts launched, but until we were pointed toward the Center for Louisiana Studies and the UL Press at the University of Louisiana at Lafayette, we were like the Saints before Benson, Finks, Mora, Hebert, Hilliard, Martin, and the Dome Patrol. We had hope but not enough good guidance. Thanks to James Wilson and his colleagues, the vision of Mulé, his dear friend and foil Ted Lewis, and a few other LSWA co-conspirators is now in your hands, even more entrancing than any of us imagined.

This publication came together, from brainstorms to bookstores, in about three years, less time than it took for Shaquille O'Neal to develop as Dale Brown dreamed, from a gigantic, phenomenal LSU freshman brimming with potential into an NBA Rookie of the Year and ultimately one of basketball's brightest superstars.

Building the Louisiana Sports Hall of Fame Museum took a bit longer, from late 2008 until the Grand Opening on June 28, 2013. Its origins trace much further back, some three-quarters of a century, and again, to a group of sportswriters. It endured an often awkward childhood. At one point, all that was the Hall was squirreled away in a broom closet in Shreveport.

There was no *Sports Illustrated*, no *USA Today*, no ESPN SportsCenter, and there were only a few TVs in any given neighborhood when state sports scribes began bantering around the idea of immortalizing Louisiana's sports greats. The first formal discussion came in a 1950 writers' meeting in Lake Charles, and although those plans didn't immediately take off, a standard was advanced that still abides today in Hall of Fame selection philosophy.

"An organization with a membership so exclusive that nobody may immediately qualify to be tapped will open for business this weekend as a going concern," wrote Otis Harris, sports editor of the *Shreveport Journal*, in a Dec. 11, 1950, column. "It is the Louisiana Hall of Fame—a hall of fame for the state's greatest athletes, men or women, amateur or professional, living or dead."

Selection would require 90 percent approval from the voting writers, with no more than two initial inductees, and just one in succeeding years, "if anyone qualifies," offered Harris.

"The purpose," he explained, "is to make the Hall of Fame mean something and limit the roll to athletes, past or present, who have become figures of national or international renown in the general sports pattern. Only the state's immortals in the sphere of athletes will be enshrined."

While Hall of Fame membership didn't prove quite so restrictive, it is reserved for the best of the best. In the 2013 voting, the thirty-member LSWA Hall of Fame committee selected nine inductees after considering a record 146 nominees from twenty-six different sport categories on a thirty-three-page ballot.

The initial list of potential Hall of Fame members cited by Harris had only thirteen names, twelve who ultimately were enshrined: baseball's Ted Lyons and Mel Ott, boxer Pete Herman, LSU track and field legends Jack Torrance and Glenn "Slats" Hardin, Tiger football All-American Gaynell Tinsley, Merryville native and Army football sensation Chris Cagle, amateur golf sharpshooter Freddie Haas Jr., and Tulane football All-Americans Bill Banker, Gerry Dalrymple, "Peggy" Flournoy, and Don Zimmerman.

Harris also foreshadowed the long-term future for the state's sports shrine. "Until a home is found for the hall of fame, it will exist only on paper and in skeletonized form," he wrote. That proved true until 1972, when Natchitoches and Northwestern State University embraced the Hall.

It took eight years after Harris' column for the concept to take root. To streamline statewide sports coverage and install a formal structure for selection of high school all-state teams, and to provide the framework to launch the Hall of Fame, the Louisiana Sports Writers Association finally was founded in 1958. The first sanctioned voting took place with boxer Tony Canozeri, baseball's Ott, and LSU's Tinsley chosen as charter Hall of Fame members. They were inducted a year later during the Ark-La-Tex Sports Awards Banquet in Shreveport in 1959.

Three more inductees were picked for the next few years, enshrined during the annual Shreveport banquet. Then ceremonies took place at LSU football games and televised basketball contests, and during the Veterans of Foreign Wars Sports Award Banquet in New Orleans. A total of forty-one Hall of Famers received plaques of induction, and portraits of each were commissioned, but until 1972, there was no permanent home for the Hall, and until a few months earlier, not a lot of consideration had been given to finding one.

LSWA titans such as Ted Castillo, Truman Stacy, Bill McIntyre, Bill Carter, and Frank Adams ensured the values of the Hall were upheld. When *Shreveport Times* writer Jim McLain was elected LSWA president, and his friend Springhill native Jerry Pierce was the young PR director at Northwestern State, they shared a common perspective.

"Sportswriters in that day weren't a very reverent bunch anyway, and they made fun of everything and everybody," said Pierce. "One of the big jokes was the Hall of Fame, that there were inductions into something that was noble enough of an idea, but didn't exist anywhere except in the newspapers."

"The Hall of Fame was homeless. I thought we could do a lot more than we had to that point," said McLain.

A raconteur with comedic timing reminiscent of his heroes Bob Hope and Johnny Carson, Pierce was master of ceremonies at LSWA dinners and a rib-busting contributor to any state sportswriters' social activity or business discussion. Annually, a half-hearted topic of discussion at the LSWA's summer conventions would be finding a home for the Hall.

"Eventually, I started making a pitch for the Hall of Fame—a tongue-in-cheek pitch. And everybody would just laugh," recalled Pierce. But over time, it began to gnaw at him that the state's sports greats were not celebrated in one place, befitting their stature. At the 1971 LSWA meetings, with McLain as the incoming president, he made his play.

"I made up my usual jokes and had fun," said Pierce, "but then I got serious and told the writers I'd talked to the administration, and Northwestern was going to support the Hall any way we could. I made a serious plea for the Hall to come to Natchitoches, and we got it in an overwhelming vote."

Then came the task of putting into shape something that had no form—or, alarmingly enough, no list of members or easily-located collection of portraits. McLain and Pierce worked diligently to assure the Hall of Fame's roll call was complete, while learning that the modest collection of portraits of five Hall of Fame members had disappeared from the Shreveport Civic Center's walls. *Shreveport Journal* sports editor Jimmy Bullock, in one of the more underrated pieces of investigative journalism in LSWA history, discovered the portraits stacked in a broom closet at the Civic Center.

"So the story went, Jimmy Bullock rescued the Hall of Fame," chuckled McLain.

The register of heroic efforts on behalf of the Hall hardly ends there. Northwestern art professor J. Clif Thorn completed thirty-five pastel portraits in a three-month span before the first induction in Natchitoches late in 1972, honoring LSU football great and Pro Football Hall of Famer Y.A. Tittle, with a ceremony at halftime of an NSU Demons basketball game and a private dinner at President Arnold Kilpatrick's home. Thorn continued to do the portraits until 1995, when the strain of Parkinson's disease overwhelmed him. He finally privately conceded a few weeks before the ceremony and coached his wife, Carolyn, an acclaimed watercolors artist who had never worked with pastels or done portraits, to complete the task. She continued the Thorn legacy until her passing shortly after the 2008 inductions.

Pierce and McLain persuaded inductees to donate memorabilia that was placed below the collection of portraits in display cases built in the lobby of Prather Coliseum, the university's multipurpose basketball arena. McLain raised money, mostly with the generosity of Hall of Fame members, to help fund elements of the start-up that NSU could not provide. Pierce added a banquet and ceremony in 1973 and, soon after, a couple of receptions and a golf tournament to the Induction Weekend.

Meanwhile, concepts for a true museum home were fleeting. University planners developed sketches for a Hall of Fame building adjoining Prather Coliseum but no serious funding options emerged. Other cities and groups inquired about hosting the Hall. Nobody had a plan good enough to consider. After nineteen years of guiding the Hall of Fame through its annual inductions, Pierce was promoted to university vice president in April 1990. At this point I assumed, in addition to my duties as NSU sports information director, responsibility for the Hall of Fame .

Ten years and a few pipe dreams later, traction finally began to develop. The LSWA accepted a joint governmental/private sector offer to shift the Induction Weekend to Shreveport-Bossier from 2000-02, accompanied by commitments to develop potential options for a permanent museum home there. An expanded schedule of events and the Hall's first significant corporate support, from Horseshoe Hotel and Casino as a lead partner and local businessman/NSU alumus Jimmy Patterson as the chief catalyst, drew notice, first from Lt. Gov. (and future Gov.) Kathleen Blanco, then soon after from Gov. Mike Foster.

After the 2002 inductions, the LSWA and its Hall of Fame committee assessed inquiries and proposals from around the state to host not only the induction activities, but to create a museum. Ultimately, the best option came from a revitalized Natchitoches community. The following spring, a formal partnership was established between the LSWA, the City of Natchitoches, the university, and the Louisiana State Museum system to build

CHICAGO
ANGELS
New Orleans
21
NO
ST. ALOYSIUS
Crusaders
1948
NATIONAL AMATEUR BASEBALL CHAMPIONSHIP
JOHNSTOWN, PENN.
JOHN ALTOBELLO - COACH
Mets
10

a Hall of Fame shrine in the oldest permanent settlement in the Louisiana Purchase. Foster's young Director of Communications, Natchitoches native Jennifer Marusak, a former collegiate track athlete then an LSWA member as sports information director at Louisiana-Monroe, helped pique the governor's interest in the long-anticipated project.

A powerful team had formed fast. Mayor Wayne McCullen spearheaded the City of Natchitoches's high level of commitment. Local legislator Taylor Townsend and his esteemed House colleague, former state champion high school basketball coach Billy Montgomery, proved a formidable backcourt, quickly forging a broad base of statewide support. Ultimately, the museum project earned the backing of nine consecutive sessions of the state legislature, three governors (Foster, Blanco, and Bobby Jindal), and Lt. Governors Blanco, Mitch Landrieu, and Jay Dardenne. It never skipped a beat as the local lineup changed when first-term Natchitoches Rep. Rick Nowlin and state Sen. Gerald Long, both avid sports fans, took office in 2008 or when Rep. Kenny Cox, another sports enthusiast, took Nowlin's seat in 2012.

At the January 2008 groundbreaking ceremonies for the museum, just as he had passionately done at Hall of Fame induction ceremonies in recent years, Landrieu outlined a grand vision for the museum: a spectacular building, featuring state of the art technology and world class exhibits. The ball was long since in motion. Four years earlier, Trahan Architects began developing a stunning, innovative design for the 27,500-square foot building. Exhibit concepts came from the internationally-renowned New York City-based firm of Thinc Design, whose other concurrent projects were the Nelson Mandela National Museum in South Africa and The 9/11 Memorial Museum on the site of the World Trade Center twin towers.

The state museum staff's professionalism endured transition in its leadership as three different directors departed during the course of the project, with veteran assistant director Robert Wheat stepping to the fore each time to steady the project. A constant dialog with the LSWA assured that dreams hatched in the years after World War II were taking shape at a level no sportswriter ever dared to imagine. The state's investment ultimately approached $23 million, with another $1.1 million privately raised by the Hall of Fame Foundation under the leadership of President/CEO Lisa Babin, greatly bolstered by Dardenne's active engagement in all aspects of the project.

For that pricetag, you'd think it's hallowed ground. And it is, in look, in feel, and the experience. As it opens for visitors July 1, 2013, the Hall of Fame Museum revives great memories and creates more of them.

The greatest accomplishments in Louisiana's sports history, and the most remarkable sports figures, are celebrated. With gripping theatrical-style films projected on pristine white curved stone walls, a collection of priceless memorabilia, storylines that evoke powerful emotions, and the ability to trace the constantly evolving panorama of Louisiana's athletic landscape, the Hall of Fame will match the credo of a great sports columnist—to provoke a strong reaction. The museum goes far past commemorating the careers of the elite who have been elected to the Hall. It embraces the state's fantastic sports culture—unique and fascinating to outsiders, a way of life for Louisianans.

If it was great in sports in the Bayou State, it's here—in this book, and in this museum. We are celebrating excellence in Louisiana, from Lake Providence to Lake Charles, from Ida to Grand Isle, in these pages and in this sensational shrine facing beautiful Cane River Lake in the cradle of Bayou State history, the Cooperstown of our state, Natchitoches. Dig in. Hold on. Savor the experience. And come back for more!

Doug Ireland
Chairman, Louisiana Sports Hall of Fame
Natchitoches, La.

Photo Credits

Grateful appreciation is expressed to all of the individuals that assisting in securing images for this project, particularly the staff members of the various university archives and sports information departments (SID).

Page vi: from *The Third Annual of the Public School Athletic League of New Orleans*; vii-viii: Tim Brando; x: James Wilson; 1: Tulane University; 2: top, Louisiana and Lower Mississippi Valley Collections, Louisiana State University; bottom, Tulane University; 3: top, University of Tennessee; bottom, by Neil Leifer, *Sports Illustrated*/Getty Images; 4: top, Topps Card Company; bottom left, Louisiana State University SID; bottom right, UPI Images; 5: top, UPI Images; bottom, James Wilson; 6: top, Louisiana State University SID; bottom left, David Browning/Wavefootball.com; bottom right, University of Louisiana at Lafayette SID; 7, 8, and 10: *New Orleans Times-Picayune*; 11-13: Grambling State University; 14: AP Images; 15: all, Grambling State University; 16: the *Sporting News* Archive; 17-18: all, Louisiana Tech University; 19 and 21: Southern University SID; 22-23: University of Louisiana at Lafayette Archives and Special Collections; 24: St. Louis Rams; 25: AP Images; 26-27: Louisiana State University SID; 29: AP Images; 30: top, Sugar Bowl; bottom, *Tiger Rag*; 31: public domain via Wikimedia Commons; 32: Classic NFL Experience; 33: University of Louisiana at Monroe SID; 34: top, Louisiana State University; bottom left, Grambling State University; bottom right, Louisiana Tech University; 36-38, Louisiana State University SID; 39-41: Tulane University Archives; 42: by Stephen Dunn, Getty Images; 43: both, Grambling State University; 44: Louisiana State University; 45: top, University of Louisiana at Lafayette SID; bottom, by Bill Frakes, *Sports Illustrated*/Getty Images; 46: New Orleans Saints; 47: AP Images; 48-49: Louisiana State University; 50-51: Grambling State University; 53: top, Louisiana Tech University; bottom, R.L. Stockard; 54: Topps Card Company; 55: Grambling State University; 57: *New Orleans Times-Picayune*; 58: top, UPI Images; bottom, Louisiana State University SID; 59: top, Bettmann Archives, Corbis Images; bottom, Topps Card Company; 60: Centenary College of Louisiana Archives and Special Collections; 61: left, Louisiana State University; right, *New Orleans Times-Picayune*; 62: left, UPI Images; right, Louisiana State University; 63-65: Tulane University; 65: center, John Stinson; 67: UPI Images; 68: top, by Neil Leifer, *Sports Illustrated*/Getty Images; bottom, left, by Sylvia Allen, Getty Images; right, by Mike Powell, Getty Images; 69-70: Tulane University; 71-72: Southeastern Louisiana University; 73-74: Louisiana State University; 75-76: Sugar Bowl; 77: James Wilson; 78: Tulane University; 79-81: Sugar Bowl; 83: both, McNeese State University; 84: Louisiana State University; 85: AP Images; 87: Tulane University SID; 88: Holy Cross School; 89: top left, Louisiana State University; top right, McNeese State University; bottom, Centenary College of Louisiana Archives and Special Collections; 90: Isidore Newman School; 91-92: John Curtis School; 93: *New Orleans Times-Picayune*; 94: top, by Tyler Kaufman, Icon SMI; bottom, Louisiana State University SID; 95: top, public domain via Wikimedia Commons; bottom Louisiana State University; 96: *New Orleans States-Item*; 97: New Orleans Saints; 98: James Wilson; 99: top, by Art Associates Illustrators, Curtis & Davis Architectural Firm; bottom, Dave Dixon; 100: top, Curtis & Davis Architectural Firm; bottom, Louisiana Superdome; 101: top, Bayou Classic; bottom, Grambling State University; 102: all, Steed Media Group; 103: New Orleans Public Library; 104: UPI Images; 105: left, the *Sporting News* Archive; top right, MLB Images; bottom right, Getty Images; 106: top left, National Baseball Hall of Fame and Museum; bottom, Archives and Manuscripts Department/John B. Cade Library/Southern University and A&M College; 107: Hoyt Powell; 108: top, Louisiana State University SID; bottom, New Orleans Zephyrs; 109: James Wilson; 110: top, Topps Card Company; bottom, Walter Iooss, Jr.; 111: Getty Images; 112: MLB Images; 113: University of Louisiana at Lafayette Archives and Special Collections; 114: *Time* & *Life* Pictures; 115: the *Sporting News* Archive; 116: UPI Images; 117: UPI Images; 118: *Boston Herald* Archives; 119: UPI Images; 120-121: by Charles M. Conlon, the *Sporting News* Archive; 122-123: University of New Orleans; 124: Louisiana State University SID; AP Images; 126-127: Nicholls State University; 128: top left, University of Louisiana at Lafayette Archives and Special Collections; top center, Louisiana State University SID; top right, Southern University SID; bottom left, Getty Images; bottom center, AP Images; bottom right, AP Images; 131: top, New Orleans Buccaneers game program; bottom left, *Sports Illustrated*; bottom center, Tulane University; bottom right, *New Orleans Times-Picayune*; 132: left, NCAA Images; right, by Susan Ragan, AP Images; 133: left, by Rich Clarkson, NCAA Photos; right, the *Sporting News* Archive; 134-136: Louisiana State University; 137: Loyola University SID; 138: Louisiana State University SID; 139: AP Images; 141: top, Louisiana tech University; bottom, Utah Jazz; 142: McNeese State University; 143: UPI Images; 144: the *Sporting News* Archive; 145: both, Louisiana State University; 146: AP Images; 147: Louisiana State University SID; 148: AP Images; 149: left, the *Sporting News* Archive; right, Focus on Sport/Getty Images; 150: NBA Cassics, Getty Images; 151: Grambling State University; 153: Xavier University; 154: Sun Belt Conference; 156: Tulane University Archives; 157: top, Southeastern Louisiana University; bottom, Louisiana Tech University SID; 158: left: Louisiana College; right, AP Images; 159: top right, Southeastern Louisiana University; middle right and bottom right, Louisiana State University SID; bottom left, Tulane University; 160: Louisiana Sports Hall of Fame Museum; 161: Frances Lyle; 162-163: Louisiana Tech University; 164: top right and bottom right, Adam Warshaw; top left, Mears Auction; middle left, John Stinson; bottom left, Curtis Perry; center, *Sports Illustrated*; 166: Loyola University; 167: both Library of Congress; 168: top, JO Sports; bottom, public domain; 169: top, the *Sporting News* Archive; bottom, from *New Orleans Mascot*; 170: top, Louisiana State Library; bottom, New Orleans Fair Grounds; 173: top, New Orleans Fair Grounds; bottom, *New Orleans Times-Picayune*; 175, both, Library of Congress; 176: Joan K. Slew; 177: Thistledown Racino; 178: *New Orleans Times-Picayune*; 179: Women's Southern Golf Association; 180: University of Louisiana at Lafayette Archives and Special Collections; 181, from *Golf World Magazine*; 182-185: *New Orleans Times-Picayune*; 186: top right, UPI Images; middle right, Louisiana State University; bottom right: *New Orleans Times-Picayune*; bottom left, University of Louisiana at Lafayette Archives and Special Collections; top left: *New Orleans Times-Picayune*; center, Louisiana Sports Hall of Fame; 188: both *Sports Illustrated*; 189-190: all, Louisiana State University; 191: U.S. Olympic Organizing Committee; 192: AP Images; 193: New Orleans Public Library; 194: Tulane University; 195: UPI Images; 196: Louisiana Sports Hall of Fame; 197: both, James Wilson; 198: Southern Yacht Club; 200-201: Louisiana College; 202-203: all, Jesuit High School; 208: Louisiana Sports Hall of Fame; 209-213, James Wilson. Front cover: top left (Pete Maravich), by Arthur Rickerby, *Time* & *Life* Pictures/Getty Images; top right (Mel Ott), UPI Images; bottom (Tom Dempsey and New Orleans Saints), AP Images. Rear cover: top left (Tank Younger), Grambling State University; top right (Kim Mulkey), AP Images; bottom (Billy Cannon), Louisiana State University SID. Endsheets: front (LSU versus Baylor, October 3, 1959), Bettmann Archives, Corbis Images/AP Images; rear (Southwestern Louisiana Industrial Institute 1912 women's basketball team), University of Louisiana at Lafayette Archives and Special Collections .